ANDREW J. BYERS serves as Lecturer in
New Testament and Free Church Tutor at
Cranmer Hall, Durham Uiversity. He has
served for thirteen years in pastoral ministry,
most recently as Chaplain of St Mary's
College, Durham University. His other
books are *TheoMedia: The Media of God and the
Digital Age* (2013) and *Faith Without Illusions:
Following Jesus as a Cynic-Saint* (2011). Andrew
blogs at hopefulrealism.com.

ECCLESIOLOGY AND THEOSIS IN THE GOSPEL OF JOHN

For the fourth evangelist, there is neither a Christless church nor a churchless Christ. Though John's Gospel has been widely understood as ambivalent towards the idea of 'church', this book argues that ecclesiology is as central a Johannine concern as christology. Rather than focusing on the community behind the text, attention is directed to the vision of community prescribed within the text. This vision is presented as a 'narrative ecclesiology' by which the concept of 'church' gradually unfolds throughout the Gospel's sequence. The theme of oneness functions within this script and draws on the Jewish theological language of the Shema. To be 'one' with this 'one God' and his 'one Shepherd' involves the believers' corporate participation within the divine family. Such participation requires an ontological transformation that warrants an ecclesial identity expressed by the bold assertion found in Jesus' citation of Psalm 82: 'you are gods'.

ANDREW J. BYERS serves as Lecturer in New Testament and Free Church Tutor at Cranmer Hall, St John's College, Durham University. He has served for thirteen years in pastoral ministry, most recently as Chaplain of St Mary's College, Durham University. His other books are *TheoMedia: The Media of God and the Digital Age* (2013) and *Faith Without Illusions: Following Jesus as a Cynic-Saint* (2011). Andrew blogs at hopefulrealism.com.

SOCIETY FOR NEW TESTAMENT STUDIES

MONOGRAPH SERIES

General Editor: Paul Trebilco

166

ECCLESIOLOGY AND THEOSIS IN THE GOSPEL OF JOHN

SOCIETY FOR NEW TESTAMENT STUDIES

MONOGRAPH SERIES

Recent titles in the series

Ecclesiology and Theosis in the Gospel of John

ANDREW J. BYERS

Cranmer Hall, St John's College, Durham University

CAMBRIDGE
UNIVERSITY PRESS

CAMBRIDGE
UNIVERSITY PRESS

University Printing House, Cambridge CB2 8BS, United Kingdom

One Liberty Plaza, 20th Floor, New York, NY 10006, USA

477 Williamstown Road, Port Melbourne, VIC 3207, Australia

4843/24, 2nd Floor, Ansari Road, Daryaganj, Delhi – 110002, India

79 Anson Road, #06–04/06, Singapore 079906

Cambridge University Press is part of the University of Cambridge.

It furthers the University's mission by disseminating knowledge in the pursuit of education, learning, and research at the highest international levels of excellence.

www.cambridge.org
Information on this title: www.cambridge.org/9781107178601
DOI: 10.1017/9781316823750

First published 2017

Printed in the United States of America by Sheridan Books, Inc.

A catalogue record for this publication is available from the British Library.

ISBN 978-1-107-17860-1 Hardback

Dedicated to Walter Arroyo, Kyle Bailey, and Joel Busby

... And in memory of Bob Waters

CONTENTS

PREFACE

For the fourth evangelist, there is neither a Christless church nor a churchless Christ. Though John's Gospel has been widely understood as ambivalent towards the idea of 'church', this book argues that ecclesiology is as central a Johannine concern as christology. Jesus is consistently depicted in John as a divine figure that destabilizes the social construct within the text and consequently generates a new communal entity. Rather than focusing on the community behind the text, the following study concentrates on the vision of community prescribed within the text. This vision is presented as a 'narrative ecclesiology' by which the prescriptive concept of 'church' gradually unfolds throughout the Gospel's sequence. Attending to this cumulative development, it will be argued that Johannine ecclesiology entails a corporate participation in the interrelation between the Father and Son, a participation helpfully described by the later patristic language of theosis. Before drawing on this (diverse and complex) theological discourse, however, rigorous exegesis will be offered on the theme of participation within an anchoring Johannine text – the Prologue – and within a primary motif, that of oneness. John 1:1–18 is recognized as one of the most influential christological texts in early Christianity, yet the passage's christology is inseparably bound to ecclesiology. The Prologue even establishes an 'ecclesial narrative script' – that is, an ongoing pattern of resocialization into the community around Jesus or, more negatively, of social re-entrenchment within the 'world' – that governs the Gospel's plot. The oneness theme functions within this script and draws on the Jewish theological language of the Shema. The Johannine claim to be 'one' signifies that Christ-devotion does not constitute a departure from the 'one God' of Jewish religious tradition; moreover, to be 'one' with this 'one God' and his 'one Shepherd' involves the believers' corporate participation within the divine family. Such participation requires an ontological transformation that warrants an ecclesial identity expressed by the bold assertion found in Jesus' citation of Psalm 82: 'you are gods'.

ACKNOWLEDGMENTS

The most difficult part of my PhD experience, of which this book is a product, was not the research and writing. The psychological, financial, logistical, and physical burdens of moving overseas to pursue an advanced degree at an awkward life-stage exceeded the intense pressures, anxieties, and labours of doctoral work. Because she endured so much of the toll with me, my wife, Miranda, deserves the foremost acknowledgment in this brief accounting of my gratitude. Thankfully, she fretted much less about the journey than I did once our hands gripped the ploughshare. Her patience, grace, and joy have provided a harbour in which my sanity remained (mostly) anchored for the longest three years of our lives.

When I reported to our four children that my thesis (the big book project Daddy worked on every day) was to be published in a distinguished monograph series, the two boys exclaimed with wonder, 'you mean the *Guinness Book of World Records*?!' My announcement, admittedly an untoward bid to boost my sense of self-importance and justify the challenging few years of unpaid labour, did not have the desired effect. Even so, they have cheered me onwards, kept me grounded, and forgiven me much since we took those one-way flights to the north of England in 2011. They deserve my thanks almost as much as Miranda.

Those flights took cousins and grandchildren away from our wider families. My gratitude to their support is inexpressible. A word of special thanks belongs to Linda Waters for all her help, which included a great deal of babysitting and washing up during her many visits.

Not a few generous friends offered financial help on occasion, especially in the few weeks before the move to England, when boarding those one-way flights seemed an impossibility. I am particularly grateful to David and Paige Adkison and to Betty and Ed Darnell.

When emergency repairs on our house in the States threatened to upend the entire PhD venture, Ron Durham and the Men's Ministry of

Mountain Brook Community Church sped to the scene. I still do not know the extent of their labours. All I know is that I have never before felt so rescued by a community of people. To each of them, I offer heartfelt thanks.

A triumvirate of close friends went beyond all others in serving and supporting my family and me. This book is dedicated to Walter Arroyo, Kyle Bailey, and Joel Busby for carrying and sustaining us at times when our reserves seemed entirely spent.

Turning now to those whose friendship and mentoring contributed most to this academic project, I thank Francis Watson whose doctoral supervision allowed me the freedom to explore and innovate but within the parameters of seasoned wisdom. It has been a treasured gift to be guided by someone whose scholarship is marked by robust theological impulses alongside precise exegetical practices. As a secondary supervisor, Lutz Doering provided helpful feedback in the early stages of my work before returning to Germany for a new post. Wendy North, Johannine exegete par excellence, was gracious enough to lend her sharp eye and read large sections of the manuscript before it was submitted as a doctoral thesis. Colleagues in the Johannine Literature group of the British New Testament Society offered affirmations and challenges that have shaped what I have written. As my viva examiners, Grant Macaskill and Dorothea Bertschmann offered a host of insights at the final stages. The (always crowded) Durham New Testament Seminar has provided rich fellowship as well as a context for learning how to think, inquire, learn, change minds, and have one's mind changed. The company of fellow postgrads in the less than glamorous study space known as '37a' proved life-giving – I am grateful for how these friends guarded me against an introverted escape into the lonely (if not less distracting!) abyss of solitary research. And I am also grateful to Richard Hays who supervised my initial forays into the seminal ideas that led to this book when he accepted my request in 2006 to join him in a directed study of John's Gospel.

Though my children would perhaps have been more excited about the *Guinness Book of World Records*, I myself could not be more pleased with Paul Trebilco's acceptance of this book into the Society of New Testament Studies Monograph Series. I am also grateful to Beatrice Rehl and her team at CUP. Rob O'Callaghan, one of my closest friends for over twenty years, has appeared in the Acknowledgments section of each of my books. Touches of his editorial and theological gifts, for which I am tremendously grateful, are scattered throughout every paragraph.

I close by expressing sorrow that Bob Waters is not here to hold this book in his hands – my father-in-law left us too early. So I submit this book into the world with his love, support, and friendship strong in my memory.

St John's College, Durham
Michaelmas, 2016

Introduction

1

THE JOHANNINE VISION OF COMMUNITY: TRENDS, APPROACHES, AND 'NARRATIVE ECCLESIOLOGY'

This book focuses not on the community that produced John's Gospel, but on the sort of community John's Gospel seeks to produce. The primary concern lies not in identifying the historical community behind the text, but in discerning the identity envisioned for that community within the text. Since that text is a story, I understand the Johannine construct of 'church' as 'narrative ecclesiology'. A comprehensive ecclesial vision is established in the Gospel's opening and then accrues expanded layers of significance and meaning as the plot unfolds. Attending to the sequential development of this narrative ecclesiology reveals an understanding of the people of God as corporate members within the interrelation of the Father and Son, an interrelation that constitutes a divine community inclusive of, and open to, human participation. Here are the primary claims central to the volume, corresponding respectively with the three major divisions:

1) ecclesiology is not a secondary or ancillary theme for John but one that appears just as prominently in the Prologue as christology and wields normative force over the entire Gospel;

2) the concept of oneness, universally recognized as a critical motif for Johannine ecclesiology, is grounded in the theological oneness of the Shema ('YHWH is one' – Deut. 6:4);

3) the Gospel portrays the human community of believers undergoing such a striking transformation for the sake of divine participation that recourse to the patristic language of 'theosis' is both warranted and exegetically promising.

Applying this later terminology associated primarily with Alexandrian Christianity is not to detract from John's early Jewish milieu. The Fourth Gospel is a 'deification narrative' that is explicitly *Jewish*: to be 'one' with the christologically reconceived divine identity refers to something more profound than a state of ecumenical harmony, internal social unity, or unity in function or will with God. Jesus' prayer in John 17 'that they may be one, as we are one' beckons believers to become 'partakers of the divine nature' (to draw from a Petrine text) of the 'one' God of Israel (to draw from the Shema).

I acknowledge that any enterprise in examining the Fourth Gospel's understanding of 'church' must come to terms with influential voices that have dismissed ecclesiology as a central Johannine concern. Rudolf Bultmann drew attention to the absence of the term ἐκκλησία[1] and attributed the Eucharistic language of John 6 to a later ecclesiastical redactor.[2] Similarly, Ernst Käsemann argued that the evangelist 'does not seem to develop an explicit ecclesiology'.[3] Yet both scholars betrayed appreciable suspicions that ecclesiology indeed bears some significance for this Gospel. Bultmann's claim that 'no specifically ecclesiological interest can be detected' seems self-corrected only a few sentences later by his affirmation that the Gospel actually evinces a 'lively interest' in the church.[4] In comparable fashion, Käsemann follows his own assessment that John lacks a clear ecclesiology with a certain degree of incredulity: 'I cannot conceive that Christian proclamation, including proclamation in which christology is so central, could be without ecclesiology'; he goes on to conclude that the 'kind of ecclesiology' on offer in John must be of the sort that simply eludes historians working with the Gospel text.[5] The equivocal sense shared by these influential interpreters that ecclesiology is virtually imperceptible in John, yet nonetheless important in some way, is broadly representative of scholarly approaches to Johannine ecclesiology. One is left to wonder if the Johannine vision of community is every bit as elusory, if not more so, than the historical details of the Johannine community.

I propose that it is not just the 'kind of ecclesiology' that confounds interpreters of the Fourth Gospel (one of participation and deification), but also the means by which that ecclesiology is presented (through sequentially developing narrative threads). Rather than offering a standard literature survey listing individual scholarly treatments, I categorize below four approaches to Johannine ecclesiology (noting representative figures and works) and briefly sketch how they relate to

[1] Rudolf Bultmann, *Theology of the New Testament*, trans. Kendrick Grobel (Waco, TX: Baylor University Press, 2007), 2:91.

[2] Rudolf Bultmann, *The Gospel of John: A Commentary*, trans. George R. Beasley-Murray, R. W. N. Hoare, and J. K. Riches (Philadelphia, PA: Westminster John Knox, 1971), 218–19; 234–37.

[3] Ernst Käsemann, *The Testament of Jesus: A Study of the Gospel of John in the Light of Chapter 17*, trans. Gerhard Krodel (Philadelphia, PA: Fortress, 1968), 27.

[4] Bultmann, *Theology*, 2:91.   [5] Käsemann, *Testament*, 27.

my own agenda of articulating the Gospel's vision of community with the patristic language of theosis.[6] This introduction will close taking a closer look at the idea of 'narrative ecclesiology' followed by a few words of orientation to the format of the project.

The Empty Search for a Formal Ecclesiology: Johannine Individualism and (Anti-)Institutionalism

The 'kind of ecclesiology' many scholars had been searching for in John when Käsemann puzzled over its liminal nature was one concerned with the formal dynamics of institutional church life. Read in comparison with the Synoptics, the omission of Jesus' baptism and the absence of a Eucharistic institution scene were at times interpreted as disinterest in (or even aversion to) sacramental rites.[7] Other interpreters, however, found strong sacramental allusions in the Bread of Life Discourse and in Jesus' language of birth from above through water and Spirit, venturing that the evangelist simply presupposed these liturgical practices along with other institutional dimensions associated with ecclesial life.[8] Still, Käsemann reasoned that a document produced by Christians around the turn of the first century would surely reflect a more appreciable degree of complexity in church order and form.[9] The absence of such

---

[6] For other literature reviews on Johannine ecclesiology, see Johan Ferreira, *Johannine Ecclesiology*, JSNTSup 160 (Sheffield: Sheffield Academic Press, 1998), 35–44 and R. Alan Culpepper, 'The Quest for the Church in the Gospel of John', *Int.* 63, no. 4 (2009): 341–54.

[7] Those (like Bultmann) viewing John as anti-sacramental or at least less interested in the sacraments include Günther Bornkamm, 'Die eucharistische Rede im Johannes-Evangelium', *ZNW* 47 (1956): 161–69; Eduard Schweizer, 'The Concept of the Church in the Gospel and Epistles of St John', in *New Testament Essays: Studies in Memory of Thomas Walter Manson, 1893–1958*, ed A. J. B. Higgins (Manchester: Manchester University Press, 1959), 230–45. For a recent monograph arguing against a eucharistic reading of John 6 see Meredith J. C. Warren, *My Flesh is Meat Indeed: A Nonsacramental Reading of John 6:51–58* (Minneapolis, MN: Fortress, 2015).

[8] Scholars who perceived a positive interest in the sacraments in John include R. H. Lightfoot, *St. John's Gospel: A Commentary*, 2nd edn. (Oxford: Oxford University Press, 1956), 154–71; Edwyn Hoskyns, *The Fourth Gospel*, ed. Francis Noel Davey, 2nd edn (London: Faber and Faber Limited, 1947), 292–307; C. K. Barrett, *The Gospel According to John: An Introduction with Commentary and Notes on the Greek Text*, 2nd edn. (London: SPCK, 1978), 82–84; and Raymond E. Brown, *The Gospel According to John: Introduction, Translation, and Notes*, AB 29, 29A (Garden City, NY: Doubleday, 1966), cxi–cxiv. Alf Corell even claimed that John's Gospel is arranged around a liturgical structure. See Alf Corell, *Consummatum Est: Eschatology and Church in the Gospel of St. John* (London: SPCK, 1958), 44–78.

[9] Käsemann, *Testament*, 27.

allusions reinforced his view that the Johannine community was aberrant and anomalous in early Christianity.

With the search for institutional ecclesiology frustrated by the Gospel's ambiguity and silence on these formal dimensions of church life, it has become axiomatic to envision Johannine Christianity as anti-institutional and, to a certain degree, akin to modern 'free church' polities in which the individual members of local communities share equally in leadership and decision-making. Corroboration for this view is found in the evangelist's emphasis on the Paraclete's sufficiency for guiding the community (lessening the need for human governance), the alleged minimization of 'the Twelve', and the 'anti-Petrinism' in which Peter's ecclesiastical authority is subordinated beneath the less official leadership status of the Beloved Disciple.[10] It appears that this anti-institutional egalitarianism contributed to the idea that 'the Fourth Gospel is one of the most strongly individualistic of all the New Testament writings'.[11] Again from Käsemann: 'Just as the concept "Church" is absent [from the Gospel] ... the disciples seem to come into focus only as individuals,

---

[10] On the issue of church offices, see Schweizer, 'Church'; Hans-Josef Klauck, 'Gemeinde ohne Amt: Erfahrungen mit der Kirche in den johanneischen Schriften', *BZ* 29, no. 2 (1985): 193–220; and Robert Kysar, *John, The Maverick Gospel* (3rd edn.; Louisville, KY: Westminster John Knox, 2007), 132–42. For the tension between Peter and the Beloved Disciple, see the overview in Harold W. Attridge, 'Johannine Christianity', in Attridge, *Essays on John and Hebrews* (Grand Rapids, MI: Baker Academic, 2010), 3–19, here at 11. For a more extreme position on Peter's subordination, see Graydon F. Snyder, 'John 13:16 and the Anti-Petrinism of the Johannine Tradition', *BR* 16 (1971): 5–15. A more expansive list of sources espousing anti-Petrinism will be provided in Chapter 10, pp. 213–20.

[11] From C. F. D. Moule, 'Individualism of the Fourth Gospel', *NovT* 5, no. 2–3 (1962): 171–90, here at 172. Moule's discussion on Johannine individualism centres on eschatology. See also Raymond E. Brown, *The Churches the Apostles Left Behind* (New York: Paulist Press, 1984), 84–85, 95; John F. O'Grady, 'Individualism and Johannine Ecclesiology', *BTB* 5, no. 3 (1975): 227–61; and Schweizer, 'Church', 235–37. More recent interpretations supporting the idea of Johannine individualism are found in Udo Schnelle, 'Johanneische Ekklesiologie', *NTS* 37 (1991): 37–50, here at 49 (though his critiques of Käsemann and Bultmann are strong and significant); Stephen S. Smalley, *John: Evangelist and Interpreter* (Exeter: Paternoster Press, 1978), 233–34 (though he allows for a balance between the individual and corporate); John P. Meier, 'The Absence and Presence of the Church in John's Gospel', *Mid-Stream* 41, no. 4 (2002): 27–34; and in Urban C. von Wahlde, *The Gospels and Letters of John*, ECC (Grand Rapids, MI: Eerdmans, 2010), 1:541. Wahlde writes, 'The second edition of the Gospel evidences a lack of concern for any sense of community organization other than the individual believer's relation to God' – ibid. A contrary voice dismissing this trend of Johannine individualism is provided by Rudolf Schnackenburg in *The Church in the New Testament*, trans. W. J. O'Hara (London: Burns & Oates, 1974), 103.

and all the titles which we miss with reference to the church organization are applied to them as individuals'.[12] Martin Hengel made a similar observation: 'Unlike Matthew, [the fourth evangelist] knows as yet no definite ecclesiology or church office, but rather the free fellowship of disciples led by the Spirit-Paraclete.'[13] The void within the text of allusions to ecclesiastical hierarchies has been filled in with the idea of Johannine individualism.[14]

Though there are grounds for doubting the supposed absence of an organized leadership structure in the historical community behind the Gospel,[15] there is no way to know definitively how this ecclesial group or network of groups was organized in terms of governance (even if vague clues may be glimpsed by lateral readings of the Gospel alongside the Johannine Epistles). The quest for formal structures and practices underlying the Fourth Gospel's concept of 'church' expects too much from its literary genre.[16] In contrast to this particular approach to Johannine ecclesiology, I contend that the sort of ecclesiology a Gospel narrative can provide is a fundamental and overarching vision of the church as a social reality. As will become clear, the evangelist is invested in a social vision that is explicitly communal, not individualistic. He certainly depicts interrelations between Jesus and specific disciples or would-be disciples; these interactions demonstrate that Johannine ecclesiology is *personal*, but they are certainly not part of an agenda promoting individualism. The Shepherd knows his individual sheep by name, but he leads them in and out *as a flock*.

---

[12] Käsemann, *Testament*, 28.

[13] Martin Hengel, 'The Old Testament in the Fourth Gospel', in *The Gospels and the Scriptures of Israel*, ed. W. Richard Stegner and Craig A. Evans, *JSNTSup* 104 (Sheffield: Sheffield Academic Press, 1994), 380–95, here at 384–85.

[14] But see the carefully nuanced approach by Richard Bauckham in his recent collection of essays, Richard Bauckham, *Gospel of Glory: Major Themes in Johannine Theology* (Grand Rapids, MI: Baker Academic, 2015), 1–29.

[15] For instance, though Ignatius of Antioch advocated an ecclesiastical leadership model based on a strong episcopacy, his comments about a bishop's authority seem largely premised on the theme of reciprocity so thematically important for the Gospel of John (see Chapter 9 in this book). It does not necessarily follow, of course, that Johannine communal life was organized within the more rigid hierarchies in place during Ignatius' ministry; but it can certainly be said that, from a particular angle, Ignatius' idea of the ecclesiastical bishop is 'Johannine'. See Ignatius, *Eph.* 3–6 (esp. 3.2) and *Magn.* 2–4; 6–7 (esp. 7.1–2).

[16] Johann Ferreira has sought to show that 'previous studies on Johannine ecclesiology have suffered under the influence of the categories of Pauline or "orthodox" ecclesiology. Scholars have approached John with theological categories that are alien to the Gospel itself' (Ferreira, *Johannine Ecclesiology*, 15). See also Brown, *John*, cvi.

Ecclesiology as Aetiology: Historical Reconstructions of the Johannine Community

The publication in 1968 of J. Louis Martyn's *History and Theology in the Fourth Gospel* significantly altered scholarly approaches to the study of John's conceptuality of 'church'.[17] The Fourth Gospel is now widely understood as a 'two-level drama'[18] that 'collapses temporal horizons, inscribing the life of the community into the story of Jesus'.[19] Though Clement of Alexandria dubbed John the 'spiritual gospel', Martyn pointed out that this narrative did not just 'drop from heaven' as if unencumbered by an historical, earthly setting.[20] Unlocking the secrets of that milieu holds enormous potential for the study of John's ecclesiology – the evangelist's ecclesial vision would surely be more accessible with an awareness of the contingencies he was attempting to address. A new trend therefore emerged in which queries concerning Johannine ecclesiology could be answered by scholarly reconstructions of the historical Johannine community. The Gospel's theological vision of the people of God became indissolubly bound to scholarly construals of actual events in the evangelist's socioreligious context.

The scholarship of Raymond Brown illustrates how this approach affected the study of Johannine ecclesiology.[21] Brown had adopted a cautious yet favourable stance in identifying possible ecclesial themes in his 1966 commentary.[22] In an article published over a decade later, he retrospectively deemed that prior search for ecclesiology within John's

---

[17] J. Louis Martyn, *History and Theology in the Fourth Gospel*, 3rd edn., NTL (Louisville, KY: Westminster John Knox, 2003). See the brief discussion on this work's impact on Johannine ecclesiology in Culpepper, 'Quest for the Church', 344–46.

[18] Martyn, *History and Theology*, 46–66.

[19] Attridge, 'Johannine Christianity', 6. To a certain degree, these developments reflected the idea already entrenched in form criticism that the Gospels are more reliable sources for understanding their ancient social contexts than they are for accessing the life of the historical Jesus. In this perspective, the Gospels are more community histories than histories of the historical Jesus. See Francis Watson's discussion of this trend in 'Toward a Literal Reading of the Gospels', in *The Gospels for All Christians: Rethinking the Gospel Audiences*, ed. Richard Bauckham (Grand Rapids, MI: Eerdmans, 1998), 195–217.

[20] Martyn, *History and Theology*, 28. Clement's well-known comment is found in Eusebius, *Hist. eccl.*, vi.14, 7.

[21] For a sustained and very recent critique of the Johannine Community hypothesis, largely targetting Brown's work, see David A. Lamb, *Text, Context, and the Johannine Community: A Sociolinguistic Analysis of the Johannine Writings* (LNTS 477; London: Bloomsbury T & T Clark, 2014).

[22] Brown, *John*, cv–cxiv.

Gospel was an exercise in following 'an argument from silence'.[23] Having exhausted that line of research, he reset his exegetical sights onto a new trajectory: 'A more fruitful approach has been opened up in Johannine scholarship of the last ten years by attempts to reconstruct the history of the church of the Fourth Gospel.'[24] Utilizing this new methodological venture, Brown's previously frustrated quest within the text for a Johannine concept of the people of God gave way to an elaborate, multi-phase history of the community behind the text.[25]

The approach epitomized in Brown's *The Community of the Beloved Disciple* has indeed been fruitful, yielding significant contributions that shed light on my own research on John's ecclesiology. It has not, however, come without a number of hermeneutical risks.[26] Attempts to understand the Johannine vision of community have not been simply informed by the *einmalige* experiences made available through the (hypothetical) historical reconstructions;[27] in some respects, a possible communal vision has been all but replaced by accounts of the community's possible origins. In many respects, *this approach tends to equate ecclesiology with aetiology.* The following is from Wayne Meeks: 'Despite the absence of ecclesiology from the Fourth Gospel, this book

[23] Raymond E. Brown, 'Johannine Ecclesiology: The Community's Origins', *Int* 31, no. 4 (1977): 379–93, here at 379.

[24] Ibid.

[25] Raymond E. Brown, *The Community of the Beloved Disciple: The Life, Loves, and Hates of an Individual Church in New Testament Times* (New York: Paulist Press, 1979).

[26] Critiques of Martyn's proposals and alternative readings are numerous. See the various works cited in Adele Reinhartz's study, 'The Johannine Community and Its Jewish Neighbors: A Reappraisal', in *'What Is John?' Volume II: Literary and Social Readings of the Fourth Gospel*, ed. Fernando F. Segovia, SBLSymS 7 (Atlanta, GA: Society of Biblical Literature, 1998), 111–38. For a more recent critique, see Raimo Hakola, *Identity Matters: John, the Jews and Jewishness*, NovTSup 118 (Leiden: Brill, 2005), 41–55 and, from a literary-rhetorical perspective, William M. Wright IV, *Rhetoric and Theology: Figural Reading of John 9*, BZNW 165 (Berlin: Walter de Gruyter, 2009).

[27] Other influential reconstruction hypotheses have been offered by Wayne A. Meeks, 'The Man from Heaven in Johannine Sectarianism', *JBL* 91, no. 1 (1972): 44–72; Oscar Cullmann, *The Johannine Circle: Its Place in Judaism, Among the Disciples of Jesus and in Early Christianity*, trans. John Bowden, NTL (London: SCM Press, 1976); Martin Hengel, *The Johannine Question*, trans. John Bowdon (London: SCM Press, 1989); and Martinus C. de Boer, *Johannine Perspectives on the Death of Jesus*, CBET 17 (Kampen: Kok-Pharos, 1996), 43–82. See the extensive overview of the quest for the Johannine community's *Sitz im Leben* in the opening chapter of Edward W. Klink III, *The Sheep of the Fold: The Audience and Origin of the Gospel of John*, SNTSMS 141 (Cambridge: Cambridge University Press, 2007).

could be called an etiology of the Johannine group.'[28] The potential
for this interpretative move of reducing ecclesiology to aetiology is
evident in the title of the article in which Brown first detailed this
'more fruitful approach': 'Johannine Ecclesiology: The Community's
Origins'. If ecclesiology is treated as no more than the construction of
a social group's aetiology, it can become an exercise of historical
description rather than a theological discipline, thus creating an unnecessary dichotomy between the 'history and theology of the Fourth
Gospel' that Martyn intended to hold together.[29]

A more obvious interpretative risk is the conscious or even unconscious prioritization of unconfirmed and ultimately hypothetical details
(however reasonable) over the content and literary aims of the existing
Gospel text. The recreated scenarios can become hermeneutical frames
wielding inordinate influence over the actual narrative. Because the
aporias within Gospel texts are valued as windows affording glimpses
into the origins of Gospel communities, John's ecclesiology has
been regularly sought not in the coherent, sequential trajectories of the
narrative, but in the disjunctive points of narrative departure.[30]
The hermeneutical move operative in this line of inquiry is a temporary
suspension of attention to the narrative in order to fashion a *Sitz im Leben*
that can then be used as a lens for rereading the narrative on a more
contextually grounded footing (as the logic goes). I am not denying
John's ostensible thematic breaks, apparent geographical disruptions,
and seemingly anachronistic temporal markers;[31] but if the fourth

[28] Meeks, 'Man from Heaven', 69.

[29] Brown went on to produce two essays on Johannine theology that were robustly
theological, even if heavily dependent on his reconstructed history. See Brown,
'The Heritage of the Beloved Disciple in the Fourth Gospel: People Personally Attached
to Jesus', in Brown, *The Churches the Apostles Left Behind*, 84–101; and 'The Heritage of
the Beloved Disciple and the Epistles: Individuals Guided by the Spirit-Paraclete', in ibid.
102–23.

[30] In response to the enthusiasm over narrative criticism, John Ashton makes the valid
point that historical critics initially approach the extant text of the Gospel but are often
compelled into diachronic directions by the unavoidable aporias – John Ashton, 'Second
Thoughts on the Fourth Gospel', in *What We Have Heard From the Beginning: The Past,
Present, and Future of Johannine Studies*, ed. Tom Thatcher (Waco, TX: Baylor University
Press, 2007), 1–18, here at 3.

[31] Wayne Meeks acknowledged that the majority of the aporias 'evidently were accep-
table to the evangelist, despite his ability to produce large, impressively unified literary
compositions' (citing the trial and passion narrative as the prime example) – see Meeks,
'Man from Heaven', 48. Similarly, Barnabas Lindars suggested that these aporias exist with
the Fourth Evangelist's editorial permission as he crafted source material in the interest of
his more expansive project of producing a Gospel – Barnabus Lindars, *Behind the Fourth*

evangelist has embedded a vision for the people of God in his narrative (as I am contending), an approach that focuses primarily on those points in the Gospel where the narrative appears to break will fall short in the exegetical task.[32]

I have no interest in dichotomizing methodological approaches, pitting the historical–critical enterprise of reconstructing the Fourth Gospel's *Sitz im Leben* against literary–narrative readings.[33] My understanding of ecclesiology as a vision for the community of God's people reconceived through Jesus presupposes the importance of historical details as well as the conceptual processes of how a social group thinks of itself theologically – the two are clearly intertwined. What I find problematic is the influential tendency to allow hypothetical reconstructions to exert such hermeneutical force in scholarly exegesis that the vision of community set forth within the narrative is suppressed or ignored. In other words, *the Johannine vision of community can easily become confused with a scholar's vision of the Johannine community*. Though the subject of ecclesiology is informed by the details behind a Gospel's composition, little information of those details is truly available, in spite of access to three epistles that circulated within the Johannine community's social networks.[34] What the Gospel does make available is a storied vision of

Gospel: Studies in Creative Criticism (London: SPCK, 1971), 15. So in spite of the diachronic markers long recognized in the text, the overall narrative structure can be heeded as an authoritative source for Johannine thought. As the conceptualization of the church, ecclesiology does not necessarily require the conjectural reconstruction of a particularized community or collection of communities.

[32] Stephen Barton provides several other related critiques of the use of historical reconstructions in discerning John's vision of community. One worth mentioning here is the 'privileging of the original text in its (reconstructed) historical context over readings of the text in its canonical context and in the light of its history of reception in the Church'. From Stephen C. Barton, 'Christian Community in the Gospel of John', in *Christology, Controversy and Community: New Testament Essays in Honour of David R. Catchpole*, ed. David G. Horrell and Christopher M. Tuckett, NovTSup 99 (Leiden: Brill, 2000), 279–301, here at 284.

[33] For the possible contributions of literary criticism to historical research, see Adele Reinhartz, 'Building Skyscrapers on Toothpicks: The Literary-Critical Challenge to Historical Criticism', in *Anatomies of Narrative Criticism: The Past, Present, and Futures of the Fourth Gospel as Literature*, ed. Tom Thatcher and Stephen D. Moore, SBLRBS 55 (Atlanta, GA: Society of Biblical Literature, 2008), 55–76. On the unfortunate dichotomization of narrative and history in Gospels scholarship, see Francis Watson's 'The Gospels as Narrated History' in Francis Watson, *Text and Truth: Redefining Biblical Theology* (Grand Rapids, MI: Eerdmans, 1997), 33–69.

[34] In the Johannine Epistles there is a small cache of historical material serviceable for a limited degree of community reconstruction (though scarcely enough, in my view, for the formulation of a community's history spanning half a century). For a representation of how

the divine–human society of 'church'. The hermeneutical circle
oscillating between the community's history and the community's text
is certainly helpful and even necessary in Gospel studies; it is the
ambiguities and gaps in the latter that press interpreters into the task of
conjecturing about the former. The general scholarly consensus that
John's Gospel evidences some form of intra-Jewish conflict in its elusive
background is assumed and affirmed throughout this study.[35] But it is
the Gospel narrative that bears primary hermeneutical weight in all
that follows.

'Christocentricity': The Eclipse of Ecclesiology by Christology

At the heart of the most prominent reconstruction theories, it is an
uncompromising devotion to a caustic high christology that precipitates
the expulsion of Johannine Christians from their Jewish socioreligious
context, a traumatic social event to be sure.[36] In contemporary biblical
scholarship the Fourth Gospel's distinctive portrayal of that christology
is therefore accentuated to such an extent that other themes or concerns
within the text can become inadvertently relegated to ancillary status.
Responding to Nils Dahl's criticism that God is the 'neglected factor
in New Testament theology',[37] Marianne Meye Thompson has argued
that an 'inadequate and imprecise' christocentricity has been applied
to John's Gospel.[38] In her view, the evangelist's presentation of Jesus
has overwhelmed the Gospel's vision of God in biblical scholarship –
theology proper (in its narrower sense as a discipline in understanding
God) has been eclipsed by a disproportionate focus on christology.

scholars frequently read the Johannine narrative through the lens of the Epistles see Stephen
S. Smalley, 'The Johannine Community and the Letters of John', in *A Vision for the
Church: Studies in Early Christian Ecclesiology*, ed. Markus Bockmuehl and Michael
B. Thompson (Edinburgh: T & T Clark, 1997), 95–104.

[35] I side with Adele Reinhartz who believes that 'the Gospel reflects the complex social
situation of the Johannine community but not the specific historical circumstances which
gave rise to that situation' – Reinhartz, 'Johannine Community', 137.

[36] The operative term in John's Gospel, of course, is ἀποσυνάγωγος, appearing in 9:22,
12:42, and 16:2.

[37] Nils A. Dahl, 'The Neglected Factor in New Testament Theology', in *Jesus the
Christ: The Historical Origins of Christological Doctrine*, ed. Donald H. Juel
(Minneapolis, MN: Fortress, 1991), 153–63.

[38] Marianne Meye Thompson, *The God of the Gospel of John* (Grand Rapids, MI:
Eerdmans, 2001), 13–14.

This christocentricity has had the same effect on ecclesiology.[39] Just as the scholarly emphasis on christology overshadows how the evangelist is reimagining the idea of 'God', his correlated programme of reimagining the people of God is eclipsed. This disproportion between christology and ecclesiology is taken as a given in Johannine scholarship. As Raymond Brown puts it, '[e]cclesiology in the Fourth Gospel is dominated by the extraordinary Johannine christology'.[40] In his Introduction to the English edition of Bultmann's commentary, Walter Schmithals writes that 'the Gospel of John fundamentally contains but a single theme: the Person of Jesus'.[41] After stating that John lacks any 'self-conscious ecclesiology', John Painter writes that John's focus is so exclusively christological that 'ecclesiology is not explicitly treated but appears only in relation to christology'.[42] For Painter and many other interpreters, ecclesiology's 'relation to christology' is incontrovertibly subordinate. Though he does believe that John touches on ecclesial themes, John Meier writes that

> John's high christology of preexistence and incarnation is an all-devouring obsession in the Fourth Gospel ... Jesus and Jesus alone stands in the spotlight of the Fourth Gospel; there is no room for anyone or anything else, including the church. And so it is not surprising that ecclesiology hardly makes an appearance on the stage ... High christology is the black hole in the Johannine universe that swallows up every other topic, including the church.[43]

The christocentricity highlighted by Thompson and epitomized in Meier's comments is so operative in Johannine scholarship that even those who do view ecclesiology as an important theme for John (like Meier) are quick to point out the thematic superiority of christology

[39] In some cases, Johannine ecclesiology is not just eclipsed by christology, but sharply polarized against it. Since high christology lies at the root of the schismatic experiences of the Johannine community in the historical reconstructions, the evangelist's portrayal of Jesus can become more associated with the negative experience of social rupture than with a positive ecclesial vision.

[40] Brown, 'Heritage of the Beloved Disciple in the Fourth Gospel', 85.

[41] Walter Schmithals, 'Introduction', in Bultmann, *John*, 5: 1–12.

[42] John Painter, 'The Church and Israel in the Gospel of John', *NTS* 25, no. 1 (1978): 103–12, here at 112.

[43] Meier, 'Church', 29.

for the Gospel.[44] D. Moody Smith's claim that ecclesiology is the 'pre-supposition' and '*sine qua non* of Johannine theology' is qualified with this: 'Clearly the Gospel of John is focused not upon ecclesiology, but upon christology.'[45] James Resseguie has recently claimed that 'the Fourth Gospel's master-plot develops the paradox of the glory in the flesh, the divine in the ordinary'.[46] My purpose is to show that this christological master-plot coincides with an integral ecclesial dimension (not a mere sub-plot) in which flesh enters divine glory, and the ordinary participates in the divine.

I agree that John's ecclesiology is related to its christology. Where I differ from other studies is in the conviction that John's christology cannot be treated as independent of, or isolated from, ecclesiology. The latter is not subsidiary to the former in a dispensable relation of thematic inferiority – both *christology and ecclesiology are weighted with parallel force*. Ecclesiology is not supplemental to christology but *complementary*. Marinus de Jonge opens an essay on 'the centrality of christology' in John with this: 'christology is without any doubt the main theme of the Fourth Gospel (20:30–31)'.[47] Yet the Gospel passage he cites binds christology and ecclesiology together. In that text, the evangelist indicates that his express purpose in narrating the signs of Jesus is to evoke a corporate response from a plural 'you' (see also 1 Jn 1:3). My point here is that the Gospel's christology bears the ecclesial task of social invitation and community formation. Though there is no ecclesiology extrinsic to christology in this Gospel, the converse is also true – christology is not extrinsic to ecclesiology. Jesus does not eclipse the church in this narrative. The two themes coinhere. As the subtitle to Part I expresses it, for the Fourth Gospel there is no Christless church nor churchless Christ.

[44] Examples include Udo Schnelle, 'Johanneische Ekklesiologie', *NTS* 37 (1991): pp. 37–50; Mark L. Appold, *The Oneness Motif in the Fourth Gospel: Motif Analysis and Exegetical Probe into the Theology of John*, 2nd edn.; WUNT 2:1 (Eugene, OR: Wipf and Stock, 1976); Ferreira, *Johannine Ecclesiology*.

[45] D. Moody Smith, *The Theology of the Gospel of John*, NTT (Cambridge: Cambridge University Press, 1995), 136–37. See also Barton, 'Community', 285–36.

[46] James L. Resseguie, 'A Narrative-Critical Approach to the Fourth Gospel', in *Characters and Characterization in the Gospel of John*, ed. Christopher W. Skinner, LNTS 461 (London: Bloomsbury, 2013), 3–17, here at 15.

[47] Marinus de Jonge, 'Christology, Controversy and Community in the Gospel of John', in *Christology, Controversy and Community: New Testament Essays in Honour of David R. Catchpole*, ed. Christopher M. Tuckett and David G. Horrell, NovTSup 99 (Leiden: Brill, 2000), 209–29, here at 209.

Ecclesiology as Sectarianism: The Relationship between Sociology and Theology

Whether a 'school',[48] 'circle',[49] 'conventicle',[50] 'community',[51] 'introversionist' sect,[52] or an 'anti-society' with an 'anti-language',[53] scholars have understood the Johannine literature as products of an insular social entity determined to define itself in contradistinction from others.[54] In some reconstruction theories, the Gospel's supposed sectarian inwardness has been understood as oriented against mainstream or Petrine Christianity[55]; most prominently, however, it is understood that the evangelist's antagonisms are, as already noted, directed against a parent Jewish community. The polemical use of Ἰουδαῖοι ('Jews') and Jesus' accusation 'you are of your father the devil' (8:44)[56] have understandably sparked a diverse array of secondary literature probing the possibility that anti-Semitism has been justified by interpretations of John and may

[48] R. Alan Culpepper, *The Johannine School: An Evaluation of the Johannine-School Hypothesis Based on an Investigation of the Nature of Ancient Schools*, SBLDS 26 (Missoula, MT: Society of Biblical Literature, 1975).

[49] Cullmann, *The Johannine Circle*.

[50] Käsemann, *Testament*, 32. Käsemann championed both Johannine individualism and Johannine sectarianism at the same time.

[51] Brown, *Community*.

[52] Philip F. Esler, 'Introverted Sectarianism at Qumran and in the Johannine Community', in *The First Christians in Their Social Worlds: Social-Scientific Approaches to New Testament Interpretation*, ed. Philip F. Esler (London: Routledge, 1994), 70–91. Esler's typology for identifying and labelling sects is drawn from Bryan R. Wilson, *Magic and the Millennium* (St Albans: Paladin, 1975).

[53] Bruce J. Malina and Richard L. Rohrbaugh, *Social-Science Commentary on the Gospel of John* (Minneapolis, MN: Fortress, 1998), 7. See also Meeks, 'Man from Heaven'.

[54] See also David Rensberger, 'Sectarianism and Theological Interpretation in John', in *'What Is John?' Volume II: Literary and Social Readings of the Fourth Gospel*, ed. Fernando F. Segovia, SBLSymS 7 (Atlanta, GA: Society of Biblical Literature, 1998), 139–56; Fernando F. Segovia, 'The Love and Hatred of Jesus and Johannine Sectarianism', *CBQ* 43, no. 2 (1981): 258–72; Meeks, 'Man from Heaven'; D. Moody Smith, *Johannine Christianity: Essays on Its Setting, Sources, and Theology* (Columbia, SC: University of South Carolina Press, 1984). For alternative reflections, see Reinhartz, 'Johannine Community'; and Gail R. O'Day, 'Johannine Theologians as Sectarians', in *"What Is John?' Volume 1: Readers and Readings of the Fourth Gospel*, ed. Fernando F. Segovia, SBLSymS 3 (Atlanta, GA: Society of Biblical Literature, 1996), 199–203.

[55] In addition to Käsemann, *Testament*, see James H. Charlesworth, *The Beloved Disciple: Whose Witness Validates the Gospel of John?* (Valley Forge, PA: Trinity Press International, 1995).

[56] Translations from the Johannine literature are mine throughout unless otherwise noted.

even underlie the entire Gospel text.[57] The historical reconstructions of
the Johannine *Sitz im Leben* have largely understood this apparent anti-
Jewish polemic as an in-house dispute between Jews and other Jews[58]
(i.e., 'Christian Jews' vs. 'Jewish Christians', to work with labels offered
by Martyn[59]).

I have already acknowledged that I embrace the widely accepted scenario
that the Johannine Christians were themselves Jews who suffered a painful
breach from the more established religious community. My study differs,
however, from standard approaches to Johannine sectarianism on at least
three points. The first is my attempt to understand the Johannine sense of
group identity with theology as my primary frame of reference. Johannine
'sectarianism' and the 'parting of the ways' between Judaism and Johannine
Christianity are certainly sociological phenomena; but they are intrinsically
related to the theological discussion of John's ecclesial vision.

David Rensberger acknowledges that the language of sectarianism
is often negative in connotation, calling to mind a group on the 'lunatic
fringe' that is 'deviant' and 'deranged'. The sociological approach of
treating John as a sectarian text also seems 'theologically barren'.[60]
The idea that John is the 'spiritual gospel' bearing theological import
for its readers 'seems hopelessly at odds with the particularism and
in-group concerns that emerge when one brings its historical origins

---

[57]   See, for instance, the collection of essays in Reimund Bieringer, Didier Pollefeyt, and
Frederique Vandecasteele-Vanneuville, eds., *Anti-Judaism and the Fourth Gospel: Papers
of the Leuven Colloquium, 2000, Jewish and Christian Heritage 1* (Assen: Van Gorcum,
2001); Johannes Beutler, Michael Labahn, and Klaus Scholtissek, eds., *Israel und seine
Heilstraditionen im Johannessevangelium: Festgabe für Johannes Beutler SJ, zum 70.
Geburtstag* (Paderborn: Schöningh, 2004).

[58]   Resseguie, 'A Narrative-Critical Approach', 15. See also D. Moody Smith,
'The Contribution of J. Louis Martyn to the Understanding of the Gospel of John', in his
introduction to Martyn, *History and Theology*, 1–23, here at 8–9.; Stephen Motyer, *Your Father
the Devil? A New Approach to John and 'the Jews'*, Paternoster Biblical and Theological
Monographs (Carlisle: Paternoster Press, 1997); Stephen Motyer, 'The Fourth Gospel and the
Salvation of the New Israel: An Appeal for a New Start', in *Anti-Judaism and the Fourth
Gospel: Papers of the Leuven Colloquium, 2000*, ed. Didier Pollefeyt, Reimund Bieringer, and
Frederique Vandecasteele-Vanneveuville (Assen: Royal van Gorcum, 2001), 92–110.

[59]   Martyn, *History and Theology*, 160–63.

[60]   Rensberger, 'Sectarianism', 140, 142. The negative connotations attached to the word
'sect' are likely drawn in part from Ernst Troeltsch's model in which a sect is defined as
a splinter group in distinct opposition to the established Church. See Troeltsch's ground-
breaking *The Social Teaching of the Christian Churches*, trans. Olive Wyon, Reprint,
2 vols. (Louisville, KY: Westminster John Knox Press, 1992). For a recent and cogent
study from a social-identity perspective, see Raimo Hakola, *Reconsidering Johannine
Christianity: A Social Identity Approach*, Bible World (London: Routledge, 2015).

to center stage'.[61] What Rensberger is observing here is the tension between sociology and theology in perspectives focusing primarily on the etic and emic phenomena of the Johannine social group. Though my understanding of Johannine ecclesiology differs from Rensberger's on many counts, I share his assessment that the social vision put forward by the evangelist is theologically grounded.[62] Since the study of early Christian communities as sects or breakaway factions requires sensitivity to 'the correlation of theological thought and social predicament',[63] sociology and theology should be wed more closely together in research on Gospel origins. Allusions to the theme of community in John are more than incidental hints of a sectarian consciousness. *They are also the fruit of a robust theological enterprise.* In my study, I purpose to remain attentive not only to this sectarian consciousness but also to the theological, christological, and ecclesial ideas that inform it. If the Gospel of John is treated primarily as a textual artifact that unlocks the etiological mysteries of an ancient religious group, then 'sectarianism' can perhaps be applied without the messy trappings of theology. But if the Gospel is regarded as a theological interpretation of an historic figure claiming divine status and written to create and shape communal identity (again, as 20:30–31 makes clear), then its purported sectarian tendencies should be understood within the broader theological frame of ecclesiology.

A second point of clarification between my study and certain others on Johannine sectarianism is my conviction that the Fourth Gospel's ecclesiology is premised on a salvation-history paradigm in which the faithful embrace of Jesus confirms legitimate membership within the people of

---

[61] Rensberger, 'Sectarianism', 140.

[62] Rensberger embraces Johannine sectarianism as a theological construct and discerns within John a sectarian theology that is inherently political and anti-establishment (vis-à-vis both local Jewish leadership and Rome). In addition to the article cited above, see David Rensberger, *Johannine Faith and Liberating Community* (Philadelphia, PA: The Westminster Press, 1998) and David Rensberger, *Overcoming the World: Politics and Community in the Gospel of John* (London: SPCK, 1989).

[63] John H. Elliott, 'Phases in the Social Formation of Early Christianity: From Faction to Sect – A Social Scientific Perspective', in *Recruitment, Conquest, and Conflict: Strategies in Judaism, Early Christianity, and the Greco-Roman World*, ed. Peder Borgen, Vernon K. Robbins, and David B. Gowler, Emory Studies in Early Christianity (Atlanta, GA: Scholars Press, 1998), 273–313, here at 279. I am drawing attention here to a potential interpretative trend that surfaces in Johannine scholarship. I acknowledge that when pressed, most scholars would draw connections between John's sectarianism and his theology.

God – a christologically reconfigured Israel.[64] A linear concept of salvation-history is certainly interrupted by the unexpected event of the Incarnation, forcing a 'conversation of the imagination' of the kind Richard Hays has observed in Pauline ecclesiology.[65] But Jesus' prayer 'that they may be one, as we are one' in John 17 demonstrates the evangelist's conviction that any departure from the local synagogue or the parent religious tradition of Judaism is not a departure from the 'One' God of Jewish faith.[66] The oneness language of the Shema denoting the divine identity is correlated in that prayer with the people of God who are relationally bound to him. In this respect, John affirms the scriptural traditions of his Jewish religious heritage, albeit a heritage now reconceived through Jesus' participation in the divine identity: 'I and the Father are one' (Jn 10:30). John is not promoting a sectarianism that

[64] This claim is by no means unique. The relation between the church and Israel in John has been a long-standing debate in New Testament scholarship. Those denying that the fourth evangelist held to a concept of salvation-history include Bultmann, Schweizer, Painter, and Ferreira, op. cit. Those who find a clear and positive presentation of Israel in John include Severino Pancaro, '"People of God" in St John's Gospel', NTS 16, no. 2 (1970): 114–29; Severino Pancaro, 'The Relationship of the Church to Israel in the Gospel of St John', NTS 21, no. 3 (1975): 396–405; Nils A. Dahl, 'The Johannine Church and History', in Nils A. Dahl, Jesus in the Memory of the Early Church: Essays by Nils Alstrup Dahl (Minneapolis, MN: Augsburg Publishing House, 1976), 99–119; John W. Pryor, 'Jesus and Israel in the Fourth Gospel – John 1:11', NovT 32, no. 3 (1990): 201–18; John W. Pryor, John: Evangelist of the Covenant People: The Narrative and Themes of the Fourth Gospel (Downers Grove, IL: InterVarsity Press, 1992); Sandra M. Schneiders, 'The Raising of the New Temple: John 20.19–23 and Johannine Ecclesiology', NTS 52, no. 3 (2006): 337–55; and more recently, see Richard Horsley and Tom Thatcher, John, Jesus and the Renewal of Israel (Grand Rapids, MI: Eerdmans, 2013) and Paul A. Rainbow, Johannine Theology: The Gospel, the Epistles and the Apocalypse (Downers Grove, IL: InterVarsity Press, 2014), 362–74.

[65] Richard B. Hays, The Conversion of the Imagination: Paul as Interpreter of Israel's Scripture (Grand Rapids, MI: Eerdmans, 2005), 5–6.

[66] Reimund Bieringer and Didier Pollefeyt offer what I believe to be the most circumspect overview of John's supposed ecclesiology of supersessionism and his idea of 'Israel': 'John does not distinguish simply in the history of salvation between the Israel of the pre-Christ period which is replaced by the community of believers in the post-Christ period . . . John's position is characterized by much more subtlety. He does not distinguish between two successive entities that one could call Israel and the Church, but between two parallel lines: true Israelites and false Israelites, faithful and unfaithful disciples of Moses. The community of disciples is not the new Israel (the position of classical supersessionism) but rather the true, genuine Israel.' From Reimund Bieringer and Didier Pollefeyt 'Open to Both Ways . . . ? Johannine Perspectives on Judaism in the Light of Jewish-Christian Dialogue', in Israel und seine Heilstraditionen im Johannesevangelium: Festgabe für Johannes Beutler SJ zum 70. Geburtstag, ed. Michael Labahn, Klaus Scholtissek, and Angelika Strotmann (Paderborn: Ferdinand Schöningh, 2004), 11–32, here at 18.

encourages anti-Semitism. He is, however, along with other Jewish Christian writers like Paul and Peter, promoting a new way to understand Jewish identity in the light of Jesus. As will become clear in Part II, my own view is that John's ecclesial vision supplies *an ecclesiology of the parting of the ways* as Christ-confession became incommensurate with the socioreligious convictions of Judaism in the Gospel's elusive setting.

A third important qualification my study brings to the discussion of Johannine sectarianism is that the social entity evoked by and centred around Johannine christology is *open and inclusive*. Rather than rigidly 'introversionist', the Fourth Gospel's ecclesiology is invitational in orientation, though appropriate Christ-confession and continual 'abiding' are undoubtedly requisite for communal membership. As will be shown, participation is the central dynamic of this ecclesial vision; and the social group is participatory in nature precisely because the divine identity is open to and inclusive of the divine figure of the Logos, Jesus. Though the evangelist certainly limns in his narrative social boundaries between a parent religious culture and the devotees of Jesus, the ecclesial community parallels the openness of the divine community.

'Narrative Ecclesiology': Gospel Writing as Group Identity Formation

I have presented four trends or approaches in the study of Johannine ecclesiology with which this present volume offers some degree of contrast (while benefiting from a number of their positive contributions). Though I will not limit myself to one particular methodological discipline, the approaches with which my work bears the most affinity are those employing the diverse range of exegetical strategies available in narrative criticism. In his overview of 'the quest for the church in the Gospel of John', R. Alan Culpepper labels the literary-critical approach as the most recent in his survey of scholarship on Johannine ecclesiology.[67] An underlying premise is the aforementioned suggestion by D. Moody Smith that John presupposes the reality of the church in his Gospel writing. For Smith, the evangelist's ecclesiology is not 'so much about what the Johannine community was as what it should be'.[68] Because John offers an ecclesiology that is more 'prescriptive' than 'descriptive',[69] readers should expect indirect ecclesial references or

---

[67] Culpepper, 'Quest for the Church', 346–50. [68] Smith, *Theology*, 137.
[69] Culpepper, 'Quest for the Church', 347.

expressions to surface in the narrative. Multiple studies are available exploring implied ecclesial meanings found in the Farewell Discourse (especially in John 17[70]), in the Eucharistic language in John 6,[71] in the enigmatic scenes and exchanges in the passion narrative,[72] or in a constellation of metaphors or images (temple/household,[73] vine,[74] etc.) that seem to convey concerns for a communal vision.

Rather than centring on one particular narrative scene, discourse, or symbolic image suggestive of ecclesiology, I am offering a more comprehensive treatment to show that the presentation of Jesus is permanently affixed to an ecclesial agenda running through the entirety of the Gospel. Ecclesiology is not to be solely identified in John with accidental references to a presupposed idea of 'church' leaked out subconsciously and at random. Both the use of the first person plural in his narration and his occasional direct addresses to the audience indicate an acute consciousness of a communal reality, one that he intends to affect and shape through his story of Jesus.[75] Though certain elements and concerns pertaining to the historical social situation are surely reflected in John, the evangelist's primary purpose in writing was not to drop clues about his context for later readers but to influence current readers through a storied presentation of Jesus and to give shape to the community forming around the testimonies

---

[70] Examples include Ferreira, *Johannine Ecclesiology* and Käsemann, *Testament*.

[71] E.g., Corell, *Consummatum Est*.

[72] E.g., R. Alan Culpepper, 'Designs for the Church in the Gospel Accounts of Jesus' Death', *NTS* 51, no. 3 (2005): 376–92; and Francis J. Moloney, 'John 18:15–27: A Johannine View of the Church', *DRev* 389 (1994): 231–48.

[73] Mary L. Coloe, *God Dwells With Us: Temple Symbolism in the Fourth Gospel* (Collegeville, MN: Liturgical Press, 2001); Mary L. Coloe, *Dwelling in the Household of God: Johannine Ecclesiology and Spirituality* (Collegeville, MN: Liturgical Press, 2007); Schneiders, 'Raising of the New Temple', 337–55.

[74] Schweizer, 'Church'.

[75] The references to John 20:30–31 and my interest in identifying 'the sort of community John's Gospel seeks to produce' would suggest an investment in the methodological perspective of reader-response criticism, particularly in the model of 'implied reader' as understood by Wolfgang Iser, et al. The author of the Fourth Gospel clearly anticipates that his narrative will generate a dynamic between text and reader with the potential for dramatic results. Though sensitive to this dynamic, my primary concern is with the vision of community the evangelist hopes to convey through his story (it should be said, however, that the evangelist certainly hopes that readers will become participants within the vision of community he narrates). On Iser's treatment of the implied reader, see Wolfgang Iser, *The Implied Reader: Patterns of Communication in Prose Fiction from Bunyan to Beckett* (London: The Johns Hopkins University Press, 1974) and *The Act of Reading: A Theory of Aesthetic Response* (London: Routledge & Kegan Paul, 1978).

about him.[76] Concrete historical situations of worshipping communities are certainly reflected in the canonical Gospels, but the evangelists wrote not to catalogue or chronicle their communities' respective experiences but to shape their communities in the midst of their ongoing circumstances.[77] My construct of 'narrative ecclesiology' looks beyond possible *Sitze im Leben* to apprehend the instructive vision for communal life within those given situations.[78]

Narrative ecclesiology locates the source for these visions of community within a complex series of developmental threads laced throughout a Gospel's story. Fundamental to any 'narrative' is a certain degree of linearity – motifs are gradually endowed with meaning, characters incrementally develop, and plotlines build and resolve.[79] As a continuous

---

[76] Again, see Culpepper, 'Quest for the Church', 347.

[77] As Mary Coloe puts it, 'The narrative is *for* the community, but is not *about* the community' (*Household of God*, 8). My approach to Johannine ecclesiology bears some similarities to Coloe's which treats the Gospel as a 'symbolic narrative' constituting a communal 'faith expression' (5).

[78] Though I do not employ a formal development of narrative social identity, my work on narrative ecclesiology assumes the identity-shaping power of a story for social groups, a conviction held by many theologians and sociologists alike. See, e.g. Part One of Stanley Hauerwas, *A Community of Character: Toward a Constructive Christian Social Ethic* (Notre Dame, IN: University of Notre Dame Press, 1981), 9–86; and Paul Ricoeur, *Time and Narrative*, vol. 3 (trans., Kathleen Blamey and David Pellauer; Chicago, IL: University of Chicago Press, 1985), 157–79. For Ricoeur's idea of narrative identity, see Kevin J. Vanhoozer, *Biblical Narrative in the Philosophy of Paul Ricoeur: A Study in Hermeneutics and Theology* (Cambridge: Cambridge University Press, 1990), 86–115. For a recent treatment of sociological and theological ideas on story-shaped identity, see Coleman A. Baker, 'A Narrative–Identity Model for Biblical Interpretation: The Role of Memory and Narrative in Social Identity Formation' in *T & T Clark Handbook to Social Identity in the New Testament*, ed. J. Brian Tucker and Coleman A. Baker (London: Bloomsbury T & T Clark, 2014), 105–18.

[79] Narrative sequence is a complicated literary phenomenon that can be interrupted or altered in pace, consequentially affecting the experience of reading in diverse ways. Events in the 'story time' can appear out of sequence in the 'narrative time', and rereadings can significantly alter the meaning of the narrative order for the reader. This basic concept that meaning is conveyed by the effect of sequence is integral to understanding narrative texts. See discussions in Iser, *Implied Reader*, 274–94; Gérard Genette, *Narrative Discourse*, trans. Jane E. Lewin (Ithaca, NY: Cornell University Press, 1980), 33–85; Menakhem Perry, 'Literary Dynamics: How the Order of a Text Creates Its Meanings', *Poetics Today* 1, no. 1/2 (1979): 35–64 and 311–61; Meir Sternberg, *The Poetics of Biblical Narrative: Ideological Literature and the Drama of Reading* (Bloomington, IN: Indiana University Press, 1985), 264–320; James L. Resseguie, *Narrative Criticism of the New Testament: An Introduction* (Grand Rapids, MI: Baker Academic, 2005), 208–13; Seymour Chapman, *Story and Discourse: Narrative Structure in Fiction and Film* (Ithaca, NY: Cornell University Press, 1978), 43–48; 59–84; Adele Reinhartz, *The Word*

narrative with a 'clear chronological framework',[80] meaning is conducted in John along the axis of its storied structure. With message and medium so inseparably bound, John offers a 'narrative christology' by which the identity of Jesus is revealed through the unfolding process of narration.[81] By the phrase 'narrative ecclesiology' I am not referring to what Hans Frei would recognize as a narrative identity in which a character (or character group) is defined by interactions with other characters and by the manifestation of intentions inside the story.[82] The Johannine community may indeed find itself mirrored inside the Gospel in particular scenes, but my use of narrative ecclesiology primarily refers not to a story about a communal entity but to the narration of a *vision* for community. Because that vision is sequentially presented, this work – as a narrative-critical exercise in theological interpretation – is cumulative in nature, tracing the conceptual and literary evolution of ecclesial themes.[83]

Brief Overview of the Work's Structure

In my attempts to offer a 'comprehensive' account of Johannine ecclesiology, I do not mean *exhaustive*. Though I believe that each episode, image, and metaphor thematically connected to the idea of 'church' must

---

in the World: The Cosmological Tale in the Fourth Gospel, Society of Biblical Literature Monograph Series 45 (Atlanta, GA: Scholars Press, 1992), 12–14.

[80] Richard A. Burridge, *What Are the Gospels? A Comparison with Greco-Roman Biography* (Grand Rapids, MI: Eerdmans, 2004), 219. This claim of a 'chronological framework' is not to deny that John's chronology often raises eyebrows for modern interpreters. The placement of the Temple protest scene in ch. 2, the geographical disjunctures, and the disruptive temporal markers indicate that John is not bound to construct an accurate chronological rendering of Jesus' life. I am working in this thesis with what Eugene Lemcio has called 'the redactional product' of the Gospel as it has been received and preserved. See Eugene E. Lemcio, *The Past of Jesus in the Gospels*, SNTSMS 68 (Cambridge: Cambridge University Press, 1991), 3.

[81] On John's 'narrative christology' see Mark W. G. Stibbe, *John as Storyteller: Narrative Criticism and the Fourth Gospel*, SNTSMS 73 (Cambridge: Cambridge University Press, 1992), 12–13. For works on narrative christology in Mark and Luke, see respectively Elizabeth Struthers Malbon, *Mark's Jesus: Characterization as Narrative Christology* (Waco, TX: Baylor University Press, 2009) and C. Kavin Rowe, *Early Narrative Christology: The Lord in the Gospel of Luke* (Grand Rapids, MI: Baker Academic, 2006).

[82] Hans W. Frei, *The Identity of Jesus Christ: The Hermeneutical Bases of Dogmatic Theology* (Eugene, OR: Cascade Books, 2013).

[83] This cumulative organization is also the approach taken by Kavin Rowe in his treatment of Luke's narrative christology – Rowe, *Early Narrative Christology*, 9–17.

be understood within John's overarching narrative ecclesiology, I do not offer a detailed synthesis of how each of these elements fits within that frame – I devote little space to the Eucharistic themes in John 6, there is barely any mention of the vine imagery in John 15, and the Paraclete is discussed only in the closing pages of the final chapter in Part III. My concentration will first be on John 1:1–18, a text that gets little attention in research on Johannine ecclesiology. Second, I will examine the Johannine concept of 'oneness'. This motif does get a lot of attention in the study of Johannine ecclesiology, but the standard interpretations of its use and meaning require serious reappraisal. A combined study of both the Prologue and the theme of oneness affords the opportunity to engage the narrative as a whole and from diverse angles, mapping the contours of a participatory ecclesial vision of corporate theosis.

Since short introductions accompany each major division of this book, it will suffice here to simply list a summary of my basic aims. In Part I, I will show that the Prologue bears as much ecclesial weight as it does christological. This narrative opening establishes the ensuing story's thematic emphases and encapsulates the Gospel's basic plotline. In short, that plotline entails the filial inclusion of believers within the divine family of the Father and the only Son, what I label as *an ecclesiology of divine participation*. Part II is where I offer a narrative rereading of the Johannine conceptuality of 'one'. The most extensive recent monograph on the ecclesial use of 'one' in John 17 and the most comprehensive treatment of the Johannine oneness motif both conclude that John's oneness language is sourced in Gnostic thought, an ideological framework now generally accepted as postdating John in its more formal developments. Furthermore, neither of these two studies utilizes narrative criticism.[84] I will propose an alternative interpretation that the theological connotations of 'one' are indebted to the Jewish profession of divine oneness in the Shema and infused with multivalent meanings through a complex process of narrative development. In the evangelist's storied account of a 'parting of the ways', the social exclusion of Johannine believers from their parent socioreligious group is not

---

[84] I am referring, respectively, to Johan Ferreira's *Johannine Ecclesiology* and Mark Appold's *Oneness*. Ferreira writes, 'the present study will by and large ignore the more recent developments in narrative or reader-response criticism' (16). Writing without the exegetical approaches that later developments in narrative criticism made available, Appold was writing before these disciplines became common practice in biblical studies. He was sensitive to literary elements but consciously addressed the oneness passages out of narrative sequence.

a departure from the One God of Israel; the oneness motif offers a *narrative ecclesiology of divine association* by which the 'one flock' is correlated with the 'one Shepherd' of messianic hopes sent from the One God of Jewish monotheistic traditions.

Part III is where I make the case that the ecclesial vision set forth in both the Prologue and the oneness motif can be appropriately expressed in the patristic language of deification. I will use this admittedly anachronistic language not to force John's Gospel into a later mould of theological discourse but to employ that discourse in the descriptive task of labelling Johannine ecclesiology. In simplified form, my primary thesis is this: 'church' according to the Fourth Gospel is a community of human beings re-originated from heaven and corporately participating within the Father–Son interrelation. To be 'one' suggests a participation in divine reality so profound that Jesus' citation of Psalm 82:6 can be addressed to Johannine believers: 'you are gods'.

PART I

**The Narrative Ecclesiology of the Prologue:
No Churchless Christ, nor Christless Church**

2

THE INCLUSIVE DIVINE COMMUNITY: THE PROLOGUE'S REINTERPRETATION OF GOD AND GOD'S PEOPLE

Introduction to Part I

The Fourth Gospel's Prologue is as much an introduction to Johannine ecclesiology as it is to Johannine christology. Admittedly, ecclesiology does not feature as a prominent subject amidst the tomes of research available on the Prologue; and few studies on Johannine ecclesiology anchor their exegesis in the Gospel's majestic beginning.[1] Those studies directly focused on John 1:1–18 are generally concerned with the source-critical questions behind the Prologue's layered, compositional pre-history and with the lofty christology recognized as thematically dominant.

That christological vision extends far beyond the Gospel it introduces, shaping the creedal and doctrinal formulations of Christian churches centuries after its composition. For Martin Hengel, 'the Prologue is the most influential christological text in the New Testament. It leads us into Johannnine christology and cannot be separated from it. Moreover, it showed the early church the way to christological truth.'[2] This appraisal

---

[1] Commenting on Jn 1:12, however, J. Ramsey Michaels writes that 'christology gives way to ecclesiology, and the Christian community to which the Gospel of John was written takes center stage' – Michaels, *The Gospel of John*, NICNT (Grand Rapids, MI: Eerdmans, 2010). For other studies that do accord some significance to ecclesiology in the Prologue, see Ernst Käsemann, 'The Structure and Purpose of the Prologue to John's Gospel', in *New Testament Questions for Today*, NTL (London: SCM Press, 1969), 138–67, particularly at 164–5; Dahl, 'The Johannine Church and History', 99–119; Paul S. Minear, 'Logos Ecclesiology in John's Gospel', in *Christological Perspectives: Essays in Honor of Harvey K. McArthur*, ed. Sarah A. Edwards and Robert F. Berkey (New York: The Pilgrim Press, 1982), 95–111. John Pryor observes that 'the thrust of the Prologue (as also of the Gospel) is not just about the person of Christ but also about the community established with him' – John Pryor, 'Of the Virgin Birth or the Birth of Christians? The Text of John 1:13 Once More', *NovT* 27, no. 4 (1985): 296–318, here at 300.

[2] Martin Hengel, 'The Prologue of the Gospel of John as the Gateway to Christological Truth', in *The Gospel of John and Christian Theology*, ed. Richard Bauckham and Carl Mosser (Grand Rapids, MI: Eerdmans, 2008), 265–94, here at 289.

of the significance of the Prologue's christology is commonly acknowledged. What is *not* commonly acknowledged is that the fourth evangelist is indicating in his opening lines that his narrative is designed to shape the church not only by a christological vision, *but also by a social vision of the renewed people of God*, a vision that serves as the basis for John's narrative ecclesiology. The arguments of the following chapters will demonstrate that ecclesiology is so intrinsic to the Prologue's christology that an emphasis on the latter to the neglect of the former is a misreading of the opening passage that serves as the foundation of the Fourth Gospel's narrative. For John, there is no churchless Christ, nor Christless church.

The Prologue's Relationship to the Rest of the Gospel

In John 1:1–2, the Fourth Gospel's audience is instantly alerted to the theological conviction that God must be reconceptualized to accommodate an interrelation with another divine figure, introduced as the Logos. This christological reimagining of God simultaneously compels *a reimagining of God's people*. At stake in the Prologue is not only the identity of Jesus, but also the identity of the people renewed or reconstituted around his appearance in the world. The Prologue's christology is therefore generative of ecclesiology, and the evangelist presents them as thematically integrated. After a brief discussion of the Prologue's relation to the rest of the Gospel, I will consider how John 1:1–18 prompts a reconfiguration of the identities of both God and God's people, drawing attention to the theme of participation. More specifically, it will be shown that the Father–Son interrelation constitutes a divine community open to and inclusive of those who respond with belief to the appearance of Jesus. As early as the Prologue the fourth evangelist indicates that divinity and humanity are discrete categories yet they are not intended to subsist outside the realm of the other.

The claim that ecclesiology is integral to the Fourth Gospel is significantly strengthened if it can be shown as integral to the Prologue. In spite of influential assessments that the Prologue serves no greater purpose than orienting Hellenistic readers to the remaining material,[3] and in spite of source-critical approaches that have interpreted the Prologue

---

[3]   E.g., Adolf von Harnack, 'Über das Verhältnis des Prologs des vierten Evangeliums zum ganzen Werk', *ZTK* 2 (1892); and C. H. Dodd, *The Interpretation of the Fourth Gospel* (Cambridge: Cambridge University Press, 1970), 296.

on the basis of its literary independence from what follows,[4] Johannine scholarship has become increasingly more inclined to conceive Prologue and Gospel as inseparably lashed together, with the former establishing foundational thematic emphases worked out and resolved in the latter.[5] C. K. Barrett's assessment below was certainly not shared universally at his time of writing, but it captures well an understanding that has gained widespread support in more recent decades:

> Prologue and gospel together are the supreme example of the coinherence of the 'that' and the 'what' of the story of Jesus. The Prologue assumes simply that the light shone in the darkness, that he came to his own, that the Word become flesh, and analyses the theological significance of the bare fact expressed in the 'that'. The gospel will tell how he came to his own, what happened when the Word became flesh. And the Prologue is necessary to the gospel, as the gospel is necessary to the Prologue. The history explicates the theology, and the theology interprets the history.[6]

Though the 'coinherence' of Prologue and Gospel was never much in doubt for John's earliest interpreters,[7] significant energy was devoted in the last century to highlighting the undeniable differences between the Gospel's opening eighteen lines and what follows. Even so, it is becoming increasingly accepted of late that the extant text should be read

[4] Raymond E. Brown renders this perspective concisely: 'The Prologue had a history independent of the Gospel and does not necessarily have the same theology as the Gospel' – Brown, *John*, 6.

[5] Minear, 'Logos Ecclesiology'; Morna D. Hooker, 'Beginnings and Endings', in *The Written Gospel (FS, Graham Stanton)*, ed. Markus Bockmuehl and D. A. Hagner (Cambridge: Cambridge University Press, 2005), 184–202; Warren Carter, 'The Prologue and John's Gospel: Function, Symbol and the Definitive Word', *JSNT* 39 (1990): 35–58; Elizabeth Harris, *Prologue and Gospel: The Theology of the Fourth Evangelist, JSNTSup* 107 (Sheffield: Sheffield University Press, 1994); Reinhartz, *The Word in the World*, 16–28; John F. O'Grady, 'The Prologue and Chapter 17 of the Gospel of John', in *What We Have Heard from the Beginning: The Past, Present, and Future of Johannine Studies*, ed. Tom Thatcher (Waco, TX: Baylor University Press, 2007), 215–28.

[6] C. K. Barrett, *The Prologue of St John's Gospel* (London: The Athlone Press, 1971), 28.

[7] Patristic commentators did not break the text up after v. 18 as has become custom. For an overview of these textual breaks in the Prologue's history of reception (and on the validity of calling the Prologue a 'prologue'), see Peter J. Williams, 'Not the Prologue of John', *JSNT* 33, no. 4 (2011): 375–86. Among the Gospel's earliest interpreters, a unit break was more likely after 1:5 than 1:18 (ibid., 378–80). This is the approach taken by J. Ramsey Michaels in his recent commentary. He reads 1:1–5 as a 'Preamble' and treats v. 6ff as part of the narrative proper (Michaels, *John*, 58–59).

as a whole.[8] The Prologue may well have been added after the bulk of the narrative was completed, and it is quite possible (perhaps even likely) that a complex amalgamation of textual or oral units underlie its formation[9]; those claims notwithstanding, 'there is no clause, no phrase, no noun, no verb'[10] in the Prologue as we have it that does not serve the express purpose of escorting readers into the unfolding concerns of the subsequent narrative. This is not to say that the evangelist expects his opening lines to encapsulate his message *in toto* – there are no direct references to Jesus' death or resurrection, and the personified Logos language noticeably fails to make an explicit reappearance. The function of the Prologue is that of a narrative opening that orients its audience by providing critical information and accentuating critical themes.

With the acknowledgment that the Johannine Prologue is foundational for the ensuing narrative, I intend to show here in Part I that ecclesiology is foundational for the Johannine Prologue. Its lofty and poetic language establishes the contours of a narrative script that will be instantiated and expanded in the circumstantial details of the following prose, which will be examined in Chapter 5. This 'script' is predicated on the immediate concern here: the reconceptualization of God's people around the christological reconceptualization of God.

Reconceiving God: The Communal Vision of 'Dyadic Theology' (John 1:1–2, 18)

John opens with the presentation of a divine dyad – God and the Logos – who have coexisted in a perpetual state of interrelation since 'the beginning'. The relational inter-dynamics of these figures are foundational for Johannine ecclesiology, setting into place the linguistic and thematic framework by which the evangelist's vision of the church is understood, presented, and even included later in the Prologue and throughout the rest of the Gospel. My purpose in this section is to provide a brief analysis of 'dyadic theology', a phrase

---

[8] See Klaus Scholtissek, 'The Johannine Gospel in Recent Research', in *The Face of New Testament Studies: A Survey of Recent Research*, ed. Grant R. Osborne and Scot McKnight (Grand Rapids, MI: Baker Academic, 2004), 444–72.

[9] Though Daniel Boyarin has made a strong case for understanding the Prologue as a self-contained narrative drawing on Jewish theology and pre-rabbinic techniques of midrash. See Daniel Boyarin, 'The Gospel of the *Memra*: Jewish Binitarianism and the Prologue to John', *HTR* 94, no. 3 (2001): 243–84.

[10] Harris, *Prologue and Gospel*, 195.

intended to evoke how the identity of Israel's 'God' is reconceived through its correlation with the Logos. The evangelist's 'narrative pneumatology' will eventually require an understanding of Johannine theology as 'triadic' (see Chapter 10); for now, I will endeavour to show how the Prologue introduces a binitarian divine community that is not exclusive to God and the Logos but is open to human participation.

Plurality and Filiation in Johannine Theology

The dyadic theology appearing in the Prologue's opening lines indicates that *plurality is constitutive of the Johannine concept of θεός/God.* Though some notions of 'binitarianism' may have held theological currency in early Judaism,[11] for early Christians within the matrices of Jewish theological traditions christology compelled a re-envisioning of 'God' that placed Jesus within the divine identity of YHWH.[12] The Prologue signals a christological rethinking of the standard interpretations of this divine identity in which Israel's God interrelates with the divine entity of the Logos. The conceptual ambiguity of the term λόγος ('word') is such that a wide range of associations could be recalled in the minds of both Greco-Roman and early Jewish readers;[13] what is *not* ambiguous about John 1:1, however, is that a narrative of cosmic proportions[14] is being introduced concerning the activity of these divine beings in the world they have jointly created. With the Logos serving as

---

[11] For the hypostasizing of Logos, Sophia/Wisdom, or the *Memra* of certain Palestinian Targumim see especially Boyarin, 'Gospel of the *Memra*'.

[12] For the phrase 'divine identity', I am relying on the work of Richard Bauckham. By divine identity, Bauckham is referring to *who God is*, a reality often conveyed in biblical and Jewish texts through the presentation of God as a person with a will and a describable series of actions. See esp. Richard Bauckham, 'God Crucified', in Bauckham, *Jesus and the God of Israel: God Crucified and Other Studies on the New Testament's Christology of Divine Identity* (Grand Rapids, MI: Eerdmans, 2008), 1–59, here at 6–11. Bauckham in turn is drawing from the work of Hans Frei (among others) on theories of identity (see Frei, *The Identity of Jesus Christ*). For Frei, the Gospels are 'realistic narratives' and must therefore portray Jesus as a character who is defined 1) by his interaction with the world and events around him over time ('self-manifestation description' – Frei, *Jesus*, 44) and 2) by his intentions as expressed in describable actions ('intention-action description' – ibid., 45). Frei observes that, as an un-substitutable character in a 'history-like' conflux of events and other realistic characters, Jesus' true identity is identifiable in the Gospel narrative – ibid., 51–57, 71, 133, 138, 143, 153.

[13] Peter M. Phillips, *The Prologue of the Fourth Gospel: A Sequential Reading*, LNTS 294 (London: T & T Clark, 2006), 143–50.

[14] See Reinhartz, *The Word in the World*.

the following story's protagonist, this particular βίος[15] is the narration of a 'god' who has determined to make a material entrance into the domain of humankind.[16] From the initial verse of the Gospel, Jewish-Christian readers (John's most probable audience) would likely have recognized that this enigmatic entity of the Logos is being retrojected into the opening of Israel's Scriptures, the sacred textual testimony to the divine identity. By embedding the Logos within the biblical creation narrative, the fourth evangelist is consciously offering an expanded interpretation of θεός[17] in which the Logos is understood as having always been on the scene protologically *with* God (πρὸς τόν θεόν) and *as* God (θεὸς ἦν ὁ λόγος).[18] Regardless of the possible interpretations of 'Logos' in the perspective of the reader (Wisdom? Divine reason? Torah?),[19] John 1:1 indicates that on offer in the Prologue is

[15] On the Fourth Gospel's similarity to Greco-Roman biographical works (*bioi*), see Burridge, *What Are the Gospels?*, esp. 213–32.

[16] As C. K. Barrett has concisely put it, 'The deeds and words of Jesus are the deeds and words of God; if this be not true the book is blasphemous' (Barrett, *John*, 156). For arguments against Jesus' divinity in the Fourth Gospel, see Margaret Davies, *Rhetoric and Reference in the Fourth Gospel*, vol. 69, *JSNTSup* (Sheffield: Sheffield Academic Press, 1992). She reads λόγος as simply 'not God in himself but God's expression of his purpose in creating and sustaining the world' (121). For a carefully nuanced view that is similar, see Wendy E. S. North, 'Monotheism and the Gospel of John: Jesus, Moses, and the Law', in *Early Jewish and Christian Monotheism*, ed. Loren T. Stuckenbruck and Wendy E. S. North, ECC 263 (London: T & T Clark, 2004), 155–66.

[17] The anarthrous form of θεός (God/god) in 1:1c after the articular form in 1:1b has been understood at times as a reference to divinity as a categorization instead of a reference to the specific person of God. For a recent example of this interpretation, see Fernando F. Segovia, 'John 1:1–18 as Entrée into Johannine Reality', in *Word, Theology, and Community in John*, ed. R. Alan Culpepper, Fernando F. Segovia, and John Painter (St. Louis, MO: Chalice Press, 2002), 33–64, here at 37–38. Bultmann's comment still seems reasonable – 'why was not θεῖος used if divinity as category were intended?' (Bultmann, *John*, 33). Though I use the anarthrous form of θεός above as that which is being defined, I have in mind the person, not the category, of 'God'.

[18] 'If you believed Moses, you would believe me, for he wrote about me' (5:46). Later on in the Gospel, Jesus is to be hermeneutically reread into the theophany in Isaiah 6 where the prophet saw Jesus in his vision of YHWH (Jn 12:39–41); and in 8:58 he is recognized as a being contemporary with Abraham.

[19] The possible background for John's Logos language is an exhaustive area of research. For a helpful treatment of Logos as Wisdom (with emphasis on ecclesiological themes), see Sharon H. Ringe, *Wisdom's Friends: Community and Christology in the Fourth Gospel* (Louisville, KY: Westminster John Knox, 1999), 53–63; Elizabeth A. Johnson, 'Jesus, the Wisdom of God: A Biblical Basis for a Non-Androcentric Christianity', *ETL* 61 (1985): 284–89; T. H. Tobin, 'The Prologue of John and Hellenistic Jewish Speculation', *CBQ* 52 (1990): 252–69; John Ashton, 'The Transformation of Wisdom: A Study of the Prologue of John's Gospel', *NTS* 32

nothing short of 'a reconceptualization of the identity of God'.[20] The evangelist is not necessarily creating a new religion around a new god; but the understanding of God/θεός must be reappraised on the basis of this '*Verbindungsidentität*'[21] (that is, a correlating identity) with the word/ὁ λόγος.[22]

The plurality of Johannine theology *establishes 'community' as a principal motif* in the Prologue – the paired introduction of God and the Logos in John 1:1–2 indicates that the divine identity actually entails a divine community. That this intra-divine relationality is central to the Prologue's dyadic theology is made clear by the familial language gradually applied throughout the Prologue's sequence to both divine figures. The plurality of Johannine theology is shown to be filial as the metaphysical language of 'God' and 'Logos' develop over the course of John 1:1–18 into the familial language of 'Father' and 'unique [or "one and only"] Son'.[23] The generalized ambiguity of 'Logos' gradually sharpens until there is a named individual for whom 'God' is 'Father'. In 1:4 the Logos is linked with the vague term ἡ ζωή (the life) and then categorized as τὸ φῶς (the light). 'Life' and 'Light' are here personifications of fundamental aspects (along with God's word) of the Genesis 1

(1986): 161–86. For an overview of the possible Hellenistic backgrounds, see Phillips, *Prologue*, 90–107. Craig Keener argues that Logos is to be understood as Torah – Craig Keener, *The Gospel of John: A Commentary* (Peabody, MA: Hendrickson, 2003), 360–63. Keener offers careful summaries of the other interpretations for Logos in pp. 339–63. For an argument that John is using λόγος in a more elevated theological sense than Philo's usage, see Hengel, 'Prologue', 272, and Richard Bauckham, 'Monotheism and Christology in the Gospel of John', in Bauckham, *The Testimony of the Beloved Disciple: Narrative, History, and Theology in the Gospel of John* (Grand Rapids, MI: Baker, 2007), 239–52, here at 240–42. Bauckham views the Logos language in the Prologue as carrying no 'metaphysical baggage' – it simply refers to God's use of his word to create according to Genesis 1 (241).

[20] The phrase is from Thompson, *God*, 51.

[21] Kavin Rowe uses this term to designate the joint coordination of Jesus' identity with God's identity in Luke's Gospel. See Rowe, *Early Narrative Christology*, 27.

[22] 'Referring to the same God implies that Jesus does not claim to bring a new god or for that matter a new religion, but that he claims to continue the true religion of the God of Abraham, Moses and Elijah' – Jan G. van der Watt, 'Salvation in the Gospel According to John', in van der Watt, *Salvation in the New Testament: Perspectives on Soteriology*, NovTSup 121 (Leiden: Brill, 2005), 101–31, here at 104.

[23] 'Unique/only Son' is my translation here of μονογενής. This term is normally understood in the LXX and elsewhere in the NT as referring to a parent's only child: LXX: Jdg 11:34; Tob 3:15; 6:11; 8:17; *Odes Sol.* 14:13; Wis 18:4 (see also the application of the term to Wisdom in Wis 7:22). For the NT: Lk 7:12; 8:42; 9:38; Heb 11:17. Though the term can be used to express non-filial uniqueness (cf. LXX Pss 21:21; 24:16; 34:17), the Johannine use is *always* filial.

cosmogony. From John 1:4b, this divine figure is identified primarily as the 'Light' (five times in 1:4b–9) until the term 'Logos' is reapplied in v. 14. There is a movement from categorizations to personifications to a *person*. Upon becoming flesh, the broader and more cosmic designations of this divine being give way to the associative language of filial relationality: he is ὡς μονογενοῦς παρὰ πατρός (the unique and only Son from the Father) in 1:15; his name is disclosed in v. 17 as Jesus Christ (Ἰησοῦς Χριστός); and he is presented in 1:18 as the only God (μονογενὴς θεός) who is 'in the bosom of the Father' (εἰς τὸν κόλπον τοῦ πατρός). The depictions of these figures disambiguates in a gradual process of *personalization* as dyadic theology is expressed in terms of family relations. The divine identity is social.

Μονογενὴς θεός and Dyadic Theology's Plurality and Unity

The phrase μονογενής θεός (transliterated into English as *monogenēs theos*, and which I would translate with the rather cumbersome, 'the one and only Son who is also God'[24]) that is applied to Jesus in 1:14 and 1:18 is densely freighted to express divine plurality and divine unity *simultaneously*. Jesus and the Father are understood as sharing the divine identity (as indicated by the latter term in the phrase, θεός, which denotes unity) while existing in an interrelation in which they are distinguishable figures (μονογενής, denoting plurality). These dual dynamics of both unity and plurality are jointly articulated in the compound title μονογενής θεός. The text-critical and interpretative complexities attending this designation betoken its theological and christological profundity.[25] While the original text is disputed, available manuscript evidence leads most interpreters to accept the more theologically loaded μονογενὴς θεός[26] over the less theologically provocative (in terms of Jewish monotheistic sensibilities) μονογενὴς υἱός (the only Son).[27] The awkwardness of the former is due to its service in compressing and epitomizing

---

[24] Though note that I will often use the more shorthand phrase 'the Only God'.

[25] See the discussion in Keener, *John*, 412–16.

[26] The earliest attestations for μονογενὴς θεός include P66 (*c*. 200) and the fourth-century Codices Sinaiticus and Vaticanus (note also the fifth-century Codex Ephraemi); the phrase appears in articular form in the third-century P75 and in the copy of Sinaiticus (א1). The earliest codex supporting ὁ μονογενὴς υἱός is Alexandrinus (fifth century). It should also be noted that the Majority Byzantine text supports the reading μονογενὴς θεός and both phrases are found in Clement of Alexandria (third century).

[27] Though Barrett acknowledges the attestation of the MSS evidence, he nonetheless argues that 'υἱός seems to be required by the following clause, and is in conformity with Johannine usage' (Barrett, *John*, 169).

the reconstrual of God that the Prologue is proposing in which unity and plurality feature simultaneously. The term μονογενής expresses affiliation *with* God yet also distinction *from* God; the pairing of μονογενής with θεός, however, constitutes a direct identification – unity – with God. So the dyadic theology that opens the entire Gospel includes careful emphases on both the distinctiveness of these two divine figures (plurality) as well as their shared identity (unity). The phrase μονογενὴς θεός is the catchphrase of the Prologue's dyadic theology, serving as a concise expression of a divine identity shared between God and the Logos/μονογενής/Jesus Christ while distinctions persist between them.

In spite of the vast array of structural arrangements posited for the Prologue, it does not appear to be widely recognized that the clauses appearing in its opening verses should be understood as intentionally designed to depict the plurality and unity of the divine identity[28]:

[Unity]: Ἐν ἀρχῇ ἦν ὁ λόγος (cf. Gen 1 [LXX]: Ἐν ἀρχῇ ἐποίησεν ὁ θεός)[29]
In the beginning was the Word (Gen 1: In the beginning God made . . .)

[Plurality]: καὶ ὁ λόγος ἦν πρὸς τὸν θεόν
And the Word was with God

[Unity]: καὶ θεός ἦν ὁ λόγος
And the Word was God

[Plurality]: οὗτος ἦν ἐν ἀρχῇ πρὸς τὸν θεόν
This one was in the beginning with God

The clauses above alternate between the idea of divine unity and divine plurality, indicating the composite nature of dyadic theology. In an attempt to honour the evangelist's interest in maintaining distinctiveness between the entities of ὁ λόγος and ὁ θεός, Francis Moloney translates θεός ἦν ὁ λόγος (1:1c) as 'what God was the Word was also'.[30] The more

---

[28] Though he does not use the terms 'plurality' and 'unity', M.-E. Boismard has a helpful discussion on the interplay of oneness and distinction in Boismard, *St John's Prologue*, trans. Carisbrooke Dominicans (London: Blackfriars' Publications, 1957), 8–10.

[29] Emphases added. Unity is implied since Jn 1:1a echoes Gen 1:1a, thereby rendering the Logos synonymous with God.

[30] Francis J. Moloney, *The Gospel of John*, vol. 4, SP (Collegeville, ME: The Liturgical Press, 1998), 35.

direct translation 'the Word was God'[31] is more preferable, however, because the distinctiveness Moloney rightly wishes to safeguard is maintained by reading θεός ἦν ὁ λόγος in sequential relation to its preceding and following clauses of 'the Word was with God' (ὁ λόγος ἦν πρὸς τὸν θεόν) and 'this one was in the beginning with God' (οὗτος ἦν ἐν ἀρχῇ πρὸς τὸν θεόν) respectively. The Logos is identified *as* God and yet remains identifiable *from* God, a dialectic denoted with remarkable precision in the phrase μονογενὴς θεός.

The extended phrase 'the only God who is in the bosom of the Father' (μονογενὴς θεός ὁ ὢν εἰς τὸν κόλπον τοῦ πατρός) that concludes the Prologue in v. 18 is simply the relational or filial reiteration of ὁ λόγος ἦν πρὸς τὸν θεόν (plurality), καὶ θεὸς ἦν ὁ λόγος (unity) affirming that Jesus and God share the divine identity as distinct yet inseparable entities. Jesus is not so subsumed within or absorbed into God that his uniquely identifiable existence dissolves into some sort of divine admixture. As noted above, the distinctions within this Johannine model are delineated and specified by the filial categorizations that eventually appear after 1:14 – God as Father/πατήρ and Jesus as the only Son/ μονογενής (and eventually as the Son/ὁ υἱός beyond the Prologue). From Richard Bauckham:

> Their unity does not erase their difference, but differentiates them in an inseparable relationship. We should also notice that the terms 'Father' and 'Son' entail each other. The Father is called Father only because Jesus is his Son, and Jesus is called Son only because he is the Son of his divine Father. Each is essential to the identity of the other. So to say that Jesus and the Father are one is to say that the unique divine identity comprises the relationship in which the Father is who he is only in relation to the Son, and vice versa.[32]

This identification of Jesus *with* God while simultaneously rendering him identifiable *from* God is among the most ambitious aims not only of the Johannine Prologue, but of the entire Gospel. Its centrality for Johannine Christianity is affirmed in 1 John: 'All those denying the Son do not have the Father; the one who confesses the Son has the Father also' (2:23). Drawing on Jewish scriptural traditions, the divine identity, which has

[31] See n. 17, above. The anarthrous θεός is normally understood by the Gospel's interpreters to indicate that θεός stands in the clause as the predicate nominative of the subject ὁ λόγος (Brown, *John*, 5).

[32] Bauckham, 'Monotheism and Christology', 251. Similarly, see Thompson, *God*, 238.

been historically characterized by unity, must now be christologically reimagined so that the divine identity comprises a degree of plurality: a community persists within that identity as these two divine figures interrelate as members of the same family.[33] Ecclesiology surfaces in relation to theology and christology when the Prologue reveals that this divine family of God the Father and Jesus the μονογενής is open to human participation.

Reconceiving God's People: Foundations of a Participatory Ecclesiology (John 1:3b–4; 9–18)

Though the reconceptualization of God is axiomatically accepted as a major programme of Johannine christology, I am suggesting in this chapter that the fourth evangelist's reconstrual of God coincides with a reconstrual of God's people. Though the focus of scholarly research on John 1:1–18 has heavily concentrated on theology and christology, anthropology[34] and ecclesiology must be recognized as themes bearing appreciable significance.[35] This is because the theology and christology of John 1:1–18 are depicted as causative of a rift within humanity. The revelation that Jesus is included within the divine identity results in a social division between those who embrace dyadic theology and those who do not.

---

[33] Many scholars have observed that a degree of plurality in conceptions of 'God' did thrive in multiple texts featuring early Jewish conceptions of 'God'. See the studies in Larry W. Hurtado, *One God, One Lord: Early Christian Devotion and Ancient Jewish Monotheism*, 2nd edn. (London: T & T Clark, 1998); James R. Davila, 'Of Methodology, Monotheism and Metatron: Introductory Reflections on Divine Mediators and the Origins of the Worship of Jesus', in *The Jewish Roots of Christological Monotheism: Papers from the St Andrews Conference on the Historical Origins of the Worship of Jesus*, ed. Carey C. Newman, James R. Davila, and Gladys S. Lewis, JSJSup 63 (Leiden: Brill, 1999), 3–18; and Loren T. Stuckenbruck, '"Angels" and "God": Exploring the Limits of Early Jewish Monotheism', in Stuckenbruck and North, eds., *Early Jewish and Christian Monotheism*, 45–70.

[34] Jeffrey A. Trumbower's monograph on Johannine anthropology is primarily concerned with the question of free will. His assessment is that the Gospel of John is 'proto-gnostic' and espouses an anthropology of 'fixed origins'; that is, when John writes of the children of God, he speaks of a unit of human beings that persisted with some affinity to the divine realm before faith commitments were made in response to Christ (Trumbower is following Heracleon against Origen along with anthropological concepts found in the Gnostic *Gospel of Truth*); see Jeffrey A. Trumbower, *Born From Above: The Anthropology of the Gospel of John*, HUT (Tübingen: Mohr Siebeck, 1992), 140–45.

[35] Brown, *John*, 23–24.

Having outlined the dynamics of theology and christology that open the Fourth Gospel in John 1:1–2, I will demonstrate below how dyadic theology generates a new social identity among human beings. In anticipation of more detailed discussions in Chapter 3, I will provide here fundamental observations about the Prologue's ecclesial vision. After tracing the transition from 'derivative anthropology' to 'participatory ecclesiology', I will discuss three signals in the logical flow of the Prologue indicating that a christological re-evaluation of the people of God is indeed underway.

Derivative Anthropology and the Inclusive Divine Community (John 1:3b–4a; 9–18)

For the Fourth Gospel, the Logos is not just the 'Light',[36] he is 'the Light of humankind' (τὸ φῶς τῶν ἀνθρώπων – 1:4). The divine figure of Jesus is presented not only in relation to God but also in relation to human beings who are collectively understood as deriving from (and eventually as participating within) some notion of divine reality. The focus in this discussion rests on four phrases[37] found in John 1:3–4, each linked together by 'staircase parallelism' or 'concatenation', a sequencing of repeated link-words regularly noted as a literary feature of the Prologue.[38] As key terms are repeated, they become slightly more defined and take on new dimensions[39]:

(1:3a) πάντα δι᾿ αὐτοῦ ἐγένετο
    (1:3b-4a) ὃ γέγονεν ἐν αὐτῷ ζωὴ ἦν
        (1:4b) καὶ ἡ ζωὴ ἦν τὸ φῶς τῶν ἀνθρώπων

(1:3a) all things came into being through him
    (1:3b-4a) what has come into being in him was life
        (1:4b) and the Life was the Light of humankind

---

[36] In the opening clause of v. 4, 'life' is said to be in the Word (ἐν αὐτῷ), but in the following clause, 'life' and 'light' seem to be used as personifications of the Word. That φῶς is intended in v. 5 to personify Jesus is confirmed by the statement in v. 8 clarifying that οὐκ ἦν . . . τὸ φῶς (For 'light' as a personification of Jesus, see 1:9; [3:19–21?]; 8:12; 9:5; 12:35; 46; 1 Jn 1:5 [of God]; for 'life' as a personification of Jesus, see 11:25; 14:6; 1 Jn 1:1; 5:20).

[37] The phrase χωρὶς αὐτοῦ ἐγένετο οὐδὲ ἕν in 1:3b is omitted in the list above since it is simply the negative affirmation (surely for emphasis) of 1:3a.

[38] Concatenation is a Jewish literary technique in which a clause closes with a specific term that is repeated in the opening of the next clause. See Boismard, *Prologue*, 12; also 5.

[39] On this literary phenomena, see Phillips, *Prologue*, 168–69; 197.

These carefully ordered phrases and link-words gradually bring the theme of anthropology to the Prologue's fore *and bind it thematically to christology*, parallelling the way christology was linked thematically to theology in John 1:1:

(1:1a) ἐν ἀρχῇ ἦν ὁ λόγος
  (1:1b) καὶ ὁ λόγος ἦν πρὸς τὸν θεόν
  (1:1c) καὶ θεὸς ἦν ὁ λόγος

(1:1a) In the beginning was the Word
  (1:1b) and the Word was with God
  (1:1c) and the Word was God

Just as the Logos (christology) is eventually correlated to God (theology) in John 1:1, that which is brought into being in John 1:3b is said to be in the Logos (ἐν αὐτῷ) then correlated in some capacity to Life and Light, terms that become emphatically christological throughout the Johannine Prologue. In linking together key terms, the literary device of concatenation also binds together key themes: christology is linked to theology in John 1:1; anthropology is linked to christology in John 1:3b–4.

In John 1:3a we read that 'all things came into being through him' (πάντα δι᾽ αὐτοῦ ἐγένετο), the plural neuter form of πᾶς (translated here as 'all things') being the most all-encompassing term possible,[40] and in which humanity is certainly included. If a full stop or pause occurs just before 'what came into being' (ὃ γέγονεν) as argued below, then the phrase in 1:3a is modified and slightly narrowed in focus in the phrase from 1:3b–4a: ὃ γέγονεν ἐν αὐτῷ ζωὴ ἦν. Read with the intended resonances of the Genesis 1 cosmogony, the 'all things' (πάντα) that came into being through the Logos would certainly include the material elements as well as the various life forms; but the phrase in 1:3b–4a narrows in on the latter, focusing on that which is characterized by 'Life'.[41] The creational categories that implicate humanity are therefore rendered sequentially as πάντα → ὃ γέγονεν ἐν αὐτῷ → ζωή. Anthropology manifestly surfaces in this movement from general to greater specificity with the direct reference to ἄνθρωποι (humankind) in the phrase ἡ ζωὴ ἦν τὸ φῶς τῶν ἀνθρώπων (1:4b).

Noting the subtle change in prepositions in 1:3 and 1:4a, it appears that anthropology *derives from* the Logos ('all things came into being *through him*'/πάντα δι᾽ αὐτοῦ ἐγένετο) but also somehow *participates within* the

---

[40] Raymond E. Brown also points out this use of πάντα appears in Rom 11:36; 1 Cor 8:6; and Col 1:16 (Brown, *John*, 25).

[41] The chronology in the Genesis 1 cosmogony, in which inanimate objects were brought into being before the animate, may well be in view here.

divine reality that the Logos shares with God ('what came into being *in him* was life'/ὃ γέγονεν ἐν αὐτῷ ζωὴ ἦν).[42] Further corroboration of this participatory character is found in that 'the Life'/ἡ ζωή references the Logos in 1:4b, rendering 'Life' a shared quality or designation between the Logos and that which was made in him. Since 'Light' is immediately indicated in 1:4b as τό φῶς τῶν ἀνθρώπων (and associated with the Logos without ambiguity in 1:9), there is some inherence between humanity and the Logos/Light/Life and therefore an inherence between christology and anthropology.

The text-critical punctuation issue referred to above affects the degree to which these phrases are read as participatory in relation to anthropology.[43] From the constructions above, it is clear that I am choosing to read ὃ γέγονεν as the opening of a sentence beginning before v. 3 ends and then continuing into v. 4, rather than as the close of the sentence in v. 3:

[1:3b]   χωρὶς αὐτοῦ ἐγένετο οὐδὲ ἕν. ὃ γέγονεν [1:4] ἐν αὐτῷ ζωὴ ἦν

[1:3b]   Apart from him came into being not one thing. That which has come into being [1:4] in him was life.

The above rendering has been adopted by NA26 and NA27[44] and has received considerable support within Johannine scholarship.[45] This is the most prominent alternative:[46]

---

[42] Emphases added.

[43] See Brown, *John*, 6–7. There are multiple text-critical issues attending 1:3b–4a, but my focus is specifically on the positioning of the full stop.

[44] See Kurt Aland, 'Eine Untersuchung zu Joh 1:3–4: Über die Bedeutung eines Punktes', *ZNW* 59 (1968): 174–209.

[45] For an extensive treatment of this text-critical issue, in addition to Aland's (previous note), see Edward L. Miller, *Salvation-History in the Prologue of John: The Significance of John 1:3/4*, NovTSup 60 (Leiden: Brill, 1989). In his review of Miller's book, D. Moody Smith points to the convincing presentation of the patristic evidence for this reading, strongly corroborated by an apparent break after οὐδὲ ἕν in P[75] (*c.* 200) – D. Moody Smith, 'Salvation-History in the Prologue of John: The Significance of John 1:3/4', *JBL* 111, no. 3 (1992): 542–44. See also the argument presented by Brown, *John*, 6. The strongest attack of this reading comes from Bruce M. Metzger, *A Textual Commentary on the Greek New Testament* (London: United Bible Societies, 1971), 195–96; J. Ramsey Michaels shares Metzger's reservations (Michaels, *John*, 51–57), but see the arguments contra his concerns in Miller, *Salvation-History*, 17–44. Peter Cohee, on the other hand, has argued that ὃ γέγονεν is simply an editorial gloss. See Peter Cohee, 'John 1.3–4', *NTS* 41, 3 (1995): 470–77.

[46] The text-critical apparatus in NA27 lists a number of other possibilities, namely the reading of οὐδέν vs. οὐδὲ ἕν or εἰσίν vs. ἦν.

[1:3b] χωρὶς αὐτοῦ ἐγένετο οὐδὲ ἕν ὃ γέγονεν. [1:4] ἐν αὐτῷ ζωὴ ἦν

[1:3b] Apart from him came into being not one thing that has come into being.
[1:4] In him was life.

But in placing the punctuation mark after οὐδέν/οὐδὲ ἕν (here, 'not one thing'), what was created through the Logos (ὃ γέγονεν) shared in the mysterious, divine Life/ζωή; and the reader will immediately become aware in 1:4b that ἄνθρωποι are specifically in mind.[47] So when introduced in John 1, human beings are not only part of that which came into being 'through him'/δι᾽ αὐτοῦ (derivative anthropology), they are 'in him'/ἐν αὐτῷ and actually identified as Life/ζωή (1:3c/4a), with which the Logos is also identified in 1:9 (participatory anthropology).

M.-E. Boismard has offered four reasons for accepting the punctuation adjustment called for here: first, that it was the reading 'universally accepted before the fourth century'; second, it maintains the 'perfect parallelism' between the phrases in v. 3; third, it utilizes the pattern of link-words seen in 1:1–2 and 1:4–5 in which a new movement in the Prologue's logic is initiated by using a word used in a previous clause; and fourth, since the first use of the other interpretation is specifically attributed to Alexandria in the midst of the Arian controversy, it makes sense that it was an interpretation purposefully chosen to counteract Arian thought.[48]

[47] That this ζωή is divine is made clear by its association with the Logos: ἡ ζωή is identified with τὸ φῶς in 1:4b which is in turn identified with the Logos in 1:9.

[48] Boismard, *Prologue*, 13–15. The earliest manuscript collection supporting the reading that breaks the sentences in 1:3 and 1:4 after ὃ γέγονεν is a sixth/seventh-century correction of Codex Sinaiticus. The Peshitta (perhaps representing a textual tradition as early as the second century) is the earliest witness among the non-Greek versions, with the seventh-century Harklensis version also in attestation. The third/fourth- and fourth-century Bohairic tradition of the Coptic and the Editio Clementina of the Vulgate, respectively, are also supportive. Manuscript support for the reading argued here (placing the full stop after οὐδὲ ἕν, indicated by punctuation or a space) include the fifth-century Codex Ephraemi and the fifth- (or possibly sixth-)century Codex Bezae. Also weighing in is the support of the Curetonian version of the Peshitta (third/fourth century) and the Wordsworth/White edition of the Vulgate (fourth century). Though one third-century Father supports the alternative reading (Adamantius), the reading called for above is found in the writings of eight second-century Fathers (Theodotus[acc to Clement], Valentinians[acc to Irenaeus and Clement], Irenaeus, Diatessaron[i,n], Ptolemy, Heracleon, Theophilus, plus the Naasenes) and in the writings of six third-century Fathers (Perateni, Clement, Tertullian, Hippolytus, Origen, and Eusebius). Miller points out that the earliest manuscripts (P[66], ℵ, A and B) have no punctuation whatsoever in John 1:3–4. But he argues that the elevated dot in P[75] just before ὃ γέγονεν need not at all be the work of a later redactor (as signified in the critical apparatus of Nestle-Aland as P[75c]). For a helpful list of the bulk of witnesses for and against, see Miller, *Salvation-History*, 28–29.

Boismard also recognizes the participatory nature of reading ὅ γέγονεν with this positioning of punctuation: the concept of 'true life' is 'envisaged as a state that is participated'. He goes on to argue that many interpreters have taken the participatory nature of the phrase as problematic since 'Life' is directly correlated to the 'Light', which, in v. 4, is clearly the Logos. The 'difficulty' of this interpretation is such that 'many have felt bound to give up the attempt to connect the words "What has begun to be" with verse 4'. Boismard resolves the issue by claiming that the dual meanings invested in the word 'Life' are not 'mutually exclusive but rather based on each other'[49] (17–18):

> In v. 4a, on the one hand, creatures are called 'life' inasmuch as they share in the life of him who is the Life par excellence. In v. 4b, on the other hand, the Word is not called 'life' on his own account, but inasmuch as he gives life to creatures, as he is the source of life (as we have seen this is the usual sense in St. John's Gospel). It seems therefore that there is no difficulty involved in St. John's passing in successive verses from the idea of contingent life to that life of the Word which is infused into the creature.[50]

Correlating human beings with the divine being of the Logos/Light/Life should not be resisted – a move that may be regarded as problematic from the perspective of certain doctrinal positions – when the Prologue's text so clearly presents them as correlated. Humanity derives from divine realities generated by dyadic theology; and if human beings, appearing as early as 1:4 (and implied in the phrase ὅ γέγονεν in 1:3b) are described as being ἐν the Logos and included within the categorization of 'Life' (1:4), then the derivative nature of Johannine anthropology is also participatory in nature. This participation will become more explicit as the familial language applied to God and the Logos is extended to humans later in the Prologue, a development suggesting that *the divine community is relationally open and thus inclusive of* humankind, at least in some capacity.

Before those filial designations appear, however, the anthropological dimensions of John 1 undergo a darkening of tone. The christological

---

[49] Boismard, *Prologue*, 17–18.

[50] Ibid., 18. It should be noted that Miller dubs Boismard's interpretation of 1:3b–4a as the 'naturalistic' interpretation that includes living creatures. Miller himself reads ὅ γέγονεν ἐν αὐτῷ as referring to the Incarnate Christ – Miller, *Salvation-History*, 17–44. I side with R. Brown's view, however, that the introduction of John the Baptist seems an important antecedent to the presentation of the Word-Become-Flesh (Brown, *John*, 26).

retelling of creation[51] taking place in the Fourth Gospel's beginning also involves a subtle retelling of the catastrophic anthropological event often referred to as 'the Fall'.[52] Just as the Creator is rejected in Eden, the Logos/Light/Life (all terms echoing Gen 1) is rejected by the realm of humankind in John 1:10–11. The primordial rejection of God that stands at the centre of biblical anthropology is being recapitulated as the one who is the Logos and the Light comes into the world. Humanity rejects its participation in the Life of this Logos/Light who, in turn, participates in the divine identity as God/θεός. Jesus, therefore, shares in the rejection of the divine identity by the world. The narrative proper will illustrate on multiple occasions what the Prologue is depicting in 1:10–11, that humanity's derivation from, and participation within, divine reality are consequently disrupted.

In John 1:12, however, a sudden turn is reported. The Prologue's focus on anthropology transitions specifically into ecclesiology because, in spite of what at first seems to be a universal rejection, a minority of

---

[51] Jan du Rand sees the theme of 'new creation' underway in the Prologue and throughout the Gospel, culminating in the re-enactment of Gen 2:7 in Jn 20:22 as Jesus breathes his Spirit into the disciples – Jan A. du Rand, 'The Creation Motif in the Fourth Gospel: Perspectives on Its Narratological Function within a Judaistic Background', in *Theology and Christology in the Fourth Gospel: Essays by Members of the SNTS Johannine Writings Seminar*, ed. P. Maritz, G. van Belle, and J. G. van der Watt, BETL 184 (Leuven: Leuven University Press, 2005), 21–46.

[52] For elements of the Fall in the Prologue, see Brown, *John*, 27, where he notes that early Christians understood the seed of woman that would overcome Satan in Gen 3:15 as referring to Christ, an interpretation represented by the imagery of Rev 12 where 'the victory of Jesus over the devil is pictured in terms of the victory of the woman's child over the serpent'. Peder Borgen, drawing on a vast array of early Jewish texts, also believes the Fall of Genesis 3 is in view in 1:5b. See Peder Borgen, 'Logos Was the True Light', in *Logos Was the True Light and Other Essays on the Gospel of John*, ed. Peder Borgen (Trondheim: Tapir Publishers, 1983), 95–110, here at 107–10. John Painter acknowledges that the Prologue's rereading of Scripture's opening cosmogony presents 'a tragic perspective not normally seen in Genesis 1–2:4a'. See John Painter, 'Earth Made Whole: John's Rereading of Genesis', in *Word, Theology, and Community in John:*, ed. R. Alan Culpepper, Fernando F. Segovia, and John Painter (St. Louis, MO: Chalice Press, 2002), 65–84, here at 67. Painter is not convinced with Borgen's interpretation of Jn 1:5b, however, noting that the Light is not withdrawn in the face of darkness, but that the darkness could not comprehend or overcome it. My own view is that darkness is indeed connected to the Fall (as Borgen contends), but the light of the Logos shone nonetheless throughout salvation-history and emerged in a new way through Jesus, the true light (as Painter would confirm). As indicated by Jesus' words in 12:35–36, the light can be shining in full view whether or not those who have it within range of their spiritual vision will notice. So, to relieve one of Painter's concerns, the Fall need not imply that darkness defeats or overcomes the Light.

humankind actually receives the Light and becomes thereby identified as a unique and special community. Ecclesiology is a central element for the Prologue because the christological reconfiguration of the divine identity generates a new social entity: 'but as many that received him, he gave to them power to become children of God' (ὅσοι δὲ ἔλαβον αὐτόν, ἔδωκεν αὐτοῖς ἐξουσίαν τέκνα θεοῦ γενέσθαι – 1:12). This formation of the 'children of God' is the consequence of receiving the Logos/Light/Life[53] as conceptually constitutive of θεός. Their re-origination ἐκ θεοῦ ('out of God') demonstrates a restored derivation; the application of filial language ('children') demonstrates a renewed (and intensified) participation. Thus begins the Fourth Gospel's agenda of reinterpreting the communal identity of God's people – just as God must be reconceptualized christologically, so must the notion of his people. The evangelist is tendering an *ecclesial* reinterpretation in correspondence with the *theological and christological* reinterpretation of dyadic theology.

Evidence for the Prologue's Reinterpretation of the People of God

I have identified anthropology as an integral theme in the Prologue. Its placement alongside theology and christology suggests that humanity derives from and was intended to participate within divine reality. The Prologue presents God and the Logos in a divine community that is somehow inclusive of humanity, but the rejection of dyadic theology leads to an anthropological crisis. Attention then turns to ecclesiology.[54] At its core, ecclesiology is a christological reconfiguring of the social identity of God's people. Three consecutive signposts build incrementally on each other to indicate that such a reconfiguration is an intentional programme being established at the Gospel's narrative foundations. Examined briefly in turn, these signposts are first, the calculated use of irony in 1:10–11; second, the negative clauses expressing how the new community is *not* formed in 1:13; and third, the correlation between this new community and Israel's covenant relationship to God in 1:14–17.

---

[53] The Light's shared identity with God is emphasized in 1:10 where once again it is claimed that this divine being is the (Co-)Creator: ὁ κόσμος δι' αὐτοῦ ἐγένετο (cf. 1:3 – πάντα δι' αὐτοῦ ἐγένετο).

[54] Sharon Ringe has argued that Wisdom (her interpretation of 'Logos') has an ecclesiological as well as christological function since its reception 'defines the center and the boundaries of the new community' (Ringe, *Wisdom's Friends*, 93).

The Irony of Rejection in John 1:10–11

The 'foundational irony of the Gospel'[55] is the anthropological crisis just described, that the Logos is rejected by the world made through his agency and by those identified as 'his own'[56] (1:11). The striking impact of the irony in 1:10–11 signals a reworking of who is to be identified legitimately as God's people and is accentuated by these prior statements: the Logos is the light of ἀνθρώπων (1:4); John the Baptist came 'in order that all might believe'/ἵνα πάντες πιστεύσωσιν (1:7); and the Logos is also the 'true Light' that shines on '*every* human being'/πάντα ἄνθρωπον (1:9; emphases added). These clauses successively create in the reader a sense of assurance that the Logos' appearance will be met with universal acceptance, yet the Light of 'all' to whom John witnesses so that 'all' might believe is received only by *some*, a mere minority. The rhetorical force of having this expectation of widespread acceptance dashed in vv. 10–11 indicates that ideas about who constitutes the people of God are under serious re-evaluation.[57]

The Negations in John 1:13

The second move the evangelist makes to signal that a redefinition of God's people is underway is found in 1:13. Here we find three emphatic negations communicating how this new social reality is *not* formed. The legitimate members are 'those *not* out of bloods and *not* out of the will of flesh and *not* out of the will of a husband'/οἳ οὐκ ἐξ αἱμάτων οὐδὲ

---

[55] R. Alan Culpepper, *Anatomy of the Fourth Gospel: A Study in Literary Design* (Philadelphia, PA: Fortress, 1983), 169.

[56] Since ἴδιος appears both in neuter and masculine forms in v. 11, Raymond E. Brown believes the dual references are to the Promised Land/Jerusalem and the people of Israel, respectively (Brown, *John*, 10). This is certainly possible, but it may be quite intentional that the terminology is still so vague. As will be seen below, a movement from broader categorizations to more concretized and relational terminology is underway in the Prologue. The neuter form of ἴδιος may simply be a more relational means of referring to κόσμος in preparation for the less generic masculine form which then precedes the explicit filial language of v. 12. For the use of ἴδιος in parallel with the use of κόσμος, see Rudolf Schnackenburg, *The Gospel According to St. John*, trans. Kevin Smyth, HTKNT (London: Burns & Oates, 1968), 1:259–61. For a detailed argument for the use of 'his own' (neuter) and 'his own' (masculine) as referring to the land of Israel and the people of Israel respectively (roughly siding with Brown), see Pryor, 'Jesus and Israel', 201–18.

[57] Craig Keener acknowledges an ecclesiological element to this ironic rejection. Building on his understanding that 'Logos' refers to Torah in the Prologue, he writes, 'That God's chosen people who celebrated Torah rejected Torah in flesh constitutes a central ecclesiological motif throughout the Fourth Gospel' (Keener, *John*, 399).

ἐκ θελήματος σαρκὸς *οὐδέ* ἐκ θελήματος ἀνδρὸς (emphases added). These negations are followed by an adversative (a contracted ἀλλά) and the positive assertion of the community members' origin: 'they were born out of God'/ἐκ θεοῦ ἐγεννήθησαν. The ecclesial entity generated by the believing reception of Jesus is described in familial terminology in 1:12 as 'the children of God'. The negations in 1:13 make explicit that this new social entity is divinely produced and not humanly *reproduced* – their genesis has nothing to do with genetics. The standard means of yielding progeny by way of human agency are flatly denied as the source for this divine family unit. The authentic people of God as envisioned by the Fourth Gospel can make no appeal whatsoever to ethnic heritage or to a patrilineage other than that of God himself (soon to be identified as πατήρ in v. 14).[58] The new divine derivation ('out of God'/ἐκ θεοῦ) effects divine participation as these children become family members within the interrelation of God and the Logos. The positive assertions about the formation of this ecclesial community – that they come about through belief in Jesus' name (1:12), which results in a divinely orchestrated birth (1:13) – are certainly important for the evangelist; but the highly concentrated succession of the three negative assertions in v. 13 suggests that expectations are being dismantled. Again, the concept of the people of God must be reappraised.

The Contrast between the Formation of the Children of God and the Formation of Israel at Sinai

Along with the emphatic negations in 1:13 and the sharp irony of 1:10–11, the evangelist continues a reconceptualization of God's people by juxtaposing the ecclesial children of God with Israel in John 1:14–17. The references to God's 'tabernacling' (from σκηνόω)[59] among his

---

[58] For the metaphorical image of God as a father who begets or produces a people, see Deut. 32:15–18; Isa 1:2; 45:9–11; Jer 2:26–27. For a more detailed discussion of these and other texts making similar references, see Matthew Vellanickal, *The Divine Sonship of Christians in the Johannine Writings*, AnBib 72 (Biblical Institute Press, 1977), 23–24.

[59] 'The Greek verb [σκηνόω] is clearly borrowed from the story of the Tabernacle in Exodus and served to translate the Hebrew word *shakan/mishkan*' – Gary A. Anderson, 'To See Where God Dwells: The Tabernacle, the Temple, and the Origins of the Christian Mystical Tradition', *Letter & Spirit* 4 (2008): 13–45. See also Brown, *John*, 33; Craig A. Evans, *Word and Glory: On the Exegetical Background of John's Prologue*, JSNTSup 89 (Sheffield: Sheffield Academic Press, 1993), 77–113; Craig R. Koester, *The Dwelling of God: The Tabernacle in the Old Testament, Intertestamental Jewish Literature, and the New Testament*, CBQMS 22 (Washington, D.C.: Catholic Biblical Association, 1989), 100–15; Alan R. Kerr, *The Temple of Jesus' Body: The Temple Theme in the Gospel of*

people during Israel's wilderness journey (1:14) and to the giving of the law through Moses (1:17–18)[60] make clear that not only must Israel's God be reinterpreted christologically, but also the constituency of Israel itself must be re-identified. Following the christological recapitulation of Creation in 1:1–5 and 1:10, the Prologue intimates in 1:14–17 that a recapitulation of God's covenant-making with Israel is also in view.[61] The Mosaic covenant joined God and his people together in a bond expressed in terms of an adoptive relationship between father and child.[62] Israel witnessed the divine presence in the wilderness tabernacle (σκηνή) after its formation, and now the renewed people of God are brought about through a believing recognition of the divine presence in the Logos who dwells among them (1:14). Accordingly, the revelation of God in Jesus is presented as more expansive than that which was supplied through Moses on Sinai (1:17–18).

Parallels between the ecclesial formation of the children of God in the Prologue and the narrative of Israel's formation as God's people[63] include the indwelling of God's presence (Exod 33 // Jn 1:14), the gift of God's words (Exod 19–20 // Jn 1:1, 14), and the mediation of God's intimately known servant (*Moses*: Exod 33 // *Jesus*: Jn 1:18). These parallels in the Prologue between the genesis of Israel and the genesis of the 'children of God', along with the intensive irony of vv. 10–11 and the insistent negations in v. 13, demonstrate the Prologue's concern to reconceptualize the people of God around dyadic theology's reconceptualization of God. This reconceptualization need not amount to a rejection or a replacement of Israel but to an imaginative reworking of Israel's identity around Christ.[64]

John, JSNTSup 220 (Sheffield: Sheffield Academic Press, 2002); Boismard, *Prologue*, 47–50.

[60] For a concise treatment of the Sinai background for John 1:14–18, see especially Boismard, *Prologue*, 135–45.

[61] Creation and covenant are central dimensions of the Jewish understanding that their God and their own identity as a people are unique. On the theological centrality of the Sinai event in Jewish self-identity, see Peder Borgen, 'The Old Testament in the Formation of New Testament Theology', in *Logos Was the True Light and Other Essays on the Gospel of John*, ed. Peder Borgen (Trondheim: Tapir Publishers, 1983), 111–20, here at 117–18. A recent thorough treatment of Israel's covenant motif in John is that of Sherri Brown, *Gift upon Gift: Covenant Though Word in the Gospel of John*, PTMS 144 (Eugene, OR: Pickwick, 2010).

[62] Exod 4:22–23; Deut 14:1–2; 32:6, 18; cf. Isa 43:6–7; 63:8; 64:8; Jer 31:9; Mal 2:10; 3:17; et al. See Vellanickal, *Divine Sonship*, 9–18.

[63] This formation could be likened to a birth. See Deut 32:15–18 and ibid., 99.

[64] Raymond Brown has pointed out that the idea of a 'new people' of God does not appear in early Christian writings until the Epistle of Barnabas (5:7). New Testament

Chapter Summary

The Prologue evokes a rethinking of the Jewish theological constructs of God. Johannine theology is initially shown as 'dyadic' (though eventually becoming triadic because of the characterization of the Spirit-Paraclete) in that the Logos shares the divine identity. Plurality and unity therefore characterize this reconfiguration of θεός because Jesus is identified *as* God while simultaneously remaining identifiable *from* God. The unity and plurality of their *Verbindungsidentität* are expressed relationally through the familial designations of 'Father' and μονογενής. Ecclesiology comes to the fore because the revelation of the Prologue's dyadic theology incites an anthropological crisis. Human beings who have derived from the Logos and even participated in the divine personification of 'Life' are depicted as rejecting the reconceived vision of God when the Logos appears in the world. But an ecclesial social entity emerges through the faithful embrace of the Logos. These 'children' are given a new divine derivation and granted participatory rights within the familial interrelation of God/Father and the Logos/μονογενής. In short, the ecclesial vision of the Johannine Prologue is of a human community enfolded into an inclusive divine community by right of supernatural birth.

---

ecclesiologies, he believes, understood the church primarily as *the renewed Israel*. My references to a reconceived people of God are intended to evoke a renewal of Israel around Christ which includes an imaginative reworking of how Israel comes into being and how this reimagined social entity is identified in the world. See Raymond E. Brown, 'Unity and Diversity in New Testament Ecclesiology', *NovT* 6, no. 4 (1963): 298–308, here at 303. Note also the comments cited in the Introduction (n. 66) by Bieringer and Pollefeyt.

3

THE ECCLESIOLOGY OF FILIATION
AND THE INCARNATION

I am making the case here in Part I that ecclesiology is so intrinsically grounded in the theology and christology of John 1:1–18 that it cannot be regarded as a negligible or tertiary motif. In this chapter, I will show that the ecclesial notion of divine–human filiation (whereby believers are accorded status as God's children) is so thematically significant that it gives shape to the Prologue's structure (pages 56–58). Through the literary techniques of sequential disambiguation/personalization and intercalation, the evangelist assigns filial participation a central place both within the Prologue's structure and within the emerging ecclesial vision. The second section of this chapter will focus on 'the ecclesiology of the Incarnation'. The Prologue's divine–human *filiation* hinges on the idea of divine–human *exchange* – humanity's assumption of divine status (as children birthed 'out of God'/ἐκ θεοῦ) is linked to the Logos' assumption of human flesh.

The Ecclesiology of Divine–Human Filiation:
Disambiguation and Intercalation

The inclusion of human beings within the familial interrelation of the Father and the μονογενής – what I am referring to as divine–human filiation – stands at the heart of Johannine ecclesiology and serves as a pivotal theme in John 1:1–18. Humankind is initially presented in the Prologue in the broadest of categorizations. The ἄνθρωποι derive from the Logos ('through him'/δι᾽ αὐτοῦ) and in some way participate in divine reality ('in him'/ἐν αὐτῷ). That participation is more specifically understood as filiation when anthropology transitions into ecclesiology and believers are identified as children of God. This theme of divine–human filiation, succinctly expressed in the phrase 'children of God'/τέκνα θεοῦ, is stylistically and structurally embedded within the Prologue and serves to coordinate ecclesiology along with christology and theology,[1] a coordination that is intentionally presented in two ways. First, the Prologue includes the identity of the people of God in the process of 'disambiguation' by which the identities of God and the Logos move from general categorizations into more focused and personalized familial language. Second, the evangelist structurally intercalates ecclesiology within the Prologue's treatment of christology and theology. These latter two themes open and close John 1:1–18, sandwiching the concentrated emphasis on the filial status of the children of God in 1:12–13. The Prologue's intentional literary techniques of intercalation and disambiguation make clear that, for the Fourth Gospel, theology, christology, and ecclesiology are coextensive.

Disambiguation and Filiation in the Prologue's Structure

I am using the term 'disambiguation' to refer to the gradual transition from the metaphysical language of God/θεός and Word/λόγος to the personalized associative terminology of family life. In other words, the language used to describe the relation of God and the Logos becomes less abstract and ambiguous, and more ordinary and familiar. In his 'sequential reading' of the Johannine Prologue, Peter Phillips uses this term to label the progression of lexemes referencing Jesus, which clarifies the identity of the Logos for the Gospel's readers. He dubs the linked designations Word – God – Life – Light (λόγος – θεός – ζωή – φῶς) as a 'matrix persona' that takes on layered dimensions as new terms are added (like Jesus' name in 1:17) and as existing terms in the matrix are qualified (e.g., 'the Word became flesh'/ὁ λόγος σὰρξ ἐγένετο).[2] In my own reading of the Prologue offered here, the term 'disambiguation' accounts not only for how the identity of Jesus is gradually specified in the Gospel, but also for how the identities of God and God's people undergo the same process.

Through the Prologue's process of sequential disambiguation and personalization, these broader theological and christological titles are eventually identified with the 'Father' and the 'only Son from the Father' (μονογενοῦς παρὰ πατρός) respectively. Jesus will not be referred to as the Logos for the rest of the Gospel; but the Father–Son

---

[1] Boismard believes the Prologue embodies a 'construction by envelopment' and sketches a parabola-shaped diagram expressing descent and ascent (Boismard, *Prologue*, 77–81). My following suggestions concerning disambiguation and intercalation do not necessarily exclude what Boismard has proposed.

[2] Phillips, *Prologue*, 168–69, 197.

Table 3.1 The Sequential Disambiguation of Jesus in the Prologue

1:1	λόγος (3 times)	Word
1:1	θεός	God
1:4	(ἡ ζωή)³	(the Life)
	τὸ φῶς τῶν ἀνθρώπων	the Light of humankind
1:5	τὸ φῶς	the Light
1:8	τό φῶς	the Light
1:9	τό φῶς τὸ ἀληθινόν	the true Light
1:14	λόγος	Word
	μονογενοῦς παρὰ πατρός	the only Son from the Father
1:15	ὁ ὀπίσω μου ἐρχόμενος⁴	the one coming after me
1:17	Ἰησοῦς Χριστός	Jesus Christ
1:18	μονογενὴς θεός	the only God
	ὁ ὢν εἰς τὸν κόλπον τοῦ πατρός	the one in the bosom of the Father

relationship between Jesus and God that the Prologue introduces will be richly integrated into every instance of 'God'/θεός from this point onwards.

After analysing how the evangelist develops this gradual delineation of christology and theology in familial terms, I will then examine how the same development is paralleled in the presentation of ecclesiology (in addition to Tables 3.1–3 below, refer also to Tables 3.4–5).

Jesus: From the Logos to the Child in the Father's Bosom

As noted above, the Prologue's references to Jesus begin with the magisterial designation Logos, continue with cosmic categorizations, and then end with an image of filial intimacy.

It has already been observed that Jesus is presented in the Prologue not only as God and co-Creator, but as a divine figure who is also understood as standing in relation to mortal beings, as well as to God: as the light *'of humans'*, as the one coming *'after me'* (that is, John the Baptist), and as the μονογενὴς θεός who is nestled within God's bosom. The progression from general terminology into that which is more specific and relational is undeniably clear.

³ The parentheses around ἡ ζωή convey that it is unclear whether Jesus is directly being equated with the 'Life' in 1:4, even though it is implied and stated more directly elsewhere (see also 11:25, 14:6).

⁴ John the Baptist is speaking here.

Table 3.2 The Sequential Disambiguation of God in the Prologue

1:1–2	θεός ('God' – 2 times, both in relation to the Logos[5])
1:6	θεός ('God' – in relation to John the Baptist: ἀπεσταλμένος παρὰ θεοῦ)
1:12	θεός ('God' – in relation to the new community: τέκνα θεοῦ)
1:14	πατήρ ('Father' – in relation to Jesus: μονογενοῦς παρὰ πατρός)
1:18	θεός ('God' – 2 times, the second in relation to Jesus: μονογενὴς θεός πατήρ ('Father' – in relation to Jesus: ὁ ὢν εἰς τὸν κόλπον τοῦ πατρός)

God: From Creator to the Father Embracing a Child

Though the term θεός is used throughout the Prologue, the identity of God is conjoined with that of the Logos in the process of disambiguation. This is not just any deity, but the God of Israel who is now revealed to be interrelated with another divine entity. The nature of this interrelation is filial since God is portrayed in 1:14 as Jesus' 'Father'. The paternal connotations for θεός actually appear earlier, however, in 1:12. Before θεός is presented as the Father of Jesus, he is implicated as the Father of believing humans (τέκνα θεοῦ). This relational resonance for θεός is sustained to the end of the Prologue:[6]

Like the presentation of Jesus after the Prologue's opening lines, God is presented in relation to others, the designations appearing four times in genitive constructions: 'one sent from God', 'children of God', 'the μονογενής of the Father', and 'in the bosom of the Father'. In the first two of these genitive phrases God is depicted in relation to John the Baptist and the new ecclesial entity; in the latter he is depicted in relation to Jesus.

So John 1:1–18 presents christology and theology in a sequential development that moves towards divine filiation. The Prologue begins with the vague designation 'Logos' and ends with the named μονογενής reclining intimately in the bosom of God, who is now recognized as 'Father'.

Humanity: From a General 'All' to the 'We All' of a Divine Family

The references to humanity follow the same disambiguating movement of personalization and narrowing of focus seen above in the references to

[5] Θεός actually appears three times in Jn 1:1–2, but the second reference is applied to the Logos.

[6] That paternal connotation also endures to the Gospel ending, powerfully captured in the words of the Resurrected Christ: 'I am ascending to my Father and your Father, to my God and your God' (20:17).

Table 3.3 The Sequential Disambiguation of Humanity in the Prologue

1:3	πᾶν (neuter)	all things
	ὃ γέγονεν ἐν αὐτῷ	what has come into being in him
1:4	ἄνθρωποι	humankind
1:7	πᾶς (masculine)	all
1:9	πάντα ἄνθρωπον	every human being
1:10	κόσμος (3 times)[7]	world
1:11	τὰ ἴδια (neuter)	his own
	οἱ ἴδιοι (masculine)	his own
1:12	τέκνα θεοῦ	children of God
1:14	ἡμεῖς	we
1:16	ἡμεῖς πάντες	we all

God and Jesus, indicating that anthropology and ecclesiology are being intentionally coordinated with the portrayal of christology and theology.[8] The progression begins with general categorizations: 'all things'/πᾶν (neuter),[9] 'what has come into being'/ὃ γέγονεν,[10] 'humankind'/ ἄνθρωποι, 'all'/πᾶς (masculine), 'world'/κόσμος, then 'his own'/τὰ ἴδια (neuter).[11] At this point (in 1:11) there occurs a transition to familial language between the use of 'his own'/τὰ ἴδια (neuter) and 'his own'/οἱ ἴδιοι (masculine). The rejection of the Logos/Light by 'his own', a term already noted as evocative of familial bonds, is answered in the text by the formation of the next reference to humankind, the 'children of God'/ τέκνα θεοῦ: though his own familial domain fails to receive him, those who do receive him form a new family unit characterized by divine–human filiation. The sequential movement of disambiguating

[7] The use of κόσμος in John's Gospel is notorious for its fluidity. In light of the prior references to Genesis 1, the term is probably being used here in a general sense to speak of humanity as representative of the wider sphere of creation.

[8] As Margaret Davies observes, 'The Prologue begins with a distant perspective and gradually moves towards the reader's present situation. It begins in eternity with God and λόγος (1.1–2), moves on to creation through the λόγος (1.3), and then mentions the λόγος's role in the lives of human creatures, as their source of life and light (1.4)'. See Davies, Rhetoric and Reference, 126.

[9] I am including this neuter instance of πᾶν from 1:3 since the creation of all things certainly includes humankind, even though the scope of generality here is admittedly vast.

[10] As discussed above in Section 1.3.3, the phrase ὃ γέγονεν in 1:3b is shown in 1:4b to include humankind.

[11] Debates surround the interpretation of the neuter and masculine instances of τὰ ἴδια / οἱ ἴδιοι in 1:11. For Fernando Segovia there is 'a concretization at play', by which he means that a directional movement between κόσμος and τὰ ἴδια is underway: 'There is a sense of emphasis . . . that points toward distinction'. See Segovia, 'John 1:1–18', 45.

categories into relational classifications then continues, *but now with first person pronouns*, beginning with 'we'/ἡμεῖς followed by the more inclusive 'we all'/ἡμεῖς πάντες. This transition to the first person indicates that the evangelist intends for the Prologue to address a communal entity with the expectation that the audience is or will become (20:30–31) enmeshed within the process of divine–human filiation currently being described through disambiguation.

The progression depicted immediately above illustrates the observation made earlier that *anthropology transitions into ecclesiology* as the focus sharpens from 'humankind'/ἄνθρωποι onto the 'children of God'/ τέκνα θεοῦ and, similarly, as 'all'/πᾶς (1:7) develops incrementally into the more radically specified '*we* all'/*ἡμεῖς* πάντες (emphasis added). The Prologue opens with the general categorizations of the Logos, God, and humankind, and within eighteen verses it concludes with Jesus intimately ensconced as a unique and only son within the Father's bosom and celebrated by a community of children who are all members of the same divine family. The ecclesial notion of divine–human filiation is therefore formative for the Prologue's entire literary movement and structure. And since theology, christology, and anthropology/ecclesiology share the same progression over the course of John 1:1–18, these categories must be recognized as inseparably bound to each other.

Ecclesiology's Critical Function in the Process of Disambiguation

It is also important to note that in this tripartite coordination *the relational language of ecclesiology* (children of God/τέκνα θεοῦ) *actually precipitates the relational denominations of christology* ('the only Son'/ μονογενής) *and theology* ('father'/πατήρ). The term 'Logos' appears only once more in the Prologue after 1:1 (v. 14), occurring just after readers are alerted to the social reality of the children of God in 1:12. It is after this introduction of God's new children that the evangelist uses phrases portraying Jesus in relation to another (mainly to God, but once to John the Baptist) and reveals Jesus' name. Similarly, the notion of God as father is introduced in the Prologue *ecclesiologically* before it appears *christologically* – by the time Jesus is presented as the μονογενοῦς παρὰ πατρός (1:14), the designation of the believing community as τέκνα in 1:12 has established God as a paternal figure. So in the process of disambiguation, it is the introduction of the children of God/τέκνα θεοῦ that initiates the language of filiation between God/θεός and the

Table 3.4 Sequential Disambiguation in the Prologue

Verses	Father	Son	Humanity	Themes Presented
1:1–2	(ὁ) θεός/God (3 times)	ὁ λόγος/the Word (3 times)		The reconceptualization of God
1:3			(πᾶν [neuter]/all things)	
1:4–5		(ἡ ζωή/the Life, τό φῶς/the Light)	ἄνθρωπου/humankind	
1:6	θεός/God			
1:7–8		τό φῶς/the Light (3 times)		
1:9–10		τὸ φῶς τὸ ἀληθινόν/ the true Light	πᾶς (masculine)/all πάντα ἄνθρωπον/every human being	The reconceptualization of God's people
1:11			ὁ κόσμος/the world (4 times) τά ἴδια (neuter)/his own οἱ ἴδιοι (masculine)/his own	
1:12	θεός/God		τέκνα θεοῦ/children of God	Introduction of filial language
1:14	πατήρ/Father	ὁ λόγος/the Word μονογενοῦς παρὰ πατρός/the only Son from the Father	ἡμεῖς (appearing in the dative, ἡμῖν)/we	
1:15		(ὁ ὀπίσω μου ἐρχόμενος/the one coming after me)		The reconceptualization of God expressed in filial terms
1:16			ἡμεῖς πάντες/we all	
1:17		Ἰησοῦς Χριστός/Jesus Christ		
1:18	θεός/God πατήρ/Father	μονογενὴς θεός/the only God		

56   *The Narrative Ecclesiology of the Prologue*

Table 3.5 Disambiguation and Intercalation of Divinity and Humanity

Verses	Divinity (A/A')	Humanity (B)
1:1–2	ὁ λόγος /the Word (3 times) (ὁ) θεός /God (3 times)	
1:3		(πᾶν [neuter]/all things)
1:4–5	(ἡ ζωή/the Life, τό φῶς/the Light)	ἄνθρωποι/humankind
1:7–8	τό φῶς /the Light (3 times)	πᾶς (masculine)/all
1:9–10	τό φῶς/the Light	πάντα ἄνθρωπον/every human being ὁ κόσμος /the world (4 times)
1:11		τά ἴδια/his own (neuter) οἱ ἴδιοι/his own (masculine)
1:12		τέκνα θεοῦ/children of God
1:14	ὁ λόγος/the Word μονογενοῦς παρὰ πατρός/the only Son from the Father	ἡμεῖς/we (appearing in the dative form, ἡμῖν)
1:15	(ὁ ὀπίσω μου ἐρχόμενος/the one coming after me)	
1:16		ἡμεῖς πάντες/we all
1:17	Ἰησοῦς Χριστός/Jesus Christ	
1:18	θεός/God μονογενὴς θεός/the only God πατήρ/Father	

Logos/Light/Life. Given the literary force ecclesiology effects in the Prologue's meticulous presentations of theology and christology, it simply cannot be regarded as a subsidiary motif.

The Intercalation of Divine–Human Filiation

The paralleled narrowing of focus in terms for both divinity and humanity coincides with an arrangement that structurally inserts the new social reality of believers within the dyadic relationship between God and Jesus. As Table 3.5 depicts, ecclesiology, theology, and christology are sequentially ordered in a simple A B A' pattern, with A/A' representing references to the divine figures and B representing humanity. The Prologue opens with a dual reference to the Logos and God (1:1) and closes with a dual reference to the μονογενὴς θεός and the Father (1:18). These paired references serve as an *inclusio* bookending the references to humanity's filial status, which, as just discussed, effect the transition to the filial dynamics of God and Jesus.

It is customary in Johannine scholarship to detect chiastic structures within the Prologue that accentuate and prioritize its themes. R. Alan Culpepper has provided detailed assessments of multiple interpreters' chiastic arrangements.[12] With certain adjustments, he has sided with Boismard's suggestion that the formation of the children of God/τέκνα θεοῦ is the Prologue's central element.[13] In Culpepper's view, this central position merits the genesis of the new social reality as 'the pivot of John's Prologue'.[14] His claim for the centrality of τέκνα θεοῦ aligns well with the observation being made here that ecclesiology is enclosed within the Prologue's christology and theology. Ecclesiology is quite literally *central* to John 1:1–18.

What I am proposing here is a reading of the Prologue not in terms of an elaborate chiasm, but in terms of a simple intercalation (that is, the encapsulation of one theme or idea within the textual bookends of another) that honours the intentional stylistic coordination of ecclesiology, christology, and theology. The ABA′ order depicted in Table 3.5 can be understood as a 'conceptual chiasm'.[15] Much simpler than the more grammatically based chiastic schemata featured in Culpepper's study, this proposal of a conceptual chiasm expressing the intercalation of ecclesiology within theology and christology retains Culpepper's own claim that the formation of the children of God serves as a pivot within the Prologue. What might the intercalation of ecclesiology within the Prologue's theology and christology indicate? I will make two brief observations.

At the very least, the ABA′ intercalation corroborates the overarching claim of Part I that ecclesiology is inalienable from the Fourth Gospel's christology and theology. Even though John 1:1–18 is regarded as one of the most intensive christological texts in early Christianity, a 'christocentricity' that overwhelms ecclesial ideas is exegetically unwarranted in the the Fourth Gospel's opening. We have just examined how the evangelist binds together the presentation of Jesus, God, and the children of God by carefully crafting a paralleled unfolding of their respective categorizations from general to relational and specific. The structural insertion of the theme of ecclesiology within the bookends of christology and theology further demands the Gospel's readers to envision the reconceptualizations of God and God's people as inextricably entwined.

---

[12] Pryor, *John*, 115.   [13] Boismard, *Prologue*, 79–80.

[14] R. Alan Culpepper, 'The Pivot of John's Prologue', *NTS* 27 (1980): 1–31.

[15] On conceptual or thematic chiasms, see again Pryor, *John*, 115.

Moreover, the intercalation of ecclesiology within christology and theology may also be intended to embody the theme of *divine inclusiveness* in that the Prologue's divine interrelations structurally and relationally encompass not only Jesus and God but also the τέκνα θεοῦ who are supernaturally born of God (note the visual arrangement of the materials in Tables 3.4 and 3.5). It was observed in the previous chapter that the statement 'what has come into being in him was life, and the life was the light of humankind' (ὃ γέγονεν ἐν αὐτῷ ζωὴ ἦν, καὶ ἡ ζωὴ ἦν τὸ φῶς τῶν ἀνθρώπων) indicates a participatory anthropology in which human beings somehow inhere within the Light and Life of divinity – that is, until the Light made a more manifest entry into the world and was not recognized. A literary arrangement that places the formation of a new humanity at the Prologue's centre seems designed to convey the divine family's openness into which the ecclesial entity can be incorporated.

Divine–Human Filiation as Participatory Ecclesiology: A Brief Summary

In Part III, I will revisit the Prologue's motif of divine–human filiation to describe Johannine ecclesiology with the later patristic language of theosis or deification. For now, it is important to note that divine–human filiation, expressed in the Prologue through paralleled disambiguation and the ABA′ intercalation, suggests a *participatory* ecclesiology in which believing humanity shares in the divine life of God and Jesus. The structural placement of ecclesiology between the Prologue's *inclusio* of christology and theology accords with the intimation that the latter categories are somehow inclusive of the former. The divine interrelation of dyadic theology is 'open' to the social reality of the new people of God.

Sharing in this divine interrelation, however, does not mean that the children of God share in the divine identity. Filiation instantiates a linguistic and thematic framework serviceable for describing a dyad that is open to humanity in some way but, for that very reason, requires internal distinctions. Though human beings participate within a divine family or community, the evangelist sets demarcations into place preserving the integrity of the reconceived divine identity. As seen in Chapter 2, identifying the Logos *with* God in such a way that the Logos remains identifiable *from* God is an agenda that opens the Prologue. It is the filial language initialized by the introduction of the children of God that becomes the primary means of maintaining the associations and distinctions not only in the dyadic interrelation of christology and theology but also in the tripartite[16] coordination of those two motifs along with ecclesiology. Jesus certainly shares kinship with the τέκνα θεοῦ since the two parties together share God as their Father; but the designation μονογενής articulates a definitive uniqueness and thus delineates Jesus from the ecclesial entity of humans.[17] Jesus is never referred to as God's 'child'/τέκνον in the Prologue (or elsewhere in the Gospel), nor are any members of the newly generated people of God ever referred to as a 'son'/υἱός.[18] Throughout the entire Gospel only Jesus will address God as *my* Father in the first person singular.[19] Though the children are brought forth (γίνομαι) through divine agency (1:12), Jesus the μονογενής (μόνος/only + γίνομαι/to become)[20] is the divine agent that coexisted with God 'in the beginning'.[21] These bonding yet distinguishing terms unite ecclesiology, christology, and theology in filial correlation while also enforcing differentiation. There persists in dyadic theology an openness, but not one in which the lines between the respective members of the divine identity and the new ecclesial entity that participates within the divine interrelation are blurred. Plurality and unity are thus constitutive of John's participatory ecclesiology as well as of his dyadic theology – there is one family (unity), but divine–human distinctions persist, preserving the divine identity (plurality).

---

[16] Just as I am using the phrases 'divine family' and 'divine identity' to account for affiliation and distinction between God, Jesus, and the children of God, I am using the term 'tripartite' rather than 'triad' quite intentionally. David Crump has argued that the people of God form a triad with God and Jesus, terminology that certainly captures the Johannine emphasis on ecclesiology but which blurs too drastically the distinctions between divinity and humanity. As already noted, the Gospel will expand dyadic theology to include the person of the Spirit. 'Tripartite' describes the interrelations between theology, christology, and ecclesiology within the divine family without inserting the people of God within the Christian Trinitarian concept of the divine identity. See David Crump, 'Re-examining the Johannine Trinity: Perichoresis or Deification?', *SJT* 59, no. 4 (2006): 395–412.

[17] See n. 23 in the previous chapter.

[18] The use of 'Divine Sonship' in the title of Vellanickal's lengthy monograph on the Johannine understanding of the people of God is thus unfortunate. He acknowledges the shortcoming of the term 'sonship', but defends its use nonetheless. See Vellanickal, *Divine Sonship*, 3.

[19] Crump, 'Re-examining', 411.

[20] The term μονογενής, however, is not to be understood as 'only begotten' in reference to Jesus as the Son, but as the *unique and singular* Son. See Brown, *John*, 13–14.

[21] Thompson, *God*, 70.

The Ecclesiology of the Incarnation: Divine–Human Exchange and the Paired 'Becomings' (John 1:12–14)

As further evidence for the coinherence of ecclesiology with christology in the Fourth Gospel's narrative opening, the Prologue's most significant christological event is inseparably bound, by shared semantics and sequential logic, to its most significant ecclesiological event. The incarnation of the Word of God in 1:14a corresponds with the formation of the children of God in 1:12–13. Werner Kelber has noted that Bultmann,[22] Käsemann,[23] and Bornkamm[24] all consider 'the prologue's announcement of Jesus' incarnational commencement as a programmatic, theological thesis which the subsequent narrative undertakes to explicate or resolve'.[25] The argument I am presenting here is that the christological Incarnation of Christ and the ecclesial formation of the children of God are presented together in an instance of divine–human exchange and cannot be viewed separately. The Prologue's unfolding rationale in 1:12–14 demands that any such claim for the Incarnation's significance for the rest of the Gospel must take note of its correlation to the genesis of the children of God with which the Incarnation is originally presented.[26] If indeed the *Fleischwerdung* of the Logos is the 'programmatic, theological thesis', then the narrative does not attempt to 'explicate or resolve' its mystery apart from the formation of the church (i.e., the children of God). After presenting exegetical grounds for treating the Incarnation and the creation of the divine children as 'paired becomings', I will then show briefly how patristic readers of the Prologue understood the connections between 1:12–13 and 1:14, a connection lost in many twentieth-century interpretations.

---

[22] Bultmann, *John*, 62–63.

[23] Käsemann is determined, however, to shift Bultmann's emphasis from the Word's becoming flesh (1:14a) to its glorious indwelling (1:14b) – Käsemann, 'Prologue'.

[24] See Günther Bornkamm, 'Towards the Interpretation of John's Gospel: A Discussion of *The Testament of Jesus* by Ernst Käsemann', in *The Interpretation of John*, ed. and trans. John Ashton, *IRT* 9 (SPCK: London, 1986), 79–98.

[25] Werner H. Kelber, 'The Birth of a Beginning: John 1:1–18', *Semeia* 52 (1990): 122–44, here at 134.

[26] Peter Phillips points out that the καί leading 1:14 could be either 'consecutive' or 'adversative', hence the reason for multiple views on the relationship between 1:12–13 and v. 14 – Phillips, *Prologue*, 195–96.

Paired 'Becomings': The Correspondence between
the Formation of God's Children and the Incarnation

The conceptual and semantic connections between the ecclesial genesis
of the τέκνα θεοῦ and the Logos' Incarnation are manifest when understood within the logic of the Prologue's sequential development. Both the
Word of God and the children of God undergo a 'becoming' (from
γίνομαι) in 1:12–14.[27] Though γίνομαι appears repeatedly throughout
the Prologue, these particular two 'becomings' are carefully correlated.
For one, they are presented in contrast to each other in terms of destination and derivation: the term σάρξ is a non-source for the children of God
and yet the destination of Christ.

τέκνα θεοῦ γενέσθαι... οὐδὲ ἐκ... σαρκός (1:12, 13) / 'to
become children of God... not out... of flesh'
ὁ λόγος σὰρξ ἐγένετο (1:14) / 'the Word became flesh'

Craig Keener observes that 'the narrative's logic implies a transferral:
the Word that had been forever "with God" (1:1–2) became "flesh"
(1:14) so others could be born not from flesh but from God (1:13;
cf. 3:6)'.[28] These two "becomings" amount to an exchange between
two entities: the divine Logos shares in human flesh, and enfleshed
humans share in the Logos' divine origin.[29] The terms 'flesh'/σάρξ and
'blood'/αἷμα are not the originating source of the children of God, yet
from 1:14 on they can apply to Jesus (e.g., 6:53–56), who has entered
the sphere of mortality. The τέκνα θεοῦ *not* deriving out of (ἐκ) flesh
stand in contrastive correspondence with the μονογενής who has
become flesh.

A coordinated pairing between the two 'becomings' in 1:12–14 is
further apparent in that the incarnate Logos, the ecclesial children, and
God – *their shared origin* – are all suddenly identified by familial terms at
this point in the Prologue:

---

[27] Whereas the openings of Matthew and Luke display interest in the successive
genealogy of Jesus, the opening of John is interested in the direct genesis of the community
of God and Jesus' status as the μονογενὴς θεός.

[28] Keener, *John*, 405.

[29] Grant Macaskill also notes that the Johannine theme of participation is largely
grounded within the divine–human transfer at work in the Incarnation – Grant Macaskill,
Union with Christ in the New Testament (Oxford: Oxford University Press, 2013), 252–54;
269–70. He places great emphasis on the revelatory significance of the term 'Logos' for
participation (252–53) and points out that 'sonship in John is not a matter of adoption, but of
transformation into a new state of intimacy with God' (270).

Εἰς τὰ ἴδια ἦλθεν, καὶ οἱ ἴδιοι αὐτὸν οὐ παρέλαβον/he came to
his own, and his own did not receive him (1:11)
τέκνα θεοῦ ... ἐκ θεοῦ ἐγεννήθησαν/children of God... born
out of God (1:12, 13)
μονογενοῦς παρὰ πατρός/the only Son from the Father]

This intense clustering of family imagery surfaces strikingly in the
Prologue's centre, with the references to 'his own' in 1:11 first signalling
connotations of family life. The birth of children out of (ἐκ) God and the
introduction of filial language that portrays Jesus as the μονογενής from
(παρά) God together evoke a scene of family formation. As the Prologue
undergoes its crucial transition here from general to filial language
through sequential disambiguation, the phrase ἐκ θεοῦ, in reference to
humanity, parallels παρὰ πατρός, in reference to Christ. Christological
Incarnation and ecclesial formation cannot be interpreted separately
because they are together part of the same overarching event: the formation of a new family unit.

It was noted in the preceding section that this filial language of
ecclesiology (children of God/τέκνα θεοῦ) precipitates the filial language
of christology (the only Son/μονογενής) and theology (Father/πατήρ).
John 1:11–14 is the pivotal moment in the Prologue when the sequential
narrowing of categorizations for divinity and humanity results in these
family designations that sustain through the remainder of the Prologue
(and the rest of the Gospel). The Logos has been unrecognized by the
world (1:9–10) and, more poignantly, rejected by his own/οἱ ἴδοι (1:11),
connoting one's family or household[30] (the term will soon recur in 1:41,
where Andrew finds Simon Peter, 'his own brother'/τὸν ἀδελφὸν τὸν
ἴδιον).[31] The surprising turn in 1:12 (note the adversative use of δέ) is that
in spite of widespread rejection, the Logos is indeed received by some.
This positive reception initiates the densely concentrated constellation in
1:12–14 of familial terms (children of God/τέκνα θεοῦ, the only Son/
μονογενής, Father/πατήρ) and the familial imagery of child rearing (out
of bloods/ἐξ αἱμάτων, out of the will of flesh/ἐκ θελήματος σαρκός, out of
the will of a husband/ἐκ θελήματος ἀνδρός, out of God they were born/ἐκ
θεοῦ ἐγγενήθησαν) that stretches into 1:18 ('the only God, the one in the
bosom of the Father'/μονογενὴς θεός ὁ ὢν εἰς τὸν κόλπον τοῦ πατρός).

---

[30] Jan G. van der Watt, *Family of the King: Dynamics of Metaphor in the Gospel
According to John*, BIS 47 (Leiden: Brill, 2000), 187. See his brief excursus on the range
of uses for the term in John on p. 309.

[31] See 19:27 where Jesus assigns his mother to the Beloved Disciple's household. Other
occasions where ἴδιος appears to indicate family relations are 5:18, 13:1; 16:32.

The dual events of ecclesial inception and christological Incarnation constitute the formation of a new family in light of the tragic rejection by his own/οἱ ἴδιοι who failed to acknowledge the Logos as a family member. In contrast, the new family unit of the children of God/τέκνα θεοῦ unmistakably makes that recognition in v. 14: 'and we saw his glory, glory as of the only Son from God' (καὶ ἐθεασάμεθα τὴν δόξαν αὐτοῦ, δόξαν ὡς μονογενοῦς παρὰ πατρός – 1:14, emphases added). What is happening here is that these believers recognize Jesus as their kin. According to 1:12–13, this reception of Jesus in the framework of dyadic theology has secured for believers a supernatural participation in the divine family.

In his extensive study on metaphor dynamics in John, Jan van der Watt observes that 'Family imagery combines and integrates different central theological themes in the Gospel by means of a network. It serves as the dominating form in which the message of the Gospel is formulated.'[32] Considering this preferential use of family imagery for solidifying and communicating the Gospel's thematic emphases, the high density and interrelated connections of associative, familial language in John 1:12–14 binds the formation of the children of God with the Incarnation of the 'the only Son from the Father' (μονογενοῦς παρὰ πατρός).

This correlation of ecclesial formation with christological Incarnation is later confirmed in Jesus' dialogue with Nicodemus (3:1–15ff.). The language of procreative family formation reappears with strong allusions to the Prologue as the nightly visitor is informed that he must undergo a new birth (3:3). Jesus explains in 3:6 that 'what has been born [τὸ γεγεννημένον] out of the flesh is flesh [ἐκ τῆς σαρκὸς σάρξ ἐστιν]', conspicuously recalling the statement in the Prologue (1:13) that the children of God are *not* born ἐκ θελήματος σαρκός ('out of the will of flesh') but ἐκ θεοῦ ἐγεννήθησαν ('were born out of God'). This new birth (ecclesial formation) is directly linked to Jesus' coming into the world (christological Incarnation) in 3:16–17.

By way of summary, the genesis of God's people corresponds with the Incarnation. The interpretation presented above is grounded in a sequential reading that 1) observes two 'becomings' in 1:12–14 paired by their contrastive relationship to 'flesh'; 2) takes into account the density of familial imagery to which the Prologue's progression of narrowing terminology points; and 3) is confirmed by similar logic and

---

[32] Van der Watt, *Family of the King*, 439.

statements found in 3:1–21. This reading is not, however, premised on a consensus position within recent Johannine scholarship.

Conjunction and Disjunction within 1:12–14 in the History of Interpretation

Modern interpreters who do hold to some sort of connection between these two 'becomings' include Keener,[33] Barrett,[34] and, perhaps most enthusiastically, Edwyn Hoskyns. In an excursus entitled 'The Birth of Jesus Christ in the Fourth Gospel', Hoskyns discusses Tertullian's well-known reading of John 1:13 based on what most scholars regard as a corrupted Latin text that rendered the οἳ οὐκ ... ἐγεννήθησαν (with the verb in the plural) as '[qui] non ... natus est' (with the verb in the singular).[35] Defending the corporeality of Christ against Valentinian detractors, Tertullian understood 1:13 as referring to Christ's virginal birth.[36] Hoskyns acknowledges that Tertullian's text is poorly attested, but he contends that the language of Christ's unique birth would have been prevalent in Christian discourse in the later first century CE to such an extent that readers of the Fourth Gospel would have recognized a direct comparison here between the birth of believers with the birth of Jesus.[37] Whether a direct correspondence to Christ's own virginal birth would have been drawn or not, Hoskyns is adamant that the two 'becomings' are connected: 'The Evangelist did not write simply *The Word became flesh*, as though he were beginning a new topic. He wrote *And the Word became flesh*. That is to say, he links v. 14 closely to v. 13. The connection of thought is not difficult to follow.'[38] Recognizing this correlation between the formation of the children of God in John 1:12–13

---

[33] Keener, *John*, 405.

[34] 'It remains probable that John was alluding to Jesus' birth, and declaring that the birth of Christians, being bloodless and rooted in God's will alone, followed the pattern of the birth of Christ himself' – Barrett, *John*, 164.

[35] The 'qui' is within brackets because it is not entirely clear whether Tertullian's text included it. For a more detailed treatment of the textual traditions and related controversies of Jn 1:13, see Pryor, 'Virgin Birth'. For examples of modern interpreters who view 1:13 as referring to Christ in the singular, see Vellanickal, *Divine Sonship*, 128–31, and Boismard, *Prologue*, 33–45.

[36] Tert., *Carn. Chr.*, xix. See Tertullian, *The Five Books of Quintus Sept. Flor. Tertullianus Against Marcion*, trans. Peter Holmes, ANCL 7 (Edinburgh: T & T Clark, 1868), 203–5, 213.

[37] See Hoskyns, *The Fourth Gospel*, 147, 163–66. His position is similar to Barrett's cited above.

[38] Hoskyns, *The Fourth Gospel*, 164.

and the Incarnation in 1:14 was a customary hermeneutical practice of the Prologue's earliest interpreters. After a brief sampling of these interpretations, I will show how the connection was overlooked and at times even read as disjunctive by major scholarly figures in the twentieth century.

Patristic Interpreters and Conjunction Between the 'Becomings'

The generation of God's children and the becoming flesh of the Logos were regularly understood by patristic theologians as a joint event in which a divine–human exchange rendered divine–human filiation possible. In his fifth-century commentary on John's Gospel, Cyril of Alexandria understood the ecclesial formation of 1:12–13 as a participation in the divine nature *directly effected by* the Incarnation:

> Is it not perfectly clear to all that he came down into that which was in slavery, not to do anything for himself but to give himself to us 'that by his poverty, we might become rich' and that we might ascend by likeness with him to his own exceptional dignity and be shown to be gods and children of God through faith? (Cyril of Alexandria, *In Jo.,* 141)[39]

For Cyril, Christ 'came down' that 'we might ascend' – the Incarnation enables a divine status for the children of God. In the citation below from one of Augustine's sermons, he also reads the two 'becomings' in John 1: 12–14 in sequential relation to each other:

> But that men might be born of God, God was first born among them ... The Word himself wished to be born of man, that you might be born safely of God, and that you might say to yourself, 'It was not without reason that God willed to be born of man, but because he thought me of some importance, so that he should make me immortal and should himself be born into mortal life for me.' So when [John's Gospel] had said, 'of God were born', in order that, as it were, we might not be astonished and terrified at such a grace so great that it might seem unbelievable to us that men were born of God, as if relieving you of anxiety, [the Gospel] says, 'and the Word became flesh, and dwelt among us'. Why then are you astonished that men are born of God?

---

[39] Cyril of Alexandria, *Commentary on John,* ed. Joel C. Elowsky, trans. David R. Maxwell, vol. 1, ACT (Downers Grove, IL: InterVarsity Press, 2013), 64.

Notice that God himself was born of men: 'And the Word was made flesh, and dwelt among us.' (Augustine, *Tract. Ev. Jo.* 2.15)[40]

John Chrysostom provides another example of reading the Incarnation and the formation of God's children as an instance of divine–human exchange:

> Having declared that they who received him were 'born of God' and had become 'sons of God', he adds *the cause and reason* of this unspeakable honor. It is that 'the Word became flesh' … For he became Son of man, who was God's own Son, in order that he might make the sons of men to be children of God. (John Chrysostom, *Hom. Jo.* II.I, emphases added)[41]

Cyril understands Christ's becoming flesh and the birth of God's children as the means and consequence, respectively, of believing humanity's salvation from its desperate state. In Augustine's sermon, he is pastorally concerned to ensure his Christian hearers that their status as children born of God is paired with Christ's becoming flesh – 'anxiety' is relieved when noting the connection. For Chrysostom, christological Incarnation is 'the cause and reason' for ecclesial formation.

These patristic interpretations of John 1:12–14 are not surprising given early Christian views on the Incarnation's soteriological implications. The writer of Hebrews draws direct connections between Christ's earthly embodiment and the salvation of believers:

> Since therefore the children have taken part in [κεκοινώνηκεν] blood and flesh [αἵματος καί σαρκός – cf. Jn 1:13], he also shared [μετέσχεν] in them, so that through death he might nullify the one having power over death (this is the devil) and that he might set these free, those who in fear of death were enslaved their entire lives. (Heb 2:14–15, translation mine)

Origen's dictum, cited by Gregory of Nazianzus (*Ep.* 101) is appropriate: 'That which [Christ] has not assumed he has not healed.'[42] So also,

---

[40] Augustine, *Tractates on the Gospel of John 1–10*, trans. John W. Rettig, FC (Washington, D.C.: The Catholic University of America Press, 1988), 72–73.

[41] John Chrysostom, *John 1–10*, ed. Joel C. Elowsky, ACCS, IVa (Downers Grove, IL: InterVarsity Press, 2006), 40.

[42] Cited in Brian E. Daley, 'Christ and Christologies', in *The Oxford Handbook of Early Christian Studies*, ed. David G. Hunter and Susan Ashbrook Harvey (Oxford: Oxford University Press, 2008), 886–905, here at 894.

Irenaeus of Lyons wrote that the Word of God 'became what we are that he might make us what he is' (*Haer.* 5, Praef.).[43] In sections 1–18 of Athanasius' treatise *De incarnatione*, he provides a series of explanations, redolent with Johannine terminology, as to how salvation hinges on Christ's taking on flesh:

> For this purpose [the recreation of fallen humanity], then, the incorporeal and incorruptible and immaterial Word of God comes into our realm ... And thus, taking from ours that which is like [human flesh], since all were liable to the corruption of death, delivering it over to death on behalf of all, he offered it to the Father, doing this in love for human beings, so that ... as human beings had turned towards corruption he might turn them again to incorruptibility and give them life from death, by making the body his own and by the grace of the resurrection banishing death from them as straw from fire. (*Inc.*, 8)[44]

Both Alexandrian theologians, Cyril[45] and Athanasius regularly discuss the Incarnation's effects in terms of deification or theosis (Athanasius: 'for he was incarnate [ἐνηνθρώπησεν] that we might be made god [θεοποιηθῶμεν]' *Inc.*, 54).[46] In anticipation of Part III's treatment of 'Johannine Theosis', it is important to note here that 1:14a bore profound soteriological dynamics for early interpreters of the Fourth Gospel that would have been viewed in natural correspondence with the ecclesial formation in John 1:12–13. And the result of these two 'becomings' is the participation of the τέκνα θεοῦ within the divine family of the πατήρ and the μονογενής.

[43] Irenaeus of Lyons, *Against the Heresies*, trans. Robert M. Grant (London: Routledge, 1997), 164.

[44] Athanasius, *On the Incarnation*, trans. John Behr, PPS 44 (Yonkers, NY: St Vladimir's Press, 2011), 65–67.

[45] See Daniel A. Keating, *The Appropriation of Divine Life in Cyril of Alexandria*, OTM (Oxford: Oxford University Press, 2005); Daniel A. Keating, 'Divinization in Cyril: The Appropriation of Divine Life', in *The Theology of St Cyril of Alexandria: A Critical Appreciation*, ed. Thomas G. Weinandy and Daniel A. Keating (London: T & T Clark, 2003), 149–85. Though focus is directed to Cyril's interpretation of Paul, see also Benjamin Blackwell's monograph which provides a helpful starting point for understanding Cyril's notion of divine participation – Benjamin C. Blackwell, *Christosis: Pauline Soteriology in Light of Deification in Irenaeus and Cyril of Alexandria*, WUNT 2/314 (Tübingen: Mohr Siebeck, 2011). Blackwell lists the following references where Cyril 'routinely refers to believers as gods in his commentary on John' (73): *Jo.* 1.3; 1.6–7; 1.9; 1.12–14; 3.33; 5.18; 6.27; 10.33–34; 15.9–10; 17.3; 17.4–5; 17.20; 17.26; 20.17.

[46] Athanasius, *On the Incarnation*, 167. See also *Inc.*, 3, 4, 5, 6, 9, 11, et al.

Twentieth-century Interpretation and Disjunction between the 'Becomings'

An association between ecclesial formation and christological Incarnation in John 1:12–14 has been missed or denied by a number of influential modern interpreters.[47] In my introductory chapter I used Marianne Meye Thompson's term 'christocentricity' to describe the tendency of emphasizing christology to such an extent that ecclesial concerns are diminished or overlooked. This line of reasoning seems operative in Bultmann, whose inattention to any connection between the 'becomings' accords with his assessment that the scandalous nature of the Revealer becoming flesh in v. 14a occasions a major thematic and stylistic rift within the Prologue.[48] Perhaps unwittingly, the consequence of this reading of the Incarnation's introduction as a rift disrupts connective seams that should be carried over into v. 14. Though the Incarnation is certainly an astonishing announcement, as Bultmann energetically championed, the text of John 1:1–18 jointly emphasizes (through irony and the use of δέ in v. 12) that just as surprising as the Logos becoming flesh is the Logos' rejection by the world and by 'his own', an appalling reality that meets its contrast with the ecclesial 'becoming' of 1:12–13.

Rudolf Schnackenburg respectfully acknowledges the interpretations of Augustine and Chrysostom, who (as noted above) seem to read the καί (normally read as 'and') of 1:14 as 'explanatory'[49]; but in the end he rejects this option:

> [such an interpretation] does not do justice to the context, and displaces the centre of gravity from v. 14 back to vv. 12f. But the main interest is centred on the Logos, and it is only at the end of this last strophe of the hymn (v. 16) that we are told how this unique event affects our salvation: through the coming of the Logos we have all received grace upon grace from his fullness.[50]

Schnackenburg's christocentric interpretation is governed in part by his understanding of 1:14 as the 'climax'[51] of the Prologue's Logos-hymn;

---

[47] M.-E. Boismard stands out as one of the exceptions. In his 'parabola'-shaped schema of the Prologue, he places the formation of the children of God in the nadir (central position), as noted earlier. It is by Christ's incarnation that he 'communicates to us that divine life which makes us children of God'. See Boismard, *Prologue*, 80.

[48] 'The character of the Prologue changes' – Bultmann, *John*, 60ff. With v. 14a begins 'the language of mythology' (61).

[49] Schnackenburg, *John*, 1:266.   [50] Ibid.   [51] Ibid.

but even if 1:14 is identified as such, its thematic and semantic connections to 1:12–13 in the extant text, perceived so naturally by Augustine and Chrysostom, need not be denied. The right to become children of God is actually the specific instantiation of what Schnackenburg labelled above the 'unique event that affects our salvation'.

The interpretative disjunction between the Incarnation in 1:14 and the divine birth of God's children in 1:12–13 also derives from source-critical convictions that a fault-line exists between 1:13 and 1:14 due to the Prologue's textual prehistory.[52] Ernst Haenchen reads vv. 12–13 as an editorial insertion[53] designed to make the simple point that 'Christians do not owe their existence as such to natural procreation'; he writes that 'there is nothing objectionable in this verse from the point of view of the Gospel of John – if it were connected to verse 14. Unfortunately, that is not the case. Verse 13 does not make it at all comprehensible that the Logos became flesh nor why it became flesh.'[54] Haenchen's appreciation of 1:13 seems to be subordinated to its efficacy for interpreting 1:14, which it presumably fails to do since it is disjointed from the original hymn material that was composed in the Prologue's textual pre-history and, as Haenchen's most recent comment above indicates, since 1:13 offers no logical grounds for 1:14 (a logic that the patristic interpreters above understood as self-evident).

No exegete, however, seems more vigorously determined to promote a thematic severance between 1:12–13 and 1:14 than Ernst Käsemann: 'Against Hoskyns ... it has to be said that the parallelism between the children of God and the Son of God is precisely what is *not* established; rather, the reference is to the Logos which is becoming flesh.'[55] Writing with Bultmann's interpretation of the Prologue targeted within his polemical sights,[56] Käsemann's contention that no parallel exists

---

[52] As Morna Hooker has pointed out, the reintroduction of the Logos in 1:14 has reinforced the sense for many scholars that something distinctively new from 1:12–13 is underway – Morna Hooker, 'John the Baptist and the Johannine Prologue', *NTS* 16, no. 4 (1970): 354–58, here at 356. But this restatement need not create such distance within the text from what precedes it. The Logos becomes flesh precisely on the heels of the statement that a new family is being produced *not* from the flesh. Thematically, the reappearance of Logos works well with my argument that 1:12–14 should be read without a disruption.

[53] 'The two verses 12 and 13 do not go well with either verse 11 or verse 14' – Ernst Haenchen, *A Commentary on the Gospel of John*, trans. Robert W. Funk, Hermeneia (Philadelphia, PA: Fortress, 1984), 1:118.

[54] Ibid.   [55] Käsemann, 'Prologue', 149.

[56] In sum, Bultmann posited that the evangelist has crafted the Prologue by polemically altering an Aramaic cultic hymn used by a sect devoted to John the Baptist. See Bultmann, *John*, 17–18. For his earlier essay exploring the religious ideas possibly drawn from by the

between Christ's Incarnation and the genesis of the children of God also seems premised on assumptions about the Prologue's underlying sources that enforce a disjuncture between 1:14 and 1:12–13. In Käsemann's assessment, vv. 1–4 and v. 5 along with vv. 9–12 are two strophes of a Christian hymn taken up by the evangelist and designed to summarize ('as a resumé'[57]) what the Revealer has accomplished.[58] Following these two strophes (and the prose interpolation of vv. 6–8) is the 'explanatory comment' of 1:13 attributed directly to the hand of the evangelist.[59] Thus ends one literary unit behind the extant form of the Prologue. Käsemann then reads 1:14–18 as an 'epilogue' penned by the evangelist for a conclusion to the preceding hymn.[60] So his rejection of parallelism between 1:12–13 and 1:14 appears to be largely founded on his view that they are disjoined at the textual partition of two discrete literary units, one a Christianized hymn, the other the evangelist's epilogue.

A theological conviction may also underlie Käsemann's resistance to relating the Incarnation to the formation of the children of God. Countering Bultmann's emphasis on 1:14a (the Logos becoming flesh), he argues with well-known vehemence that the Fourth Gospel actually places the stress on 1:14c (the enfleshed Logos' glory). One of Käsemann's legacies in New Testament scholarship is his claim that 'the humanity of Jesus recedes totally into the background'[61] of the Fourth Gospel after 1:14a.[62] Bultmann's emphasis on 1:14a may have divided christological Incarnation from ecclesial formation by augmenting the event of the Logos becoming flesh so as to overshadow the believers becoming God's children; but Käsemann's redirection of emphasis away from the Incarnation onto 1:14b intensified the effect – diminishing the Logos becoming flesh in turn obscured the stress placed on its connection to the believers becoming God's children.

In an article demonstrating the Prologue's interlacing threads with the remainder of the Gospel, Warren Carter has observed:

> The exchange between Bultmann and Käsemann which has dominated the discussion of the Prologue since Harnack, was concerned primarily with its original form and provenance. Their exegeses, marked by a focus on v. 14, treated the

---

writers responsible for the material in the Prologue, see Rudolf Bultmann, 'The History of Religions Background of the Prologue to the Gospel of John', in *The Interpretation of John*, ed. John Ashton, vol. 9, *IRT* (London: SPCK, 1986), 18–35.

[57] Käsemann, 'Prologue', 152.   [58] Ibid., 146.   [59] Ibid., 152.   [60] Ibid.

[61] Ibid., 156.

[62] Käsemann's *The Testament of Jesus*, of course, is largely an elaboration of this claim.

Prologue largely as an independent unit, with the discussion of its function as part of the Gospel receiving little attention.[63] Bultmann and Käsemann have promoted a disjointed reading of the Prologue. Not only is the Prologue itself subtly dislodged from the rest of John's Gospel (Carter's primary concern), but the focus on v. 14 has erected a partition between the paired 'becomings' in John 1:12–14. Such a disruptive reading strategy is incongruent with the exegesis of patristic theologians and misses John's 'ecclesiology of the Incarnation'.

Chapter Summary

Though a complex composition history may indeed underlie the Prologue, its extant form presents a developing sequence in which the Logos, God, and believing human beings are gradually identified and interrelated by filial designations. The Prologue structurally places ecclesiology at its centre and stylistically employs a process of disambiguation to ensure that it is read alongside christology and theology. Moreover, the most significant christological event (the Incarnation) is paired with the most significant ecclesial event (the formation of God's children). Some notion of divine–human exchange is underway as the filiation of human beings is predicated on or at least correlated with the Incarnation of Jesus. The consecutive pairing of two 'becomings' evidenced by the shared filial origin and the contrastive reference to 'flesh' conceptually and literally conjoin the Incarnation and the formation of God's reconfigured people. Again, the Johannine vision of God's people as a new family unit is not an auxiliary motif, but one prominently positioned in the Prologue and inseparably encompassed within the robust christological reworking of the divine identity and their inclusive community.

---

[63] Carter, 'Prologue', 36.

4

CHARACTERIZING THE PROLOGUE'S ECCLESIOLOGY: THE AMBIGUATION AND ASSIMILATION OF JOHN THE BAPTIST

If ecclesiology and christology are as intertwined in the Prologue as I am contending here in Part I, then it should be expected that the role of the Gospel's most vocal witness to Jesus will bear some ecclesial significance. In this section, I offer a reassessment of the Johannine characterization of John the Baptist.[1] Though I have roughly maintained a sequential reading of the Prologue in my succession of chapters, a discussion on John has been postponed until now, allowing me to treat his introduction in 1:6–8 together with his reappearance in 1:15. Consideration will be given, however, to the development of his character in the rest of Chapter 1 and beyond; extending the scope of this study beyond the Prologue will furnish a helpful transition for Chapter 5, which will show how the Prologue's ecclesial vision gives shape to the rest of the Gospel narrative. My primary point in what immediately follows is that in spite of his pronounced christological role in this Gospel, John is not just identifying the Christ – *he is also forming the church and being absorbed into its communal ranks.*

John the Baptist as Christological Witness in the Prologue

The standard interpretation of the Johannine portrayal of John is that his role is solely christological, one in which he merely serves as a foil in relation to Jesus. In comparison to the Synoptics, Jesus is not baptized by John in the Fourth Gospel,[2] and the role of Elijah *redivivus* is denied him.[3] Moreover, John is identified by *who he is not* as much by *who he is* – along with not being Elijah in the Fourth Gospel, he is also not the

---

[1] It is useful to preserve this cognomen, although it should be noted that John is never modified as 'the Baptist' in the Fourth Gospel.

[2] Jn 1:20, 25–26; Cf. Mt 3:13–17; Mk 1:9–11; it would also appear that Jesus is not baptized by John in Luke, since the former's baptism is referred to after the time of John's imprisonment (Lk 3:20–21).

[3] Jn 1:21, 25; Cf. Mt 3:4; 17:10–13; Mk 1:6; 9:11–13; (Lk 1:17).

light (1:8), not the Christ (1:20, 25), and not the prophet (1:25). These negations contribute to the fourth evangelist's subordination of John to Jesus, a programme epitomized in the former's claim, 'he must increase, but I must decrease' (3:30).

The Baptist is positively presented as a 'voice', specifically, the 'voice crying out in the wilderness' (φωνὴ βοῶντος ἐν τῇ ἐρήμῳ) from Isaiah 40:3. But the word scholars consider most representative of his Johannine portrayal is 'witness'.[4] According to Walter Wink, 'every other role is sheared away' from John in the Fourth Gospel other than the role of bearing testimony to Jesus.[5] As a christological 'witness' undergoing such a persistent minimization in the Gospel, it has been widely assumed that the evangelist has encoded into his narrative a heated polemic directed against some known group promoting cultic veneration of John.[6] This assessment offers an explanation for the Prologue's most notorious literary discontinuities: the (ostensibly) awkward lines of 1:6–8 and 1:15 are interpolations roughly incorporated into a hymn to counteract misplaced devotions to the Baptist.[7] Variations of this literary and historical interpretation have wielded considerable influence over how the Johannine Prologue has been understood.[8]

My purpose in this section is not to dispute a historical conflict between the Johannine community and a potential Baptist-sect per se.[9]

---

[4] Robert L. Webb, *John the Baptizer and Prophet: A Socio-Historical Study,* JSNTSup 62 (Sheffield: Sheffield Academic Press, 1991), 75.

[5] Walter Wink, *John the Baptist in the Gospel Tradition*, SNTSMS 7 (Cambridge: Cambridge University Press, 1968), 89.

[6] Again, see Bultmann's 'History of Religions Background', 18–35. He is building on the suggestions of Wilhelm Baldensperger, *Der Prolog des vierten Evangeliums: sein polemischer-apologetischer Zweck* (Tübingen: Mohr-Siebeck, 1898).

[7] This, of course, is Bultmann's influential interpretation. He argued that the Prologue is premised on a cultic hymn devoted to John the Baptist but co-opted by the fourth evangelist to unseat him with a focus on Christ. See Bultmann, *John*, 17–18. For arguments against Bultmann's dismissal of early Judaism as a source for the Prologue, as well as for strong grounds on seeing 1:6–8 and 1:15 as integrated rather than interpolated, see Boyarin, 'Gospel of the Memra'.

[8] Curiously, the role of John as a hermeneutical lens for understanding the Fourth Gospel's setting has quite a history. Eusebius explained the differences between John and the Synoptics by pointing to the chronological treatments of John. The Synoptics record the events in Jesus' life before John was imprisoned, and the Fourth Gospel records Jesus' ministry before that arrest. See Eusebius, *Hist. eccl.*, 3:24:12–13.

[9] Pseudo-Clementine (third century) reports that a group of Baptist devotees came into being during the ministry of Jesus: 'Some of the disciples of John who imagined they were great separated themselves from the people and proclaimed their master as Christ' (Pseudo-Clementine, *Recognitions*, 1.54). Translation from the Latin in F. Stanley Jones, *An Ancient*

Neither am I interested in ironing out the apparent intrusiveness of his references in the Prologue[10] or in downplaying the conspicuously christological role this character certainly holds in the Fourth Gospel. What I am contending is that classifying John *as no more than* a christological witness is too limiting an approach – his function in the Fourth Gospel is also ecclesiological. And the awkwardness of his introduction in the Prologue *may well be intentional and in the service of ecclesiology.*[11]

Ambiguation in the Identity and Voice of John the Baptist

I submit that the Prologue is characterizing John by a process of *ambiguation* in direct contrast to the process of disambiguation underway for God and the Logos. This proposal opens up a new way of understanding the interruptive nature of John 1:6–8 and 1:15 in the Prologue: in stark contrast to the characterizations of God, the Logos, and believing humanity in the Prologue, the Baptist's crisp, individual voice of christological witness ambiguates and then merges into the corporate voice of ecclesial confession. As a witness to Christ, John's testimonial 'voice'/φωνή is central to his identity: when the emissaries from Jerusalem ask 'who are you (σὺ τίς εἶ)'?, his one positive answer in the entire pericope is 'I am a voice' (ἐγὼ φωνή). Yet his voice is at times notoriously difficult to differentiate from other voices in the Gospel, blending with and fading into the voice of the narrator (3:31–36) or into the collective voice of the confessing community (1:15 and following). This process of blending and fading is *intentionally assigned* to the Baptist to gradually enfold Christ's most emphatic witness into the Johannine community. His introduction in 1:6 is so direct, so definitive and clear, that it has spurred the form- and source-critical enterprises prominently associated with Prologue studies. Granting that John's opening may well have

Jewish-Christian Source on the History of Christianity: Pseudo-Clementine Recognitions 1.27–71, SBLTT 37 (Atlanta, GA: Scholars Press, 1995), 88. See also Acts 19:1–7.

[10] Tom Thatcher argues that source-critical inquiries into the textual pre-history of the Prologue that isolate 1:6–8 and 1:15 fail to take into consideration the oral nature of the Fourth Gospel in its first-century media context. His recent essay on John offers a fresh rereading of John 1:1–18 in light of ancient media studies, though I am not convinced that the Prologue's foundation is to be found in the Baptist's words in 1:15. See Tom Thatcher, 'The Riddle of the Baptist and the Genesis of the Prologue: John 1:1–18 in Oral/Aural Media Culture', in *The Fourth Gospel in First-Century Media Culture*, ed. Anthony le Donne and Tom Thatcher, LNTS 426 (London: T & T Clark, 2011), 29–48.

[11] Other scholars who do not see these Baptist verses as interpolations include Barrett, *John*, 159, and Hooker, 'John the Baptist', 358.

a complex textual (and perhaps oral) pre-history involving Baptist material, it is possible to understand 1:6–8 in the present form of the text, not as an interpolation, but as a character introduction that is purposefully striking in both placement and style.[12] In contradistinction from the introduction of God and the Logos in 1: 1–5, no ambiguity is attached to John in 1:6–8.[13] His origin is unequivocally stated (from God/παρὰ θεοῦ) and he is immediately named, even though Jesus' name will not be revealed until the Prologue's ending. Readers and auditors are concisely told the purpose of his coming in no uncertain terms ('for a witness... so that all might believe through him'/εἰς μαρτυρίαν ... ἵνα πάντες πιστεύσωσιν δι' αὐτοῦ). We are additionally informed as to who he is not ('that one was not the Light'/οὐκ ἦν ἐκεῖνος τὸ φῶς). In spite of the strategic process of disambiguation marking the introductions of God, the Logos, and humanity, very little is ambiguous in the Prologue's introduction of the Baptist. This lack of ambiguity is no less strategic than the ambiguity attached to 'God', 'Logos', and the terms for general humanity in the early part of the Prologue.

When John reappears in 1:15, curiously framing the Prologue's pivotal introduction of ecclesiology (see Table 3.4 in the preceding chapter), the same vivid clarity persists. We hear in this verse John's actual voice for the first time ('[he] cried out, saying'/κέκραγεν λέγων) doing exactly what one would expect – bearing testimony to Christ. *But his individual christological testimony blends into corporate ecclesiological confession.* John's first person singular testimony comes on the heels of the first person plural voice in 1:14 – 'and we have seen his glory'/καὶ ἐθεασάμεθα τὴν δόξαν αὐτοῦ[14] – and immediately after v. 15 the first person plural resumes with 'we all received'/ἡμεῖς πάντες ἐλάβομεν (1:16). Though it is certainly possible to read 1:15 as an insertion, it is also possible that John's

---

[12] Note the similarities between the introduction of John and that of Nicodemus.

John: ἐγένετο ἄνθρωπος, ἀπεσταλμένος παρὰ θεοῦ, ὄνομα αὐτῷ Ἰωάννης· οὗτος ἦλθεν; Nicodemus: Νικόδημος ὄνομα αὐτῷ ... οὗτος ἦλθεν.

[13] *Pace* Philips, who believes that the ambiguity of 1:1–5 extends into 1:6–8 (Phillips, *Prologue*, 178). Barrett points out that the use of the preposition διά (through) indicates that John is in view, not Jesus (people 'do not not believe *through* Jesus but *in* him') – Barrett, *John*, 160. See also Michaels, *John*, 60, and Andrew T. Lincoln, *The Gospel According to Saint John*, BNTC 4 (New York: Hendrikson, 2005), 100.

[14] Several commentators have assumed that 1:15 amounts to another interpolation, since v. 16 can be read with ease if suffixed directly to 1:14, though the inclusion of 1:15 in the earliest texts is plausible for Barrett (*John*, 140).

singular voice is intentionally being incorporated into the collective voice of the narrator and that of his community. Origen,[15] Irenaeus,[16] and Theodore of Mopsuestia[17] (along with Thomas Aquinas[18] and John Calvin[19] several centuries later) held that John the Baptist's voice stretched from 1:15 at least into 1:17, evidencing the evangelist's intention to blend his witness into the first person plural voice.[20] In his study on the manuscript history behind John 1:1–18, Peter Williams makes this observation:

> Some insight into Heracleon's division of the text is provided by Origen who says, 'Heracleon takes "No one has ever seen God, etc." incorrectly, claiming that it was said, not by the Baptist, but by the disciple.' Origen thereby demonstrates that the view that John the Baptist's speech ends at 1.17 existed in the second century, a fact which may explain why second-century sources such as Tatian's *Diatessaron* and then subsequent Greek

[15] 'John too, therefore, came to bear witness concerning the light. He bore witness and "cried out saying, 'He who comes after me ranks before me, because he was before me. We all received of his fullness, even grace for grace. For the law was given by Moses; grace and truth came by Jesus Christ. No one has ever seen God; the only begotten God who is in the bosom of the Father has declared him.'" *This whole speech, therefore, was from the mouth of the Baptist* bearing witness to the Christ. This fact escapes the notice of some who think that the speech from the words, "We all received of his fullness" up to "he has declared him" was from the mouth of John the apostle' (Origen, *Comm. Jo.*, 2.212–213; emphases added). Translation from Origen, *Commentary on the Gospel According to John Books 1–10: A New Translation*, trans. Ronald E. Heine, FC 80 (Washington, D.C.: The Catholic University of America Press, 1989), 152 (see also *Comm. Jo.* 6.13–14).

[16] 'For the knowledge of salvation which was wanting to them was that of God's Son, which John gave them *when he said*, "Behold the Lamb of God, who takes away the sin of the world." This is he of whom I said, "After me comes a man who ranks before me, for he was before me" and "from his fullness have we all received"' (*Haer.*, 3.10.3; emphases added). See Irenaeus of Lyons, *Against the Heresies*, trans. Dominic J. Unger, ACW 64 (New York: The Newman Press, 2012), 49.

[17] 'These are the words the Evangelist reports were pronounced by John the Baptist: "From his fullness", he says, "we have all received."' From Theodore of Mopsuestia, *Commentary on the Gospel of John*, ed. Joel C. Elowsky, trans. Marco Conti, ACT (Downers Grove, IL: InterVarsity, 2010), 18.

[18] Thomas Aquinas, *Catena Aurea: Commentary on the Four Gospels Collected out of the Works of the Fathers by S. Thomas Aquinas*, New edn. (Oxford: James Parker, 1870), 38–39.

[19] John Calvin, *Commentary on the Gospel According to John*, vol. 1 (Edinburgh: Calvin Translation Society, 1847), 50, 55.

[20] See the discussion on the patristic texts and the use of ὅτι in Harris, *Prologue and Gospel*, 31–34.

lectionary tradition put a major division between 1.17 and 1.18, not between 1.18 and 1.19.[21]

Cyril of Alexandria,[22] John Chrysostom,[23] and Augustine,[24] however, read John 1:16 as the words not of John but of the evangelist, which is how the text is normally read today. The point made by these different readings is that *ambiguity of voice marks the text here in the Prologue*. As Elizabeth Harris points out, the ὅτι (often meaning 'that', or 'because') opening 1:16 and 1:17 could easily be read as recitative, introducing a quotation that includes the voice of John with the corporate voice of the community. And yet we could also read the passage with Augustine and Chrysostom as a transition from one distinct voice to another. The exegetical reality is that both readings are possible, creating ambiguity for the reader or auditor.

This ambiguation of the Baptist's testimonial voice/φωνή in the Prologue is intentional and consonant with his portrayal in the wider narrative. As briefly noted above, the pattern of voice-fading and voice-blending in 1:15–18 recurs in John 3 when, after stating that Jesus must increase as he diminishes (3:30), it becomes unclear whether the voice in 3:31–36 is that of the John the Baptist or of John the evangelist.[25] Receding and fading into ambiguity is the plotline assigned to John in this narrative. Unlike the Synoptic portrayals, the fourth evangelist does not record the Baptist's death, perhaps a surprising detail to omit if anti-Baptist polemics were indeed underway[26] – rather than an abrupt

---

[21] Williams, 'Not the Prologue', 379.

[22] See *Jo.*, 148 (Cyril of Alexandria, *Commentary on John*, 1:67).

[23] *Hom. Jo.* 12.1 (John Chrysostom, *John 1–10*, 73).

[24] *Tract. in Io.*, 2.16. From Thomas Aquinas, *Commentary on the Gospel of John: Chapters 1–5*, trans. Fabian Larcher and James A. Weisheipl (Washington, D.C.: The Catholic University of America Press, 2010), 74.

[25] 'The most prominent problem in these verses concerns the speaker' – Brown, *John*, 159. See his discussion (pp. 159–160) for a comparison of scholarly interpretations of who is speaking in 3:31–36.

[26] John 3:24 makes a reference to his eventual arrest, but the casual, indeterminate nature of the detail is so insignificant to the current plot that some English versions of the text render it as parenthetical. As to the validity of the broadly accepted concept of an anti-Baptist polemic in the Fourth Gospel, Brown views Baldensperger's suggestions (see n. 6) as 'uncritically' embraced and argues that the 'whole thesis of a polemic and its influence on the gospels needs re-examination'. See Raymond E. Brown, 'Three Quotations from John the Baptist in the Gospel Tradition', *CBQ* 22, no. 3 (1960): 292–98, here at 293, n. 5. Similarly, C. H. Dodd: 'there is no sufficient evidence' that a rival community accorded John the Baptist higher status than Jesus, so we must 'look in a somewhat different direction' – C. H. Dodd, *Historical Tradition in the Fourth Gospel* (Cambridge: Cambridge University Press, 1963), 298.

ending, he endures a gradual disappearance. 'He must increase and I must decrease' is the script for the John in this Gospel.

As his voice and activity fade into obscurity, the identity and voice of Jesus become louder and clearer. The sequential disambiguation of dyadic theology (Logos/Jesus; God/Father) and the ambiguation of dyadic theology's strongest witness (John) are paired together for this purpose: *to introduce a controversial christological vision of God that extends beyond scriptural theological parameters and yet is legitimated by the authority of a scriptural, prophetic voice/φωνή.* Dyadic theology is premised on a radical rereading of Israel's Scriptures, but John represents the voice of those Scriptures – C. K. Barrett viewed the Johannine John the Baptist as 'the representative'[27] and the 'μαρτυρία [witness]'[28] of the Old Testament. To make the same point, Boismard cites parallels between the Baptist's introduction in John 1:6–8 and the introduction of other scriptural heroes.[29] What is happening in the Fourth Gospel's opening chapter is a christological re-presentation of God certified by an Old Testament voice crying in the wilderness that becomes the ecclesial confession of Jesus. The paired processes of ambiguation and disambiguation are a literary instantiation of the passing of one era into a new one. So the awkward verses of 1:6–8 and 1:15 need not be read as glosses or interjections. These lines constitute a striking character introduction that is purposefully and strategically abrupt, marked by a gradual ambiguation coordinated with the gradual *dis*ambiguation underway for God, the Logos, and humankind.

Christological Witness and Ecclesial Confession: John as a Representative of Both Israel and Johannine Christianity

John the Baptist's gradual ambiguation allows him to serve as a representative figure not only of the Old Testament, but also of the ecclesial social reality of the children of God. As his character fades and blends, he shifts from the individual wilderness voice embodying Old Testament prophecy into the collective voice of the Gospel's faith community. The voice-blending that occurs between 1:15 and 1:16–17 (perhaps extending into 1:18) becomes foundational for the Baptist's

---

[27] Barrett, *John*, 171.

[28] C. K. Barrett, 'The Old Testament in the Fourth Gospel', *JTS*, no. 48 (1947): 155–69, here at 167.

[29] Boismard, *Prologue*, 24–25. Cf. Jdg 13:2; 19:1; 1 Sam 1:1.

Johannine characterization – he will soon speak not only the language of Isaianic speech; he will also use the language of the Gospel's community worship, that of 'confessing' and not 'denying'. Immediately after the Prologue, when his identity is questioned by the Pharisees' representatives, John 'confessed and did not deny, and confessed' (ὡμολόγησεν καὶ οὐκ ἠρνήσατο, καὶ ὡμολόγησεν – 1:20). This language of confession and denial is strongly ecclesial in the Johnannine literature[30] and in other New Testament texts. From C. H. Dodd:

> In view of the deep significance which the terms ὁμολογεῖν and ἀρνεῖσθαι have in the vocabulary of the New Testament, the expression in John i.20 would inevitably mean, for any Christian reader of the period, 'He confessed Christ and did not deny him'. In other words, the evangelist is claiming the Baptist as the first Christian 'confessor', in contrast to the view represented in the Synoptic Gospels that he was not 'in the Kingdom of God.[31]

John's voice therefore maintains the dual representative function of witnessing christologically in the Isaianic voice of the Old Testament while at the same time confessing ecclesiologically in the testimonial voice of the Johannine community. In the Fourth Gospel, John is not the concluding figure of the Old Testament as in the Synoptics; he is, rather, a hinge figure whose voice expresses a controversial, ecclesial confession of Jesus' divine identity that is at the same time certified in the voice of prophetic authentication.[32] This leads to two important observations. First, John's characterization is more complex than is normally allowed in Johannine character studies.[33] He represents prophetic witness simultaneously with ecclesial confession. Second, as hinted

---

[30] ὁμολογέω: Jn 9:22; 12:42; 1 Jn 1:9; 2:23; 4:2, 15. For ἀρνέομαι: Jn 13:38; 18:25–27; 1 Jn 2:22–23 (where it appears 3 times).

[31] Dodd, *Historical Tradition*, 299.

[32] As argued by Catrin H. Williams, 'John (the Baptist): The Witness on the Threshold', in *Character Studies in the Fourth Gospel: Narrative Approaches to Seventy Figures in John*, ed. Steven A. Hunt, D. Francois Tolmie, and Ruben Zimmerman, WUNT 1:314 (Tübingen: Mohr Siebeck, 2013), 60.

[33] Though Colleen Conway is keen to promote a more complex picture of Johannine characterization that exceeds the simplistic designations of 'round' or 'flat', she none-theless labels John the Baptist as a flat character whose sole function is that of bearing christological witness. Colleen M. Conway, 'Speaking through Ambiguity: Minor Characters in the Fourth Gospel', *BibInt* 10, no. 3 (2002): 324–41. She is countering what she views as overly simplistic character analyses like those found in the earlier studies of Raymond F. Collins, 'Representative Figures of the Fourth Gospel', in *These Things*

earlier, the Prologue's reconceptualization of God's people envisions *continuity with Israel* through the Baptist's scriptural and ecclesial voice, not discontinuity.

John's role as an ecclesial representative in the Prologue is confirmed later in the Gospel when his activities and relationship to Jesus become paradigmatic for the disciples. He is sent by God (1:6, 33), and the disciples will be sent (20:21) by Jesus. Just as John is the 'friend'/φίλος of the bridegroom (3:29), Jesus will call the disciples his 'friends'/φίλοι (15:14; see also 3 Jn 15). John bears witness to Jesus (1:7 et al.), but so will the faithful members of the newly formed community (15:26). I cited above Walter Wink's conviction that John's function in the Gospel of John is explicitly christological. But Wink betrays an understanding that this christological witness is tied to corporate ecclesial confession when he claims that John is not only 'the ideal witness to Christ' but that he is also 'made the normative image of the Christian preacher, apostle and missionary, the perfect prototype of the true evangelist'.[34] Dismissing the idea that the Gospel of John is counteracting a Baptist sectarian movement, Wink goes so far as to claim that 'here in the Fourth Gospel, more than anywhere else, the church is regarded as a direct outgrowth of the Baptist movement'.[35] He goes on to say, 'The Evangelist's portrait of John is thus intended more for the church than for Baptist circles.'[36] Even Käsemann would agree with these claims that an ecclesial function is attributed to John by the fourth evangelist: 'The Gospel does not exist without the confessing community, whose first representative John the Baptist was.'[37]

John the Baptist as Ecclesial Catalyst

The final point to make in arguing that John bears an ecclesial function established in the Prologue and extending into the narrative is that *the first instance of ecclesial group formation around Jesus is effected by his ministry.* In a scene that enacts the witness and confession of John in 1: 6–8 and 1:15(–17) respectively, he points to Jesus, the Lamb of God, and a transfer of group membership takes place as two of his own disciples leave him to follow Jesus instead (1:35–37). Unlike the Synoptic call narratives in which disciples become associated with Jesus over time in

Have Been Written: Studies on the Fourth Gospel, ed. Raymond F. Collins, LTPM 2 (Louvain: Peeters, 1990), 1–45; and Culpepper, *Anatomy of the Fourth Gospel,* 105–6.

[34] Wink, *John the Baptist,* 105.   [35] Ibid., 103.   [36] Ibid., 106.
[37] Käsemann, 'Prologue', 165.

multiple episodes, the Gospel of John orders a discipleship community around Jesus by the end of the opening chapter.[38] The catalyst for this virtually instantaneous group formation is not the call of Jesus as in the Synoptics but the testimony of the Baptist. So the very first ecclesial entity in the Gospel derives from John's christological witness.

Summary of the Baptist's Ecclesial Function

In keeping with the claims made throughout this chapter that the Prologue knows no christology apart from ecclesiology, we have seen that the primary christological witness in the Prologue also takes on the burden of ecclesial confession. The Fourth Gospel's agenda of subordinating John to Jesus is not achieved by obliterating this character from the narrative through a record of his death or through abruptly silencing his voice. The approach taken, rather, is that of accentuating John's preeminence as an Old Testament prophet and then assimilating his individual voice into the corporate voice of the Johannine church. If the evangelist is polemically reinterpreting John it is not by co-opting lines from a Baptist-venerating hymn and then squashing his significance as early as possible in the narrative; instead, the evangelist presents the Christ's most vocal herald positively and then appropriates his voice, assigning his testimonial function to the disciples that succeed him. Through a process of ambiguation, John is presented with a distinct dual role and a distinct dual voice that are eventually subsumed within the identity and collective voice of the reconfigured people of God.

---

[38] See the discussion in the following chapter. It should be noted that the Johannine call story takes place over a few days in narrative time.

5

THE PROLOGUE'S 'ECCLESIAL NARRATIVE SCRIPT': ECCLESIOLOGY AS STORY ARC

If the Johannine Prologue establishes thematic emphases for the ensuing narrative and if ecclesiology is as central to the Prologue as I am proposing, then an ecclesial vision should rise to appreciable prominence in the subsequent narrative. The purpose of this chapter is to show that the Fourth Gospel's opening eighteen verses set into motion a foundational narrative pattern that is explicitly ecclesial and repeatedly enacted throughout the unfolding story. This 'ecclesial narrative script' prescribes a continual process of both social disruption and community formation around Jesus. Following the trajectory launched in the Prologue, the Gospel's plotline is animated and enacted by the possibility, acceptance, or rejection of *group realignment*. Stated in the Prologue's terms, the Logos comes to 'his own', faces widespread rejection, yet is accepted by a minority that, as a result, enter (or are depicted in process of entering) a distinct family community enveloped within the filial interrelation of the Father and Son. Accordingly, the rejection and reception of Jesus forge social boundary lines throughout the narrative. The reconceptualization of God introduced in John 1:1–18 and continually proclaimed or demonstrated by Jesus in the Gospel story destabilizes the social constructs within the world of the text. Hearers and interlocutors are confronted with the decision to resocialize into the new communal entity of believing disciples or to reaffirm their social location within the unbelieving 'world'. In this narrative ecclesiology initialized by the Prologue, dyadic theology repeatedly beckons or incites communal realignments for some while reinforcing prior social allegiances for others.

The general effects of what I am calling an ecclesial narrative script are widely noted in Johannine studies. For Bultmann, Jesus' 'appearing in the world is to be conceived as an *embassage from without, an arrival from elsewhere*';[1] and those who encounter the Son 'have either

---

[1] Bultmann, *Theology*, 2:33. See also Dahl, 'The Johannine Church and History', 99–119.

anchored themselves by un-faith to their old existence or have appropriated by faith the new possibility of existing'.[2] This 'dualism of decision' erects a *'division of mankind into two groups'*.[3] Similarly, Morna Hooker has described 'the theme of John's Gospel' as 'the division caused by Christ's presence among men'.[4] According to Wayne Meeks, 'coming to faith in Jesus is for the Johannine group a change in social location. Mere belief, without joining the Johannine community, without making the decisive break with "the world", particularly the world of Judaism, is a diabolic "lie".'[5] Though communal division and subsequent resocialization are recognized by many scholars, my language of an 'ecclesial narrative script' intends to draw attention to these activities as more than metaphysical categorizations or mere social-scientific phenomena – the pattern of schism then resocialization is grounded in an ecclesial vision for a community shaped around a divisive christological vision.

The Gospel's action and its plot development are governed by the pattern detailed in those few verses of 1:11–14 as the Prologue's ecclesiology of divine–human filiation is narrated in the story as repeated acts of (or calls to) resocialization.[6] The plot in John's Gospel, therefore, is as *ecclesial* as it is *christological* since the unfolding action accords with the prospect of group formation around Jesus.[7] The coinherence of ecclesiology and christology is still in force beyond the Prologue because the ecclesial action of social division, then resocialization into a new group, is directly provoked by christology – as Klaus Scholtissek bluntly states, 'Jesus von Nazaret ist eine Provokation.'[8] Strengthening the claim that

---

[2] Bultmann, *Theology*, 2:21.

[3] Ibid. Bultmann distinguishes between the Johannine 'dualism of decision' (see also 2:71) and the cosmological dualism of Gnosticism. The determining factor of the division of humanity is the decision of faith (which is possible only through divine help, yet squarely placed within the realm of human responsibility) rather than a predetermined state pertaining to an individual's essence or nature.

[4] Hooker, 'John the Baptist' 357.   [5] Meeks, 'Man from Heaven', 69.

[6] '*All John really has to say is said in the prologue*: "He came to his own people and they did not receive him. But to all who received him he gave the power to become children of God, born ... of God, for God's Utterance has been enfleshed and has taken up residence in our midst" (1:11–14). *The vignettes in the Gospel are variations on this theme.*' Malina and Rohrbaugh, *Social-Science Commentary*, 5; emphases added.

[7] Commenting on John 1–12, C. K. Barrett wrote 'the story has been one of division, and the whole narrative turns upon the rejection of Israel – Israel's rejection of truth, and God's rejection of Israel'. From Barrett, 'Old Testament', 167.

[8] Klaus Scholtissek, '"Ich und der Vater, wir sind Eins" (Joh 10,30): Zum theologischen Potential und zur hermeneutischen Kompetenz der johanneischen Christologie', in *Theology and Christology in the Fourth Gospel: Essays by the Members of the SNTS*

ecclesiology is central to the Fourth Gospel and indivisibly bound to its bold christology is the observation that the entire narrative owes itself to the plot of group formation and social delineation (ecclesiology) around Jesus (christology) that is presented in the Prologue. The Johannine story is one of social rearrangements effected by the Son and his filial interrelation with his Father; and the action of the plot is largely a series of episodic instantiations of this ecclesial narrative script. Bound indivisibly to christology, ecclesiology is one of the Fourth Gospel's primary story arcs.

To demonstrate the programmatic significance of the ecclesial script, I will provide a brief survey of how its story arc is worked out in the Gospel and then examine three specific scenes of resocialization in John 1–9. These 'case studies' will include the Johannine call narrative of 1: 35–51, the dispute concerning Abrahamic and divine paternity in 8: 12–59, and John 9's account of the healing (and subsequent synagogue expulsion) of the man born blind. Each of these scenes manifests diverse possibilities of social formation and communal (re)alignment instigated by John's christology and predicated on the idea of divine–human filiation found in John 1:11–14. I will then show how the Shepherd Discourse in John 10 is a figural exposition of this ecclesial narrative script. Since the ecclesiology of the Johannine oneness motif is the focus of Part II, this section on John 10:1–18 will provide a transition into Chapter 6, connecting themes instituted in the Prologue to the ecclesial use of 'one' in John 10.

The Plotline of Resocialization: A Survey of the Ecclesial Narrative Script

Before taking a closer look at the three scenes mentioned above, it is important to observe in general how the Prologue's ecclesial narrative script is operative in the overall story of the Gospel. The pattern of christologically incited social rearrangement appears immediately in John 1. The call narrative, mentioned in the previous chapter and discussed in more detail below, exemplifies *the positive paradigm* of the ecclesial narrative script as members of one social group (the disciples of John the Baptist) make a voluntary exit and form a new social group around Jesus. In John 4, the evangelist's explanatory note that 'Jews have no dealings with Samaritans' (v. 9) entails two distinct (and antagonistic)

Johannine Writings Seminar, ed. Gilbert van Belle, Jan G. van der Watt, and Petrus Maritz, BETL 184 (Leuven: Leuven University Press, 2005), 315–45, here at 320.

communities; yet a positive reconfiguration of social alignments is implied when the Samaritans forsake their interests in the identity markers of ethnicity and worship location to realign with Jesus, 'the Saviour of *the world*' (4:42; emphases added). So even in the earliest movements of the narrative, John's christology intimates the formation of a new communal entity that exceeds traditional means of identifying social groupings such as ethnicity, geography, and cultic practice.

This positive paradigm of acceptance and resocialization, however, is only occasional. Tension is created in the Gospel's action when the ecclesial narrative script is left unresolved, with certain characters or character groups remaining indecisive as to whether they should transfer social membership and realign with Jesus. Nicodemus, for instance, is informed that the kingdom of God can only be seen by those whose family derivation has been redefined and sourced 'from above'; yet a departure from his own social group (identified as the Jewish leadership) and resocialization into Jesus' new community remains ambiguous over the course of the Gospel.[9]

The negative paradigm of the ecclesial narrative script ('his own did not receive him') comes to the fore in John 5–6, even though invitations for belief and therefore participation in the new community of faith are repeatedly extended. Jesus' unique relationship with God as his Father precipitates persecution and the threat of death after the invalid is healed on the Sabbath by the Bethesda pool. In John 6, a multitude makes an attempt to crown Jesus; he resists and offers such a scandalous reconceptualization of their messianic expectations that the entire Bread of Life discourse ends in the redefining and concretizing of intergroup boundaries. Some disciples fade back into the nameless crowd while the 'Twelve'[10] are delineated as true members of Jesus' new community.[11]

The harshest enactments outside of the passion narrative of 'he came to his own, and his own did not receive him' (1:11) are found

[9] His subsequent appearances, however, evince a trajectory pointing toward an eventual full membership into the social unit of Jesus' disciples (7:50; 19:39).

[10] The reference to the 'Twelve' is connotative of Israel – Horsley and Thatcher, *John, Jesus and the Renewal of Israel*, 141. Michaels, however, too easily dismisses that there is a connection between the Twelve and Israel in John as in Mt 19:28 and Lk 22:30, observing that the fourth evangelist only names seven disciples. See Michaels, *John*, 413–14. It is actually this numeric discrepancy that makes it all the more likely that the reference to the 'Twelve' is infused with some symbolic significance.

[11] For Udo Schnelle, the fissure between the disciples at the end of Jn 6 provides a transparent window into 'die aktuelle johanneischen Gemeindesituation', which he understands as a split within 'der johanneische Schule' – Schnelle, 'Johanneische Ekklesiologie', *NTS* 37 (1991): 45.

in John 7–12 (the section of the Gospel where the narrative development of the oneness motif begins). Jesus' destabilization of the social
construct in his strident interaction with the Jews is evidenced in that
his speaking regularly produces a schism (σχίσμα – 7:43; 9:16; 10:19),
a social division in which some openly reject Jesus and others remain
open to his message. In a fierce dialogue in John 8, those who reject
him are exposed as located within the social identity not of God's
household but of the devil's household.[12] In John 9, the man born blind
undergoes a forced membership transfer from his local religious community into the company of Jesus (see the case studies on John 8 and 9
below).

This repetitive pattern of communal formation or social re-
entrenchment continues beyond John 8–10. When Lazarus is raised
from death, some believe in Jesus while others rush off with apparent
misgivings and inform the Pharisees (11:45–46). By the closing of John
12, the community around Jesus is solidified and a certain number of
these disciples become the audience for the Farewell Discourse.
Another instance of group formation and membership transfer takes
place in the passion narrative when Jesus binds his mother and the
Beloved Disciple into filial relation (19:26–27). The Prologue's ecclesial narrative script is fulfilled in Jesus' resurrection when Mary is
instructed to 'go to *my brothers* and say to them, "I am ascending to
my Father and your Father, to my God and your God"' (20:17;
emphases added). The minority community that has accepted the divisive christological testimony is now sealed within the social reality of
the 'children of God' – *resocialization and divine–human filiation are
one and the same* for the Fourth Gospel. With the ecclesial narrative
script having run its course and the social identity of the disciples
finalized, the narrator turns to his readers and auditors and seems to
expect our own resocialization into the community of faith to be evoked
in the conclusion of the foregoing account (20:30–31). In sum, the
Prologue's christology compels and generates ecclesiology in the
Fourth Gospel because the identity of Jesus redefines social relation-
ships and forms a new communal identity: the children of God who are
brothers and sisters of the μονογενής.

---

[12] As noted in the Introduction, the intensity of the polemics has contributed to the
accusation that the Fourth Gospel is anti-Semitic. See the collection of essays in *Anti-
Judaism and the Fourth Gospel: Papers of the Leuven Colloquium, 2000*, ed.
Reimund Bieringer, Didier Pollefeyt, and Frederique Vandecasteele-Vanneueuville
(Assen: Royal van Gorcum, 2001).

Three Case Studies Demonstrating the Ecclesial Narrative Script

A more focused exegetical treatment of particular instantiations of the ecclesial narrative script will bring to the fore variations and nuances of the Gospel's process of group formation or social re-entrenchment. In the case studies below – each referenced briefly in the preceding survey – characters or character groups are depicted in scenes concerning group membership transfer. While the call narrative in John 1 illustrates an acceptance of the necessity of resocialization, the dialogue over paternity in John 8 provides an example of resocialization *rejected*. The removal of the formerly blind beggar from the synagogue exhibits another possibility: resocialization can, at least to some degree, be *enforced* by way of communal ejection.

Membership Transfer Accepted: The Johannine Call Narrative (John 1:35–51)

As suggested earlier, the Prologue's ecclesial narrative script of christologically provoked resocialization into a new communal realm finds an exemplary positive fulfilment in the Johannine call narrative. It was noted in the previous chapter that in the Synoptic Gospels, the discipleship community around Jesus is formed gradually through a series of disparate scenes.[13] By contrast, the Fourth Gospel offers one call narrative placed at the very beginning of its account – the reconstitution of the people of God begins taking concrete form by the end of John 1. Resocialization occurs in John 1:35–37 as Andrew and a companion extract themselves from the group associated with John the Baptist and enter the company of Jesus. This scene of membership transfer activates a rapid 'chain reaction'[14] of interpersonal encounters over a condensed span of narrative time in which five disciples are attached to Jesus, thereby forming a new (though admittedly small) social unit: 'The company of the disciples, from the first moment of their calling, forms the nucleus of a new and growing community of which Jesus is the head. Significantly, Nathanael acknowledges Jesus from the beginning as "King of Israel", the leader of the true messianic society.'[15]

Even if the evangelist had no knowledge whatsoever of the Synoptic call narratives, his compressed rendering of the calling of Jesus' disciples

---

[13] Mk 1:16–20 (Mt 4:18–22; cf. Lk 5:1–11); Mk 2:13ff. (Mt 9:9; Lk 5:27f).
[14] Brown, *John*, 76. [15] Smalley, *John*, 233.

shows signs of being highly strategic.[16] This consolidation of multiple call scenes is not just a matter of historical accuracy or storytelling convenience – the evangelist is intentionally making a point. Raymond Brown suspected that some sort of stylistic intentionality is at work in the call narrative because of the discrepancy between later portrayals of the disciples' incomplete recognition of who Jesus is and the successive expansions on christological understanding that unfold as each disciple enters the company of Jesus in the call narrative (note the series of titles applied to him[17]). The Synoptics make clear that the disciples did not enjoy such immediate christological competence – their understanding gradually develops. Yet no Gospel writer is more concerned than the fourth evangelist to demonstrate that the disciples' grasp of Jesus' identity is delayed until the resurrection;[18] and the conclusion of the call narrative with Jesus' words that greater things will be seen surely hints to the partiality of the disciples' christological understanding in John 1: 35–51, in spite of their impressive use of these loaded titles.[19] The point I am making is that some puzzling authorial agenda is at work in this call narrative. Brown's conclusion in his commentary is that the evangelist has 'used the call of the disciples to summarize discipleship in its whole development',[20] thereby 'capsulizing a longer process'.[21]

I propose that the evangelist's primary concern in compressing the call scenes of Jesus' disciples into one is to demonstrate that christology

---

[16] Harmonizing the Synoptic and Johannine call narratives is 'impossible' according to Barrett, *John*, 179. Bultmann lists the following as the main differences between Mk 1: 16–20 and Jn 1:35–51:1) there are no references to the sons of Zebedee; 2) the unknown disciple of John the Baptist who follows Jesus with Andrew is absent in Mark; 3) the Baptist's testimony precipitates the disciples' attachment to Jesus in John whereas the disciples are not called until after the forerunner's death in the Synoptics (Bultmann, *John*, 107–8). J. Ramsey Michaels notes in his commentary that although John's call narrative is condensed and confined to Jn 1, there is in Jn 21 'a kind of re-enactment of the call of the disciples, not as told in John's Gospel, but as told in the other three, Luke in particular' (cf. Lk 5:1–11) – Michaels, *John*, 1027.

[17] Rabbi (1:38); Messiah/Christ (1:41); son of Joseph (1:45); Rabbi (1:49); Son of God (1:49); King of Israel (1:49); Son of Man (given by Jesus himself in 1:51).

[18] Brown, *John*, 78. See also Richard B. Hays, 'Reading Scripture in Light of the Resurrection', in *The Art of Reading Scripture*, ed. Ellen F. Davis and Richard B. Hays (Grand Rapids, MI: Eerdmans, 2003), 216–38.

[19] Brown, *John*, 88. Jonge, 'Christology, Controversy', 217.   [20] Brown, *John*, 78.

[21] Ibid., 1:88. Brown later read the call narrative as a loose account of the Johannine community's origins, in Brown, *Community*, 26–31. Another interesting proposal is that of J. Louis Martyn, who understands John 1:35–51 as an early homily preached in the Johannine community to bring Jewish Christians to faith. See Martyn, *History and Theology*, 147–54.

provokes an extraction from one group and resocialization into another. The consolidation of the disciples' call narrative accords well with the Prologue's statement that a handful of believers accept Jesus and in so doing become a new social unit.[22] As the narrative action occurring after the Prologue indicates, *christological confession coincides with community formation.*[23] With Nathanael being hailed as a true Israelite (ἀληθῶς Ἰσραηλίτης)[24] who in turn recognizes Jesus as Israel's rightful king (βασιλεὺς ... Ἰσραήλ), it is clear that the evangelist understands this process of group formation within Jewish categories. Standard identity markers must still be redrawn, however: the guileless Nathanael (ἐν ᾧ δόλος οὐκ ἔστιν) is presented as a new representative of 'Israel', whose biblical namesake was associated with guile (δόλος, LXX Gen 27:35).[25]

The renaming of Simon to 'Peter' also connotes group extraction and resocialization. In Matthew 16:18 (cf. Mk 3:16; Lk 6:14) Peter's renaming is explicitly ecclesial: 'you are Peter, and on this rock I will build my church' (σύ εἶ Πέτρος, καί ἐπὶ ταύτῃ τῇ πέτρᾳ οἰκηδομήσω μου τὴν ἐκκλησίαν). Though the ecclesial significance of πέτρος ('rock') receives no direct attention in John,[26] the actual act of renaming occurs within the ecclesial framework of membership transfer from one social unit to another: "'you are Simon *son of John*; you will be called Cephas",

---

[22] 'The introduction of John, the witness and friend of the bridegroom, sets in motion the divine process announced in the Prologue, that believers will become children of God (1:12)' – Coloe, *Household of God*, 57.

[23] 'The disciples confer virtually all of the church's titles for Jesus upon him at the outset' – Culpepper, *Anatomy of the Fourth Gospel*, 116.

[24] Speculation persists over the enigmatic meaning of Nathanael's location under the 'fig tree'. Is the fourth evangelist simply demonstrating Jesus' prescience, suggesting that Nathanael was studying Torah (rabbinical sources have accounts of Torah being taught under a fig tree) at the moment of messianic invitation, or could this scene be a re-enactment of certain Old Testament messianic texts? See especially Craig R. Koester, 'Messianic Exegesis and the Call of Nathanael (John 1.45–51)', *JSNT* 39 (1990): 23–34.

[25] Keener, *John*, 485–6. John Painter, however, argues against this reading in Painter, 'The Church and Israel', 109. Also, Rekha Chennattu does not see 'guile' as a reference to Jacob since he is portrayed positively in John 4. Her reasoning does not stand since the OT portrays the patriarch both nobly yet also as a deceiver – Rekha M. Chennattu, *Johannine Discipleship as a Covenant Relationship* (Peabody, MA: Hendrickson, 2006), 37. For a similar position, see Schnackenburg, *John*, 1:316.

[26] This lack of a provided translation in John of Πέτρος is all the more curious since the evangelist is keen to translate other terms at this point in the narrative ('Messiah', 'rabbi', et al.). See the discussion in Markus Bockmuehl, *Simon Peter in Scripture and Memory: The New Testament Apostle in the Early Church* (Grand Rapids, MI: Baker Academic, 2012), 22.

which is translated "Peter/rock"' (σὺ εἶ Σίμων υἱὸς Ἰωάννου, σύ κληθήσῃ Κηφᾶς, ὃ ἑρμηνεύεται Πέτρος (Jn 1:42, emphases added). The familial identification 'son of John' is being superseded by a new social affiliation – Peter's new name signifies his departure from the communal realm of his family and his emerging filial status within the community of Jesus.[27] As the Prologue has indicated, the children of God are not 'out of bloods and not out of the will of flesh and not out of the will of a husband but they were born out of God' (ἐξ αἱμάτων οὐδὲ ἐκ θελήματος σαρκὸς οὐδὲ ἐκ θελήματος ἀνδρὸς ἀλλ' ἐκ θεοῦ ἐγεννήθησαν). So the Johannine call narrative is freighted with familial and national language conveying the formation of a new society that requires communal extraction from one group (e.g., the Baptist's community, one's biological family, an Israel in need of renewal) and transfer into another (a new discipleship community, a new family, a renewed Israel of which Jesus is King).[28]

Membership Transfer Rejected: A Case of Mistaken Paternity (John 8:12–59)

The Johannine call narrative depicts the *positive* instantiation of the Prologue's ecclesial narrative script – that is, resocialization into a new group ('as many as received him, he gave them the right to become children of God' – 1:12). The negative dimension of rejecting Christ ('his own did not receive him' – 1:11) amounts to a re-entrenchment of one's participation in the social realm of darkness (σκοτία) and the world (κόσμος). No episode in the Gospel exemplifies the negative elements of the ecclesial narrative script more than the dialogue in John 8 that opens with language explicitly echoing the Prologue as well as the call narrative: 'I am the Light of the world; the one who follows me will not walk in darkness but will have the light of life' (ἐγώ εἰμι τὸ φῶς τοῦ

---

[27] It may be of some interest to note that intergroup associations abound among those who are entering Jesus' company in the Johannine call narrative: Andrew and the anonymous disciples are both followers of the Baptist; Peter is the brother of Andrew; Philip is from their same hometown; Nathanael is a friend of Philip. See Hoskyns, *The Fourth Gospel*, 167.

[28] In her chapter devoted to the Johannine call narrative ('Gathering the Household'), Mary Coloe finds allusions to Pentecost's celebration of the giving of the Law at Sinai as well as nuptial imagery, all of which contribute to the idea of disciples being gathered as a new people of God (the ecclesiological community she refers to as the 'household of God'). See Coloe, *Household of God*, 39–58.

κόσμου· ὁ ἀκολουθῶν ἐμοὶ οὐ μὴ περιπατήσῃ ἐν τῇ σκοτίᾳ, ἀλλ᾽ ἕξει τὸ φῶς τῆς ζωῆς – 8:12).[29] It is in this scene that Jesus levels his most controversial statement in the Fourth Gospel against his Jewish interlocutors: 'you are of your father the devil' (8:44). These words occur within an argument over paternity and are specifically addressed to a group of 'Jews who had believed in him' (8:31). Their belief, however, is exposed as illegitimate precisely because *communal realignment never ensues*. According to the model of the call narrative, christological confession must coincide with resocialization. The vigorous antagonism of the troubling series of interchanges in John 8 stems from the refusal of these believing Jews to transfer their membership from one social entity into a new one.

Suffusing this tense dialogue is the language of Johannine dualism, and this dualism is explicitly *social*. The series of contrasting realms in John 8 are communal as much as they are cosmological: the domains of (ἐκ) 'darkness'/σκοτία, 'below'/κάτω, and 'this world'/οὗτος κόσμος are contrasted respectively with 'light'/φῶς, 'above'/ἀνά, and the realm 'not... out of this world'/οὐκ ... ἐκ τοῦ κόσμου τούτου. These cosmological realms correspond to communal spheres, with the former list of terms aligning with the household of Satan marked by slavery, and the latter aligning with the social status of freedom or freedmen (ἐλεύθεροι), the household of God, and those who are truly (ἀληθῶς) Jesus' disciples (see also 1 John 2:18–19). The cosmological dualism in John 8 is in the service of ecclesiology, serving as a means of categorizing two social realms between which genuine faith effects a membership transfer.

Midway through the dialogue of John 8, when certain Jews make their positive response to the dyadic theology of the Father–Son interrelation, Jesus urges them to 'remain in his word' (8:31) that their transfer into the new social realm of his disciples will be ensured. Abiding in this truth will set them free (ἐλευθερώσει – 8:32). But since this promise of eventual freedom implies current bondage, these believing Jews balk. In their view, they are already free/freedmen (ἐλεύθεροι) and have never been enslaved (8:33). Their bondage is to sin, but the evangelist is not primarily painting a picture of *individualistic soteriology* but one of *corporate ecclesiology*: slavery and freedom represent two communal realms (not individual states), and the soteriological issue at hand is whether the believing Jews will resocialize into the group of genuine

---

[29] The concentrated appearance of the key lexemes φῶς, κόσμος, σκοτία, and ζωή certainly recall the opening of the Prologue, and the terms ἀκολουθέω and περιπατέω appear in the call narrative (1:36, 37, 38, 40, 43).

(ἀληθῶς) disciples. They profess that their social membership is entirely sufficient: 'we are the seed of Abraham' (σπέρμα Ἀβραάμ ἐσμεν). In response to Jesus' implication that they need release from bondage through resocialization, these Jews affirm that their social identity requires no adjustment. A status change of communal membership is unnecessary.

After Jesus elevates the discussion beyond the ethnic level to the cosmic level by explaining that they are enslaved to sin (8:34), he employs the metaphor of a household and the respective positions of status between sons, slaves, and freedmen (8:35–36). Similar to Paul's symbolic reading of Abraham's household in Romans 9:6–13 and Galatians 4, Jesus is conveying that those confessing belief in him are not permanently secured as family members *until resocialization occurs*. Through the authority of the divine Son, these Jews must undergo an extraction from one group (slaves) and a transfer into another (freedmen). 'The slave does not remain in the house forever' is strong language implying that these Jews must acknowledge their status as household slaves. They need not remain in that status because the Son of the divine household has the power and will to alter it from slavery to freedom. But one cannot be truly a disciple apart from communal realignment. Along with my observation that christological confession requires community formation, the earlier quote from Wayne Meeks above is worth repeating here: 'Coming to faith in Jesus is for the Johannine group a change in social location. Mere belief, without joining the Johannine community, without making the decisive break with "the world", particularly the world of Judaism, is a diabolic "lie"'.[30]

As the dialogue intensifies, it becomes clear that the metaphorical household is dualistically divided.[31] In fact, there are actually two households corresponding to two fathers: God and the devil. Presumably, being children of Abraham is consonant with being children of God; so it is not the fatherhood of Abraham (and therefore ethnic Israel) that Jesus condemns per se, but the fatherhood of Satan.[32] In protest, the Jews claim the

---

[30] Meeks, 'Man from Heaven', 69.

[31] Curiously, there seems to be a difference between the seed of Abraham (σπέρμα Ἀβραάμ – 8:37) and the children of Abraham (τέκνα τοῦ Ἀβραάμ – 8:39). See Pancaro, '"People of God"', 126–27.

[32] Though fine distinctions are being made between paternal derivation in ch. 8, Jesus acknowledges the fatherhood of Abraham for the Jews in 8:56, even though he has accused them of not doing what Abraham did, and also accused them of having Satan as their father. The means of family identification is by way of ethics, and the ethics of ethnic Israel are summarized in their desire to have Jesus killed (something Abraham would not have done).

fatherhood of God in 8:41[33] and the oneness motif is introduced: 'We have one father: God' (ἕνα πατέρα ἔχομεν τὸν θεόν). This instance of oneness occurs within a debate over the identity of God and the Jews' familial association with him, the very essence of the oneness motif in both John 10 and John 17. In Chapter 7 I will show how this instance of oneness is premised on the Shema's monotheistic profession in Deuteronomy 6:4. For now it is enough to recognize the role of the Jews' claim in the ecclesial narrative script: Jesus is extending an invitation to dissociate from a particular filial and social realm (the patrilineage of Satan) and enter another, the filial realm of dyadic theology in which Jesus and God are both 'one' (John 10:30). In their flat refusal to acknowledge that they do not inhabit the communal realm of the latter, the ecclesial narrative script's negative pattern of social re-entrenchment rather than resocialization is patently clear ('his own did not receive him' – 1:11).

The Apostle Paul wrote that 'not all who are out of Israel are Israel, and neither are they all children of Abraham because they are his seed' (Rom 9:6–7; my translation). The fourth evangelist is making a similar claim as Jesus calls for membership transfer into the household of God, participation of which is marked by a continual abiding in the word of the Son. So the dialogue in John 8 is an explicit enactment of the negative dimension of the Prologue's ecclesial plotline in contrast to the positive dimension found in John 1:35–51.

Enforced Membership Transfer and Synagogue Expulsion (John 9)

These case studies are being offered to show that the Prologue's ecclesial narrative script of group delineation has diverse expressions in the Johannine narrative. So far we have seen that the disciples in John 1: 35–51 undergo a voluntary membership transfer and that the Jews retract their initial belief in John 8 when it becomes clear that resocialization is a requirement. In this third and final case study featuring John 9, we encounter an individual who is extracted involuntarily from one social realm and, as the text implies, invited into another. Whereas the 'believing' Jews of John 8 invalidate their belief by refusing communal realignment, the christological confession of the man born blind coincides with

---

[33] Keener points out that the Jews' claim of God's fatherhood is ironic since they have already accused Jesus of making the same claim. (5:18; cf. 10:36) – Keener, *John*, 759.

a forced membership transfer through an extreme form of communal disalignment and social disownership: *synagogue expulsion*. Resonances of family derivation and affiliation continue from John 8. The concept of 'birth' is conspicuous in its excessive repetition in John 9 and recalls the Prologue ('out of God they were born'/ἐκ θεοῦ ἐγεννήθησαν – 1:13) as well as Jesus' interaction with Nicodemus ('you must be born from above'/δεῖ ὑμᾶς γεννηθῆναι ἄνωθεν).[34] The use of γεννάω (to bear a child) in the disciples' question in 9:2 ('who sinned, this man or his parents, that he was born [γεννηθῇ] blind?') and in 9:34 ('you were born [ἐγγενήθης] entirely in sins') indicates that the idea of 'birth' is laden with cosmic and symbolic as well as physical and genetic meaning (just as blindness and seeing are also freighted with symbolism beyond their literal connotations). Though the man 'born' blind is not said to have been 'born out of God' or 'born from above' by the chapter's end, a sequential reading recalling the earlier references to group membership transfer through divine (re)generation would perceive that the birth that left the man blind is now countered by a different sort of birth. He enters the social realm of the reconceptualized people of God through the birth canal of a synagogue door: 'They answered him, 'You were born entirely in sins, and are you trying to teach us?' And they cast him out [καὶ ἐξέβαλον αὐτὸν ἔξω]' (9:34).

We have observed above that abstract cosmological terms correspond with social spheres in John 8. There is nothing abstract, however, about the social spheres appearing in John 9. The conceptuality of contrasting realms found in John 8 gets played out in the workaday lives of ordinary people in this gritty scene on Judaean streets. Along with the blind man's parents, we encounter his γείτονες (neighbours) and οἱ θεωροῦντες αὐτὸν τὸ πρότερον (those who had seen him before), that is, the passers-by for whom the blind man – who we learn is a beggar – was a regular fixture in their daily grind (9:8). This collective group brings the man to another group: the Pharisees. Social boundary lines were christologically defined in John 8 when Jesus described the families of God and Satan and used the household metaphor contrasting freedmen with slaves. Intergroup boundary lines are drawn in John 9 by the Pharisees' interrogation of the formerly blind man: 'You are his disciple, but we are disciples of Moses' (9:28).[35] In accordance with the ecclesial narrative script, christology has once again provoked a division between two distinct groups, here

---

[34] γενετή: 9:1; γεννάω: 9:2, 19, 20, 32, 34.
[35] Note the parallels between the group identity expressions: 'we are the seed of Abraham' (8:33) and 'we are the disciples of Moses'.

labelled as Jesus' disciples and Moses' disciples. The boundary lines between them are reified in the narrative action when the Pharisees eject the man born blind in 9:34 from his socioreligious context.

The neighbours and bystanders fade from view, but it is clear from the cowering of the blind man's parents that the prospect of social disalignment through synagogue expulsion was a threat of powerful effect. Their son who now sees, however, eventually confesses belief in Jesus and even worships him (9:38; for more on this, see Chapter 10). His new association with the group of Jesus' disciples (enforced by the 'disciples of Moses') is strongly implied in the phrase 'he came, seeing' (ἦλθεν βλέπων – 9:7), an echo of this Gospel's paradigmatic call to discipleship and resocialization: 'come and see' (1:39, 46; 4:29[36]). The Jews in John 8 believed Jesus but *refused to undergo a communal realignment*, thus exposing their faith as illegitimate. In John 9, the faith of the man born blind is solidified through membership transfer. Though his group extraction was coerced, the narrative account indicates some awareness of the social ramifications of his Christ-confession. To become one of Jesus' disciples (αὐτοῦ μαθηταί γενέσθαι – 9:27) is to become an ex-participant in the communal life of the synagogue (ἀποσυνάγωγος γένηται – 9:23), a social realm that denies the Gospel's dyadic theology; in avoiding this group extraction, however, one risks becoming (or remaining) blind (τυφλοὶ γένωνται – 9:39). The social lines the Gospel is drawing can cut right through not only the religious community claiming Abrahamic patrilineage (John 8) but, as apparently indicated by the man's parents in John 9, also through families formed ἐξ αἱμάτων, ἐκ θελήματος σαρκός, and ἐκ θελήματος ἀνδρός ('out of bloods, out of the will of flesh', and 'out of the will of a husband').[37]

The Shepherd Discourse as Parabolic Explanation of the Ecclesial Narrative Script (John 10:1–18)

The Shepherd Discourse of John 10:1–18 offers a figural exposition of the ecclesial narrative script's pattern of social reconfiguration around Jesus. The familial language of community formation in the Prologue is enriched and expanded in the pastoral imagery of Jesus as the Good

[36] The phrase is rendered ἔρχεσθε καὶ ὄψεσθε in 1:39, ἔρχου καὶ ἴδε in 1:46, and δεῦτε ἴδετε in 4:29.

[37] If synagogue expulsion was indeed a perennial threat to the community or network of communities associated with the fourth evangelist (and any possible redactors), then a Gospel narrating various instances of social membership transfer would have resonated deeply with its original auditors.

Shepherd who draws his sheep out from other contexts and brings them within the ecclesial realm of his flock. The entire scenario concerns the extraction and resocialization of God's people ('one flock') around a legitimate messianic figure ('one Shepherd'). Examining John 10: 1–18 here shows along with the case studies how the ecclesiology of the Prologue extends into the narrative; the Shepherd Discourse also permits a few more introductory comments (in addition to those above on John 8:41) concerning the oneness motif, the subject presently awaiting attention in Part II.

The pastoral imagery of John 10 is inextricably bound to the action of group formation and social delineation in the narrative preceding it. It is no accident that an account of social expulsion and membership transfer in John 9 is followed by the figurative portrayal of a shepherd who extracts his sheep from one social realm and gathers them into another. Though many interpreters have regarded the Shepherd Discourse as an insertion disparate from its position in the extant text of the Gospel,[38] a strong majority now views the material in John 7–10 as intentionally linked in sequence. Andrew Lincoln expresses the growing consensus in this way: 'Whatever the pre-history of this passage, in its present position Jesus' initial teaching about the sheepgate and the shepherd are now a continuation of his address to the Pharisees from the end of the previous chapter.'[39] Similarly, Raymond Brown writes:

[38] See the overview of this interpretative paradigm and the citations in Ulrich Busse, 'Open Questions on John 10', in *The Shepherd Discourse of John 10 and Its Context: Studies by Members of the Johannine Writings Seminar*, ed. Robert T. Fortna and Johannes Beutler, SNTSMS 67 (Cambridge: Cambridge University Press, 1991), 6–17. For a relatively recent argument against reading John 10 in sequential relation to what precedes it, see Mary K. Deeley, 'Ezekiel's Shepherd and John's Jesus: A Case Study in the Appropriation of Biblical Texts', in *Early Christian Interpretation of the Scriptures of Israel: Investigations and Proposals*, ed. J. A. Sanders and Craig. A. Evans, JSNTSup 148 (Sheffield: Sheffield Academic Press, 1997), 252–65.

[39] Lincoln, *John*, 291–2. For C. K. Barrett, the Shepherd Discourse is 'rather a comment upon ch. 9 than a continuation of it' (Barrett, *John*, 367). D. Moody Smith acknowledges that 'the imagery changes abruptly', yet 'the sequence of chapter 10 after 9 is not problematic' – Smith, *John*, ANTC (Nashville, TN: Abingdon Press, 1999), 202. Keener supports the connection between chapters 9 and 10 and suggests that some among John's audience would possibly be familiar with the scene in 1 Enoch 90:26–27 where blindness and sheep are correlated (Keener, *John*, 796). Also in support of the sequential connection between the Shepherd Discourse and the preceding episode in John 9 are J. Louis Martyn, 'A Gentile Mission That Replaced an Earlier Jewish Mission?', in *Exploring the Gospel of John: In Honor of D. Moody Smith*, ed. R. Alan Culpepper and C. Clifton Black (Louisville, KY: Westminster John Knox, 1996), 124–44, here at 128–29, Michaels, *John*, 571–2; Jan A. du Rand, 'A Syntactical and Narratological Reading of John 10 in Coherence with Chapter 9',

It seems quite clear that [the Shepherd Discourse] is to be related to what has preceded in ch. ix. No new audience is suggested; and as the Gospel now stands, there is no reason to believe that Jesus is not continuing his remarks to the Pharisees to whom he was speaking in viii 41. Indeed, in x 21, after Jesus has spoken about the sheepgate and the shepherd, his audience recalls the example of the blind man, while others repeat the charges of madness that we have heard hurled at Jesus during the Tabernacles discourses.[40]

In the citation above, Brown confidently calls attention to the parallels in John 10 and the foregoing scenes – the nature of the charges levelled at Jesus and the recollection of the blind man's healing in 10:21 evince a clear narrative flow. Additionally, the use of ἐκβάλλω (to cast out) in 10:4 is an echo of its twofold appearance in John 9 (vv. 34–35). Without noting John 10's narrative connections to John 9, we might end up like Jesus' audience, not knowing 'what he was saying to them' (10:6).

A primary purpose of the Shepherd Discourse is to provide a metaphoric rendering of John's ecclesial narrative script of communal re-identification around Jesus. The concern of the discourse's opening section (10:1–6) is with the leadership of God's people (the flock of sheep[41]). Portrayed as thieves and bandits (κλέπτης and ληστής), these illegitimate leaders are contrasted with the rightful 'shepherd' (ποιμήν).

---

in *The Shepherd Discourse of John 10 and Its Context: Studies by Members of the Johannine Writings Seminar*, ed. Robert T. Fortna and Johannes Beutler, SNTSMS 67 (Cambridge: Cambridge University Press, 1991), 94–115; Hoskyns, *The Fourth Gospel*, 366; D. A. Carson, *The Gospel According to John*, PNTC (Grand Rapids, MI: Eerdmans, 1991), 379–80. Schnackenburg considers a number of proposals for explaining the abrupt transition between chapters 9 and 10 (including a theory that leaves from a codex were misplaced, or perhaps that redactors incorrectly arranged the material left behind by the evangelist); even so, he concludes that 'it is more or less incontestable that there is an intrinsic relationship' between those [pastoral] discourses and the general scope of chapter 9. Indeed, those discourses 'have a bearing of the preceding healing of the man born blind' – Schnackenburg, *John*, 2:276–8.

[40] Brown, *John*, 388. Brown does go on to acknowledge, however, the two primary reasons a connection between John 9 and 10 is sometimes denied. The first is the sudden topic change and the second is the difficulty of chronologically linking the setting of the Tabernacles festival (September/October) to the Dedication festival that took place some three months later (and is identified as a time-marker in 10:22). Brown then offers cogent grounds for understanding the discourse material in 10:1–21 as an intended link of transition between Tabernacles and Dedication. See pp. 389–90.

[41] For flock imagery applied to God's people, see Num 27:16–17; LXX Ps 77:52, 70; Mic 2:12–13; 5:4; Isa 40:11; Jer 13:17; Ezek 34:12; *1 En.* 89:13–90:39; *Ps. Sol.* 17.21–44; cf. 1 Pet 5:2–3.

They are identifiable from this shepherd in the parable by their means of accessing God's people within the structural realm of the courtyard (αὐλή) – the shepherd enters via the door (θύρα) while the intruders enter illegitimately though some other way. When Jesus resumes the discourse, he specifically locates himself within the parable's symbolism with four 'I am' statements: 'I am the door' (ἐγώ εἰμι ἡ θύρα – 10:7, 9) and 'I am the good shepherd' (ἐγώ εἰμι ὁ ποιμὴν ὁ καλός – 10:11, 14). The discourse culminates with the oneness motif: 'they will become one flock, one shepherd' (γενήσονται μία ποίμνη, εἷς ποιμήν – 10:16).

The imagery and emphases of the parabolic language[42] alter and shift throughout the discourse, but the overarching theme is that Jesus is the true messianic ruler of the people of God, the community whom the current leadership establishment has failed to safeguard and care for. In 10:1–6, the Pharisees and their cohorts could be understood not only as the thief (κλέπτης) and bandit (λῃστής), but perhaps also as the door-keeper (θυρωρός), collectively. The metaphorical language is supple in John 10 and will adapt in verses 11–13 where the Jewish leaders are probably understood corporately as the hired worker (μισθωτός) and possibly also as the wolf (λύκος). The wolf may also imply the devil (cf. John 10:10) with whom these Jews are in danger of being aligned (8:44).[43] If they are to be identified with the θυρωρός in 10:1–6, then the current leaders of God's people are opposing Israel's true shepherd, seeking to block his access to the sheep.[44] In their collective portrayal as the μισθωτός, they are abandoning their posts as guardians in the face of an eminent threat (thieves, bandits/insurrectionists, and a wolf), thus exposing their illegitimacy as shepherds. The only guardianship the Jewish leaders are upholding on behalf of God's people seems to be a prohibition of the rightful shepherd.

To recognize the purpose of the shepherd discourse in expressing the ecclesial narrative script of resocialization, it must be observed that John has artfully crafted this parable by drawing from pastoral imagery in his

---

[42] 'Parable' is a loose interpretation of παροιμία in 10:6 that can also be rendered 'proverb' or 'figure of speech'. The exact meaning of the term is vague (see Brown, *John*, 385–86). I am using 'parable' for the sake of convenience and not intending to make any claims as to its technical validity as a literary term.

[43] For a detailed presentation of this interpretation, see Gary T. Manning, *Echoes of a Prophet: The Use of Ezekiel in the Gospel of John and in Literature of the Second Temple Period*, JSNTSup 270 (London: T & T Clark, 2004), 106–8.

[44] 'The beginning of the shepherd discourse rebukes the Pharisees and the chief priests for their faulty logic in rejecting Jesus, and invites them to make a correct judgment about Jesus' – Ibid., 106.

scriptural repertoire, especially that of Ezekiel 34 and Numbers 27: 12–23. In the Ezekiel passage, God critiques the rulers of Israel for dereliction of duty in shepherding the flock. Since his people have been left unfed, unattended, and unguarded from wild beasts, God himself will arise as a Shepherd and lead them out of danger into good pasture (νομῇ – LXX, Ezekiel 34:14). Moreover, he will raise up a new Davidic ruler referred to as 'one shepherd': 'I will raise up for them *one shepherd* and he will shepherd them, my servant David, and he will be their shepherd' (καὶ ἀναστήσω ἐπ'αὐτους *ποιμένα ἕνα* καὶ ποιμανεῖ αὐτούς, τὸν δοῦλόν μου Δαυιδ, καὶ ἔσται αὐτῶν ποιμήν – LXX, Ezekiel 34:23, emphases added).[45]

In Numbers 27, Joshua (LXX, Ἰησοῦς) is appointed by priestly sanction to serve as the leader of Israel. His role is described as a shepherd who will lead them out and lead them in (ὅστις ἐξελεύσεται πρὸ προσώπου αὐτῶν καὶ ὅστις εἰσελεύσεται πρό προσώπου αὐτῶν καὶ ὅστις ἐξάξει αὐτοὺς καὶ ὅστις εἰσάξει αὐτούς – LXX, Num 27:17); see the parallel phrasing of the same activities in Jn 10:9 (καὶ εἰσελεύσεται καὶ ἐξελεύσεται). Joshua/Ἰησοῦς will lead the sheep 'into' and 'out of' by the call of his voice: 'at his word [lit., mouth] they will go out and at his word they will come in, both he and the sons of Israel, of one accord, even the entire congregation [lit., synagogue]' (ἐπὶ τῷ στόματι αὐτοῦ ἐξελεύσονται καὶ ἐπὶ τῷ στόματι αὐτοῦ εἰσελεύσονται αὐτὸς καὶ οἱ υἱοὶ Ισραηλ ὁμοθυμαδὸν καὶ πᾶσα ἡ συναγωγή – LXX, Numb 27:21); see Jn 10:3–5; 10:9). The fourth evangelist is drawing a *parallel* between Jesus and Joshua as shepherds and simultaneously highlights a *contrast* between the priestly leadership of Joshua's day and the Jews in the Gospel narrative: in the Numbers passage, we have the appointment of Israel's shepherd through the priest's laying his hands on Joshua/Ἰησοῦς in consecration; but the Jewish leaders in John's Gospel have sought to lay their hands on Jesus/Ἰησοῦς not to consecrate but to punish (10:39; cf. 7:30, 44; 10:28–29).[46]

How the shepherd discourse serves as a figuration of the Prologue's foundational pattern of group transfer is all the more clear noting these echoes of Numbers 27 and Ezekiel 34. When the shepherd makes his authorized entrance into the courtyard (αὐλή) in John 10:1–6, his activity

---

[45] See Table 7.2 in Chapter 7 for a list of intertextual connections between John 10 and Ezekiel 34 and 37.

[46] Manning points out that this contrast is even more sharply seen in 11:47–50 when the high priest, Caiaphas, essentially assigns Jesus the identity of the insurrectionist (λῃστής) mentioned in 10:1, 8 rather than publicly approving him as the high priest Eleazer did for Joshua (Manning, *Echoes of a Prophet*, 108).

is *to enact a communal exodus*. He leads the sheep out of (ἐξάγω) their current structural (and also social) setting of this αὐλή. Not only does he *lead out*; he also *casts out* (ἐκβάλλω). The shepherding activity is one of removing sheep from a particular context. According to J. Ramsey Michaels, ἐκβάλλω is to be read here in its 'weaker sense of "brought out" because it merely resumes the verb "leads them out" in the preceding verse, avoiding a repetition of the same verb. It is not where the emphasis lies.'[47]

To the contrary: Jesus has already cast out sheep in this Gospel, and the scene was tumultuous: 'he cast out of the temple. . . the sheep' (ἐξέβαλεν ἐκ τοῦ ἱεροῦ τά. . . πρόβατα – 2:15). More importantly, the cogency of the ἐκ (out of) prefix[48] at the beginning of both ἐξάγω and ἐκβάλλω accords with the activity of the divine shepherd in Ezekiel 34 who forcibly enacts a programme of extracting sheep from the domain of Israel's negligent leaders. The prophet's language includes ἐκ- and ἀπό- verbs like ἐκζητέω (34:10, 11, 12), ἐξαιρέω (34:10, 27), ἐξάγω (34:13), ἀπελαύνω (34:12), and ἀποστρέφω (34:10). As the true Shepherd, God will dynamically remove his sheep 'out of [their] hands' (ἐκ τῶν χειρῶν) and 'out of their mouths' (ἐκ τοῦ στόματος αὐτῶν), expelling them from their present context: 'I will expel them from every place [ἀπελάσω αὐτὰ ἀπὸ παντὸς τόπου] to which they have been scattered' (34:12). This forceful pastoral activity matches exactly the activity of the shepherd in John 10:1–6 and *recalls what just happened in the narrative to the man born blind*. In the opening of the Shepherd Discourse, the evangelist is commenting on the episode in John 9 while also providing a parabolic portrait of his ecclesial vision. The legitimate shepherd has appeared on the scene and is effecting an expulsion from the courtyard/αὐλή by which the legitimate people of God will be identified.[49] The use of ἐκβάλλω in 10:4 must be understood as retaining the associations from its very recent appearances in 9:34–35.[50] And as Jesus continues the parable and makes adjustments within its symbolic framework, we learn that the work of the legitimate

---

[47] Michaels, *John*, 580.

[48] For a study of the freighted meaning of ἐκ in John's Gospel, see Leander E. Keck, 'Derivation as Destiny: "Of-Ness" in Johannine Christology, Anthropology, and Soteriology', in *Exploring the Gospel of John: In Honor of D. Moody Smith*, ed. R. Alan Culpepper and C. Clifton Black (Louisville, KY: Westminster John Knox, 1996), 274–88.

[49] Grant Macaskill interprets the Gate as the place where sheep are sorted after coming in from the pasture and corralled into their respective folds – Macaskill, *Union*, 261–62.

[50] Michaels points out that it is the Pharisees who cast the formerly blind man out of the synagogue, not Jesus (Michaels, *John*, 580). This misses the point that the overarching reason for the blind man's removal is his testimony to the true shepherd.

shepherd is not just that of extracting sheep from one setting but also gathering them into another: 'Jesus' description of himself as the "door" suggests another sheepfold that the chief priests and Pharisees have no control over, and indeed one that currently excludes them.'[51]

We have seen that it was as Jesus was *exiting the Temple* that he encountered the man born blind who was then *expelled from the synagogue*. In the pastoral imagery of John 10, the shepherd is legitimately entering the structural realm of the courtyard/αὐλή and effecting membership transfer. Later in the Gospel, an αὐλή guarded by a θυρωρός (doorkeeper) will reappear – the scene will be the courtyard of the high priest (18:16), a centralized location embodying in the narrative the legitimate shepherd's blatant rejection. Although an αὐλή can refer simply to a standard house court, Gary Manning observes that its predominant use in the LXX and the NT is to refer to the Temple courts or the court of the high priest.[52] The role of the Shepherd Discourse in the ecclesial narrative script is clear: this παροιμία is an explanatory depiction of Jesus' programme in the Gospel of generating a new community by way of expulsion and extraction from the communal life of 'the Jews', a social realm emblematized in the structural contexts of the Temple, the synagogue, and the αὐλή.[53]

A Narrative Ecclesiology of Divine Participation: Chapter Summary and Conclusion to Part I

The aim of Part I has been to show that the Prologue is the foundation of Johannine ecclesiology and that ecclesiology is foundational for the Johannine Prologue. The reconceived vision of God (dyadic theology) necessitates a reimagining of the identity of God's people. This ecclesial vision is structurally and literarily embedded within the Prologue evidencing a thematic dominance coinherent with theology and christology. As broader, metaphysical categorizations (God, Logos, humankind) give way to filial designations, the Prologue narrates the enfolding of a human community within the divine community by right of supernatural birth. The Incarnation and the testimony of John the Baptist are freighted with ecclesial as well as christological significance as their agency allows for

---

[51] Manning, *Echoes of a Prophet*, 109.

[52] By his reckoning, αὐλή is used 45 times in the LXX to refer to a house court, but 141 times to designate the courts of the Temple. In the NT, it refers to the Temple once, to a house court twice, and to the high priest's court seven times (ibid., 110, n. 28).

[53] On the αὐλή representing 'the Jewish nation', see Pancaro, 'Relationship of the Church', 403.

the participation of believers within the Father–Son interrelation. That corporate participation within the open divine community is the heart of Johannine ecclesiology.

In this chapter, I have shown how the ecclesiology established in the Prologue asserts itself in the remainder of the Gospel (hence the namesake of Part I, 'The Narrative Ecclesiology of the Prologue'). The 'ecclesial narrative script' is a pattern of either social re-entrenchment within an existing group or resocialization into a new communal realm (provoked by christology) that governs the plotline of the wider story. The call narrative in John 1:35–51 begins with an instance of membership transfer as two disciples from the group of Baptist followers leave their rabbi and attach themselves to Jesus. Simon, 'son of John', becomes 'Cephas/Peter' in a scene suggestive of family realignment. The true Israelite Nathanael recognizes Jesus as the rightful king of Israel, suggesting a redefinition of the people of God. These departures from various communal contexts into the community of Jesus are positive instantiations of the ecclesial narrative script.

A negative instantiation occurs in John 8. The heated exchange between Jesus and the Jews demonstrates that christological confession is invalid without a commitment to group extraction and resocialization. In John 9, the evangelist makes clear that group extraction may not be voluntary as in the call narrative or openly resisted as in John 8 – membership transfer may be coerced by one's own social unit. In short, the possibility of membership transfer in the ecclesial narrative script is accepted in John 1, rejected in John 8, and largely coerced in John 9. These three case studies demonstrate the consistent, foundational presence of the ecclesial narrative script and the diverse ways it can be played out in the Gospel's action.

The παροιμία (parable or figure of speech) in 10:1–6 is a figural rendering of this programme of group realignment incited by Jesus. Oneness language, the subject of Part II, is used to label the new communal reality resulting from resocialization: through the process of casting out and gathering in, Jesus and his followers are together recognized as 'one flock' under 'one Shepherd'. The pastoral imagery in John 10 serves the same function as the Prologue's familial imagery in expressing a participatory ecclesial vision. For the Fourth Gospel, community formation around Jesus – whether as an ecclesial flock or family – is a controlling story arc.

PART II

**The Narrative Ecclesiology of the Shema: A Reappraisal
of the Johannine Oneness Motif**

6

THE SHEMA AS THE FOUNDATION FOR JOHN'S THEOLOGICAL USE OF 'ONE': IDENTIFYING AND ADDRESSING RESERVATIONS

Introduction to Part II

Along with the filial language of the Prologue (and the pastoral imagery in John 10), oneness is another primary motif expressing ecclesiology in the Fourth Gospel.[1] In John's ecclesial vision, kinship and oneness convey *participatory or incorporative possibilities*. The participatory dynamic of the former is self-evident – a family consists of multiple members mutually participating within its social reality. The incorporative nature of oneness is perhaps less obvious. In a strictly numeric sense 'one' denotes singularity and uniqueness. In Johannine usage, these expected properties of the cardinal number retain in a theological sense while simultaneously allowing for the plurality of multiple participants (e.g., Jesus and God's children/ flock). Just as the divine family is a community that is open to human membership, John's oneness motif is 'open' and 'social'. So along with the idea of divine–human kinship, the theme of open or social oneness designates the new communal entity being formed around Jesus and also entails that entity's incorporation within the divine fellowship of the Father and Son.

The purpose of Part II is to offer a reinterpretation of the Johannine oneness motif. Contrary to those studies contending that the evangelist's use of εἷς ('one') stems from Gnostic or Greco-Roman conceptual frames, I will argue below in Chapter 7 that the Fourth Gospel's oneness motif *develops out of a creative hermeneutical interplay of Jewish scriptural texts – most prominently the Shema and Ezekiel 34 and 37.* John's literary coordination of theological oneness in Deuteronomy 6:4 alongside the messianic and national oneness of Ezekiel freights εἷς with connotations of *theology, christology, and ecclesiology.* These threefold resonances must be retained when reading the climactic expression of oneness in John 17. Not only does the fourth evangelist make the

---

[1] See the Introduction where references are made to studies on other motifs expressing Johannine ecclesiology.

controversial move of including Jesus within the Shema's language of divine identity ('I and the Father are one' – 10:30); in a move perhaps no less astonishing, he also includes within that language the social reality of the faith community ('that they may be one even as we are one' – John 17:11, 22). Oneness in John portrays the divine identity as somehow interlinked with ecclesiology, and conversely, the oneness language expressing ecclesiology in this Gospel is always grounded in the oneness of divine identity.

A thematic rift between the oneness motif in John 10 and John 17 has been inadvertently promoted in Johannine studies, with the oneness of John 10:30 having negligible interpretative impact on the oneness language in Jesus' lengthy prayer closing the Farewell Discourse. Though 'one' is recognized as some sort of expression of Father–Son unity in 10:30, readers of the Gospel regularly understand 'one' in John 17 as a call to social harmony among believers, divorced from connotations established earlier in the narrative. Such readings overlook the evangelist's *careful, cumulative development of oneness*. This sequential narrative development compels an interpretation in which the resonances of 'one' in John 10 sustain into John 17, with oneness encompassing an indivisible interplay between theology, christology, and ecclesiology. Reflecting a pattern established in the Prologue, the divine interrelation between Father and Son somehow comprises the social unit of the 'one flock' of Jesus' 'sheep' (John 10); and the social reality of these believers is somehow constitutive of that divine interrelation (John 17).

It is customary in Johannine scholarship to understand the prayer for oneness in John 17 as evidence of a historical schism that threatened the integrity of the Johannine community (e.g., why else would the evangelist have Jesus praying so intensely for unity unless he faced a situation of *dis*unity?). Quite naturally, this reading of John 17 reinforces the influential interpretative tradition in ecumenical dialogue where Jesus' prayer is treated as a foundational text for building church unity. My reading of the oneness motif presented here proposes a reappraisal of these standard interpretations: *Johannine oneness is informed by the language of the Shema, meaning that the prayer for believers to become one as Jesus is one with the Father is ultimately a call not so much to social harmony but to social identity construction around Israel's God.* I will suggest at the end of Chapter 7 that the prayer in John 17 'that they may be one', is also a call *to corporate participation within the divine interrelation of Father and Son*, setting up the discussion of 'Johannine theosis' in Part III. For now, the more immediate task is to build the case for associating the Fourth Gospel's concept of oneness with the Shema. Before working out the ecclesiology of participation offered by the oneness motif in Part III, I will first explore its ecclesiology of *association* – the term 'one' is a means of group identity construction correlating the Johannine disciples with the 'one' God of Israel.

By the end of these next two chapters it should be clear that, in grounding his christology within Jewish monotheistic categorizations,[2] the evangelist has also grounded his ecclesiology within a Jewish framework of communal self-identification. John locates Jesus' ministry within the symbolic structures (namely, Temple and synagogue) and significant temporal settings (namely, the Feasts) of Judaism not just to express christology. He is also constructing a social identity, crafting a vision for a community that is becoming (or has become) extracted from the more mainstream communal life of Judaism but is nonetheless bound to the one God of Jewish monotheistic confession now revealed to be 'one' with Jesus. The overall picture that will emerge is that, in Johannine communal self-understanding, it is not they who have parted ways with Judaism; on the contrary, the polemicized 'Jews' have parted ways with the one God who encompasses the one Shepherd Jesus Christ, and in this rejection of 'dyadic theology' certain Ἰουδαῖοι (Jews) have negated their right to be identified as 'children of God'. So the Gospel of John uses the term 'one' *to indicate that the experience of group extraction and resocialization does not amount to a departure from the 'one' God of Israel.* If influential reconstruction theories like those of Brown and Martyn are at least partially correct, the social crisis evoked by christology among Johannine Christians would have been severely distressing for them as Jews suddenly finding themselves at odds with their communal identity and long-standing religious traditions.[3] The oneness language grounded in Ezekiel 34 and 37 and in the Shema's language of divine identity are jointly employed to express an *ecclesiology of divine association.* The consequences of the ecclesial narrative script repositions these Christ-confessing Jews within a theologically valid community ('one flock') aligned with the 'one' God and his 'one' Shepherd.

---

[2] I am aware that controversy surrounds the terms monotheism and monolatry in reference to the Shema. See R. W. L. Moberly, 'How Appropriate Is "Monotheism" as a Category for Biblical Interpretation', in *Early Jewish and Christian Monotheism*, ECC 263 (London: T & T Clark, 2004), 216–34.

[3] This social distress is certainly happening within the narrative world of the Gospel, with or without the specific details of the *Sitze im Leben* proposed in the historical reconstructions.

The Shema and the Gospel of John: The State of the Question

I begin my treatment of John's oneness motif by identifying and addressing reservations that may be preventing scholars from understanding Jewish monotheism as its primary theological source. It is surely an oddity that oneness features so strongly in this ancient Jewish text with so few commentators drawing connections to the Shema.[4] Birger Gerhardsson's *The Shema in the New Testament* is an impressive collection of no fewer than seventeen essays exploring the use of Deuteronomy 6:4 in early Christianity, yet the Johannine writings receive little more than a dismissive paragraph in the final pages, a paragraph that concludes with the observation, 'We do not get much help from the Johannine writings for the Shema question.'[5] Similarly, in an essay broadly entitled 'The Shema and Early Christianity', Kim Huat Tan includes no discussion on the Gospel of John.[6] Tan alerts his readers that 'tight controls' must be imposed to avoid an unwieldy study, so 'we must only use those passages where the Shema is explicitly cited or referred to'.[7] This qualification apparently rules out John's Gospel. Tan's 'Jesus and the Shema' is a more recently published essay that would appear to afford more space; yet these 'tight controls' apparently remain in force since his discussion is again limited to the Synoptics.[8] As noted earlier, claiming that the Shema features at all in the Fourth Gospel is a minority position.[9]

There are, however, significant voices within this minority. C. K. Barrett suggested in 1947 that the Shema should be recognized

---

[4] By 'Shema', I am referring to Deuteronomy 6:4–9, with the acknowledgment that this text was also associated closely with Deuteronomy 11:13–21 and Numbers 15:37–41 in Jewish tradition. See R. W. L. Moberly, 'Toward an Interpretation of the Shema', in *Theological Exegesis: Essays in Honor of Brevard S. Childs*, ed. Christopher Seitz and Kathryn Greene-McCreight (Grand Rapids, MI: Eerdmans, 1999), 124–44, here at 125, n. 2.

[5] Birger Gerhardsson, *The Shema in the New Testament: Deut 6:4–5 in Significant Passages* (Lund: Novapress, 1996), 315.

[6] Kim Huat Tan, 'The Shema and Early Christianity', *TynBul* 59, no. 2 (2008): 181–206. He does mention in a footnote Richard Bauckham's suggestion that the Shema is in view in John 10:30, yet once again the 'tight controls' make their imposition: 'For the sake of keeping to our tight controls, and to keep this essay within manageable proportions, discussion of this will not be carried out' (Bauckham, 'Monotheism and Christology', 200, n. 83).

[7] Ibid., 183.

[8] Kim Huat Tan, 'Jesus and the Shema', in *Handbook for the Study of the Historical Jesus*, ed. Tom Holmén and Stanley E. Porter, vol. 3 (Leiden: Brill, 2011), 2677–707.

[9] Note also this 2005 essay collection where only the Synoptics feature in the study of the Shema: Perry B. Yoder, ed., *Take This Word to Heart: The Shema in Torah and Gospel* (Scottdale, PA: Herald, 2005).

as the fourth evangelist's source for Jesus' striking self-identification with God in John 10:30.[10] Though Barrett's article has been influential in terms of John's use of Old Testament texts and themes, his suggestion concerning the Shema has made little impact and seems to have escaped notice within the field of Johannine studies for decades[11] – only in recent years have multiple scholars begun to argue similarly that the oneness motif is somehow related to the divine oneness of the Shema. Among these interpreters[12] are Stephen Barton,[13] Andreas Köstenberger,[14] Craig Keener,[15] Jane Heath,[16] Thomas Söding,[17] Richard Hays,[18] and Richard Bauckham.[19] Apart from a recently published essay by Bauckham (see immediately below), the works

[10] Barrett, 'Old Testament', 161–2. I am thankful to Joel Marcus for directing me to this source.

[11] Bauckham: 'Although, so far as I am aware, *it has not been suggested by other scholars*, it seems to me very probable that this saying of Jesus alludes to the Jewish confession of faith in the one God, the Shema.' Bauckham, 'Monotheism and Christology', 250 (emphases added).

[12] In addition to the scholars listed here who find the Shema referred to in Jn 10:30, some have also suggested that the Shema underlies the phrase τοῦ μόνου θεοῦ (Jn 5:44) in the controversy over what the Jews believe is Jesus' claim to be 'equal' (ἴσος) with God. This was argued by Lori Baron in 'Reinterpreting the Shema: The Battle over the Unity of God in the Fourth Gospel' (a Paper at the Annual Meeting of the Society of Biblical Literature, Boston, Massachusetts), 2008; see also Alicia D. Myers, *Characterizing Jesus: A Rhetorical Analysis on the Fourth Gospel's Use of Scripture in Its Presentation of Jesus*, LNTS 458 (London: T & T Clark, 2012), 103. A reference to the Shema is strengthened when it is observed that love for God (the corollary of his oneness) forms the immediate context. See Jörg Augenstein, *Das Liebesgebot im Johannesevangelium und in den Johannesbriefen*, BWANT 134 (Stuttgart: Kohlhammer, 1994), 60–62.

[13] Barton, 'Community', 290–4 and Stephen C. Barton, 'The Unity of Humankind as a Theme in Biblical Theology', in *Out of Egypt: Biblical Theology and Biblical Interpretation*, ed. Craig Bartholomew et al., vol. 5, Scripture and Hermeneutics Series (Grand Rapids, MI: Zondervan, 2004), 233–58.

[14] Andreas J. Köstenberger, *John*, BECNT (Grand Rapids, MI: Baker Academic, 2004), 312. See also Andreas J. Köstenberger and Scott R. Swain, *Father, Son and Spirit: The Trinity and John's Gospel*, NSBT 24 (Downers Grove, IL: InterVarsity Press, 2008), 24–44, 67, 82, 174, 175.

[15] Keener, *John*, 826.

[16] Jane Heath, 'Some Were Saying, "He Is Good" (John 7:12b): "Good" Christology in John's Gospel?' *NTS* 56, no. 4 (2010): 513–35.

[17] Thomas Söding, '"Ich und der Vater sind Eins" (Joh 10,30): Die johanneische Christologie vor dem Anspruch des Hauptgebotes (Dtn 6,4f)', *ZNW* 93, no. 3–4 (2002): 177–99.

[18] Richard B. Hays, *Reading Backwards: Figural Christology and the Fourfold Gospel Witness* (London: SPCK, 2015), 101.

[19] Bauckham, 'Monotheism and Christology', 250; Richard Bauckham, 'Biblical Theology and the Problems of Monotheism', in Bauckham, *Jesus and the God of Israel*, 104–6.

cited by the foregoing authors note possible connections between Deuteronomy 6:4 and John 10 but little interest is shown in pressing for the possibility that those connections obtain in Jesus' prayer 'that they may be one, as we are one' in John 17:21–23.[20] As Bauckham shows in 'Divine and Human Community', those connections are indeed in force.[21] The Shema's influence must be regarded as extending beyond John 10 if the Gospel's narrative sequence is taken seriously.

I will now address a range of anticipated apprehensions that may inhibit a more widespread acceptance of this Gospel's use of 'one' in Deuteronomy 6:4. Fundamental questions to consider include whether the fourth evangelist would have been familiar with the Shema and thus writing in a context in which oneness references would have been naturally associated with its language. I conclude below that ignoring or denying the Shema's influence on the Fourth Gospel is untenable in light of the Jewish monotheistic convictions in early Judaism, convictions regularly expressed through the Johannine rhetoric of oneness.

The Shema in Early Jewish Religious Life: The Evangelist's Potential Awareness of Deuteronomy 6:4

Though the term εἷς held a vast range of meanings in the Greco-Roman world (beyond its use as the cardinal number '1'),[22] the most conspicuous Jewish source for a claim pairing 'one' with God (as John does) would have most certainly been the language of the Shema.[23] According to Stig Hanson,

---

[20] Michael Labahn affirms the prominence of the Shema for the Gospel's Jewish milieu, finding possible evidence of its use in Jn 5 and Jn 8, but does not draw connections between Deut 6:5 and Jn 10 or Jn 17 – Labahn, 'Deuteronomy in John's Gospel', in *Deuteronomy in the New Testament*, ed. Maarten J. J. Menken and Steve Moyise, LNTS 358 (London: T & T Clark, 2007), 82–98.

[21] Bauckham, *Gospel*, 21–41. Bauckham's arguments about the Shema in John in the chapter entitled 'Divine and Human Community' (pp. 21–41), published just before my own manuscript went into the publication phase, are largely consonant with my own here in this chapter. Our primary difference, it seems, is that I press beyond an *analogical* reading of divine and human oneness in John 17 for a *participatory* reading, to be discussed in detail in Part III.

[22] See Larry W. Hurtado, 'First-century Jewish Monotheism', *JSNT*, no. 71 (1998): 3–26. Also helpful is the study of oneness in various religious contexts provided by Appold, *Oneness*, 163–93.

[23] Bauckham, 'Divine and Human Community', in Bauckham, *Gospel*, 23 and 32.

in trying to penetrate the thought of unity in Judaism, we are always referred to the idea of one God. Monotheism is, as we shall see, the source of all other unity, whether it be unity in cosmos or in Israel, the unity of the cult or of the Law in Judaism. The oneness of God is the common foundation of all other unity, and the various ideas of unity are different expressions or consequences of this oneness of God.[24]

Moreover, Stephen Barton notes the following,

> That unity or 'oneness' is a pervasive motif in biblical thought is impossible to deny. Without doubt, its foundation in belief and cult is monotheism, the oneness of God as given classical expression in the Shema ... The body of the people of God is to be one people in love of God because the God they worship is one. As such, the people's oneness is testimony to the oneness of God.[25]

Though first-century Jewish audiences did not live within an intellectual or linguistic environment hermetically sealed off from wider cultural influences, they would surely connect theological oneness language to the Shema more readily than to the oneness language of Hellenistic philosophy or Greco-Roman religious sects.[26] In fact, the Shema's oneness theology is understood as a primary means of religious self-identification and communal preservation for Jews living within a Greco-Roman milieu offering so many theological and philosophical options. In terms of cultural and religious resonance, there is nothing shocking or surprising in claiming that the oneness motif of the Fourth Gospel is in some fashion related to the expression, 'Hear, Israel: YHWH our God; YHWH is one'.[27]

The recent debate as to whether Deuteronomy 6:4ff was used liturgically in Jewish synagogues during the first century CE may be unnecessarily (and unwittingly) complicating the issue as to whether or not the Shema appears in the Fourth Gospel. Joachim Jeremias made the claim in *The Prayers of Jesus* that the Shema was recited twice daily as a Jewish liturgical prayer during the second Temple period.[28] Because the

[24] Stig Hanson, *The Unity of the Church in the New Testament: Colossians and Ephesians*, ASNU (Copenhagen: Einar Munskgaard, 1946), 5.

[25] Barton, 'Unity', 238.   [26] Keener, *John*, 826.

[27] On this translation, see R. W. L. Moberly, '"YHWH Is One": The Translation of the Shema', in *Studies in the Pentateuch*, ed. J. A. Emerton (Leiden: Brill, 1990), 209–15.

[28] Joachim Jeremias, *The Prayers of Jesus*, SBT Second Series, 6 (London: SCM Press, n.d.), 78–81. A similar case is made by E. P. Sanders in *Judaism: Practice and Belief, 63 BCE – 66 CE* (London: SCM Press, 1992), 195–208.

Synoptic Gospels' citations of the Shema deviate awkwardly from each other as well as from Deuteronomy 6:4 in the Septuagint, Jeremias assumed that early Christian churches that maintained the Jewish practice of reciting prayers nonetheless dispensed with the Shema (he attributes the variance in the Synoptic citations of Deuteronomy 6:4–5 as evidence for this phasing out).[29] The question this raises concerns the familiarity with the Shema during the ministry of Jesus and, perhaps more importantly, during the time of the evangelists' writing – if it can be shown that Jewish synagogues were indeed praying the Shema, then the chances are higher that the term 'one' would have been associated with the monotheist confession of Deuteronomy 6:4 for Jewish Christians reared within the worship life of the synagogue (the most likely audience for John's Gospel).

This liturgical usage has been questioned. Jeremias' claim that the Shema was a part of the synagogue worship in Jesus' day is attacked by some as a mere assumption that, however reasonable, lacks verifiable proof.[30] Though the Shema was certainly a feature of synagogue liturgies in Rabbinic Judaism, the final form of the Mishnah cannot be dated much earlier than the start of the third century CE. The opening sections of *Berakoth* (1–3) give diverse details for the Shema's recitation, but the evidence that the same liturgical use was underway during the writing of New Testament texts is patchy. Tan asks the pertinent question: 'To what extent can the evidence of the Mishnah be retrojected back to Jesus' ministry?'[31] Daniel Falk appeals to 'corroborating evidence' justifying a pre-Rabbinic use of the Shema in Jewish worship,[32] and Donald

---

[29] Jeremias, *Prayers*, 80–81. Daniel Falk, however, dismisses Jeremias' observation, pointing out that 'liturgical items often exist in varying forms from the earliest periods'. See Daniel K. Falk, 'Jewish Prayer Literature and the Jerusalem Church in Acts', in *The Book of Acts in Its Palestinian Setting*, ed. Richard Bauckham, vol. 4 (Carlisle: Paternoster, 1995), 267–301, here at 276, n. 28. For a critique of Falk's critique of Jeremias (on the grounds that Falk fails to offer any evidence as to why the Shema never gained ground in Christian worship if it was so important in Jewish worship in the same time period), see Paul Foster, 'Why Did Matthew Get the Shema Wrong? A Study of Matthew 22:37', *JBL* 122, no. 2 (2003): 309–33, here at 327. For a more recent assessment of the early church's reception of the Shema, see R. W. L. Moberly, *Old Testament Theology: Reading the Hebrew Bible as Christian Scripture* (Grand Rapids, MI: Baker Academic, 2013), 7–40.

[30] See especially Foster, 'Shema'.   [31] Tan, 'Jesus and the Shema', 2677.

[32] The evidence to which he refers is the Nash Papyrus, 4QDeut^{j,n}, 1QS 10, and a collection of *tefillin* found at Qumran – Falk, 'Jewish Prayer Literature', 287–88. For a careful overview of these texts (and others) decidedly in favour of the Shema's liturgical use in early Jewish worship, see Tan's subsection 'Did the Shema Have the Status of a Creed pre-70 CE?' – Tan, 'Jesus and the Shema', 2682–90.

Verseput points to some lines from Josephus as confirmation that the Shema held a fixed position as a liturgical text before 70 CE.[33] Paul Foster, however, remains unconvinced and vigorously reasserts the lateness of the most reliable textual witnesses to this liturgical usage.[34] His arguments are strong, but less cogent in light of the information more recently provided by David Instone-Brewer. Though a fixed prayer tradition by which the Shema was formally recited in synagogue gatherings during John's day is unlikely, Instone-Brewer offers detailed, line-by-line commentary on *m. Ber* 1–3 tracing many of the instructions on the recitation of the Shema back to pre-70 CE religious life.[35] The later formalization of the Shema as a liturgical prayer derived from traditions actively in force during the first century.[36]

This ongoing debate on the Shema's possible liturgical function before the Temple's destruction can obscure the question as to the significance of the Shema during the first century CE. The actual words of the wider passage in Deuteronomy 6:6–9 envision specifically a private or domestic setting for recital more so than a liturgical setting,[37] so the absence of the Shema in the latter context would therefore in no way deny its influence in early Jewish life. Josephus seems to offer evidence for the regular use of the Shema in Jewish devotional practice during his lifetime.[38] In his retelling of Moses' giving of the law in Deuteronomy, Josephus denotes a temporal marker for the daily commemorations of the Shema ('twice every day'), a schedule drawn logically from the instructions in Deuteronomy 6:7.

---

[33] Donald J. Verseput, 'James 1:17 and the Jewish Morning Prayers', *NovT* 39, no. 2 (1997): 177–91, here at 179–86. See Josephus, *Ant*. 4.212–13.

[34] Foster, 'Shema'. Also sceptical of a developed used of the Shema in pre-70 Jewish worship is Stefan C. Reif, *Judaism and Hebrew Prayer: New Perspectives on Jewish Liturgical History* (Cambridge: Cambridge University Press, 1993), 83–84.

[35] David Instone-Brewer, *Prayer and Agriculture: Traditions of the Rabbis from the Era of the New Testament*, vol. 1. (Grand Rapids, MI: Eerdmans, 2004), 41–52. He does not argue for a fixed tradition of liturgical prayers dating before the destruction of the Temple, but the reasoning behind his early dating of much of the material in *m. Ber* 1–3 seems convincing.

[36] See Tan, 'Jesus and the Shema', 2687–90, and James D. G. Dunn, 'Was Jesus a Monotheist? A Contribution to the Discussion of Christian Monotheism', in Stuckenbruck and North, *Early Jewish and Christian Monotheism*, 104–119.

[37] Jutta Leonhardt-Balzer, *Jewish Worship in Philo of Alexandria* (Tübingen: Mohr Siebeck, 2001), 98–99. See also Falk, 'Jewish Prayer Literature', 293, 296, 300.

[38] A similar argument is made in Christopher R. Bruno, *'God Is One': The Function of Eis Ho Theos as a Ground for Gentile Inclusion in Paul's Letters*, LNTS 497 (London: Bloomsbury, 2013), 97.

Twice each day [δὶς δ᾽ ἑκάστης ἡμέρας], at the dawn and when
the hour comes for turning to rest, let all acknowledge before
God the bounties which he has bestowed on them through their
deliverance from the land of Egypt ... They shall inscribe on
their doors the greatest of the benefits which they have received
from God and each shall display them on his arms; and all that
can show forth the power of God and his goodwill towards
them, let them bear a record written on the head and on the
arm, so that men may see on every side the loving care with
which God surrounds them.[39]

Verseput argues strongly that this text betrays an established practice in
the formal prayer life of Jewish *worship*.[40] Jutta Leonhardt-Balzer,
however, believes this is a reference more to private practice, albeit
a practice active for Jews during Josephus' time of writing.[41]

Philo also seems to prescribe first-century Jewish devotional practices
tied to the Shema:[42]

The law tells us that we must set the rules of justice *in the heart*
[τῇ καρδίᾳ] and *fasten them for a sign upon the hand* [ἐξάπτειν
εἰς σημεῖον ἐπὶ τῆς χειρός] and have them shaking *before the
eyes* [πρὸ ὀφθαλμῶν].[43] The first of these is a parable indicating
that the rules of justice must not be committed to untrustworthy
ears since no trust can be placed in the sense of hearing but that
these best of all lessons must be impressed upon our lordliest
part, stamped too with genuine seals. The second shows that we
must not only receive conceptions of the good but express our
approval of them in unhesitating action, for the hand is the
symbol of action, and on this the law bids us fasten and hang
the rules of justice for a sign ... The third means that always and

---

[39] Josephus, *Ant.* 4.212–13. Translation (slightly modified) from Flavius Josephus, *Jewish Antiquities*, 2 vols., trans. H. St. J. Thackery, LCL (London: William Heinemann, 1930–34), 1.578–79.

[40] Verseput, 'Jewish Morning Prayers', 183.

[41] Leonhardt-Balzer, *Jewish Worship*, 140.

[42] Leonhardt-Balzer (previous note) finds convincing Naomi Cohen's argument from *Spec.* IV.137–139 that Philo was familiar with the daily recitation of the Shema – Naomi G. Cohen, *Philo Judaeus: His Universe of Discourse* (Frankfurt am Main: Peter Lang, 1995), 129–55; 167–77; 294–96.

[43] I have provided the Greek text of the italicized portions above that correspond almost exactly with Dt 6:4, LXX (though Philo uses ἐξάπτω in line 137 above where Dt 6:8 has ἀφάπτω the meaning is essentially the same).

everywhere we must have the vision of them as it were close to the eyes.[44]

Philo comments on the Shema's prescribed practices as if they were in force for his audience.

These first-century Jewish references to Deuteronomy 6:6–9 from Philo and Josephus may not offer proof for Jeremias' claim that the Shema was *formally* used in pre-Rabbinic Judaism. But they do provide evidence for suggesting that the devotional practices of the Shema were known at least in private, informal settings. Whether or not the Shema was actually recited in Jewish worship settings is a non-issue for the question of the fourth evangelist's familiarity with its influence and use.

Along with Philo and Josephus, the first-century Jewish writers of the New Testament demonstrate familiarity with the Shema and an eagerness to affirm and promote its significance.[45] Christian devotion to Jesus could have eventually motivated an eclipse of the Shema's emphasis on God as 'one', but many of the earliest Christian writers were keen to present Jesus' work and identity as consonant with the Shema's theology. Mark has Jesus citing the oneness formula in Deuteronomy 6:4 after he has been associated with εἷς ὁ θεός (lit., 'one, the God' or 'the one God', though often translated as 'God alone') because of his authority to forgive sins (Mk 2:7).[46] Similarly, Paul offers an innovative christological reinterpretation of the Shema's oneness in 1 Corinthians 8:6.[47] Regardless as to whether or not the Shema was recited twice daily in the synagogue's worship or even in the Jewish home, it is clear that the Shema was a significant text for early Christian writers – including the first, second, and third evangelists. There is nothing fanciful in proposing that the fourth evangelist was very likely familiar with the Shema and, like Paul and Mark, was concerned to offer an innovative christological reinterpretation of the theological meaning of oneness in Deuteronomy 6:4.

---

[44] Philo, *Spec.* IV.137–39; emphases added. From Philo of Alexandria, *Works*, vol. 7, ed. T. E. Page et al., trans. F. H. Colson, LCL (Harvard University Press, 1939), 93–95.

[45] Mt 19:16–17; 22:34–40; 23:8–10; Mk 2:7; 10:17–18; 12:28–33; Lk 10:25–28; 18:19; Rom 3:30; 1 Cor 8:6; Gal 3:20; 1 Tim 2:5; (Heb 2:11); Jam 2:19; 4:12.

[46] See Joel Marcus, 'Authority to Forgive Sins upon the Earth: The Shema in the Gospel of Mark', in *The Gospels and the Scriptures of Israel*, ed. W. Richard Stegner and Craig A. Evans, *JSNTSup* 104 (Sheffield: Sheffield Academic Press, 1994), 196–211.

[47] See N. T. Wright, 'Monotheism, Christology and Ethics: 1 Corinthians 8', in *The Climax of the Covenant: Christ and the Law in Pauline Theology* (Minneapolis, MN: Fortress, 1991), 120–36.

In claiming that the fourth evangelist draws on the Shema for his oneness motif, I am referring not just to a phrase or a collection of verses in Deuteronomy but to a comprehensive theological construct widely recognized as conceptually normative for the context in which the Fourth Gospel was produced.[48] The references to God as 'one' in early Jewish literature serve as theological abbreviations dense with religious meaning.[49] Indeed, for a first-century Jew to be unfamiliar with the Shema's oneness theology was to be ignorant of the first commandment stating 'that there is but one God, and that we ought to worship him only' (Josephus, *Ant.* 3.91). Though we are not sure how the Shema may have been used ritually in the first century, the Gospel of John was produced within a Jewish socioreligious setting in which the oneness language of Deuteronomy 6:4 held considerable purchase for theological expression. Was the fourth evangelist familiar with the Shema? There can be little doubt.

Other Possible Reservations in Accepting the Shema's Influence on John

In spite of the prevalence of the Shema's oneness theology in early Judaism, doubts may still persist about its presence in John's Gospel. Certain grounds for reservation have been identified in the previous section as matters of no consequence on the question, namely the range of meanings for 'one' in Greco-Roman religion and philosophy and the lack of evidence for the Shema's liturgical use in first-century synagogues. These concerns can be dismissed when it is acknowledged that John is a Jewish text produced in a socioreligious milieu familiar with the Shema's oneness theology. Here in this section, I identify three other

---

[48] See, e.g., *Letter of Aristeas* 132: '(Eleazar) began first of all by demonstrating that God is one.' From 'Letter of Aristeas', trans. R. J. H. Shutt, in *The Old Testament Pseudepigrapha: Expansions of the 'Old Testament' and Legends, Wisdom and Philosophical Literature, Prayers, Psalms and Odes, Fragments of Lost Judeo-Hellenistic Works*, edited by James H. Charlesworth, vol. 2 (New York: Doubleday, 1985), 7–34, here at 21. And also, Josephus, *Ant.* 5.112: 'they recognized but the one God, owned by all Hebrews alike'. Translation from Josephus, *Jewish Antiquities*, 2.53.

[49] For a recent survey of early Jewish texts on divine oneness, see Bruno, *God Is One* and Erik Waaler, *The Shema and the First Commandment in First Corinthians: An Intertextual Approach to Paul's Re-reading of Deuteronomy*, WUNT 253 (Tübingen: Mohr Siebeck, 2008). Helpful studies on oneness and Jewish monotheism include the essays in Stuckenbruck and North, eds., *Early Jewish and Christian Monotheism*. See also Larry W. Hurtado, *Lord Jesus Christ: Devotion to Jesus in Earliest Christianity* (Grand Rapids, MI: Eerdmans, 2003) and Bauckham, 'Problems of Monotheism'.

reasons that could serve as a means of doubting Deuteronomy 6:4 as a source of Johannine oneness. The first potential concern is that John does not explicitly cite the Shema like Mark, Matthew, and Luke. Second, the form of 'one' in the Septuagint rendering of the Shema is the masculine εἷς whereas John uses the neuter ἕν in 10:30 and in chapter 17. I will conclude discussing apprehensions towards the corporate identification of human beings with the 'one' God of Jewish monotheism – a phenomenon I contend is underway in Jesus' prayer that the believers will be 'one' as he and the Father are 'one'.

The lack of direct scriptural citations of the Shema

Unlike the Synoptics,[50] the fourth evangelist does not refer to the Shema directly.[51] The inability to bracket quotation marks around Greek phrases from Deuteronomy 6 may contribute to reservations about finding the Shema in John. Yet also unlike the Synoptics, the Fourth Gospel is openly recognized as having oneness as a significant motif. Even without the quotation marks, my argument that the theological language of Deuteronomy 6:4 lies at the source of this carefully developed theme still stands. As pointed out in the previous section, John is drawing not just from a specific proof-text but from a dense conceptual base expressing monotheistic theology. 'One' is a cipher for this theology requiring no footnote or chapter-and-verse references.

Echoes and allusions are more common instances than direct citations in the phenomenon of intertextuality and often just as influential in establishing connections.[52] And suggestive references as opposed to verbatim quotations are precisely what should be expected according to the fourth evangelist's overall use of Israel's Scriptures:[53] 'The Evangelist does not mainly rely on quotations and proof-texts, but he has, so to speak, absorbed the whole of the Old Testament into his system.'[54] Martin Hengel writes that 'in accordance with his esoteric,

---

[50] Mk 12:28–33; Mt 22:24–40; Lk 10:25–28. On the variance between the evangelists' citations and the text of the LXX, see the aforementioned study of Jeremias, *Prayers*, 78–81.

[51] Johannes Beutler, SJ, 'Das Hauptgebot im Johannesevangelium', in *Das Gesetz im Neuen Testament*, ed. Karl Kertelge, QD 108 (Freiburg: Herder, 1986), 236.

[52] John J. O'Rourke, 'Possible Uses of the Old Testament in the Gospels: An Overview', in *The Gospels and the Scriptures of Israel*, ed. Craig A. Evans and W. Richard Stegner, *JSNTSup* 104 (Sheffield: Sheffield Academic Press, 1994), 15–25, here at 25.

[53] Barrett, 'Old Testament', 168.

[54] This quote is from T. F. Glasson as a summary of Barrett's finding in 'The Old Testament in the Fourth Gospel' – T. F. Glasson, *Moses in the Fourth Gospel*, SBT

indirectly suggestive style, the emphasis in John (in contrast to Matthew) is on "allusions". He prefers the bare, terse clue or allusion, the use of metaphor or motif, to the full citation.'[55] C. K. Barrett points out that we should actually *expect* to find scriptural passages that are directly quoted in the Synoptics merely alluded to by the fourth evangelist. John esteemed the Old Testament as a 'comprehensive unity, not a mere quarry from which isolated fragments of useful material might be hewn'.[56] According to A. T. Hanson,

> It could perhaps be said of the Synoptic Gospels that they are quasi-historical accounts of the life of Jesus, helped out by fairly frequent recourse to prophecy in the Old Testament. But this will hardly serve as a description of the Fourth Gospel. For the author of the Fourth Gospel Scripture is not a prop, an addition. It is constitutive for this work. Indeed we may guess that one of the main reasons that he wrote his Gospel was that he wanted to show to what extent the career and person of Jesus Christ was the fulfilment of Scripture.[57]

He goes on to write, 'Far more than any of the other three, this work is concerned with Scripture and the fulfilment of Scripture.'[58] Johannes Beutler points out that in the sharp controversy scenes between Jesus and the Jews (where the oneness motif often surfaces), precise citations from Scripture are less apparent than elsewhere in John's Gospel, though the evangelist seems to be making the larger case that the entirety of the Scriptures find fulfilment in Jesus:

> Apparently, the 'fulfillment' of scripture in Jesus is so self-evident that individual texts have only a limited importance for the argument. What seems to stand behind this perspective

40 (London: SCM Press, 1963), 36, n. 1. A. T. Hanson cites Glasson on this point as well, providing the qualification that John did not have access to all the documents which we associate with OT today. See A. T. Hanson, 'John's Use of Scripture', in *The Gospels and the Scriptures of Israel*, ed. Craig A. Evans and W. Richard Stegner, *JSNTSup* 104 (Sheffield: Sheffield Academic Press, 1994), 358–79, here at 373.

[55] Hengel, 'Old Testament', 392. Hengel points out that Moses' name is actually mentioned more in the Fourth Gospel than in the Synoptics or in Paul (11 times in John – see p. 387); also, the 'concepts νόμος and γραφή' both are found more in John than in the Synoptics (388).

[56] Barrett, 'Old Testament', 168. Barrett is building on a section in Hoskyns' commentary where he demonstrates that scripture passages cited by the Synoptics are taken by John and embedded within his Gospel as major themes rather than mere textual references – Hoskyns, *The Fourth Gospel*, 58–85.

[57] Hanson, 'John's Use of Scripture', 379.   [58] Ibid.

is the controversy between church and synagogue at the end of the first century, where the question was no longer whether some isolated texts could be used as proof texts for or against Jesus, but whether scripture as such found its ultimate meaning in a Christian or in a merely Jewish perspective.[59]

Similarly, Beutler observes that in John's 'documentation of controversies between Johannine Christianity and Judaism, he has reached a kind of "meta-level," where the individual proof text no longer counts, but rather, the whole of scripture is at stake'.[60] In his recent study on the evangelists' use of Scripture, Richard Hays asserts that, 'because John engages Israel's Scripture chiefly as a source of symbols, he often references the biblical stories not through direct quotation of texts but through allusions and echoes'.[61]

Since the Fourth Gospel is dense with intertextual connections maintained by allusive echoes, the absence of direct citations (as found in the Synoptics) cannot be used as grounds for dismissing the Shema as a background for Johannine oneness. As will become more clear in Chapter 7, the repeated references to 'one' indicate instead that the Shema's oneness theology has been actively appropriated by the evangelist and carefully developed into a major theme of his work, even if quotation marks cannot be easily inscribed around his references.

I hinted previously that John's scriptural allusions to the Shema are reinforced by the Johannine love commands.[62] Two German scholars have identified links between Deuteronomy 6:4–5 and John's theme of loving God (and one another). In his article 'Das Hauptgebot im Johannesevangelium', Beutler makes a convincing case that the Shema underlies John 5:39–47, 8:41–44, and the love commands in chapter 14.[63] John, for instance, makes reference in 5:44 to 'the only God [τοῦ μόνου θεοῦ]', whom Jesus accuses the Jews of failing to love (5:42). Since the corollary of God's singularity and uniqueness is love

---

[59] Johannes Beutler, SJ, 'The Use of "Scripture" in the Gospel of John', in *Exploring the Gospel of John: In Honor of D. Moody Smith*, ed. R. Alan Culpepper and C. Clifton Black (Louisville, KY: Westminster John Knox, 1996), 147–62, here at 156.

[60] Ibid.

[61] Richard B. Hays, *Echoes of Scripture in the Gospels* (Waco, TX: Baylor University Press, 2016), 343.

[62] Jane Heath, however, believes that a primary contrast between John's use of the Shema and the Synoptics' use is with the difference in emphases: John emphasizes God's oneness and the others emphasize the love command. See Heath, '"Good" Christology', 534.

[63] Beutler, 'Hauptgebot'.

(Deuteronomy 6:5), failing to love him (and Jesus who has come in his name) is nothing short of a breach of the Shema. Beutler reinforces his claim that the Shema is in view here by pointing out that the accusation of failing to love the one God is bracketed by a reference to the Scriptures in 5:37 and more specifically to the scriptural writing of Moses in 5:45–46; for Beutler, the command to love the 'only God', abrogated by the Jews in their failure to love Jesus, is most epitomized in the Mosaic writing of Deuteronomy 6:4–5.[64] In 8:41 the Jews claim to be descendants from Abraham, and therefore also from 'one father: God' (ἕνα πατέρα . . . τὸν θεόν). Jesus denies their self-ascribed communal identity on the basis of their lack of love. As in 5:39–47, the Jews are breaking the Shema, failing to love God and Jesus, his divine agent and Son, thus invalidating their allegiance to the 'one' God from whom they claim patrilineal descent.[65] Later in this discourse, Jesus explains that he is glorified by his father 'of whom you claim, "he is our God [θεὸς ἡμῶν ἐστιν]"'. (8:54). Michael Labahn suggests that the phrase 'he is our God' is a loose quotation of Deuteronomy 6:4 (κύριος ὁ θεὸς ἡμῶν κύριος εἷς ἐστιν).[66] The Jews, therefore, seem to be claiming their 'one' father to be the God confessed in the Shema. Though a direct citation is lacking, Beutler is convinced of the connections: 'Steht es deutlich erkennbar hinter zwei Abschnitten der großen Auseinandersetzungen zwischen Jesus und "den Juden" in Jerusalem, nämlich hinter Joh 5,41–44 und 8,41f.'[67]

Though their interpretations on various texts differ at times, Jörg Augenstein agrees with Beutler that the Johannine literature shares along with the Synoptics the pairing of the Shema's love for God with the love of neighbour commanded in Leviticus 19:17.[68] The most concise demonstration of this pairing may well be 1 John 4:19–21: 'If anyone says, "I love God", yet hates his brother, he is a liar. For the one who does not love his brother whom he has seen is not able to love God whom he

---

[64]   Ibid., 227–28. According to Beutler, the claim that Deut 6:4–5 underlies John 5:41–44 is mentioned only by Josef Blank, *Das Evangelium nach Johannes*, Geistliche Schriftlesung 1b (Düsseldorf: Patmos, 1981), 52, n. 8; and Friedrich Büchsel, *Das Evangelium nach Johannes*, NTD 4 (Göttingen: Vandenhoeck & Ruprecht, 1937), 80. More recently, Michael Labahn has accepted this reading with confidence – Labahn, 'Deuteronomy', 88.

[65]   Beutler, 'Hauptgebot', 229–31.

[66]   Labahn, 'Deuteronomy', 87. He is clear that John's use of the Shema in 8:54 cannot be determined with certainty.

[67]   Beutler, 'Hauptgebot', 236.   [68]   Augenstein, *Das Liebesgebot*, 61, 66, 183–85.

has not seen. And this commandment we have from him, that the one who loves God should also love his brother.'[69] The epistle's theological and ethical vision of the Shema is embedded within the substructure of the Gospel: 'That love is the chief command of Jesus in St. John's Gospel no one need deny; but … it should probably be carefully scrutinized in the setting of Jewish understanding of the Shema.'[70]

The absence of direct scriptural citations cannot be adduced as grounds for dismissing this Gospel's intentional appropriation of the Shema. Indeed, since John is invested in demonstrating Jesus as a divine figure who comes in fulfilment of the Old Testament's overarching message and story, *he is virtually compelled to employ the Shema*. To present a deity who has appeared on the scene as scripture's fulfilment dictates a reworking of the Shema's theology of 'one'. If the 'Word was God' (1:1) and if Jesus seems to make himself 'equal with God' (5:18), then the Shema cannot be easily overlooked or disregarded by a Jewish apologist of Christ-devotion. In light of John's 'high' christology, we should expect to find him demonstrating how his presentation of Jesus' identity comports with (or redefines) the Shema.[71] So in spite of the scarceness of direct quotes, when it comes to the Gospel's theological expressions of oneness (8:41; 10:30; 17:11, 22) the fourth evangelist is drawing from the rich fund of monotheistic theology for which Deuteronomy 6:4 stands irrefutably as the most quintessential textual rendering: Ἄκουε Ἰσραήλ· κύριος ὁ θεὸς ἡμῶν κύριος εἷς ἐστιν ('Hear, O Israel: the Lord is our God, the Lord is one').

Ἕν rather than Εἷς: The Neuter Form of 'One' in John 10:30 and Chapter 17

The neuter use of 'one' is the second of three possible grounds for reservation in accepting John's reliance on Deuteronomy 6:4 for his oneness motif addressed here in this section. In the LXX rendering of

---

[69] Judith Lieu also believes the love command of the Shema is paired here in 1 John with the love of neighbour called for in Lev 19:18. See Judith M. Lieu, *I, II, & III John: A Commentary*, NTL (Louisville, KY: Westminster John Knox, 2008), 198–99.

[70] C. T. R. Hayward, ''The LORD Is One': Reflections on the Theme of Unity in John's Gospel from a Jewish Perspective', in Stuckenbruck and North, eds., *Early Jewish and Christian Monotheism*, 138–54, here at 154.

[71] Though he does not mention the Shema, Scholtissek has pointed out that John has Jesus engaging his Jewish interlocutors at precisely the points at which Jewish theological convictions clash with the Fourth Gospel's high christology. See Scholtissek, '''Ich und der Vater'''.

Deuteronomy 6:5, the word for 'one' appears in the masculine form (εἷς). Though this is the form used in the reference to God's divine oneness in John 8:41, other uses of 'one' connotative of theology in John 10 and John 17 appear in the neuter form (ἕν). Does the alteration in gender signify a departure from the Shema as a source for theological oneness?[72]

Debating the meaning of the exact parsing of oneness in John 10:30 and in chapter 17 has a long history, serving as a pivotal matter of exegesis during the Trinitarian controversies of the third and fourth centuries.[73] Monarchianists capitalized on John 10:30 in their convictions that Christ and God were to be understood as the same. Countering this position, Hippolytus, Novatian, and Tertullian saw the plural form of εἰμί ('I am', from the verbal idea 'to be') and the neuter form of εἷς as grounds for emphasizing the distinction of two persons ('we are'/ἐσμεν) sharing the same essence (ἕν).[74] Athanasius, however, could still look to John 10:30 as evidence of divine unity between Jesus and the Father in refuting Arian claims that Jesus was a created being not to be characterized as the one God.[75] After recounting the role of John 10:30 in these christological debates, T. E. Pollard admits that 'the evangelist himself was content to leave the problem in the paradox of *distinction-within-unity*, a paradox which is stated most explicitly in "I and the Father are one"'.[76]

Though the neuter use of 'one' and the plural form of εἰμί in John 10:30 proved serviceable for the trinitarian hermeneutics of later interpreters, they stand in accord with the fourth evangelist's dyadic theology. As discussed earlier in Chapter 2, both unity and plurality are constitutive of the Johannine concept of θεός. The evangelist takes considerable pains in deftly coordinating Jesus with God in such a way that they share the divine identity without one absorbing into the other. Recalling the discussion in Chapter 2, the Prologue's opening phrase 'In the beginning was the Word' emphasizes unity – the Logos seems here to be equated with Israel's Creator God. Yet the following phrase 'and the Word was with God' emphasizes plurality by drawing distinctions between the λόγος and θεός. With 'the Word was God', the emphasis on unity resumes, only to be balanced with the plurality of the following line: 'this one was in the beginning with God'. The dual dynamic of

---

[72] On the basis of this gender issue Söding remarks that the term 'one' in Jn 10:30 'ist selbstverständlich keine Identität' (Söding, 'Ich und der Vater', 197).

[73] See the detailed account provided in T. E. Pollard, 'The Exegesis of John X. 30 in the Early Trinitarian Controversies', *NTS* 3, no. 4 (1957): 334–49.

[74] See Tertullian, *Prax.*, 22, 25; Novatian, *De Trin.*, 15; Hippolytus, *Noet.*, 3.

[75] See Athanasius, *C. Ar.*, 3.   [76] Pollard, 'John X. 30', 348.

plurality and unity marking John's christological monotheism is succinctly encompassed in the title μονογενὴς θεός. Jesus is clearly identified as θεός, but he is simultaneously identifiable from God by the filial
term μονογενής. Dyadic theology places Jesus within the divine identity
while drawing certain boundary lines to prevent a fusion of the two
entities.

I review these previous observations simply to claim here that the
neuter ἕν serves the exact same purpose as the phrase μονογενὴς θεός
and as the evangelist's delicate alteration between the unity and
plurality of the Logos and God in John 1:1–2.[77] Just as we should
expect John to present Jesus in terms of the Shema because of his high
christology, so we should expect his use of the Shema's oneness
language to reflect his agenda of including Jesus within the divine
identity while maintaining a distinctiveness between Jesus and God.
The neuter rendering of εἷς is perfectly suited for such an agenda.
The Trinitarian hermeneutics of 'one' in later years need not be viewed
as fanciful appropriations of John's text for the sake of christological
convenience. The preservation of distinct 'persons' within a divine
unity honours the evangelist's vision of dyadic (and eventually triadic)
theology.

For Richard Bauckham, the neuter use of 'one' in John's Gospel
is 'a necessary adaption of language' since 'Jesus is not saying that
he and the Father are a single person, but that together they are one
God'.[78] Similarly, J. Ramsey Michaels sees very little at stake in the
gender alternation – the term 'one' has a degree of fluidity already at
work in John 10 (cf. v. 16), and there is no mistake that Jesus
is somehow including himself within the identity of Israel's 'only'
God.[79] Considering the axiomatic association of 'one' with Deuteronomy
6:4 in early Jewish theology and noting the strong hints of the Shema
in John 5:39–47 and 8:41, the Shema is still the most natural basis
for the theological oneness of John 10:30. The neuter form of 'one' is
simply a result of how the evangelist is creatively employing this
fundamental understanding of God's identity and incorporating
Jesus within it.

---

[77] Brown points out that it is odd for John to use ἕν rather than ἑνοτῆς (unity) as Ignatius
of Antioch occasionally did (*Eph.* 4:3, 14:1; et al.) – Brown, *John*, 759.

[78] Bauckham, 'Monotheism and Christology', 251. As Bauckham points out, there is no
need to be surprised that a Christian author writing around the turn of the first century would
include Jesus within the Shema since Paul did so years before John. See also Wright,
'Monotheism'.

[79] Michaels, *John*, 601.

'That they may be one, as we are one': Human Identification
with the One God?

The lack of direct scriptural citations and the use of ἕν rather than εἰς
are both unnecessary grounds for doubting the Shema as a source
for Johannine oneness. The integration of the disciples into this
oneness in John 17, however, may seem to contradict fundamental
convictions of early Jewish monotheism every bit as striking as the
inclusion of Jesus within the divine identity. If, as Appold has
pointed out, 'any self-identification with God was foreign to the
Hebrew mentality',[80] then a conceptuality of oneness in which
humans participate – that is, 'that they may be one, as we are
one' – cannot derive from the Shema.[81]

This basis for doubting the indebtedness of Johannine oneness to the
Shema is also unfounded.[82] The monotheistic oneness language of
Deuteronomy 6:4 could assume a certain degree of versatility in which
the term 'one' correlated a thing, place, or a people with the 'one' God.
This versatility of theological oneness has biblical precedence in
Jeremiah 32:37–41 (LXX, Jer. 39:37–41) where we find what Gerald
Janzen has called a 'redistribution of the terms of the *Shema*'.[83]

> See, I am going to gather them from all the lands to which
> I drove them in my anger and my wrath and in great indignation;
> I will bring them back to this place, and I will settle them in
> safety. They shall be my people, and I will be their God. I will
> give them *one* heart [καρδίαν ἑτέραν / לב אחד] and *one* way
> [ὁδὸν ἑτέραν / ודרך אחד], that they may fear me for all time, for
> their own good and the good of their children after them. I will
> make an everlasting covenant with them, never to draw back
> from doing good to them; and I will put the fear of me in their
> hearts, so that they may not turn from me. I will rejoice in doing

---

[80] Appold, *Oneness*, 174.

[81] Bauckham acknowledges that John's human integration into divine oneness has led
many interpreters to dismiss the Shema as a background text for 'one' – again, see
Bauckham, 'Problems of Monotheism', 104.

[82] In what follows I am drawing in part from my article, Andrew Byers, 'The One Body
of the Shema in 1 Corinthians: An Ecclesiology of Christological Monotheism', *NTS* 62,
no. 4 (2016): 517–32.

[83] J. Gerald Janzen, 'An Echo of the Shema in Isaiah 51.13', *JSOT* 43 (1989): 69–82,
here at 77. Janzen's purpose is not to point out ways that God's people are associated with
the oneness motif, but to argue that the oneness motif of the *Shema* can be found in the exilic
literature. His focus is primarily on Isa 51:1–3.

good to them, and I will plant them in this land in faithfulness, *with all my heart and all my soul* [ἐν πάσῃ καρδίᾳ καί ἐν πάσῃ ψυχῇ].[84]

In this passage, the Shema's language of 'all my heart and all my soul' is on God's lips, and – according to the Hebrew text – Israel will have 'one heart and one way'.[85] The theological oneness of Deuteronomy 6:4 is here applied to the social entity of Israel.[86]

Josephus' rhetoric of theological oneness was also marked at times by this versatility of correspondence: 'We have but one temple for the one God [εἷς ναὸς ἑνὸς θεοῦ] (for like ever loves like), common to all as God is common to all'.[87] The idea that 'like ever loves like' (a loose transla- tion of φίλον γὰρ ἀεὶ παντὶ τὸ ὅμοιον) seems to indicate an analogical use of divine oneness – just as God is One, that which pertains to or correlates with him can also be 'one'. Here Josephus punctuates Mosaic speech with analogical uses of the Shema's oneness: 'Let there be one holy city [πόλις . . . μία] in that place in the land of Canaan . . . And let there be one temple [νεὼς εἷς] there, and one altar [βωμὸς εἷς] . . . In no other city let there be either altar or temple; for God is one [θεὸς γὰρ εἷς], and the Hebrew race is one [γένος ἕν]'.[88] This passage is immediately followed with the injunction, 'He that blasphemes God, let him be stoned, and let him be hanged upon a tree all that day, and then let him be buried in an ignominious and obscure manner'[89] (4.202). Josephus is using Deuteronomic language in recounting that ancient scene on the plains of Moab, but his oneness theology manifests a developed and seasoned expansion in which other places, items, and even his ethnic group are included within the idea that 'the Lord is one'.[90]

Philo explains that the reason Moses banned foreigners from lead- ing God's people was due to the bond of kinship between fellow Hebrews who shared 'one citizenship [πολιτεία μία] and the same law and one God [εἷς θεός] who has taken all members of the nation

---

[84] Jer. 32:37–41, NRSV (LXX, Jer. 39:37–41), emphases added (cf. Deut 6:5 LXX). The last line of this passage indicates that the Shema is indeed in view when the term 'one' is applied to Israel.

[85] In Hebrew, the word for one is the cardinal number אחד, used for the term 'one' in the Shema. In the LXX (Jer. 39:37–41), the word translating אחד is ἕτερος not εἷς.

[86] See also the Hebrew text of Malachi 2:15 where the oneness of man and wife (אחד) is correlated to 'the One' (האחד) God. Cf. Mal 2:10.

[87] Josephus, *C. Ap.*, 2.193. Translation (slightly modified) from Josephus, *Against Apion*, ed. H. St. J. Thackery (William Heineman, 1926), 371. See also Philo, *Spec. leg.*, 1.67.

[88] Josephus, *Ant.* 4.200–201 (slightly modified from *Antiquities*, 1.571–73).

[89] Josephus, *Ant.* 4.202 (*Antiquities*, 1.573).   [90] See also Josephus, *Ant.* 5.111–12.

for his portion'.[91] Written not long after the Temple's destruction in 70 CE, the author of 2 Baruch also used this versatile range of theological oneness: 'For we are all one celebrated people, who have received one Law from the One' (48:24).[92] This social use of oneness grounded in theological oneness is also found in certain Qumran texts – according to C. T. R. Hayward, the communal self-designation *Yahad* is consciously tied to the identity of the 'one' God.[93]

This inclusive, analogical versatility of the Shema's theological oneness in early Jewish thought invalidates any dismissal of the Fourth Gospel's indebtedness to the Shema on the basis of the human identification of oneness in Jesus' prayer, 'that they may be one, as we are one' (17:22). Contrary to Appold's comment above, the language of divine oneness stemming from Deuteronomy 6:4 possessed a degree of fluidity in which 'one' was a means of expressing *social identity* as well as monotheistic convictions.[94] In the wake of Hellenization,

> it was precisely their single devotion to the One God, their abhorrence of sharing his worship with that of any other, that gave to the Jews their sense of being a unique people. That exclusive monotheism was part of the very fabric of the life within which the earliest followers of Jesus grew up, and it was no less a part of the premises with which the Pauline wing began. For them, as for the Jews in a Greek city, it served as the focus of their difference from others and signified also the basis of unity among believers.[95]

---

[91] Philo, *Spec. leg.*, 4.159 (*Works*, 107). In 2 Sam 7:22–23 the reference to God's people as 'one' stands in correspondence with God's singularity and uniqueness: 'Therefore you are great, O Lord God. For there is none like you, and there is no God besides you, according to all that we have heard with our ears. And who is like your people Israel, the one nation [גוי אחד / ἔθνος ἄλλο] on earth whom God went to redeem to be his people.'

[92] Daniel M. Gurtner, *Second Baruch: A Critical Edition of the Syriac Text, with Greek and Latin Fragments, English Translation, Introduction, and Concordances*, vol. 5, T & T Clark Jewish and Christian Texts Series (London: T & T Clark, 2009), 84–85. I am grateful to Dr Matthew Crawford for his help with the Syriac of this text.

[93] See the section 'Unity at Qumran' in Hayward, '"The LORD Is One"', 142–49.

[94] Larry W. Hurtado, 'Monotheism', *The Eerdmans Dictionary of Early Judaism*, ed. John J. Collins and Daniel C. Harlow (Grand Rapids, MI: Eerdmans, 2010), 961–64, here at 964.

[95] Wayne Meeks, *The First Urban Christians: The Social World of the Apostle Paul*, 2nd edn. (New Haven: Yale University Press, 2003), 91–92.

As this citation from Wayne Meeks makes clear, the theological oneness of the Shema was a means of *social identity construction* – Jewish communities often defined themselves on the basis of the uniqueness of God.[96] Larry Hurtado writes, 'Ancient Jewish religious belief and practice had major social consequences. The monotheistic stance of early Judaism distinguished the Jewish people religiously, and, thus, socially and contributed to their sense of being a distinctive people with a shared identity.'[97] Tan makes the same point when he writes that 'the Shema and the doctrine of monotheism were used around the time of Jesus to shore up Jewish identity and to differentiate them from other people'.[98] Along with expecting the fourth evangelist to engage with the oneness of the Shema in his bold christology, we should also expect the resulting christological monotheism to have social (and thus ecclesial) implications. In anticipation of what follows in Chapter 7, the correlation of human and divine oneness in John 17 is a theological expression of Jewish social identity. The one true God is establishing a new people: the one flock of the one true Messiah.

Chapter Summary

Christology compels theological as well as ecclesial innovation. Confronted with the Christ event and the community formed in its aftermath, John took recourse to his scriptural tradition and found theological, christological, and ecclesial utility in the oneness motif of the Shema. In this chapter I have identified – and sought to allay – concerns for scepticism towards drawing connections between the Johannine oneness motif and the Shema's foundational claim, 'YHWH is one'. Given the prevalence of this monotheistic theology of oneness in early Judaism, it would be unreasonable to view the fourth evangelist's use of 'one' as unrelated. Apprehensions arising from John's lack of direct citations of Deuteronomy 6:4–5 are insubstantial on the widely accepted grounds that John's use of the Old Testament is strongly allusive in character. Additionally, the love command bound to God's oneness is embedded within the Johannine narrative and, like the Synoptics, paired with love for others. Reservations over the neuter use of 'one' (ἕν) in John 10:30 and in chapter 17 as opposed to the masculine use of 'one' (εἷς) – as in Deuteronomy 6:4 – are also unfounded. In accordance with his dyadic

---

[96] Söding, '"Ich und der Vater"', 185–6.   [97] Hurtado, 'Monotheism', 964.

[98] Tan, 'Jesus and the Shema', 2702. Tan does not, however, explore the social/ecclesial ramifications of this observation, as pointed out by Bruno, *God Is One*, 4.

theology, the evangelist employs the language of oneness to express simultaneously a distinction between the Father and Son and their joint constitution of the divine identity.

The versatility of theological oneness language enables John to offer an 'ecclesiology of the Shema'. The new social reality created through Christ-belief and highlighted in the Gospel through the ecclesial narrative script is designated as 'one' without eviscerating the term of its theological connotations. The 'parting of the ways' that seems to underlie the Fourth Gospel embodied in some form of synagogue conflict resulted not in a disownership of prior theological commitments; this new community, rather, was to understand itself as the legitimate children of the one true God gathered into one by the one Shepherd. Ecclesial oneness, therefore, is to be understood as a theologically grounded expression of Jewish social identity reshaped by christology and offering an ecclesiology of divine association.

7

THE SHEMA, JOHN 17, AND JEWISH-CHRISTIAN IDENTITY: ONENESS IN NARRATIVE DEVELOPMENT

Having made the case that the Shema lies at the root of John's theological use of 'one', I will now sketch the narrative development of oneness within the Gospel to affirm my argument that the distressing communal crises of schism in the story (and possibly behind it on the historical plane) are to be understood as a function of Israel's one God (10:30) sending the one Davidic Ruler ('one shepherd'/εἷς ποιμήν) to renew his one people ('one flock'/μία ποίμνη). Each instance of oneness in John is treated below in relation to a patterned sequence of intertextual echoes from Deuteronomy 6:4 and Ezekiel 34 and 37. Since *every appearance of 'one' in this Gospel builds on its previous appearances and anticipates its forthcoming iterations*, the narrative ecclesiology of oneness calls for a reassessment of what may well be the Fourth Gospel's most eminent text on ecclesial identity: John 17. To be 'one' with Jesus and God is to be identified with a social entity correspondent with Israel's 'one' Lord.

Tracing the Narrative Development of 'One' in John 8–11: The Alternation between Oneness from Deuteronomy 6:4 and from Ezekiel 34 and 37

As previously observed, the oneness motif is emphatically theological when it first appears in 8:41, modifying God – 'we have one Father: God' (ἕνα πατέρα ἔχομεν τὸν θεόν). Yet in the next instance of oneness – the formula 'one flock, one shepherd' (μία ποίμνη, εἷς ποιμήν) in 10:16 – the denotations are ecclesial (flock) and christological (shepherd). Has the evangelist abandoned the theological resonances of 'one'/εἷς in 8:41 in his narrative sequence, thereby demonstrating that the oneness motif is so semantically plastic in his Gospel that it can be used to express a number of unrelated categorizations? At first glance, it may appear that the Gospel writer is haphazard in his uses of oneness, isolating the connotations of ecclesiology, christology, and theology from one another on an ad hoc basis.

Table 7.1 The Narrative Development of Johannine Oneness

Verses	Oneness Connotation	OT Text	From the Gospel Texts
8:41	Theology	Deut 6:4	The Jews: ἕνα πατέρα ἔχομεν τὸν θεόν[1]
10:16	Ecclesiology + christology	Ezek 34/37	Jesus: μία ποίμνη, εἷς ποιμήν[2]
10:30	Theology + christology	Deut 6:4 + Ezek 34/37	Jesus: ἐγὼ καὶ ὁ πατὴρ ἕν ἐσμεν[3]
11:49–52	Ecclesiology + christology	Ezek 34/37	Caiaphas: συμφέρει ὑμῖν ἵνα εἷς ἄνθρωπος ἀποθάνη Narrator: ἵνα... τὰ τέκνα τοῦ θεοῦ... συναγάγη εἰς ἕν[4]
17:11, 21–23	Theology + christology + ecclesiology	Deut 6:4 + Ezek 34/37	Jesus: ἵνα ὦσιν ἕν καθὼς ἡμεῖς ἕν[5]

Instead, the evangelist is methodically developing this motif of oneness through creative exegesis of his primary oneness texts from Israel's scriptures, most importantly Deuteronomy 6:4 and Ezekiel 34 and 37. It is not that these texts are directly cited or the only texts within the evangelist's hermeneutical range for oneness. These passages, however, do serve collectively as a foundational scriptural reserve for his purposes. As seen in the discussion of the Shepherd Discourse in Chapter 5, oneness in the Ezekiel passages is both a) *messianic* and b) *national*, becoming christological and ecclesial, respectively, in their textual collocation in the Gospel story. John gradually pressures an integration of these ecclesial and christological meanings into the Shema's theological concept of oneness through a process of intertextual interplay in the narrative sequence. The oneness motif develops cumulatively in John 8–11 along this hermeneutical programme. What John means by 'one' cannot be properly understood without attending to this narrative process and taking into account the intertextual dynamics attached to each stage of its development.

Table 7.1 portrays how in John 8–11 the evangelist underscores the theological, christological, and ecclesial dimensions of oneness by

---

[1] 'We have one Father: God.'   [2] 'One flock, one shepherd'.

[3] 'I and the Father are one.'

[4] Caiaphas: 'It is to your advantage that one man die'; Narrator: 'In order that ... the children of God ... may be gathered into one'.

[5] 'In order that they may be one as we are one'.

alternately drawing from both Deuteronomy 6:4 and Ezekiel 34 and 37. Theology is indeed the prominent connotation in 8:41, with christology and ecclesiology featuring in the oneness formula of 10:16. In the controversial claim of 10:30, oneness expands to comprise both christology and theology. The collocation of christology and ecclesiology reappears in John 11. In the final appearance of the oneness motif in John 17, the evangelist *climactically binds all those dimensions together* in a thematic coup d'état.

John 8:41 | Theological Oneness from the Shema

As argued in the preceding chapter, the Johannine oneness motif derives from the Shema when it first appears in 8:41. The Jews have already claimed Abraham as their father in 8:39 (see also 8:33), so to use the term 'one' in the phrase ἕνα πατέρα ἔχομεν τὸν θεόν in 8:41 seems out of place if a non-theological numerical use is intended (since numerically these Jews would have now laid claim to *two* fathers, not 'one'). The use of εἷς is superfluous here unless Jesus' interlocutors are making a direct reference to the one God of the Shema[6] (note the similar use of the Shema in Malachi 2:10 – 'Did not one God [θεὸς εἷς] create you? Do you not have one Father [πατὴρ εἷς]?'[7]).

In 8:42, Jesus immediately challenges the Jews' filial association with the one God by pointing out their lack of love; and love is the corollary of God's oneness in Deuteronomy 6:5 – 'love YHWH your God with all your heart, and with all your soul, and with all your might'. John has already paired the love command with the phrase 'the only God' (ὁ μόνος θεός) in 5:41–44, language conceptually parallel with Deuteronomy 6:4–5.[8] If these Jews are claiming the paternity of the one God, then they should love Jesus who, as will become clear in John 10:30, shares in the divine oneness and therefore deserves the same devotion of love:[9]

---

[6] Scholars seeing the Shema in 8:41 include Bauckham, 'Problems of Monotheism', 104; Lincoln, *John*, 272; Herman Ridderbos, *The Gospel of John: A Theological Commentary*, trans. John Vriend (Grand Rapids, MI: Eerdmans, 1997), 313. Though he does not use the term 'Shema', Michaels links the use of 'one' in 8:41 to Jewish monotheism and cites 1 Cor 8:6 as a comparable example of this instance of oneness (Michaels, *John*, 515).

[7] Oneness language is paired with God's fatherhood elsewhere in the NT: Mt 23:8–10; Eph 4:6; 1 Cor 8:6; and Heb 2:11.

[8] See Chapter 6, pp. 117–21, where I cited Augenstein, *Das Liebesgebot*, 60–61, and Beutler, 'Hauptgebot', 226–9.

[9] Andrew Lincoln draws a connection between the Shema and the Jews' statement that they have not been born of πορνεία (Lincoln, *John*, 272). In their scriptures, Israel's claim

'If God were your Father, you would love me, for I came from God and I am here' (8:42). Their lack of love for Jesus nullifies the Jews' appeal to God's fatherhood.[10] In other words, authentic affiliation with the one God is demonstrated by loving Jesus as God's divine agent in whom he has the right to share obeisance. So in John 8, the initial appearance of 'one' derives from the Shema. The term is conceptually grounded from the start in theological oneness (with hints of christological participation within that oneness latently present).

When the oneness motif is introduced here,[11] its appearance is entirely fitting within a Jewish conceptual framework. Though appearing in the midst of a charged controversy, there is nothing controversial about its theological use. The claim 'we have one Father: God' is voiced by Jews who would be quite at home associating 'one' with the divine identity. This reference to the one God on the lips of the Jewish antagonists is entirely harmonious with the monotheistic sensibilities of their scriptural traditions. The reason they take recourse to oneness is to validate before Jesus their membership in the household of the 'one' true God. They are not born from multiple fathers through sexual immorality (πορνεία), and they are not merely the genetic offspring of Abraham; indeed, they feel

---

to God's paternity was nullified by idolatry, a practice metaphorically cast as sexual immorality (Jer 3:1–3; Ezek 16:28–41; Hos 1:2; 2:4–6, LXX; in the Hosea passages, note the twice-used phrase τέκνα πορνείας (see also Wis 14:12). The defensive avowal in 8:41 that ἡμεῖς ἐκ πορνείας οὐ γεγεννήμεθα but are legitimately children of the ἕνα πατέρα is an assertion of identity status: these Jews are staunch monotheists worshipping only one God and therefore entitled to be recognized as his people.

[10] Augenstein sees here a divorce between the two dimensions of the love command: love of God (Deut 6:4f) and love of neighbour (Lev 19:17f). For him, the Jew's self-identification with God is nullified in this case not because they fail to love Jesus as a participant within the divine identity, but because of their failure to love Jesus as a neighbour. See Augenstein, *Das Liebesgebot*, 61–62.

[11] Though I am attributing 8:41 with the introduction of the oneness motif, I acknowledge that the actual term εἷς has already appeared a number of times in the Gospel (Jn 1:3, 40; 3:27; 6:8, 22, 70; 7:21, 50; 8:9; 9:25; cf. also 12:2, 4, 12:21, 23; 18:14, 22, 26, 39; 19:34; 20:1, 7, 12, 19, 24; 21:25). John's use of lexemes can certainly be suggestive of resonances that extend beyond the standard lexical definitions; and there are a few instances when εἷς may connote such an extension (as in Jn 1:3 and 9:25). Even so, it would be hard to make a solid case that oneness as a motif begins earlier than 8:41. In his comparative study of oneness in Ephesians and John's Gospel, Ulrich Heckel acknowledges soundings of oneness throughout the Gospel, but does not believe the theme is formally broached until John 10 – Ulrich Heckel, 'Die Einheit der Kirche im Johannesevangelium und im Epheserbrief: ein Vergleich der ekklesiologischen Strukturen', in *Kontexte des Johannesevangelium: Das vierte Evangelium in religions- und traditionsgeschichtlicher Perspektive*, ed. Jörg Frey and Udo Schnelle, WUNT 175 (Tübingen: Mohr Siebeck, 2004), 614.

within their rights to make an even higher appeal, claiming to be the
legitimate children of God himself, the heavenly Patriarch of their
historic family. The Jews' self-identification with their divine father
indicates that the evangelist's understanding of theological oneness
quite naturally derives from the standard Jewish understanding of oneness most classically formulated in Deuteronomy 6:4.

Mark Appold believes that John 8:41 is one of the only passages in the
Fourth Gospel in which εἷς has 'theological implications'; yet 8:41 is not
merited the status of a oneness passage in his detailed monograph. This is
due to his explicit rejection of Jewish monotheism as a basis for Johannine
oneness. Since 'the idea of self-identification with God was foreign to the
Hebrew mentality' (quoted earlier in Chapter 6), then 'the language of
oneness and reciprocity, as evidenced in the Gnostic formulae and in the
Johannine expressions, *does not at all develop within the framework of
Hebrew thought*'.[12] So even though Appold finds connotations of the one
God of Israel in 8:41, this particular use of oneness is 'extraneous to the
Johannine oneness complex since the evangelist shows no interest in using
the oneness term to express the monotheistic aspect of faith'.[13] His
hermeneutical lenses for reading all the Johannine oneness passages are
established by John 17, where believers become one with Jesus and God;
this inclusivity of oneness compels Appold to rule out the Old Testament
and early Jewish theology as foundational influences for each instance of
the theme throughout the Gospel. As discussed in Chapter 6, it is this
(supposed) incompatibility of human participation in Jewish ideas of
oneness that drives him to find 'the language of Gnostic phenomenology'
as the motif's 'closest parallel'.[14] But there is no need to look to Gnostic
(or proto-Gnostic) uses of 'one' when early Jewish speakers such as Jesus'
interlocutors could refer quite naturally to God as their 'one' father. In not
allowing the sequential process of narrative development to guide his
thinking about John's oneness motif, Appold misses an uncontroversial
reference to the theological oneness of the Shema in John 8:41.

There are two more related points to be made here before proceeding to
the oneness formulae in John 10. First, as a function of the ecclesial narrative
script, *the oneness motif ignites controversy in the Fourth Gospel.*[15] Though
the appeal to theological oneness in 8:41 is harmonious with Jewish
monotheistic sensibilities, it is discordant with Jesus' *ecclesial* sensibilities –
the Jews cannot claim social membership within the divine family if they do

---

[12] Appold, *Oneness*, 174 (emphases added). See also 162; 174–75; 191–92; 243–45;
259–60.
[13] Ibid., 13, n. 1.   [14] Ibid., 190.   [15] Barton, ''Community', 290–4.

not love the Son who shares the divine identity. This is the immediate context of the polemical remark: 'you are out of your father the devil' (ὑμεῖς ἐκ τοῦ πατρὸς τοῦ διαβόλου ἐστέ – 8:44). From its first instance in the Gospel narrative, the Johannine oneness motif is divisive.

A second point is that the theological use of oneness in 8:41 serves the sociological (and ecclesial) function of redefining social groups. It may seem ironic that a term normally associated with unity should be so volatile. Stephen Barton offers some clarity:

> The irony is that the discourse of unity – precisely because it is always embedded in particular cultures and sub-cultures and is always the expression of particular interests – is at one and the same time a means of articulating *difference*. As a way of saying 'yes' to one way of seeing the world, it is necessarily also a way of saying 'no' to other ways. As a way of saying who 'we' are and to whom 'we' belong in unity, it is also a way of saying who 'they' are and from whom we are (in unity!) separating.[16]

Barton expands on this observation with the assertion that 'claims about unity are a way of establishing *boundaries* ... The discourse of unity is an ordering discourse: it helps to define not only those outsiders with whom we are not "one" but also what it means to be a member of those who claim to be united together as "one".'[17] In sum, 'unity is invariably unity *up to a point*'.[18] Though I prefer to use the term 'oneness' over 'unity' to maintain the grounding theological connotations drawn from Deuteronomy 6:4, it is important to recognize that the Jews' appeal to their 'one' Father is to be understood as a sociological move in keeping with the ecclesial narrative script of resocialization or, as in this case, social re-entrenchment.

John 10:16 | Ecclesial and Christological Oneness from Ezekiel 34 and 37

When oneness makes a reappearance in John 10:16 the hermeneutics of 'one' take on a new dimension as the evangelists draws from a different set of scriptural texts. In the formula 'one flock, one shepherd' (μία ποίμνη, εἷς ποιμήν), the Old Testament pretexts emphasize *messianic* oneness and *national* oneness, rather than *theological* oneness as in Deuteronomy 6:4 (and in Malachi 2:10), though John is still operating within standard Jewish categorizations. As in 8:41, there is little dispute

---

[16] Barton, 'Unity', 235.   [17] Ibid.   [18] Ibid.

in regard to the conceptual use of 'one' in this pastoral expression of the one flock and one shepherd. Though a schism/σχίσμα soon results 'on account of these words' (διὰ τοὺς λόγους τούτους) in 10:19, the 'words' causing offence are not the words of the oneness formula, per se; what generates the ire and resentment is the messianic application of 'these words' to Jesus and their implied call for resocialization into a new communal realm (an application that is ecclesial[19]) associated with his messianic identity.

That the wording of the oneness formula in 10:16 comes out of Ezekiel is unmistakable.[20] In Chapter 5 (pages 98–101) I referenced Ezekial 34:23 where God promised to his dispersed people, struggling to define and consolidate their identity, that he would raise up 'one shepherd' (ποιμένα ἕνα), a phrase referring to a Davidic, and hence messianic, king (see Table 7.2). In Ezekiel 37, the oneness of this royal figure is coordinated with the reunification and restoration of the nation. After tasking the prophet with the symbolic act of piecing two rods together to form 'one rod' (ῥάβδον μίαν), God declares his intentions to gather his people from the midst of the nations ('I will gather them'/συνάξω αὐτούς) and lead them ('I will bring them into'/εἰσάξω αὐτούς) into the land of Israel, making them one nation.[21] As previously discussed, this divine programme of pastorally leading out and bringing in is strikingly echoed in John's Shepherd Discourse. In Ezekiel 37, over this 'one nation' (ἔθνος ἕν) will be 'one ruler' (ἄρχων εἷς), the same Davidic ruler referred to in Ezekiel 34. With the reign of this 'one shepherd' (ποιμὴν εἷς – Ezek 37:24, LXX) established, the one people of God will be reconstituted – 'I will be God to them, and they will be my people' (καὶ ἔσομαι αὐτοῖς θεός, καὶ αὐτοί μου ἔσονται λαός – Ezek 37:27, LXX).

The points to be observed here in this instance of the oneness motif's gradual development are that 1) the evangelist's use of 'one' is once again a direct accomplice in the ecclesial narrative script, inciting an immediate social divide; and 2) the formula in 10:16 is an uncontroversial use of oneness drawn from Israel's Scriptures, *except that* it is christologically applied to Jesus and to his own social (that is, ecclesial) activity in gathering and reconfiguring the people of God.

---

[19] I appreciate Heckel's comment that the one flock ('die eine Herde') is John's paraphrase ('Umschreibung') for the missing term ἐκκλησία – Heckel, 'Die Einheit der Kirche', 614.

[20] See the recent study on 10:16 offered by Richard B. Hays in *Echoes of Scripture*, 340–43.

[21] LXX, Ezek 37:21–22.

Table 7.2 Intertextuality between Ezekiel 34/37 and the Johannine Shepherd Discourse

John 10	Ezekiel 34, 37 (LXX)
νομὴν εὑρήσει/he will find pasture (10:9)	ἐν νομῇ ἀγαθῇ βοσκήσω αὐτούς/in good pasture I will feed them (34:14)
ἐκ τῆς χειρός μοῦ /out of my hand (10:28)	ἐκ τῶν χειρῶν αὐτῶν/out of their hands (34:10)
μία ποίμνη/one flock (10:16)	ἔθνος ἕν/one nation (37:22)
	ῥάβδον μίαν/one rod (37:17, 19)
εἷς ποιμήν/one shepherd (10:16)	ποιμένα ἕνα/one shepherd (34:23)
	ποιμήν εἷς/one shepherd (37:24)
	ἄρχων εἷς/one ruler (37:22)
καὶ ἐξάγει αὐτά/and he leads them out (10:3)	καί ἐξάξω αὐτούς ... καί εἰσάξω αὐτούς/and I will lead them out ... and I will bring them in (34:13)
εἰσελεύσεται καί ἐξελεύσεται/he will go in and come out (10:9)	
ὅταν τά ἴδια πάντα ἐκβάλῃ/whenever he casts out his own (10:4)	ἀπελάσω[a] αὐτά ἀπὸ παντὸς τόπου/I will expel them from every place (34:12)
ἐάν τις εἰσέλθῃ σωθήσεται/if anyone may enter, he will be saved (10:9)	καὶ σώσω τὰ πρόβατά μου/and I will save my sheep (34:22)
σκορπίζω/to scatter (10:12)	διαχωρίζω/to separate (34:12), διασπείρω/to scatter abroad (34:5)

[a] Ἀπελαύνω and ἐκβάλω can both refer to expelling or driving out.

John 10:30 | Theological Oneness from the Shema

The next instance of oneness results not in a schism/σχίσμα but in an attempted execution. Tensions reach an apex in 10:30 when Jesus' self-identification with the one Davidic king expands to include a self-identification with the one God of Israel: ἐγὼ καὶ ὁ πατὴρ ἕν ἐσμεν ('I and the Father are one'). As we have seen, the idea of national/communal oneness affiliated with 'one' messianic figure has warrant on the basis of Ezekiel. The pairing of communal formation (ecclesiology) with christology under the rubric of 'one' is an appropriate use of oneness within a Jewish scriptural framework when Ezekiel 34 and 37 are understood as the exegetical background, even if the social implications and the direct messianic application to Jesus in 10:16 prove collectively divisive. But pairing a 'oneness christology' with the 'oneness theology' of Jewish monotheism has no warrant in the Shema and Jesus' statement is instantly recognized as blasphemous and punishable by stoning: ἐβάστασαν πάλιν λίθους οἱ Ἰουδαῖοι ἵνα λιθάσωσιν αὐτόν ('the Jews again took up stones in order that they might stone him').

By pairing christology with theology within the semantic and conceptual range of ἕν (one) in John 10:30, the evangelist ceases operating within the standard scriptural parameters of oneness.[22] This terminology of εἷς is appropriate for messianic and nationalistic discourse, as in Ezekiel 34 and 37. It is also suitable for identifying God, as in Deuteronomy 6:4. John has alternately employed both of these uses drawing from these respective texts. In 10:30 the process of fusing the connotations of oneness begins (though it was intimated in 8:41). So over the course of its narrative development, oneness is becoming increasingly *open* and *social*.[23] The moment Jesus correlates messianic and national oneness with the theological oneness of the Shema, his rhetoric becomes not just controversial but intolerable. It could be said that the oneness motif of Ezekiel 34 and 37 is deemed incompatible with the oneness motif of Deuteronomy 6:4 when applied to Jesus. The Jews will not embrace these porous hermeneutics of 'one'.

The theme's multivalence, however, is entirely sensible within the dyadic theology of John's Gospel and its implications for ecclesiology: Jesus cannot be recognized as Messiah/Christ (εἷς ποιμήν/one shepherd) without also being directly identified with God (ἐγὼ καὶ ὁ πατὴρ ἕν ἐσμεν/I and the Father are one), a correlation that compels a reconceptualization of God's people (μία ποίμνη/one flock). The identity and work of Jesus pressures the integration of these varied models of oneness.

The leap from less controversial uses of oneness to an explicit inclusion of christology within the theological oneness of the Shema is not arbitrarily presented in John 10. This is a move anticipated within the immediate narrative context because the Gospel author does more in the Shepherd Discourse than identify the Jewish leaders with the corrupt shepherds of Israel's past, new believers with the abused and scattered sheep, and Jesus with both a new Joshua and a new Davidic king. In his christological rereading of Ezekiel's shepherd oracles in John 10, *the evangelist identifies Jesus with God well before verse 30*.[24] He does this in at least two ways: through the christological 'I am/ ἐγώ εἰμι'

---

[22] Richard Bauckham on John 10:30: 'It is in the portrayal of this intra-divine relationship that John's christology steps outside the Jewish monotheistic definition of the unique identity of the one God' (Bauckham, 'Problems of Monotheism', 106).

[23] We will see later in Chapter 9 that the openness and porosity is limited. Within Johannine oneness are carefully demarcated boundaries.

[24] This observation is also made by Macaskill, *Union*, 261.

statements, and through the reciprocal relationship between Jesus' 'hand' and the 'hand' of the father.

The ἐγώ εἰμι formula is spoken by God three times in the Ezekiel passages (34:15, 20; 37:28) and four times by Jesus in John 10 (vv. 7, 9, 11, 14). In the former set of texts, God claims that he himself will become Israel's Shepherd (Ezekiel 34:11–16) even though he will also appoint the Davidic king as the 'one shepherd' (Ezekiel 34:23). In John's Shepherd Discourse we find a merging of the oneness concepts found in the Shema and Ezekiel as Jesus conflates these two distinct shepherd roles and assumes them both. This composite role is clear when reading ἐγώ εἰμι ὁ ποιμὴν ὁ καλός/'I am the good shepherd' (10:11, 14) and μία ποίμνη, εἷς ποιμήν/'one flock, one shepherd' (10:16) in their sequential connections – Jesus simultaneously appropriates the messianic role of the new Davidic ruler while also laying claim to the divine identity with his 'I am' statements. Since Jesus' claim in John 8:58, πρὶν Ἀβραὰμ γενέσθαι ἐγὼ εἰμί ('before Abraham was, I am'), the Johannine 'I am' phrase has become theologically freighted within the Gospel.[25] So whereas the oneness formula in 10:16 echoes Ezekiel's description of the *Davidic* shepherd (cf. 34:23; 37:22, 24), the predicated ἐγώ εἰμι statement is suggestive of Jesus' co-identification with Ezekiel's description of the *divine* shepherd. Once again, christology and theology cannot be divorced in this Gospel; and it is in response to whether or not he is the Christ that Jesus identifies himself as 'one' with God (εἰ σὺ εἶ ὁ χριστός, εἰπὲ ἡμῖν παρρησίᾳ/'if you are the Christ, tell us plainly' – 10:24).

Building on these theological associations, the evangelist has Jesus reaffirm in 10:28 his power to give eternal life to the sheep (the giving of life being the task and prerogative of God – John 5:21, 26; 6:57). He also figuratively parallels his own hand with God's hand in 10:28–29:[26] καὶ οὐχ ἁρπάσει τις αὐτά ἐκ τῆς χειρός μου. ὁ πατήρ μου ὃ δέδωκέν μοι πάντων μεῖζόν ἐστιν, και οὐδεὶς δύναται ἁρπάζειν ἐκ τῆς χειρός τοῦ πατρός.[27] The portrayal of God as a Shepherd with an unassailable,

[25] See the discussion in David Mark Ball, *'I Am' In John's Gospel: Literary Function, Background and Theological Implications*, JSNTSup 124 (Sheffield: Sheffield Academic, 1996), 195–98.

[26] Brown, *John*, 407.

[27] 'And no one will snatch them out of my hand. What my Father has given me is greater than all things, and no one is able to snatch it out of the hand of the Father.' I am choosing here with NA27 the neuter relative pronoun ὅ (rather than ὅς or ὁ) along with the neuter adjective μεῖζον (rather than the masculine μείζων). In this reading of the text-critical options, it is that which the Father has given to Jesus that is greatest, rather than the Father himself. See the discussion in Michaels, *John*, 599–601.

protective grasp is strongly rooted in monotheistic texts like
Deuteronomy 32:39 and Isaiah 43:13:[28]

ἴδετε ἴδετε ὅτι ἐγώ εἰμι,
καί οὐχ ἔστιν θεὸς πλὴν ἐμοῦ·
ἐγὼ ἀποκτενῶ καὶ ζῆν ποιήσω,
πατάξω κἀγὼ ἰάσομαι,
καί οὐκ ἔστιν ὃς ἐξελεῖται ἐκ τῶν χειρῶν μου (Deut 32:39).[29]

καὶ οὐκ ἔστιν ὁ ἐκ τῶν χειρῶν μου ἐξαιρούμενος· ποιήσω, καὶ
τίς ἀποστρέψει αὐτό (Isa 43:13).[30]

In the 'syllogism'[31] of God's hand and Jesus' hand, the evangelist is
coordinating the identity of Jesus with the divine identity of God, the
great Shepherd. Along with the 'I am' statements, this association anticipates in the flow of John 10 the climactic statement ἐγὼ καὶ ὁ πατὴρ ἕν
ἐσμεν ('I and the Father are one').

Questions are raised concerning the nature and scope of this theological oneness. Is it a functional oneness of 'power and operation',[32] an
ethical or moral unity,[33] a oneness in deed/action (*'Handlungseinheit'*),[34]
a oneness of sending,[35] or simply 'the agreement he has with the
Father'?[36] Is something more metaphysical or ontological at work?[37]

[28] See also Ps 95:7 (LXX 94:7). Hoskyns sees Isa 43:13 (along with Isa 49:2 and Wis 3:1) at work but does not mention Ps 94 (Hoskyns, *The Fourth Gospel*, 388). Keener references Ps 94 and Wis 3:1, but does not mention others (Keener, *John*, 825). Andreas Köstenberger references Isa 43:13 and Wis 3:1, but also points to possible connections in Ezekiel 37:15–19 where the rods representing Judah and Ephraim respectively become 'one rod' (ῥάβδον μίαν) 'in your hand' (ἐν τῇ χειρί σου) – Köstenberger, *John*, 312. See also Ezek 37:19 – ῥάβδον μίαν ἐν τῇ χειρὶ Ιουδα.
[29] 'Look, look, that I am / and there is no God except me / I will kill and I will make alive / I will wound and I will heal / And there is no one who can take out of my hand'. The concept that God gives life (ζῆν ποιήσω) is found in Jn 10:28 (5:21, 26; 6:57), and the ἐγὼ εἰμι statement certainly fits the wider context of ch. 10. That God gives life (ζῆν ποιήσω) and heals (ἰάσομαι) is certainly demonstrated in the narrative about Jesus in the resurrection of Lazarus and in the healing of the blind man, respectively.
[30] 'And there is not the one who can take out of my hands; I act, and who can turn it away?'
[31] Michaels, *John*, 600.   [32] Brown, *John*, 412; Lincoln, *John*, 306.
[33] Barnabus Lindars, *The Gospel of John*, NCB (London: Oliphants, 1972), 370–71.
[34] Heckel, 'Die Einheit der Kirche', 615–16 and Scholtissek, '"Ich und Der Vater"', 337.
[35] Paul W. Meyer, '"The Father": The Presentation of God in the Fourth Gospel', in *Exploring the Gospel of John: In Honor of D. Moody Smith*, ed. R. Alan Culpepper and C. Clifton Black (Louisville, KY: Westminster John Knox, 1996), 255–73, here at 261–62.
[36] Hoskyns, *The Fourth Gospel*, 389.
[37] A concise discussion on the functional and ontological dimensions of oneness in 10:30 is provided by Carson, *John*, 394–95. See also Ridderbos, *John*, 371.

These varied means of labelling bleed together when the Shema is recognized as the basis for the oneness formula in 10:30. Richard Bauckham's language of 'divine identity' used throughout this study is, in my view, the most helpful means of expressing the dyadic theology presented in John 10:30. Because Jesus shares the identity of the one God of Israel, he also shares in divine power, will, mission, ethical vision, and works.

In sum, in John 10:30 the evangelist transitions from the national and messianic oneness of Ezekiel 34 and 37 back to the theological oneness language of Deuteronomy 6:4 first broached in John 8:41. This alternation marks a critical point in the evangelist's meticulous development of the oneness motif. The theological resonances of oneness in 8:41 and the christological and ecclesial resonances of oneness in 10:16 could stand on their own within the narrative as related but ultimately quite different models of oneness drawn from two different biblical texts. Yet what we find in 10:30 is that John carefully coordinates the 'I am' statements along with the oneness motif to justify his process of coordinating the theological and christological connotations of oneness.

John 11:47–53 | Ecclesial and Christological Oneness from Ezekiel 34 and 37

In the final instance of oneness in John 8–11, the connotations alternate once again with a shift from the theological oneness of the Shema back to the combined ecclesial and christological oneness drawn from Ezekiel 34 and 37. In the immediate narrative context, the potential import of Lazarus' recent resurrection is understood by the Jewish leadership as disastrous: all the people will end up believing in Jesus and then 'the Romans will come and take away from us both our place [τὸν τόπον] and our nation [τὸ ἔθνος]' (11:48). The urgency of this collective awareness propels the Sanhedrin into high alert and their plans for taking the emergency measure of executing Jesus are formalized. Caiaphas, high priest and 'one' of the Sanhedrin, reports in 11:50 the prophecy that one (εἷς) man is to die a death that, as it is explained in 11:52, will not only spare the nation, but will also gather into one (ἕν) the dispersed 'children of God/τέκνα τοῦ θεοῦ'. The language of the prophetic statement and the evangelist's accompanying commentary recall the Prologue and, most prominently, the Shepherd Discourse – the coinciding of an individual, christological 'one' and a corporate, ecclesial 'one' echoes the oneness formula of 10:16 (μία ποίμνη, εἷς ποιμήν/'one flock, one shepherd') and its background in Ezekiel 34 and 37.

In John's christological (and ecclesial) expansions on these prophetic passages, the ultimate means by which the Shepherd establishes a new community is through his own death (10:11). Jesus repeatedly described himself in the Shepherd Discourse as one who would give his own life on behalf of (ὑπέρ) his sheep (10:11, 15; cf. vv. 17–18). The Sanhedrin now assumes agency for that death, and the beneficiaries of Jesus' sacrifice are identified in 11:47–53 in communal terms: the 'people' (λαός) and the 'nation' (ἔθνος). In the narrative's sequential unfolding it seems clear that the 'sheep' of ch. 10 and the 'children of God' in the Prologue are one and the same.[38] The 'other sheep that do not belong to this fold' (10:16), who will become united with the one flock under the one Shepherd, would naturally be explained as the 'dispersed children of God' of 11:52.

The prophecies of both Caiaphas and Ezekiel express the same divine concern that the scattered people of God be united. For Ezekiel, the flock (ποίμνη) is not only scattered and dispersed (διασπείρω – 34:5–6; διαχωρίζω – 34:12), but the remnant still attached to their geographical domain is split into two nations: Judah and Ephraim. Ezekiel's prophecy offers the same solution as Caiaphas' prophecy, that of 'one' figure who will unite and gather these dispersed and divided into one. The pertinent text is worth revisiting here:

> Thus says the Lord God: Behold I will take the entire house of Israel out of the midst of the nations [ἐκ μέσου τῶν ἐθνῶν] into which they entered, and will gather them [συνάξω αὐτούς] from all sides, and bring them [εἰσάξω αὐτούς] to the land of Israel. I will make them one nation [ἔθνος ἕν] in my land, on the mountains of Israel; and one ruler [ἄρχων εἷς] shall be over them all. They will never again be two nations, and they will never again be split into two kingdoms... They will be my people [λαόν], and I the Lord will be their God. My servant David will be the ruler in their midst; and he will be one shepherd [ποιμήν εἷς] over all (from Ezek 37:21–24, LXX; my translation).

The death of this one shepherd – identified with Jesus – is one of the many unique features of the Johannine hermeneutics of 'one'. With its imminence now formalized by the Sanhedrin, Jesus departs to the geographical fringes. Once more the oneness motif intensifies division (and foreshadows death).

---

[38] Michaels, *John*, 654.

The painful reality of God's people being scattered abroad and the audacious hope of an ingathering are found throughout biblical and early Jewish texts.[39] In this final use of oneness before John 17, the evangelist is drawing on the long-standing tradition in Israel's heritage of dispersal and hopeful regathering, a poignant motif rife with pathos and vividly depicted in the Ezekiel texts on which he has been heavily relying. The ecclesial vision being cast, however, is unbound to a physical place (τόπος) and disentangled from Jewish nationalism. As the new temple (John 2:14–21), Jesus is becoming the new divine place, the new 'locus of God's presence with his people',[40] a people who are now to be understood not so much in nationalistic or genetic terms (τό ἔθνος) but in terms of oneness and family kinship (τέκνα τοῦ θεοῦ). The one Shepherd of the one God is gathering together their one people.

Summary: Narrative Development of Oneness in John 8–11

The oneness motif cannot be abstracted from its embedded location within the Gospel narrative. I have made the case above that John consciously develops this theme over the consecutive unfolding of his storied presentation of Jesus. Every instance of oneness builds on its former use and anticipates its forthcoming appearances. Neglecting this cumulative development leads to misguided conclusions about oneness that downplay or neglect the multivalent connotations of theology, christology, and ecclesiology. These dimensions are attached to the term 'one' by an intertextual process of alternating between and eventually integrating the meanings of 'one' in two sets of scriptural pretexts. In these Johannine hermeneutics of 'one', the evangelist shifts between the oneness theology of the Shema and the national (and thus ecclesial) and messianic (and thus christological) oneness of Ezekiel 34 and 37. In order to express Jesus' identity and the identity of those resocialized around him, the evangelist expands the theological parameters of the Shema's oneness to include Ezekiel's messianic language of the 'one' Davidic ruler as well as the nationalistic language of the reconstituted people of God. Oneness is a fluid theme – both *open* and *social* – and is serviceable for both dyadic theology and ecclesiology.

---

[39] See, e.g., Isa 11:12; 43:5; 60:4; Jer 23:2; 31:8–11; Ezek 34:12, 16; Mic 2:12; *Ps. Sol* 8:34; 4 Ezra 13:8, 47; cf. also Philo, *Praem.*, 163–72; Tob 14:4–5; 2 Macc. 1.27; 2.7, 18. In spite of this evidence, Mark Appold denies a Jewish background for the oneness motif in John 11, pointing instead to the mystery religions and Gnostic sects (Appold, *Oneness*, 243–44).

[40] Keener, *John*, 527.

Jesus Prays the Shema: Oneness as Social Identity Construction in John 17

Jesus' prayer at the end of the Farewell Discourse has generated a range of ecclesiological interpretations in modern biblical scholarship. When it was assumed that the fourth evangelist was writing from a more Hellenistic milieu, the prayer for oneness was sometimes understood as a mystical absorption into divinity.[41] This idea of oneness still has residual impact today,[42] even though it runs roughshod over the explicitly Jewish nature of John's narrative development of oneness, a development that appreciably draws from pertinent texts in Israel's scriptures.[43] Others have minimized any mystical elements of oneness and stressed the believers' unity of will or a functional unity of mission with the Father and Son.[44] Another influential paradigm understands Jesus' prayer for oneness as a call to social harmony for a Johannine community whose internal cohesion is threatened with schism.[45] The ecumenical movement, of course, has taken this prayer for internal harmony and issued a global call for Christian unity within and among existing church traditions.[46]

---

[41] Whereas most commentators today identify the genre of the prayer as a Jewish 'testament', Bultmann pointed to the prayer of the departing Messenger in Gnostic literature as a suitable comparison for John 17. The oneness is therefore a heavenly, divine unity, and thus not of the sort expressed in church creeds or institutional structures (Bultmann, *John*, 489). Käsemann believes that it is in this prayer for unity that 'one perceives most clearly John's naïve Docetism which extends to his ecclesiology also'. The integration of believers into the unity of Father and Son 'must be called gnosticizing' (Käsemann, *Testament*, 68–71).

[42] Note the regular citation of Appold's monograph (Appold, *Oneness)* in the commentaries, in spite of his conclusions that Gnostic spirituality lies at the heart of Johannine concepts of oneness. Though reading Gnosticism in the Gospel of John has fallen largely out of fashion, one of the most extensive monographs on John 17 has reinforced this Gnostic conceptuality of oneness, namely Ferreira, *Johannine Ecclesiology,*.

[43] This is not to say, however, that early Judaism was a monolithic phenomenon sealed off from any Gnostic (or proto-gnostic) ideas. For the confluence of gnostic thought patterns and early Jewish thinking, see John C. Reeves, 'Gnosticism', in *The Eerdmans Dictionary of Early Judaism*, ed. John J. Collins and Daniel C. Harlow (Grand Rapids, MI: Eerdmans, 2010), 678–81.

[44] Protestant scholars seem less keen on participatory dimensions of oneness; see, e.g., Ridderbos, *John*, 563. Catholic scholars, on the other hand, seem to be more likely to accept a Christian unity that derives from some form of participatory union with God – e.g., Schnackenburg, *John*, 3:192–93.

[45] E.g., Heckel, 'Die Einheit der Kirche', 617, and David L. Mealand, 'The Language of Mystical Union in the Johannine Writings', *DRev* 95 (1977): 19–34, here at 21, 32.

[46] For a critique of ecumenical and evangelistic readings of John 17, see Paul S. Minear, 'Evangelism, Ecumenism, and John Seventeen', *ThTo* 35, no. 1 (1978): 5–13.

This complex history of diverse interpretations notwithstanding, by the time Jesus prays 'that they may be one, as we are one' in John 17:22, the concept of oneness has already undergone the careful, complex development within the Gospel's sequence just discussed. Approaches that understand 'one' as signifying a unity of social harmony or a unity of function or mission *do not sufficiently take this prior narrative development into interpretative account.* Because oneness formulae are often isolated from their complementary iterations elsewhere in the Gospel, a narrative disjuncture has been unwittingly erected between the use of 'one' in Jesus' climactic prayer and in its previous instances in John 8–11.[47] Such an approach divorces the categories of ecclesiology, christology, and theology from one another, when in fact they are inextricably encompassed within the rubric 'one' through the evangelist's careful process of narrative development.

My purpose in this section is to show that the narrative development of oneness found in John 8–11 extends into John 17. In Jesus' prayer, the multilayered strands of ecclesial, christological, and theological oneness interfuse in an abbreviated but complex polyphony. The scriptural resonances from Deuteronomy 6:4 as well as Ezekiel 34 and 37 are not dropped here at the end of the Farewell Discourse; their contributions to oneness are sustained into this concise formula, creating a dense compression of all three of the motif's prior connotations. In the Johannine hermeneutics of 'one', the pattern of alternating between these Old Testament texts ends in John 17 where they are forced to be read as coextensive. Noting this programmatic narrative development, I make the case below that oneness in Jesus' prayer in John 17 is 1) a theological expression of Jewish Christian social identity rather than a call to internal social harmony (that is, oneness as social and in some way analogous to the divine identity); and 2) a call for the believers' integration within the divine interrelation of Father and Son

---

[47] As I have repeatedly observed, the neglect of narrative context is a standard hermeneutical misstep in interpreting Johannine oneness. Mark Appold tends to treat the oneness passages in John as discrete units. Addressing them out of narrative order, he seems more invested in highlighting the 'interactive traditive layers' behind the sayings material than in noting the interactive connections of the oneness passages within the extant narrative. To be fair, Appold certainly expresses a concern for literary connections; even so, his treatment of John 17, 11:49–52, and 10:16, 30 are conducted in reverse order from their appearance in the Gospel, circumventing the opportunity to observe the unfolding logic of narrative sequence. See Appold, *Oneness*, 139. Likewise, Johann Ferreira announces that 'the task of the interpreter… is *to isolate Johannine motifs* in their particular *religionsgeschichtliche* .context' – *Johannine Ecclesiology*, 28. A methodology of isolating passages is counterintuitive to the logic of narrative criticism employed here.

(that is, oneness as social and participatory). The Fourth Gospel's 'narrative ecclesiology of the Shema' will now come into full view.

The 'Shepherd's Prayer': John 17's Narrative Connections with John 8–11

It is important to note the narrative connections between oneness in John 17 and in John 8–11 so that the careful process of the theme's earlier development in the Gospel is not lost on interpreters by the deluge of material in the Farewell Discourse. A number of concepts appearing in Jesus' lofty prayer draw directly from the Shepherd Discourse and the related oneness formulae of 10:16, 10:30, and 11:47–53. The thematic connections are so strong between Jesus' self-presentation as the Good Shepherd and his prayer for the disciples in John 17 that J. Ramsey Michaels has proposed that the 'High Priestly Prayer' could also be called the 'Shepherd's Prayer', since pastoral imagery is just as prevalent as priestly imagery.[48]

The priestly function of offering consecration, however, is among the points of connection with John 10: only in 10:36 and 17:17–19 do we find the use of ἁγιάζω. In the former text Jesus claims that he is consecrated by the Father for his mission in the world; in chapter 17 Jesus speaks of consecrating himself that the disciples may also be consecrated. Along with other reciprocal themes appearing in the prayer (e.g., the disciples are sent just as Jesus has been sent, the disciples can pray directly to the Father just as Jesus, the disciples are not from the world just as Jesus is not from the world) the theme of consecration is entailed within the term 'one', which encompasses these reciprocal parallels.[49]

The concept of 'other sheep' is also a point of connection, intended as a reference to those who have yet to hear the message of the Shepherd but soon will:

> καὶ ἄλλα πρόβατα ἔχω ἃ οὐκ ἔστιν ἐκ τῆς αὐλῆς ταύτης· κἀκεῖνα δεῖ με ἀγαγεῖν καὶ τῆς φωνῆς μου ἀκούσουσιν, καὶ γενήσονται μία ποίμνη, εἷς ποιμήν. (10:16)[50]

---

[48] Michaels, *John*, 857; also 868, 871, 873–74; 878; 882.

[49] Michaels notes that consecration and the oneness motif also appear in Heb 2:11 – ὅ τε γὰρ ἁγιάζων καὶ οἱ ἁγιαζόμενοι ἐξ ἑνὸς πάντες (ibid., 874, n. 63).

[50] 'And other sheep I have who are not out of this fold; and I must bring them also and they will hear my voice, and they will become one flock, one shepherd.'

καὶ οὐκ ὑπὲρ τοῦ ἔθνους μόνον ἀλλ' ἵνα καὶ τὰ τέκνα τοῦ
θεοῦ τὰ διεσκορπισμένα συναγάγῃ εἰς ἕν. (11:52)[51]

Οὐ περὶ τούτων δὲ ἐρωτῶ μόνον, ἀλλὰ καὶ περὶ τῶν
πιστευόντων διὰ τοῦ λόγου αὐτῶν εἰς ἐμέ, ἵνα πάντες ἕν ὦσιν.
(17:20–21a)[52]

In each of these texts Jesus is expressing concern for future members
of the believing community who lie beyond the geographical and/or
the temporal sphere of his ministry.[53] The goal or hope in all three
passages is the same: that they might become 'one'.[54] The statement
in 10:28 that the sheep of Jesus will not be 'lost' is echoed in 17:12
(the Greek verb ἀπόλλυμι appears in both statements);[55] and in 10:28
and 17:3 the believers are promised the gift of 'eternal life'. Only in
the Shepherd Discourse and in the 'Shepherd's Prayer' do we find the
plural possessive neuter of τὰ ἐμά, a possessive term used by Jesus to
refer to the sheep/believers as his own.[56]

These connecting threads between John 17 and John 10–11 affirm
that oneness in Jesus' prayer must be read in light of previous oneness
formulae. This claim is strengthened when it is acknowledged that
Jesus' request 'that they may be one, just as we are' is a direct response
to a pastoral crisis that can only be understood within the frame of
reference provided by the statements concerning ecclesial and christological oneness in 10:16 and 11:47–53: the crisis addressed by John
17 is the dispersal of the flock at the death of the Shepherd. To be 'one'
in Johannine perspective is to be (re)gathered into the divine community of the Father (Israel's 'one' God) and Jesus (the 'one' messianic
king).

[51] 'And not on behalf of the nations only, but in order that he might gather all the
scattered children of God into one.'

[52] 'But I do not ask concerning these only, but also concerning those who are believing
in me through their word, in order that they may all become one.'

[53] Though a majority of interpreters envision some form of a Gentile mission within this
scope, J. Louis Martyn believes the 'other sheep' of Jn 10:16 refers to other Jewish
communities (Martyn, 'Gentile Mission').

[54] Again, see the discussion on this in Michaels, *John*, 874–75.

[55] This connection is noted by Ridderbos, *John*, 553.

[56] Michaels, *John*, 865–66. Schnackenburg supposes that the possessive language of that
which belongs to God and Jesus draws from the idea in John 10 that the sheep are 'his own'
(from ἴδιος – cf. 10:3, 12 with 17:6, 10) – Schnackenburg, *John*, 3:212. See also the
language of mutual indwelling in 10:38 and 17:11 (see 14:20 as well). And it should be
noted here that the phrase τὰ ἐμά does appear in 3 Jn 4.

The Crisis Precipitating Jesus' Prayer for Oneness: External
Dispersal, not Internal Disunity

The context for oneness in John 17 is established in 16:32 – ἰδοὺ ἔρχεται
ὥρα καὶ ἐλήλυθεν ἵνα σκορπισθῆτε ἕκαστος εἰς τὰ ἴδια κἀμὲ μόνον
ἀφῆτε ('behold, the hour is coming – and has now come – when each
of you will be scattered to his own, and will leave me alone'). This
imminent crisis of dispersal is what prompts the 'Shepherd's Prayer'.
Though Jesus' affiliation with the Father will remain intact ('I am not
alone, because the Father is with me' – 16:32b), his fellowship with the
disciples will be temporarily severed. The ominous temporal marker of
Jesus' 'hour' has referred to the crucifixion throughout the Gospel; and it
becomes manifest here in 16:32 that this christological event creates an
interim period of communal vulnerability between Jesus' departure and
his resurrection and subsequent sending of the Paraclete.

This theme of dispersal is directly related to the ecclesial dimensions
of oneness in the Fourth Gospel and connects John 17 with both the
Shepherd Discourse and the prophecy of Caiaphas (the verb σκορπίζω/
scatter appears in 10:12 and 16:32 and the related verb διασκορπίζω/
scatter in 11:52). In John 10 the Shepherd's flock are scattered when the
hired worker observes the approach of a wolf and abandons his entrusted
position as a guard. Through the pastoral imagery of that extended figure
of speech, Jesus draws from Ezekiel 34 and 37 to describe Israel's
ravaged status as a nation placed under the negligent watch of illegitimate leaders. And as Caiaphas prophesied, many of these sheep have
been scattered (11:52). The unique vocation of the Good Shepherd is to
call out to the flock (10:3), including the scattered sheep (10:16), and
gather them into 'one' (11:52) to form a messianic community of 'one
flock, one Shepherd'. In both Caiaphas' prophecy and Jesus' pastoral
imagery in John 10, the formation of this ecclesial entity is effected by
the Shepherd's death (10:11; 11:50–51).

As the Farewell Discourse draws to a close, Jesus indicates that
the hour of that death has arrived. It would appear from 16:32 that before
(the post-'hour') *community formation* occurs the initial impact of that
death is *community dispersal*. Rather than abandoning his flock like the
hired worker, the Shepherd in John 10 endures death on their behalf; but
the flock of Jesus' disciples are about to abandon the Shepherd when that
death takes place. Jesus expects the precarious state induced by his death
and departure to be stabilized eventually: the disciples' grief will give
way to joy, just as the mother forgets her prior birth-pains when her child
is born (16:20–22). Furthermore, the Paraclete will be sent to provide

comfort, wisdom, and guidance, extending Jesus' ministry throughout the believing community. In spite of these forthcoming consolations, though, Jesus' prayer in John 17 expresses a more immediate concern: the fragile state his return to the Father will naturally create for the discipleship community. The threat of communal dispersal is therefore the immediate crisis precipitating the prayer for oneness:

> I am no longer in the world, but they are in the world, and I am coming to you. Holy Father, keep them in your name that you have given to me, in order that they may be one just as we are. When I was with them I was keeping them in your name that you have given to me, and I guarded them ... But now I am coming to you. (17:11–13a)

The state of dispersal Jesus warns against in 16:32 has been presented in John 10:16 and 11:47–53 as the antithesis to ecclesial oneness. Conversely, ecclesial oneness is presented as the intended *telos* for the dispersed condition of the new communal identity associated with Jesus. Both instances of ecclesial oneness before John 17 (10:16 and 11:47–53) address the same threat of dispersal. Jesus' farewell prayer continues this pattern.

Significantly, in neither the Shepherd Discourse nor Caiaphas' prophecy has the scattered state of the sheep addressed by ecclesial oneness *resulted from internal strife or discord*. For the Fourth Gospel, *dispersal* is not the same as *disharmony*. In John 10:16 and 11:52, the sheep are scattered by external forces, either by negligent pastoral leadership (as in 10:11–13) or simply by geographical or temporal contingencies that have placed the sheep momentarily beyond the range of the Shepherd's voice. Reading the Gospel vis-à-vis the Johannine Epistles, where the Elder must address fractious internal behaviour, it is easy to assume that the oneness language in John 17 betrays an underlying church schism behind the textual curtain. Surely discord and disunity mark the *Sitz im Leben*: 'wird Einheit so stark betont, so muß sie bedroht sein'.[57] This threat is regularly deemed in Johannine scholarship to be internal. Ecumenical readings of John 17 reinforce this interpretative trend, reading oneness as a call to harmony among divided Christians. Though the evidence provided in the Epistles should not be ignored, hypothetical scenarios of church conflict behind the text should not be allowed to overshadow the patent thematic threads that come together in John 17's narrative context.

---

[57] Heckel, 'Die Einheit der Kirche', 617.

It is impossible to know with certainty what may lie historically behind the composition of John 17.[58] But in light of the foregoing study, it can be acknowledged with confidence that the ecclesial issue addressed at the level of the narrative by oneness in John 17 is not that of *schism from within*, but *dispersion from without*. There is nothing in the narrative context of John 17 that clearly indicates, beneath the textual surface, an intra-church conflict dividing the Johannine community, which the evangelist hopes to restore to unity or social oneness. In fact, *the oneness language of this Gospel does not address schism as much as it incites schism*. If the evangelist is pastorally addressing a conflict at the level of his actual experience, it is more reasonable to assume that this is a threat posed by unbelievers on the community around Jesus (a scenario that accords well with those models envisioning a church–synagogue split). 'One' is a term designating the community extracted from antagonistic social domains and regathered around Jesus: 'they will become one flock' (10:16); 'that the scattered children of God might be gathered into one' (11:52); 'that they may be one' (17:21, 22).

In summary, Johannine oneness in John 8–11 and 17 is primarily about 1) community formation and 2) the preservation of that community from external threats. Jesus' 'hour' creates a new situation that breaks up the disciples (16:32) and thereby necessitates a prayer for their protection and consolidation; but preservation from disunity created by internal strife is not envisioned. The problem addressed is the circumstance of Jesus' departure, a traumatic event that allows a host of external pressures to endanger the community's integrity as it inhabits the hostile and alien realm of the world, the domain of the evil one (17:15–16). When Jesus repeats the prayer, 'that they may be one', in 17:21–23, the thrust of oneness is once again community formation. He does not pray 'concerning these alone' (17:20). The Shepherd anticipates the ingathering of dispersed sheep lying outside the present circle of his disciples, those who will come to belief through the disciples' witness. So ecclesial oneness is ultimately concerned with the formation of a new community around Jesus and its ongoing preservation. But that which challenges the social integrity of the flock with dispersal are external rather than internal forces. Discord and schism may well have marked the Johannine communal network at certain times on the historical level behind the

---

[58] Schnackenburg cautions against reading the prayer for oneness in John 17 in light of 1 John. Acknowledging that 'inner tensions within the community' could be in view, he concludes that 'we do not know the concrete background and no information is provided about a possible threat to the unity of the community by the positive formulation of the petition [for oneness]' (Schnackenburg, *John*, 3:190).

text, but within the text oneness is not a call to internal social harmony. It is instead a call for the ingathering of a new community associated with Jesus and a prayer for their protection. In a christological enactment of Ezekiel 34 and 37, John 17 depicts the one Shepherd's desire for his sheep to be gathered out of their state of dispersion and vulnerability to be formed into one people.

A Narrative Ecclesiology of Divine Association: Chapter Summary and Conclusion to Part II

In the Johannine hermeneutics of 'one', two sets of scriptural texts emphasizing particular dimensions of oneness alternate back and forth and accrue expanded meanings through a narrative process. When these dimensions of oneness first appear they accord with standard Jewish expectations: the monotheistic oneness of the Shema is uncontroversial in John 8:41, and in 10:16 Jesus draws on messianic and nationalistic ideas of oneness in Ezekiel 34 and 37. Although these initial oneness formulae draw from uncontroversial sources, their application becomes a function of the ecclesial narrative script in which Jesus' work and identity destabilize the social construct and induce either group re-entrenchment or resocialization into the communal entity of the new people of God. In John 8–11, the oneness motif is a primary element of this script: along with igniting controversies that accentuate boundary lines, the term 'one' also becomes a means of labelling the social entity aligned with Jesus (e.g., μία ποίμνη/one flock).

The theological implications of the Shema in John 17 are not to be drowned out by the messianic and national connotations of Ezekiel 34 and 37 discussed immediately above. 'One' still retains its function as an expression of Jewish monotheism in John 17. Concurrent with the prayer of the 'one' Shepherd for the ingathering of the 'one' community is a prayer for divine association with Israel's 'One' God. Oneness still bears in this prayer the theological weight of John 8:41 ('we have one Father: God') and 10:30 ('I and the Father are one'). Jesus' address to the Father as 'the only true God' (τὸν μόνον ἀληθινὸν θεὸν) in 17:3 recalls the statement in 5:44, a text convincingly argued by Jörg Augenstein[59] and Johannes Beutler[60] as referring to the Shema.[61] Jesus' prayer for

---

[59] Augenstein, *Das Liebesgebot*, 60–61.   [60] Beutler, 'Hauptgebot', 226–29.

[61] Michaels sees this phrase as stemming from Jewish monotheism (Michaels, *John*, 860). So also Raymond Brown (citing LXX Isa 37:20), *John*, 741. In his study of the Shema in 1 Corinthians, Erik Waaler notes that the phrase μόνος θεός was used by early Jewish writers as a way of distinguishing the God of Israel from other deities. He does not cite

oneness is a compound formula of prior oneness formulae – 'one Father, even God' plus 'one flock, one Shepherd' plus 'I and the Father are one' plus the idea in John 11 that 'one' must die to gather the people into 'one'. These are all compressed in the phrase 'that they may be one, as we are one'. Contrary to readings of John 17 that regard oneness primarily as a call to internal or intra-church unity, the theological freight of the Shema cannot be jettisoned as the ecclesial and christological strands are joined to it.

Recognizing the retention of the Shema in John 17:11, 21–23 prompts a reappraisal of Johannine oneness. I reaffirm here one of my primary claims repeated in this chapter and in Chapter 5: *the term 'one' in Jesus' prayer is a theological expression of Jewish Christian social identity*. As argued above, the situation addressed by oneness in John 17 is not so much a schism within the Christian church, but a schism within the Jewish synagogue. Oneness addresses 'the parting of the ways' ignited by Christ-confession among Jewish Christians. Jesus is so closely associated with the one God of Israel in this Gospel that divisions are erected within the parent milieu of Jewish religious life in the text (and possibly behind it). The fourth evangelist vigorously and creatively appropriated the oneness motif of the Shema for the sake of classifying the social identity of Jewish Christians finding themselves at odds with a parent religious community historically correlated to the one and only God. I discussed in the previous chapter how theological oneness could bear associative or analogical implications for social identity. Corresponding with the 'One God' could be 'one law',[62] 'one citizenship',[63] 'one Temple', 'one altar', and 'one nation'.[64] The Fourth Gospel has employed this analogical use of oneness as a means of affirming allegiance to Jewish religious heritage, albeit reconfigured around the christological conviction that Jesus is the one ruler shepherd whom the prophet Ezekiel portrayed as David's

---

examples, but Philo uses the phrase εἷς ὁ μόνος θεὸς δημιουργός in his discussion of Creation in *De fuga et inventione*, 71. Variations of the phrase μόνος θεός also appear in 2 Kgs 19:14–19; Ps 85:10 (LXX); *Odes Sol.* 7:45 (LXX); Isa. 37:16, 20; Dan 3:45 (LXX; or 'Azariah and the Three Jews', 22); 2 Macc. 7:37 (see also 1:24); *4 Macc.* 5:24; 1 Tim 1:17; Jude 25. Waaler points to Gerhard Delling who has argued that the phrase μόνος θεός could be an interpretation of the Shema. Conceptually, μόνος θεός certainly expresses the monotheistic convictions of Deuteronomy 6:4. See 'Excursus: The Only God' in Waaler, *Shema*, 397.

[62] 2 Bar. 48:24.   [63] Philo, *Spec. leg.*, 4.159.

[64] These three phrases come from Josephus, *Ant.* 4.200–1. See Chapter 6, pp. 124–27.

regal heir. With his oneness motif, he is presenting *a narrative eccle-siology of divine association.*

The Shema's resonance in Jesus' prayer, however, betokens a dimension of Johannine oneness more comprehensive than associa-tion or correspondence. The formula 'that they may be one, as we are one' expresses *participation* within the divine reality of the Father–Son interrelation. Jesus does not just pray that the disciples will share in his mission; beyond a task-oriented or functional unity, Jesus prays that this new social entity *will actually share in his preexistent divine glory.* The Prologue presents a 'high ecclesiology' in which the new people of God become divinely birthed members of a divine family. In similar fashion, oneness is a motif with integrative possibilities by which this new ecclesial community can enjoy a divine status. This participatory ecclesiology can be classified with the later patristic language of 'theosis'. To this 'high ecclesiology' of divine participation we now turn.

John's Narrative Ecclesiology of Participation and Deification

8

THE FOURTH GOSPEL AND DEIFICATION IN PATRISTIC WRITINGS

Introduction to Part III

I have endeavoured in Parts I and II to demonstrate ecclesiology as a principal theme for John's Gospel by underscoring the ecclesial emphases in a foundational text (John 1:1–18) and in an overarching theme (oneness). In the Prologue, filiation inspires a participatory ecclesiology – those who receive the Logos undergo a re-origination that sources them in God as 'children' within the divine family (see also John 3:1–8). With the oneness motif deriving in part from the Shema, the ecclesial use of 'one' correlates the community of believers with the God of their religious heritage. This aspect of Johannine ecclesiology is more *association* than *participation*. But I suggested that something more is underway, closing the previous chapter with the claim that Jesus' prayer in John 17 'that they may be one, as we are one' extends beyond a mere analogical, associative, or functional notion of oneness. While identifying Johannine Christians with the 'one' God of Jewish monotheism, thus legitimating their allegiance to Jesus as the 'one' messianic king, the evangelist is also envisioning the disciples' participation within the divine interrelation of the Father and Son. The ontological and relational dynamics of this integration invite the use of *theosis* language for expressing the Johannine vision of the people of God. Having shown that the Prologue puts forward an ecclesiology of participation and that the oneness motif conveys an ecclesiology of association, I now turn to the task of demonstrating that this associative ecclesiology of oneness (one flock, one Shepherd, one God) includes a form of participation worthy of the term 'deification'.

I stated in the Introduction that my use of 'theosis' or 'deification' (used interchangeably throughout[1]) is not to force John's Gospel

---

[1] Scholars sometimes use the terms 'theosis' and 'deification' to refer to different categories, with the former sometimes used to represent the more formal doctrines of

into a later mould of theological discourse but to employ that discourse in the descriptive task of labelling Johannine ecclesiology.[2] Though the theme of participation has surfaced repeatedly in this study, I have intentionally delayed applying the term 'theosis' to my findings for the purpose of grounding my research firmly within the exegesis of the Gospel text. Having sought to establish ecclesiology as central to John and having identified its most essential dynamic as participation within the Father–Son interrelation, I will now utilize the language of deification, but anchor the particularities of its meaning to the Gospel narrative. The focus of this study is not theosis per se, but theosis that is specifically 'Johannine'.

With the descriptive task at hand of bringing the foregoing material on Johannine ecclesiology into a more coherent synthesis, I will provide grounds here in Chapter 8 for legitimately applying patristic terminology to Johannine ecclesiology, even though the idea of theosis bears a complicated history of development and usage that post-dates the Gospel. In the opening of Chapter 9 I will outline essential characteristics of the Johannine version of deification (pp. 169–79) and then revisit the Prologue and oneness motif to show how they contribute to the Gospel's narrative ecclesiology of deification (pp. 183–85). Part III will close considering how various characters embody Johannine theosis within the Gospel narrative. These

---

participation that developed after the patristic period in the Eastern church – i.e., Carl Mosser, 'The Earliest Patristic Interpretations of Psalm 82, Jewish Antecedents, and the Origin of Christian Deification', *JTS* 56, no. 1 (2005): 30–74, here at 31, n. 3. Because the term 'divinization' has connotations with the mystical and philosophical concepts of a more Hellenistic milieu, I use it sparingly. This is not to suggest, however, that Hellenistic ideas and early Christian theology were rigidly distinct from one another. But recent interpreters of patristic deification have taken pains to point out that the early Christian theologians were quite capable of identifying the Judaeo-Christian and Hellenistic strands of thought informing their subject matter, and could sift through the helpful and not so helpful elements of their diverse cultural contexts (on this, see Macaskill, *Union*, 73). For an earlier work counteracting the claim that Hellenism co-opted early Christianity in the area of deification, see Jules Gross, *The Divinization of the Christian According to the Greek Fathers*, trans. Paul A. Onica (Anaheim, CA: A&C Press, 2002), 11–92.

[2] Gösta Hallonsten urges writers employing theosis language today to note the difference between theosis as a doctrine and theosis as a theme. I will be using theosis more thematically than doctrinally in what follows. See Gösta Hallonsten, '*Theosis* in Recent Research: A Renewal of Interest and a Need for Clarity', in *Partakers of the Divine Nature: The History and Development of Deification in the Christian Tradition*, ed. Michael J. Christensen and Jeffrey A. Wittung (Grand Rapids, MI: Baker Academic, 2007), 281–93, here at 283–4.

characterizations are constituent of the wider theme of reciprocity in John's Gospel whereby believers enjoy similar relational and vocational privileges and responsibilities that parallel Jesus' own relationship with the Father. After considering the man born blind, Peter, and the Beloved Disciple (Chapter 10), the final character to be considered is the one who enables Johannine deification: the Spirit-Paraclete (Chapter 11).

Deification as 'Foreground' for the Fourth Gospel

Richard Hays has suggested that 'a careful study of participation motifs in patristic theology' might illuminate New Testament texts.[3] The appreciable surge of interest within current biblical scholarship in reading patristic deification discourses as hermeneutically helpful indicates that his suggestion has been taken seriously.[4] Cognizant that theosis language developed well after the era of earliest Christianity, such scholarly studies require a defence of some kind against anticipated accusations of chronological impropriety. I will briefly make my own defence and broadly indicate how I am using the concepts of participation and deification for describing Johannine ecclesiology.

The lexical repository associated with deification in the Greek (and largely Alexandrian) writings of the patristic era – θεοποιέω, θεοποίησις, θειάζω, ἐκθειάζω, θεοποιΐα, ἀποθεόω, ἀποθέωσις, θέωσις, et al. – make no appearance in the Gospel of John.[5] The absence of this technical or quasi-technical terminology, however, has certainly not prevented the application of theosis language to other New Textament texts. From Michael Gorman:

---

[3] Richard B. Hays, *The Faith of Jesus Christ: The Narrative Substructure of Galatians 3:1–4:11*, 2nd edn., The Biblical Resource Series (Grand Rapids, MI: Eerdmans, 2002), xxxii.

[4] Scholars who make appeal to Hays' comments include Michael Gorman, *Inhabiting the Cruciform God: Kenosis, Justification, and Theosis in Paul's Narrative Soteriology* (Grand Rapids, MI: Eerdmans, 2009), 3, n. 6.; Macaskill, *Union*, 26; and Blackwell, *Christosis*, 23.

[5] Various patristic exegetes expressed different meanings in their uses of these terms, and some terms are consistently used to indicate certain *types* of divinization (e.g., the pagan deification of heroes or the elevation of an emperor to divine status). For a detailed synthesis of the semantics of theosis, see Appendix 2 ('The Greek Vocabulary of Deification') in Norman Russell, *The Doctrine of Deification in the Greek Patristic Tradition* (Oxford: Oxford University Press, 2004), 333–4.

'*Theosis* ... should be seen not as anachronistic but as retrospectively appropriate. Now, I would add that it should also be seen as retrospectively *accurate*.'[6] David Litwa offers a similar defence for his associations of Paul with deification language: 'The debate is not whether Paul had a "doctrine" or "theory" or "idea" of deification. Rather, the question is whether an aspect of Paul's soteriology can be called "deification", by which I mean "sharing in God's reality through Christ."'[7] Indeed, for Paul Collins, deification is itself a metaphor that 'arises from reflections on New Testament witness'.[8]

Grant Macaskill, however, voices strong cautions against the use of theosis language in New Testament exegesis. In affirmation of Gösta Hallonsten's warnings (cited in note 2), he observes that 'if the word [theosis] is used without sufficient reference to its theological advocates and their cautionary moves, it can lead to categorical errors in describing the nature of participation'.[9] So along with the risk of anachronism, correlating theosis language with the New Testament corpus also risks haphazardly appropriating later theological terminology without recourse to conceptual developments spanning diverse patristic writers over multiple centuries in varied locales.[10] Macaskill offers the following elaboration on the suitability of using the term 'theosis' in biblical studies:

> For the purposes of describing the New Testament material, the word is both 'under-determined' and 'over-determined.' It is under-determined in the sense that the terminology of theosis can be applied to a broad range of theological accounts that vary in significant ways. As such, to apply the term to the New Testament writers does not clarify anything unless a specific account of the word's meaning (as it is deployed by the scholar) is provided. It is over-determined in the sense that the modern doctrine, with all its varieties, has come to operate within a certain conceptual framework that may not be directly mapped onto that of the New Testament writers. That framework may be

---

[6] Michael J. Gorman, 'Romans: The First Christian Treatise on Theosis', *JTI* 5, no. 1 (2011): 13–34, here at 18.

[7] M. David Litwa, '2 Corinthians 3:18 and its Implications for Theosis', *JTI* 2, no. 1 (2008): 117–33, here at 117.

[8] Paul M. Collins, *Partaking in Divine Nature: Deification and Communion* (London: T & T Clark, 2010), 38.

[9] Macaskill, *Union*, 76.

[10] This neglect in identifying the specific linguistic contexts of deification language is one of Macaskill's critiques of Gorman, *Inhabiting*. See Macaskill, *Union*, 26–28; 75–76.

valid as a theological structure, but once terminology is taken out of that framework and applied to writings that operate within a different intellectual culture, it becomes potentially misleading.

Taking these concerns into serious consideration, I am choosing nonetheless to employ theosis language, though not without offering 'a specific account of the word's meaning' (which is the remit of the following chapter). My reasons are as follows. For one, the language of 'participation' and 'union' also bears potential for anachronistic interpretations that can be either 'under-' or 'over-determined'. I have been using the term participation regularly. It is a vague term that will now receive fuller definition with the language of deification – in the Fourth Gospel, participation involves an ontological re-origination (ἐκ θεοῦ/'out of God') by which human participants in the divine interrelation actually become divine beings. The term 'union' is one I have thus far avoided (along with 'unity') to preserve my interpretation that 'one' stems from the Shema's profession of the one God of Israel. While attempting to provide the appropriate qualifications of the kind Macaskill calls for, I am writing with the conviction that patristic concepts of theosis can indeed serve as fruitful *articulations* and *clarifications* of biblical themes like union and participation.

I am also comfortable using terms of discourse that locate my exegesis within interpretative theological traditions. In this regard, the hermeneutical interplay between canonical texts and their later interpreters is regarded by Markus Bockmuehl as an advantageous 'foreground' for reading the New Testament.[11] New Testament texts are not simply historical artifacts isolated to one era in history – they have generated an 'effective history'.[12] The New Testament 'comprises not just an original setting but a history of lived responses to the historical and eternal realities to which it testifies'.[13]

---

[11] Markus Bockmuehl, *Seeing the Word: Refocusing New Testament Study*, Studies in Theological Interpretation (Grand Rapids, MI: Baker, 2006), 64–65. See also Macaskill's discussion of this quotation (Macaskill, *Union*, 3–4).

[12] The phrase 'effective history' (*Wirkungsgeschichte*) draws from Hans-Georg Gadamer, *Truth and Method*, 2nd edn. (London: Sheed & Ward, 1989), 300–307. Bockmuehl uses the phrase to refer to the impact of scriptural interpretation within and throughout the history of reception. See Bockmuehl, *Seeing the Word*, 66.

[13] Ibid., 65.

Though I will certainly draw some attention to the 'effective history' of the Fourth Gospel's participatory ecclesiology in the subsequent material, my primary interest lies not in recounting patristic readings of John but in describing the ecclesial vision set forth within the Gospel's text. In this descriptive task, I enlist the language of deification and theosis found in the 'foreground' of patristic interpretation, but the terminology and conceptualization will be decidedly shaped by the particular Johannine usage as found within the Gospel text. Broadly speaking, 'deification' refers to some form of participation within divine reality, a phenomenon at the heart of Johannine ecclesiology and outlined in more detail in Chapter 9.[14]

The Fourth Gospel as a Background for Patristic Deification

Deification is manifestly a Johannine concept. This claim is far from extraordinary – it is openly acknowledged that patristic writers consciously used John as a source for their reflection on theosis (not least while writing commentaries on its text, as with Origen and Cyril). But the current emphasis in New Testament scholarship on deification and participation in Paul, with little attention placed on the Johannine literature, is disproportionate and hardly representative of the patristic writings.[15] Macaskill has recently made the same observation about

---

[14] 'The core or the very point of a doctrine of deification is defined as participation in divine life or union with God' – Gösta Hallonsten, *'Theosis'*, 282.

[15] Some of the attention to Paul is due to recent approaches that link deification with Pauline justification. Finnish interpreters have been particularly keen to note potential connections. See, e.g., Veli-Matti Kärkkäinen, *One with God: Salvation as Deification and Justification* (Collegeville, MN: Liturgical Press, 2004); and the essays in Carl E. Braaten and Robert W. Jenson, eds., *Union with Christ: The New Finnish Interpretation of Luther* (Grand Rapids, MI: W. B. Eerdmans, 1998). For studies on Paul and theosis (some of which have already been cited) see Stephen Finlan, 'Can We Speak of Theosis in Paul?', in Christensen and Wittung, *Partakers of the Divine Nature* (Grand Rapids, MI: Baker Academic, 2008), 68–80; Litwa, '2 Corinthians 3'; M. David Litwa, *We Are Being Transformed: Deification in Paul's Soteriology* (BZNW 187; Berlin: De Gruyter, 2012); John Pester, 'The Gospel of the Promised Seed: Deification According to the Organic Pattern in Romans 8 and Philippians 2', *Affirmation & Critique* 7: 2 (2002), 55–69; Roland Chia, 'Salvation as Justification and Deification', *SJT* 64: 2 (2011), 125–39; Gorman, *Inhabiting*; Benjamin C. Blackwell, 'Immortal Glory and the Problem of Death in Romans 3.23', *JSNT* 32: 3 (2010): 285–308; and Blackwell, *Christosis*. This list of sources is by no means exhaustive.

the theme of participation in the current scholarly climate: 'This [emphasis on Paul] reflects the increasing specialization or, more pejoratively, fragmentation of New Testament scholarship during the modern period and particularly during the twentieth century.'[16] The concern is that the themes of participation and divine union are being limited too narrowly within a constricted range of canonical texts. As an example, a number of recent works providing a survey of theosis as a patristic theme give John marginal attention.[17] Paul Collins grants a paragraph to the Johannine literature (less space than he gives to Matthew's Gospel) after more than four pages on Paul.[18] The most authoritative contemporary work on theosis is Norman Russell's monograph, repeatedly cited in this chapter and the next. In his brief section on the Johannine literature as a background for patristic theosis he suggests that John was a rather aberrant text until it was wrested from Gnosticism in the third century.[19] This account of the Fourth Gospel's late acceptance in orthodox Christianity no longer holds the day,[20] a reality confirmed (ironically) by Russell's own identification of multiple Johannine influences in his treatment of second-century theologians writing from a rigorously Christian perspective.

Writers who do give considerable attention to John's Gospel as a source for patristic theosis include Jules Gross (writing in 1938)[21] and, most recently, Macaskill.[22] Stephen Finlan grants John some significance as a text with deification themes,[23] and David Crump

---

[16] Macaskill, *Union*, 17. For Harnack's claims, see Adolf von Harnack, *History of Dogma*, Theological Translation Library (London: Williams & Norgate, 1894), 121–304.

[17] In a fairly recent (and very helpful) collection of essays devoted to theosis covering the historical span of the classical period to the modern era, two are devoted to New Testament texts. One looks at Paul and the other at 2 Peter 1:4. The Johannine literature is excluded. See Christensen and Wittung, eds., *Partakers of the Divine Nature*.

[18] Collins, *Divine Nature*, 46–47; cf. 42.   [19] Russell, *Deification*, 88.

[20] For a history of this construal of John's reception, including references to significant biblical scholars who have challenged it, see Charles E. Hill, *The Johannine Corpus in the Early Church* (Oxford: Oxford University Press), 2004 and Tuomas Rasimus, 'Introduction', in *The Legacy of John: Second-Century Reception of the Fourth Gospel* (ed. Tuomas Rasimus; NovTSup 132; Leiden: Brill, 2010), 1–16. See, however, the critiques of Hill in Francis Watson, *Gospel Writing: A Canonical Perspective* (Grand Rapids, MI: Eerdmans, 2013), 473–93.

[21] Gross, *Divinization*, 88–90.   [22] Macaskill, *Union*, 251–70.

[23] Stephen Finlan, 'Deification in Jesus' Teaching', in *Theosis: Deification in Christian Theology*, ed. Vladimir Kharlamov, vol. 2 (Cambridge: James Clarke & Co., 2012), 21–41, here at 31–35.

employs theosis language to describe the disciples' union with the Father and Son.[24] David Litwa argues that Pilate's exclamation, 'Behold the man' in John 19:5 may imply the divine nature of prelapsarian Adam.[25] In comparison to the growing literature on theosis in Paul, however, the deification narrative of the Fourth Gospel is not receiving the attention it is due.[26] Supplying an exhaustive analysis of John's contributions to deification in the later centuries of the church is well beyond the scope of my own study on participatory ecclesiology within the Gospel's narrative. But to corroborate my point that deification is as Johannine as it is Pauline, I will take three thematic elements central to patristic deification discourses and briefly demonstrate their resonance with the Fourth Gospel. The themes of filiation and exchange discussed below have already been demonstrated as central features of the Prologue. In the next chapter, I will show how these patristic ideas, along with the patristic use of Psalm 82, relate to Parts I and II of this study.

The Use of Psalm 82 [LXX, 81]

With its ascription of divine status to beings other than YHWH, 'Psalm 82 is the single most significant text for the development of a theology of deification.'[27] It should certainly be of some significance that the Gospel of John is *the only New Testament text to cite this psalm* (John 10:34–35). The most relevant verses are 1, 6, and 7:

> God [ὁ θεός] stood in the congregation of gods [θεῶν];
> In the midst of the gods [θεούς] he enacts judgment . . .
> I said, 'You are gods [θεοί], and all of you are sons of the most high;
> But you will die like humans, and fall as one of the rulers.'

---

[24] Crump, 'Re-examining'.

[25] M. David Litwa, 'Behold Adam: A Reading of John 19:5', *HBT* 32 (2010): 129–43.

[26] There is also John A. Sanford's *Mystical Christianity: A Psychological Commentary on the Gospel of John* (New York: Crossroad, 1993). Sanford uses the term 'deification' to refer to Johannine mysticism (279, 294, 299, 302–5), but he draws primarily from Hellenistic cults and reads the Gospel in reference to Carl Jung and diverse psychological concerns.

[27] Macaskill, *Union*, 73. Gösta Hallonsten claims that Ps 82:6 was a more important theosis text in the patristic literature than 2 Pet 1.4 (Hallonsten, *'Theosis'*, 283, n. 19).

The earliest patristic expositions of Psalm 82 by Justin Martyr[28] and Clement of Alexandria[29] do not discuss the text in explicit dialogue with John 10:34–35 – an interpretative tradition was becoming established around this psalm in early Judaism well before it was cited by the fourth evangelist and by Christian theologians in the second century and beyond.[30] Its stretching of divine categories was in the hermeneutical air, so to speak. Origen, Didymus the Blind, Athanasius, and Cyril of Alexandria, however, certainly did read the psalm in light of Jesus' citation in John.[31] In the second of his three references to Psalm 82 (*Haer.* 3.19.1; see also 3.6.1 and 4.38.4), Irenaeus of Lyons (writing earlier than Clement and later than Justin) clearly has John 10:34–35 in

---

[28] Justin Martyr, *Dial.* 124. Justin understands the divine beings in Ps 82 to refer to humanity prior to the disobedience in Eden. Adam and Eve 'were considered worthy to become gods, and to have the capability of becoming sons of the Most High' (124.4). From St Justin Martyr, *Dialogue with Trypho*, ed. Michael Slusser, trans. Thomas B. Falls, vol. 3, Selections from the Fathers of the Church (Washington, D.C.: The Catholic University of America Press, 2003), 187. Though he does not imply a reliance on John 10:34–35, his language is in some respects Johannine. He introduces his citation of Ps 82 by pointing out his Jewish audience's discomfort with the claim that Christians are also θεοῦ τέκνα. Aside from two instances in *Dial.* (123.9, 124.1), the phrase θεοῦ τέκνα also appears in Gregory of Nyssa, *Contra Eunomium*, 3.1.118. The phrase τέκνα [τοῦ] θεοῦ is found three times in Paul (Rom 8:16, 21; 9:8; Phil 2:15). The phrase is more common in the Johannine literature (1:12; 11:52; 1 Jn 3:1, 10; 5:2). It is also tempting to find a connection between Justin and John since the ecclesial designation of 'children of God' is immediately preceded by the phrase τὰς ἐντολὰς τοῦ Χριστοῦ (123.9). The concept of Christ's commandments is exclusively Johannine in the New Testament corpus: 14:15, 21; 15:10; cf. 1 Jn 2:3; 3:22; 5:2. Even so, there is no way to determine with confidence whether Justin had John's citation of Psalm 82 in mind in *Dial.*, 124. There is debate as to whether Justin even had access to John. For arguments that he did indeed draw on the Fourth Gospel in his writings, see Charles E. Hill, 'Was John's Gospel Among Justin's 'Apostolic Memoirs'?', in *Justin Martyr and His Worlds*, ed. Sara Parvis and Paul Foster (Minneapolis, MN: Fortress, 2007), 88–94; Hill also cites (88, n. 2) Graham Stanton who allows for the possibility of Justin's use of John in Graham N. Stanton, 'Jesus Traditions and Gospels in Justin Martyr and Irenaeus', in *The Biblical Canons* (ed. J.-M. Auwers and H. J. de Jonge; BETL 163; Leuven: Leuven University Press, 2003), 353–70. For arguments against, see A. J. Bellinzoni, *The Sayings of Jesus in the Writings of Justin Martyr* (Leiden: E. J. Brill, 1967) and Helmut Koester, *Ancient Christian Gospels: Their History and Development* (Philadelphia, PA: TPI, 1990), 246.

[29] Clement of Alexandria, *Paed.* 1.26.1; Clement of Alexandria, *Strom.* 2.145.4–5; 4.149.8–4.150.1. See Russell, *Deification*, 129.

[30] Mosser, 'Psalm 82', 34, n. 12.

[31] See the relevant discussions in Russell, *Deification.*, esp. 146, 156, 170, 180, 185, 194, 196, 197, 199. For Origen, see *Comm. Jo.*, 1.31. For Didymus, *In Zach.* 94–95; 267; *In Gen.*, 246; 248. For Athanasius, see *C. Ar.*,1.11.39; 1.39; 3.19–20; *Inc.*, 4.32; *Ep. Serap.*, 1.4; *Ep. Afros* 7. For Cyril: *Jo.* 1.12.133; cf. 12.1.

mind.[32] After directly citing John 8:36 and using Johannine language like 'eternal life', he recalls a scene when 'the Word' (a reference to Jesus here) quoted Psalm 82:6 to those who had rejected his incarnate identity. Like much patristic writing on theosis, Irenaeus' exposition of this psalm in 3.19.1 is a fluid admixture of language ringing with both Johannine and Pauline resonances. Though the segment below is large, it provides a representative example of how this psalm was read in patristic interpretation with recourse to both Paul and John. Citations of Scripture are italicized for ease of identification.

> Furthermore, those are liable to death who bluntly assert that [Jesus] is a mere man, begotten of Joseph, since they remain in the slavery of the former disobedience; for they have not yet been united with the Word of God the Father, nor have they received liberty through the Son, as he himself said, *If therefore the Son makes you free, you will be free indeed.*[33] But since they are ignorant of the Emmanuel who was born of the Virgin, they are deprived of his gift, which is eternal life.[34] And since they do not receive the Word of imperishability, they continue in the mortal flesh and are debtors to death, because they do not accept the antidote to life. In reference to them the Word, speaking of his gift of grace, said, I have said, *'You are gods, sons of the Most High, all of you; nevertheless, you shall die like men.'* Doubtless he speaks these words to those who have not received the gift of adoption, but who despise the incarnation of the pure generation of the Word of God, defraud humankind of its ascent to God, and are ungrateful to the Word of God who was incarnate for their sakes. For the Word of God became man, and he who is God's Son became the Son of Man to this end, [that man,] having been united with the Word of God and

[32] *Pace* Mosser, 'Psalm 82', 34–35, n. 12. But see also his comments on p. 41 where he does attribute Irenaeus' 'Word of God' language to John's Gospel.

[33] Bernhard Mutschler argues that the reference to 'the Word of God' (*Verbum Dei*) in the opening lines of 3.19.1 is directly linked to John 1:1. The phrase 'liberty through the Son' (*per filium ... libertatem*) is drawing from the line of thought in John 8 (see vv. 31–32) preceding Irenaeus' 'wörtlich und explizit' citation of 8:36 (see vv.31–32). See Bernhard Mutschler, *Das Corpus Johanneum bei Irenäus von Lyon: Studien und Kommentar zum Dritten Buch von Adversus Haereses*, WUNT 189 (Tübingen: Mohr Siebeck, 2006), 415.

[34] The Matthean ('Emmanuel') and Lukan ('Virgin') language coincides here with the Johannine theme of the divine gift of eternal life, which Mutschler argues is drawn from John 4:10, 14 (ibid., 417–19.).

receiving adoption, might become a son of God.[35] Certainly, in no other way could we have received imperishability and immortality unless imperishability and immortality had first become what we are, in order that the perishable might be swallowed up by imperishability, and the mortal by immortality, that *we might receive the adoption as sons*?[36]

Irenaeus is undeniably aware of Jesus' citation of Psalm 82 in the Fourth Gospel. Detailed attention will be given to the Johannine use of this psalm in Chapter 9. For now it is important to observe that Jesus views as 'gods' those 'to whom the word of God came' in John 10:35. Irenaeus understands the word of God to be Jesus himself – to receive this incarnate Word is to become adopted as a son and thus made divine.

The 'Exchange Formula'

As exemplified in Irenaeus' interpretation of Psalm 82:6 above, the dynamic of 'exchange' is central to patristic notions of deification. The general idea derives from the salvific effects of Jesus' Incarnation implied in John 1:14 – by taking on our humanity, the divinity of the Son is somehow communicable to human beings. There are multiple expressions of this concept among patristic writers, often manifested in an 'exchange formula' that has become recognized by historical theologians as a specific genre of theosis discourse. From Irenaeus: 'Jesus Christ our Lord ... became what we are in order to make us what he is';[37] Athanasius: 'He became human that we might become divine' (αὐτὸς γὰρ ἐνηνθρώπησεν, ἵνα ἡμεῖς θεοποιηθῶμεν);[38] Cyril of Alexandria: 'The Only Begotten Word of God became like us, that we too might become like him so far as is possible for human nature ... He became like us, that is, a human being, that we might become like him, I mean gods and sons.'[39]

Norman Russell ascribes an exclusively Pauline background to the patristic concept of divine–human exchange (see, e.g., 2 Corinthians 8:9

---

[35] Though the term 'adoption' is Pauline (see Gal 4:5), Mutschler writes that 'die Vorstellung der Fleischwerdung des Wortes' draws from John 1:14, which is Irenaeus' most commonly used verse from the Johannine corpus (ibid., 420–21), and it is often paired conceptually with Gal 4:5 (ibid., 425).

[36] Translation by Robert M. Grant, in Irenaeus of Lyons, *Against the Heresies*, 3:92–93.

[37] Irenaeus of Lyons, *Haer.*, 5 (praef). From ibid., 164.

[38] Athanasius, *Inc.*, 54. See also *c. Ar.* 3.33–34; 38, 39, 48; *Ep. Adelph.* 4.

[39] Cyril of Alexandria, *Commentary on John*. 12.1. Cited in Russell, *Deification*, 199. See also Clement of Alexandria, *Prot.* 1.8.4.

and Philippians 2:6–8).[40] The Johannine influence, however, is unmistakable. Though Pauline and Johannine language often intertwine in patristic deification texts, it must be acknowledged that the fundamental dynamic of divine–human exchange is the Incarnation for which John 1:14 is the classic expression. In his comments on Irenaeus' use of Psalm 82 in *Haer.*, 3.19.1, Bernhard Mutschler draws attention to the indispensability of Johannine Incarnation christology for Irenaeus: 'Zeigt Irenäus nachdrücklich, dass alle Soteriologie (ἡ δωρεά, Joh 4,10; ἡ υἱοθεσία, Gal 4,5) grundsätzlich von einer qualifizierten christologie abhängt, die auf der 'Fleischwerdung des Wortes Gottes' (Joh 1,1f.14a) basiert. Diese zu missachten, heißt, das Heil zu verfehlen.'[41] Moreover, Athanasius draws heavily on the Johannine Logos language in his treatise *On the Incarnation*; and it must not be forgotten that Cyril's exchange formula appears in his commentary on the Fourth Gospel.

Divine Filiation

The identification of Christians as 'sons' or 'children' of God – filiation – is another theme integral to theosis in the patristic tradition.[42] The idea of deification through filiation is explicit in Psalm 82:6 – 'I said, "You are gods [θεοί], and all of you are sons [υἱοί] of the most high."' As Justin writes in his succinct interpretation of this verse, it is clear that filiation and deification are understood as parallel to the other: 'all men are deemed worthy of becoming "gods",' and of having power to become sons of the Highest'.[43] To be a child of God is to be divine in some capacity.

Having outlined the concept of divine filiation in the Old Testament writings (whereby Israel is identified collectively as God's 'son'), Jules Gross writes,

> By his incarnation, the Son of God has become the brother of humankind in order to save them. To that end, he reconciles them to his Father, who consequently adopts them as children.

---

[40] 'The 'exchange formula' has its roots in Pauline thinking' (Russell, *Deification*, 108).

[41] Mutschler, *Das Corpus Johanneum*, 427.

[42] Macaskill can say that by the time of Clement of Alexandria, filiation's thematic correlation with deification is 'a consistent theme in patristic writings' (Macaskill, *Union*, 63.).

[43] Justin Martyr, *Dial.*, 124. Mosser identifies three verses from 1 John that Justin cites in this wider passage (Mosser, 'Psalm 82', 40–41).

> Thus, by the appearance of Christ, the Judaic concept of divine filiation is transformed and raised up to a genuine participation. Barely sketched out in the Synoptics, this transformation becomes manifest in Saint Paul and Saint John.[44]

As Gross indicates above, the Pauline concept of adoption and the Johannine concept of children of God born from above provide the basis for the conceptual foundations of filiation in patristic thought. Like the concept of divine–human exchange, deification through filiation derives largely from Jesus' Incarnation: by uniting himself with mortal flesh, Jesus secures for believing humans a divine, filial status by uniting them to God.[45] Characteristic of the confluence of both Pauline and Johannine language in patristic writings on theosis are Cyril of Alexandria's comments on John 1:13 as it pertains to divine filiation[46]:

> He [the Word] joins what is human to himself through the flesh that was united to him, and he is joined by nature to the Father since he is by nature God. In this way, the slaves ascend to sonship through participation in the true Son since they are called and so to speak raised to the honour that is in the Son by nature. Therefore, we who received the new birth through the Spirit by faith are called born of God, and that is what we are.[47]

As with the exchange formula and the use of Psalm 86, the deification theme of filiation is central to patristic theosis discourse. All three are key elements in Johannine ecclesiology.

Chapter Summary

This short introduction to the idea of Johannine theosis has attempted to retrospectively situate the Fourth Gospel within the trajectory of later patristic thinking about deification. In spite of its later developments, theosis offers a repository of ideas and vocabulary for articulating John's

---

[44] Gross, *Divinization*, 80.

[45] Contrary to the observations of Mutschler cited above, both Russell and Macaskill attribute Irenaeus' understanding of deification through filiation to Paul's adoption language and not to John's idea of the children of God (Russell, *Deification*, 106; Macaskill, *Union*, 61).

[46] 'Cyril's perspective is profoundly Pauline as well as Johannine' – Russell, *Deification*, 197.

[47] *In Joh.* 1:13, 136. Translation from Cyril of Alexandria, *Commentary on John*, 61.

participatory ecclesiology. If believers are integrated into the divine interrelation of Father and Son, generated by God himself 'from above', and enabled to share in activities and authority readily classified as divine, then Johannine ecclesiology offers nothing short of 'divinization'. Because John provides such a robust vision of theosis in his narrative, and because patristic theologians constructed their ideas of theosis while reflecting on major Johannine themes, applying theosis language to Paul with minimal regard to John is canonically lopsided and historically inaccurate. With the use of Psalm 82 and the thematic significance of divine–human exchange and filiation, the fourth evangelist stands in the history of early Christianity as one of the first theologians of deification.

9

JOHANNINE THEOSIS: DEIFICATION AS ECCLESIOLOGY

I have made clear that my purpose is not to conform John's Gospel to the later concepts and semantics of patristic theosis, but to demonstrate the conceptual and semantic serviceability of patristic theosis for describing the fourth evangelist's ecclesial vision. The subject of my study is not theosis per se, but theosis that is explicitly *Johannine*. The purpose of this chapter is to outline the contours of Johannine theosis. I will then revisit participatory themes in the narrative ecclesiology of the Prologue and show how the ecclesial model of oneness as association is at the same time a oneness of participation and deification – Jesus' prayer in John 17 'that they may be one' is a plea for corporate theosis.

The Nature of Johannine Theosis: Jewish, Narrative, and Communal

Divinity is an inclusive category in the Fourth Gospel (see Chapter 2). As will be made clear below, the *divine identity* shared between Jesus and God is exclusive; but the *divine interrelation* between Father and Son is communally open, creating the possibility of a divine society of human family members. The models of ecclesiology that have been emerging throughout this study of the Fourth Gospel can be succinctly listed as *participation through filiation* and *association through oneness*. Both filial participation and associative oneness, however, are dimensions of the broader event of the deification of Johannine believers: 'filiation' refers to their participation in the Father–Son interrelation; 'deification' is the ontological transformation that filiation entails or requires and the believers' social identity of association with the 'one' God entails some form of divine status. Johannine ecclesiology is ultimately deification because believers collectively participate in the Father–Son union by becoming divine beings born from above. Along with his narrative christology, the fourth evangelist is narrating the creation of a new humanity enabled by divine (re)birth to participate in the speech, activities, and filial joy of the one God, Father and Son.[1] This narrative pattern is established in the Prologue and extended throughout the Gospel in the motif of oneness.

Though serviceable for the descriptive task of outlining Johannine ecclesiology, theosis language notoriously lends itself to misconstrual in contemporary ecclesial and theological contexts (as highlighted in the discussion of Macaskill's comments in the previous chapter). I will therefore provide three qualifying and descriptive statements on the nature of Johannine deification (that it is Jewish, narrative, and communal) and then show that the evangelist does not envision the dissolving of human beings into some ethereal, generic category of divinity. Though the Johannine idea of divinity is inclusive of human participation in the Fourth Gospel, divine–human parameters and distinctions are carefully maintained.

Johannine Theosis as Jewish Theosis

The first clarification to make about Johannine theosis is that this Gospel's vision of participation and deification is explicitly *Jewish*. I argued in Part II that the fourth evangelist's primary theological source for the oneness motif is the scriptural affirmation of the Shema rather than the oneness conceptuality found in Hellenistic philosophy and Greco-Roman mystery religions. It may seem incongruent to apply now to John's Gospel the language of theosis, a category normally associated with Alexandrian Christianity and therefore also with (Middle and Neo-)Platonic philosophy. Adolf Harnack was famously suspicious of deification, regarding it as a Hellenistic idea imported into post-apostolic Christianity: 'The notion of the redemption as a deification of mortal nature is subchristian'; therefore, 'the whole doctrine is inadmissible' having 'scarcely any connection with the Jesus Christ of the Gospel'. Since deification 'is connected with the real Christ only by

---

[1] Norman Russell classifies patristic ideas of deification along a continuum moving from imitation (*homoiosis*) to participation (*methexis*). Within his category of participation he denotes another range of intensity. The appropriation of divine life can be simply 'in principle', though not experientially evident. This appropriation can also be 'dynamic' in such a way that human beings actually experience certain elements of the deified life. Johannine theosis entails a level of participation that extends beyond mere metaphor and principle and involves both an actual re-origination in the cosmic realm of 'above' and an experiential filial union with the divine figures of God and the Logos. See Russell, *Deification*, 1–3. NB: I am using 'ontological' in a less technically nuanced sense, understanding it to represent the nature of anthropological being.

uncertain threads, it leads us away from him' and is 'not founded in truth'.[2]

Norman Russell notes[3] that Harnack's negative assessment of deification endures among some scholars of Christian origins, even though the trend of attributing early Christianity to an unconscious syncretism of Hellenistic ideas is less tenable today. Hans Boersma, for instance, celebrates what he calls the 'Platonist–Christian synthesis' whereby patristic thinkers employed Greek religious and philosophical language and ideas but, with varying degrees of care, modified them in accordance to a vast array of convictions that were explicitly *Christian*.[4] The Platonist tradition was actually found as an 'ally rather than an opponent'; by no means was everything Platonic 'incompatible with the gospel'. According to Boersma, the church fathers were not naïve about the Platonist tradition.[5] The syncretism of disparate ideas certainly occurred at times, but patristic writers generally reworked Platonist values and concepts in accordance with their christology.[6]

The early Christian reception of the Platonic tradition also coincided with the reception of diverse Jewish traditions with certain conceptual roots that had developed quite independently of Hellenism.[7] Identifying firm demarcations between the boundary lines of Greek, Christian, and Jewish thinking is a tedious and perhaps impossible exercise; the point here is that Hellenistic influences in the first centuries of the church remained in tension with both Christian and Jewish theology. On the

---

[2] Adolf Harnack, *What Is Christianity?*, trans. Thomas Bailey Saunders, 3rd edn. (London: Williams & Norgate, 1912), 238.

[3] Russell, *Deification*, 3

[4] Hans Boersma, *Heavenly Participation: The Weaving of a Sacramental Tapestry* (Grand Rapids, MI: Eerdmans, 2011), see esp. 19–39.

[5] Ibid., 36.

[6] Ibid. Preserving ontological distinctions remains a distinctive legacy in early Jewish and early Christian ideas of participation or deification, a distinction John certainly honours. Some early theologians writing on theosis were more reliant on Platonic language and ideas than others (e.g., Origen and Clement of Alexandria), but the ontological gulf between human beings and the one supreme God of Jewish/Christian theology was eventually identified and then largely maintained in the Greek patristic tradition. The emphasis on *creatio ex nihilo* beginning with Athanasius established the primary conceptual basis for this gulf and reconceived divinization in accordance with Jewish creation theology. See Andrew Louth, *The Origins of the Christian Mystical Tradition: From Plato to Denys* (Oxford: Oxford University Press, 1981), 78–80; 196–98.

[7] In reference to deification, Russell lists three early Jewish ideas that owed very little to Greek thought: 'the peopling of heaven with the angelic orders, the revelation of divine mysteries to a representative human figure, and the participation of the elect in a new exalted life beyond the grave' (Russell, *Deification*, 65).

topics of theosis and participation, both Macaskill and Russell take pains to show that these themes derive from sources spanning Athens and Jerusalem.[8] For writers in early Christianity and Judaism, Jewish theology exerted conforming pressure on Hellenistic religious and philosophical ideas. Though a range of variance was inevitable, concepts imported from outside the Jewish cultural and religious matrices were largely assimilated into the more dominant convictions that the God of Israel was singular and unique.

Writing on Clement of Alexandria's understanding of Psalm 82, Carl Mosser similarly grants that Hellenistic ideas are detectable. But his overall conclusion is that 'the patristic citation of this Psalm was not an *ex post facto* attempt to provide warrant for alien terminology imported into the Christian tradition by well-meaning Hellenizers'.[9] The recapitulation of salvation-history in Psalm 82 'might look very Hellenistic', but the 'eschatological hope and the theological story in which it is embedded have their roots deep in early Judaism'.[10] Noting how the Psalm is cited in John 10 and in other Jewish writings, Mosser argues that this primary text of patristic deification discourse constitutes an adaption of 'an interpretation of Psalm 82 that was common currency in the Second Temple era'.[11] The following citations from early Jewish texts indicate that certain ideas about human divinization were operative in early Judaism (see also pp. 176–77 below for more examples):

> For in the heights of the world shall they dwell,
> And they shall be made like the angels,
> And be made equal to the stars;
> And they shall be changed into whatever form they will,
> From beauty into holiness,
> And from light into the splendor of glory.
>
> *(2 Bar. 51:10)*[12]

> He [God] caused some of the sons of the world to draw near (him) ... to be counted with Him in the com[munity of the 'g]ods' as a congregation of holiness in service for eternal life and (sharing) the lot of his holy ones. (From DSS, 4Q181)[13]

---

[8] Macaskill, *Union*, see esp. 100–27; Russell, *Deification*, 53–78. See also Collins, *Divine Nature*, 27–32.

[9] Mosser, 'Psalm 82', 58.   [10] Ibid., 60.   [11] Ibid., 62.

[12] Cited in Russell, *Deification*, 70.

[13] Cited in ibid., 69. Translation from Geza Vermes, *The Complete Dead Sea Scrolls in English* (Harmondsworth: Penguin, 2011), 183.

My [a human speaker] glory is incomparable, and apart from me none is exalted. None shall come to me, for I dwell in . . . in heaven . . . I shall be reckoned with the 'gods' and my dwelling place is in the congregation of holiness . . . [F]or I am reckoned among the 'gods,' and my glory is with the sons of the King. (From DSS, 4Q491 fr. 11)[14]

Under the rubric of 'angelomorphism', Crispin Fletcher-Louis has written extensively on the divine–human interdynamics found in the Qumran texts and throughout early Jewish literature.[15] In his study of Psalm 82 in the Fourth Gospel, Martinus J. J. Menken provides extensive evidence from Old Testament, early Jewish, and early Christian texts to show that before and around John's time the idea was readily available that 'individual human recipients of special revelation were supposed to be present in the heavenly council'.[16] Naturally, Moses was a primary candidate, whom God appointed 'as/like God' before Pharaoh (ἰδοὺ δέδωκά σε θεὸν Φαραω) in Exodus 7:1 and whose face shone with the radiance of divine glory in Exodus 34:29–35. Ben Sira writes of Moses that '[God] made him equal in glory to the holy ones' (Sir 45:2).[17] Yet even Philo's exaltation of Moses to godlike status resists certain divinizing trends in the Hellenistic milieu, to which he is otherwise so open:

In spite of a doctrine of the soul which is thoroughly Greek, and in spite of a predicative use of the word θεός, which is also thoroughly Greek, Philo is unwilling to say that Moses is a god except by title or analogy. And without biblical

---

[14] Partially cited as 4QM^a in Russell, *Deification*, 69–70 and by Martinus J. J. Menken, 'The Use of the Septuagint in Three Quotations in John: Jn 10,34; 12,38; 19,24', in *The Scriptures in the Gospels*, ed. Christopher M. Tuckett (Leuven: Leuven University Press, 1997), 367–93, here at 377. Translation above from Vermes, *Complete Dead Sea Scrolls*, 342–43. For a closer look at this passage as a deification text, see Morton Smith, 'Ascent to the Heavens and Deification in 4QM^a', in *Archaeology and History in the Dead Sea Scrolls*, ed. Lawrence H. Schiffman, JSPSup 8 (Sheffield: Sheffield Academic, 1990), 181–88.

[15] See, e.g., Crispin Fletcher-Louis, *Luke-Acts: Angels, Christology and Soteriology*, WUNT 94 (Tübingen: Mohr Siebeck, 1997), esp. Part II, 109–215: and Crispin Fletcher-Louis, *All the Glory of Adam: Liturgical Anthropology in the Dead Sea Scrolls* (STDJ 42; Leiden: Brill, 2002).

[16] Menken, 'Septuagint', 379; see 376–79.

[17] Translation from Michael D. Coogan, ed., 'Ecclesiasticus, or The Wisdom of Jesus, Son of Sirach', in *The New Oxford Annotated Apocrypha*, trans. Daniel J. Harrington, Revised Fourth Edition (Oxford: Oxford University Press, 2010), 99–169, here at 159.

>   authority he would not have ventured to say even that – so
>   eager is he to qualify the statement – even though Moses
>   shared in the kingship and glory of God through his ascent
>   of Mount Sinai.[18]

The two related points to be observed here are 1) that the themes of
participation and deification are not isolated to the Platonic tradition in
the Hellenistic world; and 2) that the appropriation by early Jewish
writers of Hellenistic ideas about these themes often involved their
modification to Jewish convictions about theology and anthropology.
Though a conscious Jewish–Hellenistic interchange is certainly evident
in John,[19] the fourth evangelist's theological and anthropological perspectives are most appropriately situated within the scriptural and cultic
traditions of early Judaism.[20] The themes of family kinship and oneness,
both central to the Gospel's ecclesial vision, are sourced respectively in
the Jewish understanding of God's relationship to Israel and in the
monotheistic confession of the Shema. In my use of patristic deification
discourse to describe the Fourth Gospel's ecclesiology, Johannine
theosis is *Jewish* theosis.

Johannine Theosis as Narrative Theosis

Deification is a theme associated primarily with the genres of patristic-
era theological treatises and brought to expression by an array of
recognizable, quasi-technical vocabulary.[21] Identifying the theme of
deification in John requires a degree of genre-translation because
Johannine theosis is *narrative* theosis. The fourth evangelist did
not craft a treatise with a set list of formally recognized theological
keywords. His ecclesial vision of participation is embedded within the
unfolding sequence of his Gospel story.[22] For this reason, many
patristic writers worked out their own ideas about deification as they

---

[18] Russell, *Deification*, 64.

[19] Specifically I am thinking of the translation of Jewish terms into Greek (e.g., μεσσίας/
χριστός), the theme of the Jewish Diaspora (7:35; 10:16; 11:45–53), the Έλληνες who seek
Jesus in 12:20, and the multilingual inscription on the titulus, which is unique to John
(19:20; cf. Mt 27:37; Mk 15:26; Lk 23:38).

[20] I say this with the recognition that intrinsic to the rubric 'early Judaism' is some
degree of Hellenistic influence.

[21] It should be noted, however, that Justin makes references to the theme of deification
through the genre of discourse in his *Dialogue with Trypho*.

[22] In his study of Cyril's ideas of participation and divinization, Daniel Keating notes
that there is a narrative dynamic to theosis. The 'narrative of divine life' involves the

wrote Gospel commentaries. Theosis, therefore, is in many respects a *narrative concept*.

In his *Inhabiting the Cruciform God*, Michael Gorman contextualizes his arguments for Pauline theosis within a narrative framework.[23] For Gorman, the theme of participation in Christ includes a participation in 'the story of Christ', that is, an overarching narrative that possibly generates and governs the discursive material in the apostle's letters.[24] This approach to Pauline theosis makes important contributions; it is, however, to some degree experimental because Gorman must work primarily with non-narrative material.[25]

To find theosis operative in a narrative frame in the New Testament, we are on surer textual footing when we turn to the Fourth Gospel. Johannine theosis does not require excavating or constructing a liminal narrative 'substructure'. The Gospel is itself a 'story of Christ' in which deification serves as a major function of the narrative programme. Gorman proposes a 'narrative soteriology' for Paul, the heart of which is theosis. My proposal is that the fourth evangelist presents a 'narrative ecclesiology' (which naturally includes soteriology) with theosis as a defining developmental theme. John offers what could be called 'narrative theosis' because it is along the plot sequence of the Gospel that believers are gradually included as participants of divine reality. Linearity and deification go hand in hand as the disciples' integration within the Father–Son union occurs over the course of the narrative, a narrative in which the audience outside the text is invited to participate.[26] When it comes to the narrative dynamic of participating

biblical creation story, the event of the Incarnation, and then the gradual appropriation of divine life over the course of a believer's life. See Keating, *Appropriation*, 7–9.

[23] Gorman, *Inhabiting*.   [24] Ibid., 167.

[25] In narrative readings of Paul, the narrative in question is external to the literary corpus of his letters and is usually identified as the salvation-history resolved in the linear events of Christ's death, resurrection, and glorification.

[26] The fourth evangelist encourages audience participation by at least three different ways: 1) the use of first person plurals, particularly in the Prologue (1:14, 16; 3:11; cf. 4:22); 2) the direct address of the narrator who presents himself as a trustworthy witness (19:35–37); and 3) the stated purpose of the Gospel addressed to 'you' in the plural form (20:30–31). Reader participation is even more pronounced if, as Martyn has suggested, John indeed narrates a 'two-level drama' by which the account of Jesus' life is intentionally mapped onto the contemporary community experience (in Martyn, *History and Theology*). For reader entrapment in John's Gospel, see Jeffrey Lloyd Staley, *The Print's First Kiss: A Rhetorical Investigation of the Implied Reader in the Fourth Gospel*, SBLDS 82 (Atlanta, GA: Scholars Press, 1988).

within divine reality and 'the story of Christ', the Gospel of John is the quintessential New Testament text.

So unlike the patristic theologians (and, arguably, unlike Paul), the fourth evangelist binds the theme of deification to a narrative process of sequential development. To understand the Johannine themes of participatory ecclesiology ('Johannine theosis'), attention must be given to how deification is grounded in the conceptualization of Israel in early Judaism ('Jewish theosis') and developed through a storied sequence ('narrative theosis'). As noted earlier, the ecclesial vision of corporate participation in divinity is so embedded within the Gospel story that John can be regarded as a 'deification narrative'.

Johannine Theosis as Communal Theosis

I have thus far addressed two potential areas of misunderstanding for John's theme of deification: 1) the associations of theosis with Hellenistic religion and philosophy as opposed to early Judaism, and 2) the associations of theosis with the genres of patristic commentary and theological treatise. A third potential area of misunderstanding is the association of theosis with *individual* exaltation or soteriology. In Greco-Roman concepts of apotheosis, divinization is usually an isolated event experienced by a particular figure. The same is often true for biblical and early Jewish literature where divine qualities are attributed to key individuals. As already observed, Moses is appointed to serve as a 'god' to Pharaoh (Exod 7:1) and his face later radiates with the divine glory (Exod 34:29–35). In the Synoptic Gospels, Moses and Elijah appear alongside Jesus clothed in divine light (Mt 17:1–13; Mk 9:2–8; Lk 9:28–36). In the *Similitudes of Enoch*, the prophetic figure undergoes a mysterious transformation and is then designated as *a* 'son of man' in some way parallel to *the* 'Son of Man' (1 Enoch 71:11–17).[27] In 2 Enoch, the face of Methusalam shines like the sun from behind the altar (69:10). In the *Testament of Abraham*, the eponymous protagonist sees 'a man seated on a golden throne. And the appearance of that man was terrifying, like the Master's' (11:4).[28] In reply to Abraham's 'who is this wondrous man ... ?', the 'Commander-in-chief' explains that it is Adam (11:8–9). In *Joseph*

---

[27] From 'Recension J', trans. E. Isaac in '1 Enoch: A New Translation and Introduction', in Charlesworth, ed., *The Old Testament Pseudepigrapha*, vol. 1, 5–89.

[28] From Recension A; trans. E. P. Sanders, in 'Testament of Abraham: A New Translation and Introduction', in Charlesworth, ed., *The Old Testament Pseudepigrapha*, vol. 1, 871–902.

and Aseneth, Joseph's physical features are mirrored in the chief angel who visits Aseneth in her repentance,[29] a heavenly being she calls a 'god' (17:9). This divine figure speeds away in a 'chariot of four horses' (17:8), a description parallel with that of Joseph's own chariot (5:4).[30] After partaking of the 'bread of life', 'the cup of immortality', and the 'ointment of incorruptibility' (16:16), Aseneth is depicted in terms of heavenly splendour (18:5–11; 20:6); and both Joseph and the angel place their right hand on Aseneth's head as a paralleled action (8:9; 16:13; cf. 21:6). This sampling conveys that human mimesis of divine beings and even divine communicability surface in a diverse range of Jewish texts with features or activities of heavenly figures ascribed to human beings.[31]

In John's Gospel, divine communicability is not limited, however, to one distinct mortal character such as Moses, Enoch, Adam, a prophet, a patriarch, or even to Jesus the Logos; included within the category of divinity are the children of God, who collectively participate in the filial bond of Israel's God and his Son. There is no individual apotheosis of an ancient biblical hero (and no Transfiguration account).[32] Instead, the fourth evangelist identifies the unique Word as a pre-existent being who has always been included in the divine identity and then narrates the collective integration of believers into a corporate family ontologically regenerated from the heavenly realm and constituting the one people of the one God. The evangelist is clear that Moses did not see God, but since the disciples have seen Jesus, they are jointly granted divine status as God's children (1:18; 14:8–9; cf. 5:37).[33] Soteriology, a concept usually associated with individual salvation, *is ultimately*

---

[29] 'A man in every respect similar to Joseph ... except that his face was like lightning, and his eyes like sunshine, and the hairs of his head like a flame of fire of a burning torch, and hands and feet like iron shining forth from a fire, and sparks shot forth from his hands and feet.' *JosAs*, 14.9.

[30] Aseneth describes Joseph as a 'son of God' (6:3, 5), and 'nothing escapes him, because of the great light that is inside him' (6:6). Translations C. Burchard from 'Joseph and Aseneth: A New Translation and Introduction', in Charlesworth, ed., *The Old Testament Pseudepigrapha*, vol. 2, 177–247.

[31] See also Ezekiel the Tragedian's *Exagōgē* 70, where Moses sees in a vision a 'man' (φώς, a poetic term for ἀνήρ) seated on what appears to be a divine throne – Alan F. Segal, 'Mysticism', ed. John J. Collins and Daniel C. Harlow, *The Eerdmans Dictionary of Early Judaism* (Grand Rapids, MI: Eerdmans, 2010), 982–86, here at 984.

[32] 'No one has ascended into heaven except the one who descended from heaven, the Son of Man' (3:13).

[33] It is possible that John's emphasis on Jesus as the sole revealer of divine reality is a critique against the trend in post–70 Judaism to emphasize heavenly ascents as requisite for spiritual insight. See James D. G. Dunn, 'Let John Be John: A Gospel for Its Time', in

ecclesiology in John's Gospel because the central salvific effect is to be resocialized into the community of a new divine family. Jan van der Watt captures this communal nature of salvation in this excerpt from an essay on Johannine soteriology:

> Having [eternal] life implies being enabled to consciously and existentially partake in the reality of the family of God. To live in this ordinary world means being able to eat, drink, enter into relations with others, act, and obey. The same applies to eternal life. Receiving this life through birth means that a person becomes able to participate in the heavenly reality of God. He or she becomes a child of God within the family of God – through birth – which implies participation in all the associated rights. In this heavenly reality, believers can act, enter relations, and experience the heavenly reality in the form of peace and love. Having eternal life, therefore, means that we can participate fully in the familial reality of God. Being born into that family, and thus having eternal life in that family, namely the figurative family of God, determines their lives within those communities.[34]

Van der Watt's comments imply that *salvation is filiation and resocialization*. Johannine soteriology extends beyond the scope of a personal salvific event or experience and, likewise, deification in John does not point to the divinization or salvation of a sole individual. Certain characters in John do manifest divine attributes at specific points in the narrative; but as will be shown in the next chapter, these individuals are paradigmatic and representative of the wider sphere of believers (it will be argued presently that this is the case even for the honoured role of the Beloved Disciple). Unique to the Fourth Gospel is the occasional, yet powerfully suggestive, first person plural: 'we have seen his glory' (1:14); 'out of his fullness we all have received' (1:16); 'we have found the Messiah' (1:41); 'we have found the one whom Moses wrote about in the Law and the Prophets, the Messiah' (1:45); 'we speak of what we know, and we bear witness to what we have seen' (3:2); 'we worship what we know' (4:22); 'It is no longer because of what you said that we believe, for we ourselves have heard, and we know that this is indeed the Saviour of the world' (4:42); 'Lord, to whom shall we go? You have the

---

The Gospel and the Gospels, ed. Peter Stuhlmacher (Grand Rapids, MI: Eerdmans, 1991), 293–322, here at 310.

[34] Van der Watt, 'Salvation in the Gospel', 124.

words of eternal life, and we have believed, and we have come to know, that you are the Holy One of God' (6:68); 'we must work the works of him who sent me' (9:4) 'Let us also go, that we may die with him' (11:16); 'Lord, we wish to see Jesus' (12:21); 'Now we know that you know all things and do not need anyone to question you; this is why we believe that you came from God' (16:30); 'we have seen the Lord' (20:25); 'Simon Peter said to them, "I am going fishing." They said to him, "we also are coming with you" (21:3); 'this is the disciple who is bearing witness about these things, and who has written these things, and we know that his testimony is true' (21:24).

Johannine theosis is communal, and thus also ecclesial. The claim that this Gospel emphasizes individualism breaks apart on the evangelist's explicit concerns to narrate the formation of a new social group around Jesus. Though John highlights the actions and words of certain individuals and perhaps beckons the reader into some form of personal introspection,[35] the evangelist knows nothing of 'the introspective conscience' of Western culture, as Krister Stendahl has put it.[36] In fact, John actively resists individualistic language for believers – Jesus alone is the Son while believers are collectively labelled 'children', 'flock', and so forth. Moreover, it is the objective of the evangelist's writing that you, *plural*, may believe ($\pi\iota\sigma\tau\epsilon\acute{\upsilon}[\sigma]\eta\tau\epsilon$[37]). Ecclesiology in this Gospel is a social vision of a divine family that persists as 'one' within the society of the Father and the Son. Put differently, the *Fourth Gospel's ecclesial vision consists of the corporate deification of believers to form a new humanity.* And this Johannine theosis is expressed in Jewish categories and worked out in the unfolding sequence of the Gospel's narrative.

---

[35] Though we tend to regard reading as an individual and even solitary activity, reading would have been primarily a communal exercise in John's ancient media culture. See the chapter 'Literacy and Literary Culture in Early Christianity', in Harry Y. Gamble, *Books and Readers in the Early Church: A History of Early Christian Texts* (New Haven, CT: Yale University Press, 1995), 1–42. See also the collection of essays in Holly E. Hearon and Philip Ruge-Jones, eds., *The Bible in Ancient and Modern Media: Story and Performance*, vol. 1, *Biblical Performance Criticism* (Eugene, OR: Cascade Books, 2009).; and in Donne and Thatcher, eds., *The Fourth Gospel in First-Century Media Culture.*

[36] Stendahl was addressing the inward anxiety that has driven the hermeneutical approach to Paul's idea of justification; though he is not specifically addressing communal versus individual perspectives, the individuality of Western culture certainly goes hand in hand with its 'introspective conscience'. See Krister Stendahl, *Paul Among Jews and Gentiles, and Other Essays* (London: SCM Press, 1977), 16–17.

[37] Regardless of whether this verb was originally present (P^{66vid}, א, B, Θ) or aorist subjunctive (as in the rest of the MSS), the number is unmistakably plural.

Boundaries within the Inclusive Divine Community

The concept of theosis implies that divine–human boundaries become porous. Resistance to a categorization of divinity inclusive of human participants has been noted in Chapter 6 (pp. 124 – 27). For the most part, patristic writers were not unaware of this provocative nature of deification – the concept strikingly conveyed the extraordinary nature of Christian identity. But the risk taken was to threaten the uniqueness of the identity of the one (Triune) God. Qualifications therefore abound among the early theologians who were eager to 'provide an account of divine–human communion that [did] not compromise the essential uniqueness of God'.[38] Irenaeus of Lyons, for instance, directly refers to believers 'who received the filial adoption' as the 'gods' referred to in Psalm 82 (*Haer.*, 3.6.1), but then clarifies his meaning by pointing out that when 'Scripture calls those gods who really are not, it does not ... present them as gods absolutely, but with certain modification and indication by which they are shown not to be gods' (*Haer.*, 3.6.3).[39] In his commentary on the phrase 'he was the true light' in John 1:9, Cyril writes that the

> divine Evangelist ... makes a clear distinction between that which is something by nature and those that are the same thing by grace; between that which is participated in and those that participate in it; between that which supplies itself to those in need and those that receive the abundance. If the Son is the true light, then nothing else besides him is truly light. Originate beings will not produce what I just indicated as a fruit of their own nature. Just as they exist from [former] nonexistence, so also they rise up to being light when they were [formerly] not light. They will receive the beams of the true light and be made to shine brightly by participation in the divine nature. By imitation of that nature, they will be called and will be light. The Word of God is light in his substance. He is not light by participation, that is, by grace, nor does he have this dignity in himself as an accident.[40]

Though Cyril can refer to human believers as 'gods' (*Jo.* 12.1), his comments above show that the divinity of human beings is entirely

---

[38] Macaskill, *Union*, 75.

[39] From Irenaeus of Lyons, *Against the Heresies* (trans. Grant), 39. See also *Haer.*, 3.19.2.

[40] Cyril of Alexandria, *Jo.* 96. From Cyril of Alexandria, *Commentary on John*, 1:43.

derivative and accessed by way of participation in that which is divine naturally or sui generis. In spite of the tremendous grace that relaxes the boundaries between divinity and mortality, an ontological gulf is still affirmed: 'the Only Begotten is different from us and from creation, as far as the identity of nature is concerned' (*Jo.*, 99).[41] Commenting on John 1:12 he goes on to say that 'being something by nature is different from being something by adoption, and being something truly is different from being something by imitation. We are called sons by adoption and imitation' (*Jo.*, 134).[42]

Cyril's joint affirmations of both the participation of humans in the divine life and the persistence of divine–human boundaries are entirely appropriate for a commentary on John, a Gospel in which these affirmations receive careful treatment. It has already been observed that plurality is constitutive of divine unity (see Chapter 2). In other words, Jesus is correlated with God but not in such a way that the two dissolve into one another: Jesus may be 'one' with the Father (10:30), but the Father is 'greater' (14:28); the Word 'was God', and was also 'with God' (1:1–2). Plurality is intrinsic to the Johannine conceptualization of inclusive divinity: *christological* space is provided for including Jesus within the divine identity; *ecclesial* space is provided for including believers *not within the divine identity*, but within the *divine family*. Delineations between these participants in divinity are limned throughout the Gospel, affirming a gulf between the divine identity comprising Jesus and God and the divine family into which human beings are integrated.

On certain occasions, Jesus will speak directly of exclusive privileges and roles he shares with the Father in a reciprocal sense. These reciprocity statements are heavily concentrated in Jesus' discourse in John 5: 'For just as [ὥσπερ γάρ] the Father raises the dead and gives them life, so also [οὕτως καί] the Son gives life to whom he wishes' (5:21); 'that all may honour the Son just as [καθώς] they honour the Father' (5:23); 'for just as [ὥσπερ γάρ] the Father has life in himself, so also [οὕτως καί] he has granted the Son to have life in himself' (5:26). The authority to raise the dead, to give out divine life, and to receive the honour due to the Father, is limited to Jesus in John's Gospel.[43] Yet there are instances

---

[41] Ibid., 1:44.

[42] Ibid., 1:60. For a discussion on Clement of Alexandria's clarifications on divine–human boundaries, see Russell, *Deification*, 134–38. For Origen's (which are less strict than Clement's) see ibid., 144–52.

[43] In addition, the reciprocal relationship between the disciples and the Father and Son is maintained through continual obedience and abiding (6:56; 15:4–10), 'whereas this

when elements of Jesus' divinity become inclusive. The blind man says 'I am' (9:9); Peter is given a role as shepherd (21:15–19); and the privileged access to the Father Jesus has in prayer is extended to the disciples (11:22, 41–42; cf. 14:13–14; 15:7, 16–17; 16:23–24). The extension of divine speech, privileges, and activities to include the disciples will be discussed in the next chapter. It is important to observe here that the evangelist is attempting to narrate a unique divine entity while simultaneously presenting a robust vision of ecclesial divinization. So how does John maintain a gulf between the divine identity consisting of Jesus and the divine family consisting of believers?

This gulf is pictured through metaphorical imagery, enacted by narrative events, and ordered by the language of filiation. As for the imagery, Jesus is clearly the vine and the disciples are cast in the derivative position of branches (15:1–11); Jesus is the bridegroom and believers are collectively the bride (3:29); Jesus is the Shepherd while the ecclesial entity is the flock (10:1–18). In each of these images, Jesus stands as a singular figure and the believers are identified corporately as dependants. Narrative events that draw distinctions between Jesus and believers include the blind man's act of worship (9:38) and the collapse of the armed guard at the final 'I am' statements (18:4–8). Filial language also maintains a gulf between the divine identity and human beings while allowing the ecclesial vision of a participatory and divinized family. The linguistic precision is impressive. Only Jesus is referred to as ὁ μονογενής (the only Son) and ὁ υἱός (the Son), both in the singular. The filial term of reference for believers is the collective τέκνα (and on one occasion 'sons' in the plural – υἱοὶ φωτός/'sons of light' – in 12:36). Though John the Baptist is referred to as being sent from 'God' (1:6), only Jesus is referred to as being sent by the 'Father'. Jesus is also the only character in John's Gospel to refer to God as 'my Father' (ὁ πατήρ μου, occurring 25 times in John[44]). When he affirms the filial incorporation of the disciples within the divine family, the language is not 'I am ascending to our Father and our God', but 'I am ascending to my Father and your Father [πατέρα μου καὶ πατέρα ὑμῶν], my God and your God [θεόν μου καὶ θεὸν ὑμῶν]' (20:17). So although the disciples are actualized as members of the divine family through the death and resurrection of Jesus, the juxtaposition of the singular first person possessive ('my') alongside the plural second person possessive ('your') preserves

---

condition is never posited of the Father and the Son who simply share (an eternal) reciprocal union 'in' each other' – Crump, 'Re-examining', 401–2.

[44] Meyer, "The Father"', 260.

a subtle, yet significant, degree of distinction between Jesus' relationship to God and that of his disciples.

Johannine theosis, therefore, does not envision the divinization of human beings in such a way that they are merged with the identity of the one God of Jewish scriptural traditions. Divinity is indeed inclusive in John, but it is appropriated through filiation as believers share in the interrelation of Father and Son. While an ontological transformation (deification) enables believers to become members of the divine family, the filial terminology, narrated action, and rich metaphors define parameters in the divine–human fellowship.[45]

The Prologue as a Deification Text

Having outlined the basic contours of Johannine theosis, I will now revisit the Prologue and then the oneness motif (in the following section) to show how their ecclesial dynamics can be helpfully labelled as deification. We have seen that John 1:1–18 functions as a narrative opening establishing John's participatory ecclesiology as a major theme. Filiation, a central ecclesial theme for the Prologue, has been identified in the previous chapter as a major component of patristic deification discourse. It was also observed that the idea of divine–human exchange among the early theologians is largely premised on John 1:12–14. This exchange and filiation result in a deification of the children of God because they are ontologically regenerated and accorded a divine status. What follows is a cursory review of the Prologue's ecclesiology that shows how John 1:1–18 is indeed a deification text.

---

[45] Writing from a social Trinitarian perspective, Jürgen Moltmann takes up the Trinitarian term 'perichoresis' to account for the preservation of divine–human boundaries in the relational 'interpenetration' of the Father, Son, believers, and the Spirit: their mutual indwelling 'is not the inner-Trinitarian perichoresis of different Persons of the same nature, but the perichoresis of persons of a different nature with each other . . . In this perichoretic community between the Trinity and the human community there is also simultaneous unity and difference. We are not swallowed up in a divine ocean as finite beings in the infinite being, as some mystics tell us.' From Jürgen Moltmann, 'God in the World – the World in God: Perichoresis in Trinity and Eschatology', in *The Gospel of John and Christian Theology*, ed. Richard Bauckham and Carl Mosser (Grand Rapids, MI: Eerdmans, 2008), 369–81, here at 376. David Crump would argue against this reading, pointing out that the Trinitarian terms of Moltmann's understanding of perichoresis (at least according to John) are unfounded because mutual indwelling or interpenetration in John follows the triadic pattern not of 'Father–Son–Spirit' but 'Father–Son–Disciples'. See Crump, 'Re-examining the Johannine Trinity' (for the quotations, see 412). For a critique of Moltmann's use of perichoresis see Randall E. Otto, 'The Use and Abuse of Perichoresis in Recent Theology', *SJT* 54: 3 (2001): 366–84.

First, it should be noted that the theme of participation is initially christological in the Prologue. Using cosmological language, the author makes clear that the Logos participated in the divine activity of creation and also shares the divine identity. This christological participation is later portrayed as filial in John 1:18 as Jesus, the μονογενής, is embraced within the bosom (κολπός) of the Father.

The Prologue's participatory ecclesiology parallels this participatory christology. Both the Logos and humanity (ἄνθρωποι) are presented cosmologically in the opening of the text and both are depicted in relational imagery by the end of the text (through a process of disambiguation). The Logos shares the divine identity ('the Word was God'), and humankind shares in divine reality ('what came into being in him was life, and the life was the light of human beings'). The phrase 'in him' bears just as much participatory meaning as Paul's 'in Christ', a phrase associated with Pauline theosis.[46] And John's phrase ὃ γέγονεν ἐν αὐτῷ ζωὴ ἦν locates humankind (indicated subsequently in 1:4b as the focal subject of ὃ γέγονεν) within the sphere of divinity because 'life' here is a divine category.[47] Consonant with later patristic readings of salvation-history (often appearing in expositions on Psalm 82), the Prologue presents a participatory anthropology in which humanity was initially created as divine. Commenting on Justin's *Dialogue with Trypho* (124), Carl Mosser summarizes the early Jewish interpretation of Psalm 82 that captures what also seems to be happening in the Johannine Prologue:

> The basic line of thought seems to have been something like this: in the beginning humanity (in the persons of Adam and Eve) was created like God immortal and impassible and would have remained *in* this state if they had obeyed God's commandments. They did not obey and therefore in judgment they fell from their immortal state to suffer death. This appears to be a traditional interpretation that the testimony source has expanded or adapted by indicating (apparently) that in Christ

---

[46] For instance: 'Thus Paul can say that, in Christ, believers are transformed into the righteousness *of God* (2 Cor 5:21). He means, I propose, that Christians are deified.' From Litwa, '2 Corinthians 3', 132; see also 121. The phrase also has strong participatory meaning in 1 John – 2:5, 27, 28; 3:24; 4:13, 15.

[47] By way of review, here is how the text should be rendered:

[1:3b]   χωρὶς αὐτοῦ ἐγένετο οὐδὲ ἕν. ὃ γέγονεν [1:4a] ἐν αὐτῷ ζωὴ ἦν

[1:3b]   Apart from him came into being not one thing. That which has come into being [1:4a] in him was life.

all humans have the opportunity to regain what was lost. Because of the Son of God, humans can be made sons of God and thereby restored to immortality, i.e. made 'gods'.[48]

Human beings, therefore, were understood as participants within divine reality (John 1:1–5), but the Logos' decisive appearance in the world provoked a crisis as collective humanity rejected him (1:9–10). Alternatively, those who received him became participants in a new social reality that is explicitly described as divine since these believers have not been generated through any earthly or mortal agency but through God himself (1:12–13). So the participatory anthropology in the Prologue's opening gives way to a participatory ecclesiology by its closing.

This idea of divine filiation, so integral in patristic theosis texts, is paired with the filial status of the Logos in the dynamic of divine–human exchange, the other major deification theme among patristic writers discussed in the previous chapter along with filiation and the use of Psalm 82. In Chapter 3 I laboured to point out that the evangelist intentionally correlates the 'two becomings' in John 1: 12–14 (the generation of the children of God and the incarnation of the Logos), a correlation readily noted in patristic interpretation. Immediately after the Prologue describes the formation of the divine children, the Logos is identified as a human entity participating (as the μονογενής) in a filial relation to God. And God is in turn now identified in the Prologue's sequence as 'Father'. The exchange dynamic is clear: human believers become divine (1:12–13) because the divine Logos becomes human (1:14). Filiation and exchange are the foundational elements of the Prologue's ecclesiology, and these two themes are foundational for later ideas of deification. Believers derive from a divine paternal source (plus a divine sphere, as the phrase 'born from above' indicates in 3:3) and participate within the social sphere of a divine family comprising the children, the μονογενής, and the Father. Filiation involves deification in the Prologue because membership in this new family includes a divine re-origination ἐκ θεοῦ ('out of God') and a relational participation within a divine social entity. Having made the case in Part I that the Prologue is the foundation of Johannine ecclesiology, the point can now be made that this ecclesiology is one of filiation and theosis. The Prologue is not only an ecclesial text; it is also a deification text.

---

[48] Mosser, 'Psalm 82', 38–39.

Oneness as Deification: Narrative Ecclesiology
in Psalm 82 and John 17

My argument in Part II was that the Johannine motif of oneness constitutes *an ecclesiology of association by which Jewish Christian social
identity is expressed.* Ultimately, Jesus is not praying in John 17 for
a unity of social harmony in light of internal ecclesial schisms. He is
instead identifying Jewish believers as the one people of the one Messiah
of the one God who face claims of social and religious illegitimacy by
fellow Jews. The schism oneness addresses is not internal church strife
among Christians but a wider conflict between Jews and Jewish
Christians. In John 17, oneness is analogously employed, correlating
the believing Christians accused of blasphemy on account of their Christ-
worship with the God of their cultic and scriptural heritage. My study on
oneness in Part II concluded, however, suggesting that the evangelist has
in view not only a oneness of association, but one of participation and
theosis. I will now build my case for understanding *Johannine oneness as
deification* by allowing the evangelist's use of Psalm 82 in conjunction
with the oneness of the Shema in John 10 to inform my reading of
oneness in John 17.

When Jesus is accused of blasphemy after claiming 'I and the Father
are one' in 10:30, he cites Psalm 82 in response to this accusation levelled
by his potential executioners: σὺ ἄνθρωπος ὢν ποιεῖς σεαυτὸν θεόν
('you, being a man, are making yourself God' – 10:33).[49] This charge
lies at the heart of later christological controversies for which John's
Gospel is adduced as an instructive resource. The question in these
controversies and to a large degree in John 10 is this: how can Jesus
exist as both human and God? The fourth evangelist does not provide in
his narrative a Trinitarian formula in reply, of course. In his final words to
the Jews in the entire Gospel – whose hands are clutching stones – Jesus
gives warrant to his explicit self-identification with the one God of the
Shema by appealing to Psalm 82, already noted in this study as the most
important deification text in patristic theology.

> Is it not written in your law, 'I said, you are gods' [ἐγὼ εἶπα· θεοί
> ἐστε]? If he called them 'gods' [θεούς] to whom the word of
> God [ὁ λόγος τοῦ θεοῦ] came (and the scripture is not able to be
> broken), how can you say of whom the Father consecrated and

---

[49] The anarthrous use of θεόν ('a god') is virtually universal in the manuscript witnesses.
But uncorrected P[66] adds the article (τόν) indicating that the god whom Jesus makes himself
out to be is the one God of Israel.

sent into the world, 'you blaspheme', because I said, 'I am a son of God?' (Jn 10:34b–36)[50]

The appeal to Psalm 82 associates Jesus not so much with the one God of Israel (with whom he has just identified himself in 10:30), but with a more general category of divine being: θεοί (LXX, Ps. 81:6). These gods appear in the Psalm as a plurality, and Jesus maintains the collective nature of their identity (note the plural ἐκεῖνοί/those). What I will argue below is that Jesus is drawing on a Jewish tradition associated with Psalm 82 that not only legitimates his own claim to divine status, but also indicates that his coming into the world will result in the plural, collective deification of a new people.

Psalm 82 in Rabbinic Exegesis: The Deification of Israel (and Adam)

Turning to the rabbinical literature for elucidating New Testament texts risks the same accusation of anachronistic exegesis that attends the use of patristic writings. The notorious challenge of reading Paul or the canonical evangelists vis-à-vis the rabbis is determining whether the interpretative traditions found in the latter were operative during the first century. Similar to the previously examined case of the Shema, John's Gospel seems to confirm trends in the rabbinical exegesis of Psalm 82:6 as later iterations of long-standing hermeneutical ideas.

Specifically, these ideas concern the deification of Adam and Israel. I cited earlier[51] Carl Mosser's general synopsis of how patristics and early Jews viewed Psalm 82 as a retelling of salvation-history. Though the Psalm's original intended meaning probably involved God's judgment of angels or other deities,[52] Mosser points out that it was eventually understood that the 'gods' referred to pre-fallen humans who were originally created as divine beings, but lost their immortality after heeding the serpent. The connection to humanity's edenic status is quite natural since Psalm 82:7 begins with 'surely you will die

---

[50] In the phrase υἱὸς τοῦ θεοῦ in 10:36, 'son' is anarthrous in virtually all manuscripts (the exception is P[45]).

[51] pp. 184–85.

[52] Mosser, 'Psalm 82', 65–72. In addition to Mosser's comments, see Joel S. Kaminsky, 'Paradise Regained: Rabbinic Reflections on Israel at Sinai', in *Jews, Christians, and the Theology of the Hebrew Scriptures*, ed. Alice Ogden Bellis and Joel S. Kaminsky, SBLSymS 8 (Atlanta, GA: Society of Biblical Literature, 2000), 15–43, here at 20.

like אדם' (LXX, ἄνθρωποι). Though אדם could certainly be representative
of general humanity (as rendered in the LXX) and not just the biblical
character of Adam, the reference to a punitive death could be understood
as an echo of God's warning about eating from the tree of knowledge in
Genesis 2:17. On this reading, Psalm 82 depicts the fall of Adam and
Eve, divine beings who were stripped of their immunity from death and
reduced to mortal existence.

This interpretation was regularly paired in rabbinical exegesis alongside another featuring Israel on Mount Sinai. In this tradition, the claim of
Psalm 82:6 that θεοί ἐστε καὶ υἱοὶ ὑψίστου πάντες ('you are gods, and all
of you are sons of the most high') refers to Israel's corporate deification
that resulted from the reception of the Law.[53] But because they turned
to the metal calf, their divine status was lost. They were consequently
consigned, as 82:7 reports, to 'die like [mortal] humans'. The paralleled
pattern of deification-then-fall between Israel and Adam is obvious.[54]
Psalm 82 was repeatedly used as a proof text binding these dual exalta-
tion/fall stories in rabbinic thought.[55]

Joel Kaminsky has offered a detailed (though not exhaustive)
treatment of the rabbinic texts in which Psalm 82 serves as
a textual rubric for the deification and fall of both Adam and Israel.
For the sake of my discussion on Jesus' use of Psalm 82 in John's
Gospel, I only engage with a small sampling of these texts. The first
is from *Midrash Rabbah* on Exodus 23:20 ('Behold, I am sending an
angel before you to guard you on the way and to bring you to the
place which I have prepared'):[56]

---

[53] From Kaminsky: 'The rabbis tended to be troubled by all references to other gods and
thus they developed readings, sometimes a bit forced, to fit these texts into their monotheistic worldview ... So when this psalm [82] uses language that implies the existence of
many gods, the rabbis interpret it as referring to humans in an exalted state' (ibid). I have
found other rabbinic passages that envision mortals constituting the divine congregation:
e.g., 'R. Halafta b. Dosa of Kefar Hanania said: If ten men sit together and occupy
themselves in the Law, the Divine Presence rests among them, for it is written, *God stands
in the congregation of God*' (*Ab* 3.6). Translation from Herbert Danby, *The Mishnah:
Translated from the Hebrew with Introduction and Brief Explanatory Notes* (Oxford:
Oxford University Press, 1933), 450.

[54] On Psalm 82:6–7, James Ackerman observes that 'what we have here is a new Fall
story'. From James S. Ackerman, 'The Rabbinic Interpretation of Psalm 82 and the Gospel
of John', *HTR* 59, 2 (1966): 187–91, here at 187. The idea of a 'fall' is explicit in the final
clause of 82:7 – 'you shall fall [נפל/πίπτω] like one of the princes'.

[55] Kaminsky, 'Paradise Regained', 18.

[56] Italicized words indicate scriptural citations.

Thus it is written, *I said: Ye are godlike beings* (Ps 82:6). Had Israel waited for Moses and not perpetrated that act [the worship of the calf], there would have been no exile, neither would the Angel of Death have had any power over them ... When Israel exclaimed: *All that the Lord has spoken will we do, and hearken* (24:7), the Holy One, blessed be he, said: 'If I gave but one commandment to Adam that he might fulfil it, and I made him equal to the ministering angels – for it says *behold the man was one of us* (Gen 3:22) – how much more so should those who practice and fulfil all the six hundred and thirteen commandments – not to mention their general principles, details and minutiae – be deserving of eternal life?' ... As soon, however, as they said, *This is thy god, O Israel* (Exod 32:4), death came upon them. God said: 'You have followed the footsteps of Adam who did not withstand his trials for more than three hours, and at nine hours death was decreed upon him. I said: "Ye are godlike beings", but since you have followed the footsteps of Adam, *Nevertheless ye shall die like men.*' What is the meaning of *And fall like one of the princes*? R. Judah said: Either as Adam or as Eve.[57] (Exod. Rab. 32:1)

The citation from Psalm 82:6, quoted by Jesus in John 10:34, is here understood to be addressed to Israel at Sinai. Their divine status rendered them immune from the Angel of Death. This exalted state was short-lived, annulled by the sinful act of idol worship. A link is immediately drawn to Adam's own divine status before the breach of the one commandment issued in Eden. The gift of the Law bore the potential for restoring Israel to this glorified status. Indeed, the six hundred and thirteen statutes were regarded as more efficacious in redemption than the one statute of the garden. Choosing the calf, however, invited death back into their humanity, just as Adam's sin precipitated his own demise. To 'fall like one of the princes', a phrase taken straight out of Psalm 82:7, is to recapitulate the fall of the immortal Adam.

The connection between Genesis 2–3 and Exodus 19–34 is also made in a midrash reflecting the question in Ecclesiastes 8:1, 'Who is like the

---

[57] *Midrash Rabbah: Exodus*, trans., S. M. Lehrman, in H. Freedman et al., *Midrash Rabbah* 2nd edn. (London and Bournemouth: Soncino Press, 1951), 404–5. A second explanation is also supplied – 'God said to them: "You have brought about your own downfall. In the past, you were served by direct inspiration; now however, you will be served only by an angel" – as it says, *Behold, I send an angel before thee.*' (Ibid.)

wise [person]?'[58] The writer supplies two answers, the first being Adam, whose wisdom was manifest in the divine radiance that emitted even from his feet ('the ball of Adam's heel outshone the sun'), a reading that connects to the later statement in Ecclesiastes 8:1 that 'the wisdom of a man [חכמת אדם] causes his face to shine'. Adam's emission of glorious light fades when he sins. This parallels the scene at Sinai: 'Another interpretation of *who is as the wise man?* This alludes to Israel.' It is reported that when Israel received the Law on Sinai, 'there was granted them something of the lustre of the Shechinah of the Most High'. When the newly divinized people sinned, though, 'the words applied to them into what is written, *Nevertheless you shall die like men* (Ps 82:7)'. So once again, in the giving of the Law Israel is accorded a divine status similar to that which Adam enjoyed in paradise; but in both cases sin effected the loss of divinity (expressed in this midrash as the cessation of the emission of supernatural light).

A concise summary of the rabbinical trend of associating Psalm 82 with Israel at Sinai is provided in *Tanna Debe Eliyyahu*: 'After the giving of Torah, Israel possessed themselves of a false god, and because they worshiped a false god, the angel of death came upon them. Thus, at first God said [to Israel], *You are godlike beings* (Ps 82:6), but after their deeds became corrupt, God went on to say, *Surely, ye shall die like men* (Ps 82:7).' In this text, Rabbi Ishmael ben Eleazar reports that what Adam and Israel lost due to sin will be restored when the Messiah comes. This messianic salvation will accompany the reception of Torah by all peoples: 'each and every nation and kingdom would come and accept the Torah and so live and endure forever and ever and ever'.[59]

Other texts could be adduced to demonstrate the rabbinic use of Psalm 82 as a deification text referring to both Adam in paradise and Israel at Sinai.[60] For the purposes of John's use of Psalm 82, it is important to recognize two points. The first is that 'gods' in 82:6 is understood as addressing human beings – not angels or other deities – who collectively

[58] See *Midrash Rabbah, Ecclesiastes*, trans. A. Cohen, in H. Freedman et al., *Midrash Rabbah* 2nd edn, 213–14.

[59] W. G. Braude and I. J. Kapstein (trans.), *Tanna Debe Eliyyahu* (Philadelphia, PA: Jewish Publication Society of America, 1981), 382–83.

[60] See *Lev. Rab.* 11:1, 3 where God empowered Adam and Eve 'to fly and designated them as deities', a divine privilege and status lost when they sinned, a scenario linked to the people of Israel whom God granted 'divine qualities'. Their exalted state is confirmed by the citation of Ps. 82:6, 'You are godlike beings', a state lost when they turned to the golden calf and thus fell under the condemnation of Ps. 82:7, 'you shall die like humans'. Cited and discussed in Kaminsky, 'Paradise Regained', 33–35.

enjoy some sort of divine status. In other words, Israel can be corporately identified as 'god'/'gods'. The second point to note here is that what deifies Israel at Sinai is the coming of Torah. Israel is made divine by receiving the definitive form of divine revelation. It now remains to ask how these rabbinical readings of Psalm 82 may evidence an interpretative tradition reflected in John 10:34–36, and then to explore the christological – as well as the ecclesial – implications for the evangelist's use of the psalm as a possible deification text.

Psalm 82 in John 10: Christological Apology and Ecclesial Vision

New Testament scholars have repeatedly turned to the rabbinical literature in search of clues for reading Jesus' citation of Psalm 82.[61] Though it has been proposed that the term 'gods' refers to angels[62] or judges[63] in John's context, the strongest arguments come from those interpreters who believe the Sinai tradition just discussed lies at the heart of the fourth evangelist's usage.[64] When Jesus cites the phrase θεοί ἐστε from Psalm 82:6, he also supplies the basis for the divine status of these θεοί: they are

[61] Ps 82 enjoyed some degree of prominence among some rabbis (and perhaps for ancient Israel) – *Tamid* 7.4 reports that this psalm was one of the daily texts sung by the Levites in the Temple (the 3rd day).

[62] See J. A. Emerton, 'Some New Testament Notes', *JTS* 11, 2 (1960): 329–36, here at 329–32. After the association with 'gods' (הימאלו) in Psalm 82 with Melchizedeck was discovered in the DSS (11QMelchizedek), Emerton wrote another brief note expressing his confidence that the Qumran text confirmed his earlier argument. Since הימאלו refers to Belial and evil angels when it does not refer to Melchizedek, he feels confirmed in interpreting 'gods' in John 10:34 as angels. See J. A. Emerton, 'Melchizedek and the Gods: Fresh Evidence for the Jewish Background of John X.34–36', *JTS* 17, 2 (1966): 399–401.

[63] B. F. Westcott, *The Gospel According to St. John* (London: John Murray, 1908), 70; Lightfoot, *St. John's Gospel*, 209. The applicability of this interpretation to John 10:34–36 is flatly rejected by all the specialist studies cited immediately below.

[64] See Hermann L. Strack and Paul Billerbeck, *Kommentar zum neuen Testament aus Talmud und Midrash* (Munich: C. H. Beck'sche Verlagsbuchhandlung, 1965), 543; Dahl, 'The Johannine Church and History', 109–10; Ackerman, 'Rabbinic Interpretation'; A. T. Hanson, 'John's Citation of Psalm 82', *NTS* 11, 2 (1965): 158–62; A. T. Hanson, 'John's Citation of Psalm 82 Reconsidered', *NTS* 13, 4 (1967): 363–67; and Jerome H. Neyrey, '"I Said, You Are Gods": Psalm 82:6 and John 10', *JBL* 108, 4 (1989): 647–63. Added to these focused treatments of John 10:34–36 are several major commentators: Keener, *John*, 829; Carson, *John*, 398. Schnackenburg, *John*, 2:311; Barrett, *John*, 384. A dissenting voice is Ridderbos, *John*, 376. Brown accepts the Sinai tradition as a plausible source for John 10:34–36, but admits that this background cannot be proven – Brown, *John*, 410–11.

those 'to whom the word of God came'.[65] Deification through the reception of verbal, divine revelation accords with the Sinai tradition attached to Psalm 82 in the later rabbinic writings where Israel is depicted as deified at the giving of Torah: 'So Moses came and called the elders of the people and set before them all these words [τοὺς λόγους τούτους] which God had appointed to him' (Exod 19:7, LXX). As Carl Mosser writes, 'Almost all scholars today accept that this tradition [of Psalm 82's connection to Exodus 19] very likely goes back to the Second Temple period and that "those to whom the word of God came" refers to Israel when the Law was given.'[66]

Jerome Neyrey is surely right in observing that 'we must investigate how [Psalm 82] functions as an apology to a specific charge in the forensic dynamics of John 10'.[67] The immediate context of Jesus' citation of the psalm responds to the accusation that he is a man making himself God, an act of blasphemy concisely expressed in the oneness formula of 10:30. Though a *christological* apology is certainly in view in John 10:34–36, the Sinai tradition affixed to Psalm 82 bears implications for *ecclesiology* that seem to have gone largely unconsidered – the current exegesis of John 10:34–36 in biblical studies, therefore, serves as another example of the eclipse of ecclesiology by christology. In the interpretation I provide below, I will supply a reading of John's use of Psalm 82 that is both christological and ecclesial. Along with affirming the deity of Jesus, the evangelist draws from this scriptural text to enrich his ecclesial vision of a new people deified by the coming of the Word of God.

First, it should be acknowledged that Psalm 82 is ultimately a psalm of judgment. Whether the 'gods' are understood as deities, angels, mortal judges, Adam and Eve, or Israel at Sinai, Psalm 82 indicts a group of divine or divinized beings for walking in darkness [בחשכה יתהלכו/ἐν σκότει διαπορεύονται], failing to judge correctly, and neglecting to rescue the vulnerable from the hand of the wicked [מיד רשעים/ἐκ χειρὸς ἁμαρτωλοῦ]. The scene of Hannukah/Dedication in John 10:22–39 in

---

[65] 'The characteristic which qualifies these people as gods, and identifies them as a group, is the fact that the Word of God had come to them' – Ackerman, 'Rabbinic Interpretation', 187.

[66] Mosser, 'Psalm 82', 67–68. Also from Neyrey: 'Although the midrashim studied above were written considerably later than the Fourth Gospel, the understanding of Ps 82:6 in John 10:34–36 belongs in that same trajectory of interpretation. It might be the earliest extant witness of that tradition, although not the most complete example' (Neyrey, 'You Are Gods', 663).

[67] Ibid., 649.

which the psalm is cited is the final direct interchange between Jesus and the Jews in the Fourth Gospel.[68] The climactic scene epitomizes the foregoing dialogues in which Jesus' divine agency and identity are dismissed, thus bringing his opponents into judgment.[69] The divine revelation of the Light of the world is rejected and 'the one who follows me will not walk in darkness [οὐ μὴ περιπατήσῃ ἐν τῇ σκοτίᾳ]' (8:12), an image parallel with Psalm 82:5.[70] Jesus flatly proclaimed in John 8 that the failure to receive him results in the same consequence found in Psalm 82:7, that of death: 'unless you believe that I am, you will die in your sins' (8:24; see also v. 21). Jesus has also identified himself as the great divine Shepherd who protects the vulnerable sheep: 'no one will snatch them out of my hand [ἐκ τῆς χειρός μου]' (10:28).

Grant Macaskill's observation that Johannine participation 'is set firmly in a framework of revelation' accords well with the evangelist's likely use of the Sinai tradition in Psalm 82.[71] The 'noetic incapacity' of the Jews in the Gospel parallels that of Israel in Exodus as both refused to embrace the respective means of divine revelation.[72] Indeed, to reject Jesus is to reject the Jewish scriptural legacy, because repeatedly throughout John the words of Jesus are elevated to scriptural status.[73] In John 7, Jesus implicated the Jews in the same predicament the Sinai tradition of Psalm 82 portrays for Israel: 'Has not Moses given you the Law? Yet none of you keeps the Law' (v. 19). After the prediction of his Resurrection in John 2, it is reported that the disciples eventually 'believed the Scripture and the word that Jesus had spoken' (v. 22) – Jewish γραφή ('Scripture') and Jesus' λόγος ('word') are here paralleled. In John 5, Jesus tried to reason with the Jews about his identity on the basis of Torah: 'If you believed Moses, you would believe me, for he wrote of me. But if you do not believe his writings [γράμμασιν], how will you believe my words [ῥήμασιν]?' (vv. 46–47). Again, the Jewish

[68] Michaels, *John*, 606.
[69] Stephen Motyer points out that John 10 is rarely read with appropriate attention to the themes of Dedication/Hannukah. Jesus is being related to Antiochus Epiphanes IV who, being a man, made himself God, and the Jewish leaders are taking on the role of the Maccabees who purified the Temple and defended monolatry. For my purposes, these connections accentuate the Johannine agenda of forming a new people of the 'one' true God. See 2 Macc 10:6–8 and Stephen Motyer, 'The Fourth Gospel', 99.
[70] Cf. John 12:35–36.   [71] Macaskill, *Union*, 256.   [72] Ibid., 253.
[73] See Beutler, 'The Use of 'Scripture'', 154. As noted previously, Martin Hengel points out that Moses' name is mentioned more in the Fourth Gospel than in the Synoptics or in Paul (11 times); also, the 'concepts νόμος and γραφή' both are found more in John than in the Synoptics. See Hengel, 'Old Testament', 387–88.

Scriptures and Jesus' words are placed on the same plane of revelatory authority. Throughout the discourses leading up to John 10:
34–36, the words of Jesus are repeatedly presented as divine revelation received by some ('when they heard these words [τῶν λόγων
τούτων], some of the people said, "this really is the Prophet"' –
7:40) but ultimately rejected by the Jews ('my word [ὁ λόγος ὁ
ἐμός] finds no place in you' – 8:37; 'you cannot bear to hear my
word [τὸν λόγον τὸν ἐμόν]' – 8:43). Remaining in the word of Jesus
leads to life (8:51), authenticates discipleship, and brings freedom
(8:31–32). Jesus makes the positive consequence of receiving his
word doubly clear: 'if anyone keeps my word, he will never see
death ... if anyone keeps my word, he will never taste death' (8:
51–52). The negative corollary is the same found in the Sinai
tradition of Psalm 82: the rejection of divine revelation (Torah)
results in death ('you will die like humans' – v. 7).

The use of Psalm 82 in John 10:34–36, therefore, is not just to provide
a christological apology for Jesus' supposed blasphemy in John 10:30,
justifying Jesus' claim to divinity; the citation reaffirms the developing
ecclesial vision in which a new society is created by the divine revelation
provided by Jesus. The standard christological interpretation of John 10:
34–36 among Johannine scholars follows the line of a 'from the lesser to
the greater' method of argumentation: if mortal beings can in some way
be referred to as 'gods' and 'sons of the Most High' (a phrase parallel to
'gods' in Ps. 82:6), then *a fortiori* surely Jesus in his unique vocation as
'*the* Son of God'[74] and consecrated divine agent can be legitimately
designated as 'god'.[75]

My own proposal here is that the citation of Psalm 82 allows Jesus to
make an *ecclesiological* statement as well as a *christological* one. He is
indeed a divine being, but in citing Psalm 82 with its likely connections to
the scene at Sinai, he highlights not only his own divine status, *but also
the divine status granted to those who receive him as the definitive
revelation of God* (see John 1:18). The ecclesial significance of this
psalm in John's Gospel is noted by Käsemann, for whom the 'community
under the Word' is a 'heavenly reality':

---

[74] Though the article is missing in the phrase 'son of god' in 10:36, Jesus' identity as *the*
Son of God has been well established by this point in the Gospel narrative.

[75] Perhaps most recently, see Hays, *Echoes of Scripture*, 330–1. Against the
majority of commentators, Ridderbos does not accept the *a fortiori* argumentation
(Ridderbos, *John*, 374). Neyrey argues that Jesus' primary use of the psalm is to
demonstrate that he does not make himself God – it is God who makes Jesus God
(Neyrey, 'You Are Gods', 661).

This idea is expressed in the most astonishing form in 10.34f. There the statement of Ps. 82.6, 'You are gods,' is justified through the reception of the divine Word. To be sure, this verse has a christological slant, but it cannot be limited to christology only, since it already had validity for the community of the old covenant. The accepted Word of God produces an extension of heavenly reality on earth, for the Word participates in the communion of Father and Son. This unity of Father and Son is the quality and mark of the heavenly world. It projects itself to the earth in the Word in order to create the community there which, through rebirth from above, becomes integrated into the unity of Father and Son.[76]

Käsemann, however, understands the evangelist's ecclesiological use of Psalm 82 to betray a 'frightening understanding of the Johannine community' that amounts to 'gnosticizing' and claims that 'his interpretation of the Old Testament is also gnosticizing' in regards to Psalm 82 and elsewhere.[77] Though he discerns some loose idea of a participatory ecclesiology, Käsemann enlists the citation of Psalm 82 as another example of the Fourth Gospel's aberrant trends towards Docetism and Gnosticism. Recognizing John's Jewish milieu and the Jewish interpretative traditions likely affixed to Psalm 82 leads to different conclusions. The participatory ecclesiology in view is that of a renewed Israel established by the faithful reception of the supreme revelation of Israel's one God.

The foregoing discussion affirms that Psalm 82 was not employed in John as a haphazard christological proof text.[78] At a critical point in the narrative where the clash with the Jews has reached a climactic pinnacle, the citation of this psalm – freighted with connections to the giving of Torah – provides a summative reflection on the ecclesial narrative script established in the Prologue.[79] The Word of God – Jesus – has appeared in history as the ultimate disclosure of divine reality whose rejection leads to death, but whose acceptance leads to filiation and deification ('you are gods' and 'sons of the Most High'). Just as Israel's inception was associated with receiving the words of Torah at Sinai, the faithful

---

[76] Käsemann, *Testament*, 69.   [77] Ibid., 70.

[78] Bultmann, *John*, 389. Mosser, however, writes that Psalm 82 expresses themes 'embedded in the narrative theology of John' – see his interpretation, similar to my own, in Mosser, 'Psalm 82', 63.

[79] Ackerman has viewed the Prologue as thematically connected to the Sinai motif attached to Psalm 82 (Ackerman, 'Rabbinic Interpretation', 188–91).

reception of the words of Jesus, who is himself the Word, creates a new people of God who enjoy the divine gift of eternal life.[80] If the deification and fall of Adam is also evoked by John's use of Psalm 82, a possible resonance with this psalm as discussed above, it would suit well the theme of new creation climactically depicted in Jesus' re-enactment of Genesis 2:7 by breathing his breath/Spirit into his disciples in John 20:22, thereby forming a new humanity. And this new humanity consists of the 'children of God', that is, those 'to whom the Word of God came' and who received him; conversely, those 'to whom the Word of God came' but who rejected him will 'die in [their] sins' (8:24); or, as Psalm 82:7 puts it, they will 'die like humans' (Ps. 82:7).

In sum, the evangelist's use of Psalm 82 makes this statement about believers: 'you are gods'.

Psalm 82 and John 17: The Prayer for Oneness as a Prayer for Theosis

Psalm 82 helps make narrative connections between the theological, christological, and ecclesial overtones of oneness in John 17. In John 10, the word 'one' becomes freighted with all three connotations: the 'one flock, one Shepherd' formula succinctly expresses the ecclesial and christological; the phrase 'I and the Father are one' expresses the christological and theological. By appealing to Psalm 82, a deification text linked to the Sinai tradition that seems to have been readily available in the first century, Jesus answers the accusation of blasphemy by including a wider social entity within the sphere of divinity: 'gods' in the plural. Though Jesus is included within the divine identity and thus superior to any other 'god' (1:1, 18; 10:30), the use of Psalm 82 suggests the formation of a new Israel deified through receiving him as the ultimate revelation of God. The plural 'gods' indicates that divinity is to some degree inclusive and open to the wider community of Jesus' recipients. In anticipation of the triadic coordination of ecclesiology, christology, and theology in John 17, the use of Psalm 82 presses for a more open and inclusive conceptualization of divinity, allowing the possibility for mortals to be called 'gods'. In fact, the two distinctive qualifications Jesus provides for himself in his citation of Psalm 82 – that he is consecrated

---

[80] Didymus the Blind offers a similar reading. See Didymus the Blind, *Commentary on Zechariah*, trans. Robert C. Hill, The Fathers of the Church (Washington, D.C.: Catholic University of America Press, 2006), 115.

and sent by the Father – are both used to qualify the believers who are made 'one' with the Father and Son in John 17:[81]

ὃν ὁ πατὴρ **ἡγίασεν** καὶ ἀπέστειλεν εἰς τὸν κόσμον (10:36)[82]
ἁγίασον αὐτοὺς ἐν τῇ ἀληθείᾳ· ὁ λόγος ὁ σὸς ἀλήθειά ἐστιν.
καθὼς ἐμὲ ἀπέστειλας εἰς τὸν κόσμον, κἀγὼ ἀπέστειλα αὐτοὺς
εἰς τὸν κόσμον· καὶ ὑπὲρ αὐτῶν ἐγὼ **ἁγιάζω** ἐμαυτόν, ἵνα ὦσιν
καὶ αὐτοὶ **ἡγιασμένοι** ἐν ἀληθείᾳ (17:17–19)[83]

Jesus' 'god'-status in John 10:34–36 is characterized by his being consecrated and sent into the world by God. These same characteristics are extended to the believers in John 17. Jesus sends them into the world and consecrates himself that they may be consecrated. So, being 'one' with God (10:30), Jesus is also the Word of God – consecrated and sent into the world – whose reception results in deification (10:34–36). In John 17, this divine 'oneness' is expanded to include the faithful recipients who are themselves consecrated and sent into the world (17:11, 17–19, 21–23). For the Fourth Gospel, oneness means deification.

The claim that oneness with God means to be deified is further affirmed by Jesus' prayer for the disciples to share in his divine glory. In 17:4, Jesus attests that he has glorified God, having completed the work assigned to him during his earthly ministry. In v. 5 he asks that God will glorify him 'with yourself' in the heavenly glory he shared with God in his preexistence. The prayer for oneness in 17:22 includes the imparting of this heavenly, preexistent glory to the disciples: κἀγὼ τὴν δόξαν ἥν δέδωκάς μοι δέδωκα αὐτοῖς, ἵνα ὦσιν ἓν καθὼς ἡμεῖς ἕν ('and the glory which you have given to me, I have given to them, in order that they may be one, just as we are one').[84] Though he acknowledges that the heavenly, preexistent glory fitting for divinity is in view in 17:5, Herman Ridderbos assumes that the glory given to the disciples in 17:22 is of a different sort, that of a functional glory of Jesus' mission and work.[85]

---

[81] See also 1 Jn 3:3. [82] 'whom the Father consecrated and sent into the world...'

[83] 'Consecrate them in truth; your word is truth. Just as you sent me into the world, I also have sent them into the world; and on behalf of them I consecrate myself, in order that they may also be consecrated in truth.'

[84] David Mealand sees the mutual indwelling of Father, Son, and disciples as stemming from the theme of God's presence amidst Israel as outlined in Leviticus – Mealand, 'Language of Mystical Union', 19–34.

[85] 'In v. 22 ... the reference is not to this preexistent (and postexistent) glory of Jesus ... but to the glory with which the Father clothed and equipped him as the Son of Man for his mission in the world ... So when Jesus speaks here of the glory given to him by the Father as something he then gives to the disciples, this can hardly refer to anything other than that in their association with him they will be involved in the performance of that task, and not

The text, however, does not delineate between two types of glory, one exclusive to divinity (and thus unshareable with the disciples) and one merely functional or associative (which *is* shareable with the disciples). There is no distinction made in the prayer between a heavenly glory of preexistence and a functional glory of divine activity in the world. The glory befitting divinity that Isaiah saw clothing the preexistent Christ (John 12:41) is bestowed on the deified believers who are one with the one God of Israel.[86] Because Jesus' glory is so closely associated with his death on the cross, however, Käsemann's claim referenced above, namely that Johannine theosis envisions an ecclesiology of heavenly participation of such a (naïvely) docetic nature that bodily life is disparaged, cannot be maintained.[87] For the Fourth Gospel, divine glory is most prominently manifested not in Isaiah's glorious vision but in the scene on Golgotha where the embodied Word was crucified and through which eternal life was granted.[88] The prayer for oneness is precipitated by warnings in the Farewell Discourse that to participate in Jesus is to share in his sufferings (15:18–25; 16:1–4). The deification of Johannine oneness does not promote an escapist flight from this world; its dynamics are decisively operative within this world, a reality that motivates Jesus' prayer in John 17: 'I am not asking that you take them out of this world' (v.15).

The oneness of the disciples in John 17 certainly entails a participation in Jesus' mission and activity. But the theological basis of the Shema behind the term 'one', the expansion of the boundaries of divinity pressed by Psalm 82, and the participation of mortals in the divine and heavenly glory of Jesus all require an understanding of oneness that extends beyond a call to social harmony or a functional imitation of Jesus' earthly ministry. The oneness of John 17 calls for the communal deification of

only for their own salvation but also as fellow agents in carrying out Jesus' task' – Ridderbos, *John*, 563.

[86] Augustine understands the gift of glory in John 17:22 as immortality (See *Tract. Ev. Jo.*, 110.3). William Countryman: 'The unity into which believers are now called is that of the primordial glory, the beauty and power of the godhead, before the foundation of the cosmos.' From L. William Countryman, *The Mystical Way in the Fourth Gospel: Crossing Over into God*, revised edn. (Valley Forge, PA: Trinity Press International, 1994), 116.

[87] Käsemann, *Testament*, 69–70. What he calls 'gnosticizing' I am calling filiation and deification.

[88] So Francis Watson, who rhetorically asks, 'is eternal life disembodied life?' He provides multiple grounds for rejecting Käsemann's attributions of Docetism to John's Gospel that include, along with the death of Jesus, the preexistence of Jesus' humanity and the materiality of speech. See Watson, 'Trinity and Community: A Reading of John 17', *JST* 1, 2 (1999): 176.

those who have received and will receive the divine revelation of the Word of God.

An Ecclesiology of Deification: Chapter Summary

Though deification language is borrowed from later patristic sources, what I have provided in this chapter is an overview of theosis that is explicitly Johannine and bound to the Gospel text. This Johannine theosis is explicitly Jewish, presented through the unfolding sequence of a narrative, and corporate rather than individualistic. Building on the research presented in Part I, I briefly showed above that deification is suggested in the Prologue's ecclesiology of participation through filiation, a model that establishes an ecclesial trajectory for the ensuing story. Building on the arguments and observations of Part II, I treated the oneness motif alongside the deification themes implied by Jesus' citation of Psalm 82. Jesus is 'one' with the God confessed in the Shema, but his own divinity – and the divine revelation he brings – allows for the divinization of others as 'gods'. The deification of Israel at Sinai, a rabbinical reading of Psalm 82 of which the evangelist seems aware, brings an ecclesial dimension to the christological citation. Jesus is the Word of God whose reception leads to a corporate divine status for the disciples just as the reception of Torah divinized Israel. Though divine–human boundaries are delineated throughout the Gospel narrative to protect the divine identity shared by the Father and Son, the use of Psalm 82 in conjunction with the Shema in John 10:30 expands the category of divinity to include those who are 'one' with them as 'gods'. The prayer for oneness in John 17 expresses more than an ecclesiology of divine association, and the sort of participation envisioned amounts to theosis. The Gospel of John is a deification narrative, and two of its most important ecclesial passages, the Prologue and the prayer of Jesus in John 17, are both deification texts.

10

CHARACTERIZING JOHANNINE THEOSIS: DIVINIZED CHARACTERS WITHIN THE NARRATIVE

To further demonstrate the claim that John is a 'deification narrative' in which divine participation constitutes the major function of the narrative programme, these final chapters will show how Johannine theosis is a central feature of the ecclesial narrative script. The argument will proceed by demonstrating that the Fourth Gospel incorporates theosis into its ecclesial narrative through the technique of *characterization*, that is, how literary characters are presented and developed. If the Gospel opens with an ecclesial vision suggestive of deification, then we should expect in the narrative proper to find divine attributes in the portrayal of certain believers as they are resocialized into the Father–Son interrelation according to the ecclesial narrative script. Character studies have become a popular trend in current Johannine scholarship, and I have already discussed the ecclesial role of John the Baptist. The contribution to these discussions on Johannine characterization that I hope to make in this chapter is the suggestion that the fourth evangelist's narrative ecclesiology of theosis is the overarching frame of reference for understanding his literary representations of believing disciples.

The deification of these believers is implied or at times clearly signalled by a literary device I am calling 'inclusive parallelism' in which divine actions or words of Jesus become mirrored in particular human characters or character groups. These parallels are 'inclusive' because they suggest some degree of participation in (and not merely imitation of) divine reality or activity. Before sketching the inclusive parallels central to the characterizations of the man born blind, Peter, and the Beloved Disciple, I will show how their shared speech and activities are part of the wider Johannine theme of 'reciprocity'. Throughout the narrative proper, reciprocal bonds between Jesus and the Father are expanded to include not just individual protagonists, but all those who receive Jesus as God's Son. Narrative sequence is critical for understanding Johannine reciprocity since the parallels and reciprocal statements work by building on previous occurrences and sayings earlier in the Gospel's linear development. I will make the case that this reciprocity should be understood as 'filial assimilation' and therefore also as a function of Johannine theosis – the collective effect of the inclusive parallels and reciprocal statements throughout the narrative is to evoke the theme of deification as believers become assimilated as divine beings into the divine family. In the following chapter, I will consider the characterization of the Paraclete, whose presence and activity enable Johannine theosis and sustain filial participation.

Theosis and the Ecclesial Narrative Script: The Prologue as the Frame for Johannine Characterization

Since motifs and trajectories explicit in John 1:1–18 bear enormous significance for the narrative proper, it stands to reason that the Prologue also establishes a frame for the Gospel's presentation of characters. In a recent article on Johannine characterization, Christopher Skinner shows that 'the Prologue provides a grid through which to read the entire narrative, *especially misunderstanding characters*'.[1] Though his focus on the negative dimension of misunderstanding is important, I would add to his overall argument that *positive* Johannine characterizations should also be read in light of John 1:12–13 – certain people do receive him, and, as a result, they become divine beings by virtue of their birth not out of human will or processes but through the agency of God. The Prologue's vision of participatory ecclesiology, in which believers are generated by God as divine members of the Father–Son interrelation, establishes the expectation that some Gospel characters will be portrayed as divinized in some way, or as undergoing a process of divinization.

The positive narrative pattern or template established in the Prologue and closely followed in the wider Gospel's sequence is as follows: first, Jesus participates in the divine identity (1:1–5; 18); then, believers eventually participate in the divine interrelation of Jesus with God (1:12–13) precisely because Jesus participates in their mortality (1:14). Since the social sphere into which potential believers are resocialized

---

[1] Christopher W. Skinner, 'Misunderstanding, Christology, and Johannine Characterization: Reading John's Characters through the Lens of the Prologue', in *Characters and Characterization in the Gospel of John*, ed. Christopher W. Skinner, LNTS 461 (London: T & T Clark, 2013), 126; italics are mine. In his monograph on John's 'I am' sayings, David Mark Ball highlights the importance of the Prologue in establishing patterns for Jesus' characterization in the rest of the Gospel – Ball, '*I Am*', 50–51.

through this ongoing ecclesial narrative script is that of a divine family sourced in God, the new ecclesial community is not just another alternative group among many in the horizontal social plane of the Gospel's story world. It is a community marked by a new vertically generated identity. Having identified theosis as the fundamental vision of Johannine ecclesiology, it can now be observed that *the positive resocializing activity of the ecclesial narrative script leads to (or at least points to) the deification of those who believe.*

Beyond the Prologue, Jesus repeatedly speaks of his filial interrelation with the Father; then, gradually, the same language is used to identify believers' incorporation within this filial interrelation. *This incorporation is a central feature for Johannine characterization*, and the pattern of Father–Son participation that opens to Father–Son–*believer* interrelation is anchored in the Prologue's sequence and re-enacted in broader narrative scale in the story that follows, a story that finds fulfilment by the plot resolving with the formation of a divine family: 'Go to my brothers and say to them, "I am ascending to my Father and your Father, to my God and your God"' (John 20:17). The integration of human beings into the filial bond of Father and Son is a primary plotline – theosis is the narrative trajectory of the Fourth Gospel (its ecclesial story arc) and *the theme within which positive character responses to Jesus are portrayed.*

Reciprocity Statements and Inclusive Parallels: Mimesis as Theosis

As just noted, 'inclusive parallelism' refers to certain actions, descriptions, or statements used in portraying dyadic (and triadic) theology that are repeated later in the narrative but applied to certain human characters or character groups. These parallels serve the programme of narrative theosis by portraying believers as participants in divine speech and activity. The following verses about prayer serve as an example:

MARTHA TO JESUS: 'But even now I know that whatever you ask from God, God will give you.' (11:22; see also 11:41–42)

JESUS TO THE DISCIPLES: 'Whatever you ask the Father in my name, he may give it to you.' (15:16; see also 14:13–14; 15:7, 17; 16:23–24)

Collective parallels of this kind between Jesus and the disciples are consonant with a theme often referred to as 'reciprocity', mentioned already in the previous chapter.[2] In the early scenes and discourses of the Gospel, a number of reciprocity statements correlate Jesus with his Father. Though he does not limit himself to a rigid stylistic form, the evangelist sometimes renders the reciprocity of his dyadic theology in recognizable patterns. A simple example already encountered is found in John 5:26 – 'For just as [ὥσπερ] the Father has life in himself, so also [οὕτως καί] he has granted the Son to have life in himself.' The preponderance of reciprocity statements similar in style, content, or theme throughout the Gospel continually upholds dyadic theology as the unmistakable conceptual frame for the narrative.[3] John's story proclaims the divine identity of Jesus in the Prologue, sustains this christological claim in the plot action and discourse material, and accents the narrative denouement with Thomas' confession: 'My Lord and my God!' (20:28).

In a move that also follows the template of the Prologue, dyadic theology's reciprocity is gradually extended in scope at later points in the Gospel to include the believing disciples (through the work of the Spirit-Paraclete whose portrayal, discussed in the following chapter, expands dyadic theology to triadic theology). The communal inclusiveness of Johannine divinity is evidenced by inclusive reciprocity statements like this one from John 6:57 – 'just as [καθώς] the living Father sent me, and I [κἀγώ] live because of the Father, also [καί] whoever eats me will live because of me'. In this example, the divine life inherent to dyadic theology (as indicated in 5:26 immediately above) is available for human participation. Here is another instance where dyadic theology's reciprocity is extended later in the Gospel to include believers:

10:38   The Father is in me and *I am in the Father.*
14:20   *I am in my Father,* and you in me, and I in you.[4]

Both sets of reciprocity statements differ in form and style. The former passages on divine life follow a generic formula of 'just as ... so (also)', employing some combination in the Greek of the terms ὥσπερ or καθώς and καί. The style of both John 10:38 and 14:20 just listed is that of a balanced dualism conveying the idea of 'mutual indwelling'. Note how these reciprocity statements function *in narrative sequence*. In these two sets of

---

[2] See the chapter 'Oneness and the Reciprocity Statements' in Appold, *Oneness*, 18–47.

[3] For the connections between the oneness motif and reciprocity, see Söding, '"Ich und der Vater"',198–9.

[4] The italicized phrases above read in Greek as κἀγὼ ἐν τῷ πατρί and ἐγὼ ἐν τῷ πατρί μου, respectively.

examples, the participatory expressions build on aforementioned references to Jesus' interrelation with his Father. Just as in the Prologue, so also in the narrative proper: dyadic theology is the established thematic reference frame and participatory ecclesiology is gradually enfolded within it.

In sum, the Father and Son exist in reciprocal connection to one another, but their internal relation opens to include an external entity – the social unit of those who believe in Jesus and, by reciprocal extension, also believe in the Father. This expanding of the Father–Son communal sphere to include the disciples within their shared activity, work, and filial bond is participation, but also deification since, as repeatedly observed, their inclusion involves ontological reconfiguration. The evangelist familiarizes his readers with dyadic theology through the high frequency of Jesus' reciprocal status with God. Then he subtly and gradually begins applying the familiar language of this christological and theological dynamic to human believers. Because these reciprocal statements have their narrative roots in the Prologue's opening references to the divine family, and since the narrative closes with Jesus' pronouncement that his death and resurrection have somehow solidified the disciples' filial status (20:17), *Johannine reciprocity should be understood as the filial assimilation intrinsic to Johannine theosis*. The gradual opening up of the Son's reciprocal relationship with the Father to include the children of God is central to the ecclesial narrative script and, by definition, an act of filiation.

The point was made in the previous chapter that the Fourth Gospel ultimately narrates the deification of a *community*, not the apotheosis or glorification of one mortal figure. Though emblematic for others[5] and presented within the broader ecclesial vision of participation and deification that extends to all believers, certain characters display divine attributes particular to their own roles within the Gospel:

Jesus ‖ Philip ‖ Samaritan Woman ‖ Mary and the mourners

Jesus to the Baptist's Disciples in 1:39: 'come and you will see' ἔρχεσθε καὶ ὄψεσθε

Philip to Nathanael in 1:46:	'come and see'	ἔρχου καὶ ἴδε
Samaritan woman in 4:29:	'come see'	δεῦτε ἴδετε[6]
Mary and the mourners in 11:34	'come and see'	ἔρχου καὶ ἴδε

---

[5] On the representative function of individuals in the Fourth Gospel, see Barton, 'Community', 294–5.

[6] The difference in terms for 'come' and 'see' are not grounds to dismiss parallelism. Keener notes that 'variation was common' and cites multiple instances from the canonical Gospels in which δεῦτε means 'come' (Keener, *John*, 622, n. 393).

Jesus ‖ Man Born Blind

Jesus in multiple scenes[7]   'I am'   ἐγώ εἰμι
The Man Born Blind in 9:9   'I am'   ἐγώ εἰμι

Jesus ‖ Beloved Disciple

No one has ever seen God. God the only Son who is in the bosom of the Father [ὁ ὢν εἰς τὸν κόλπον τοῦ πατρός] has made him known. (1:18)

One of his disciples – the one whom Jesus loved – was reclining in the bosom of Jesus [ἐν τῷ κόλπῳ τοῦ Ἰησοῦ] next to him. (13:23)[8]

Jesus ‖ Peter

He said this to show by what kind of death [σημαίνων ποίῳ θανάτῳ] he [Jesus] was going to die. (12:33)

This was to fulfil the word that Jesus had spoken to show by what kind of death [σημαίνων ποίῳ θανάτῳ] he [Jesus] was going to die. (18:32)

This he said to show by what kind of death [σημαίνων ποίῳ θανάτῳ] he [Peter] was to glorify God. (21:19)

Speech ('come and see'; 'I am'), actions (shepherding, death by execution), and relational imagery ('bosom') associated with Jesus are later in the narrative sequence associated with certain Gospel characters. Taken on their own, each occurrence of parallelism could perhaps be understood as no more than an artistic flourish. But since multiple characters are implicated in these inclusive parallels and since the Prologue sets the expectation for some element of divine communicability, it is best to understand them as related instances conveying reciprocal participation. The repetitive language makes the parallel associations recognizable for readers and auditors, alerting the audience to the possibility of participating within the divine prerogatives and activities of the Logos.

These instances of inclusive parallelism and reciprocity raise a pertinent question: are they indicative of *mimesis* rather than *theosis*? The parallels in the call language of 'come and see'[9] could certainly be read as no more than instances of the former. Imitation, after all, is a theme strongly pressed by

---

[7] The unpredicated 'I am' sayings appear in 4:26; 6:20; 8:24; 8:58; 13:19; 18:5–6, 8.

[8] In both 1:18 ('who is close to the Father's heart') and 13:23 ('was reclining next to him') the clear parallel in the Greek is profoundly obscured by the NRSV (and many other translations).

[9] For detailed lists on the use of this phrase in the LXX, rabbinic, early Jewish, and Greco-Roman literature, see Keener, *John*, 471–72, 485.

Jesus in the Farewell Discourse. He refers to the act of footwashing as a ὑπόδειγμα, a pattern or example to be emulated (13:15); and many of the reciprocity statements are certainly mimetic in character (as in Jesus' explanation of the act of footwashing: 'if therefore I washed your feet as the Lord and Teacher, you also ought to wash one another's feet' – 13:14). Like many other apparent calls to mimesis in John's Gospel, if the shared invitational language ('come and see') in 1:39, 46, and 4:39 is allowed to stand on its own within the narrative, then they may be categorized merely as imitational.[10]

Yet the Gospel's mimetic language cannot be isolated from the narrative's wider theme of participation. Johannine mimesis is grounded in the ontological reconfiguration established in the Prologue. Because the call to believers ultimately includes a divine transformation and re-origination along with membership within the divine community of Father and Son, imitation is grounded within the dual themes of filiation and deification. The disciples do not just imitate Jesus' ministry (14:12); they re-enact it as filial participants within the divine family (20:17) who are eventually filled with the re-creating breath/Spirit of Jesus (20:22).[11] As will be shown in the following two sections, the inclusive parallels involving the blind man, Peter, and the Beloved disciple imply that imitation is ultimately participation, that mimesis is sourced in theosis.

The Man Born Blind: Ἐγώ Εἰμι

Only Jesus voices the theologically weighted phrase ἐγώ εἰμι ('I am') in John with one exception: the man born blind in 9:9.[12] Most

---

[10] See 3 Jn 11: Ἀγαπητέ, μὴ μιμοῦ [from μιμέομαι] τὸ κακὸν ἀλλὰ τὸ ἀγαθόν.

[11] For understanding John 20:22 as a re-enactment of Gen 2:7 and thus an act of re-creation, see Marianne Meye Thompson, 'The Breath of Life: John 20:22–23 Once More', in *The Holy Spirit and Christian Origins: Essays in Honor of James D. G. Dunn*, ed. Stephen C. Barton, Bruce W. Longenecker, and Graham N. Stanton (Grand Rapids, MI: Eerdmans, 2004), 69–78; and du Rand, 'The Creation Motif', 21–46.

[12] In her extensive monograph on the 'I am' sayings in early Judaism and Christianity, Catrin Williams explains:

> Since ἐγώ εἰμι serves as a succinct expression of the unique and exclusive divinity of Yahweh in both Deut. 32:39 and the poetry of Deutero-Isaiah, its appropriation by Jesus in the Fourth Gospel demonstrates that John is expounding the central theme that Jesus is the definitive revelation of God, which signifies his unity with the Father. Indeed, each occurrence of ἐγώ εἰμι is complemented by a statement stressing the Son's dependence on, and unity with, the Father.

commentators either pass over this curious 'I am' statement entirely or dismissively regard it as no more than a 'purely secular use of the phrase'[13] for self-identification[14] and thus empty of 'divine connotations'.[15] The formula can certainly be understood as common parlance conveying presence ('it is I'[16]) or confirming one's identity ('I am [he]'[17]). In John's Gospel, however, the words ἐγώ ('I') and εἰμι ('I am') appear together on multiple occasions, but are not rendered in the exact bipartite order of ἐγώ εἰμι except in Jesus' expressions implying christological monotheism ... and in 9:9.[18] When Jesus pairs these two words in a 'secular', non-theological sense, the order is either reversed as εἰμι ἐγώ (7:34; 12:26; 14:2; 17:24) or the phrase is interrupted by the negative particle: ἐγώ οὐκ [not] εἰμι (8:23; 17:14).[19] Negative εἰμι statements paired with ἐγώ also appear on the lips of John the Baptist and Pilate. In each case, the phrase undergoes the same rendering as in its non-theological use by Jesus: the order is reversed as εἰμι ἐγώ (3:28) or it is interrupted by a different word (ἐγώ οὐκ [not] εἰμι – 1:20; μήτι ἐγώ Ἰουδαῖός εἰμι?[20] – 18:35). Though there is nothing grammatically amiss about these configurations, it is significant that John reserves Jesus' use of the exact phrasing of ἐγώ εἰμι as a christological expression of dyadic

See Catrin H. Williams, *I Am He: The Interpretation of 'Anî Hû' in Jewish and Early Christian Literature*, WUNT 113 (Tübingen: Mohr Siebeck, 2000), 302. In spite of this assessment that the ἐγώ εἰμι formula in John's Gospel is directly linked to the divine identity of Israel's God, Williams does not believe that Jesus' use of 'I am' requires the interpretation that he is 'an independent divine being'. Jesus, rather, is a representative of God who speaks and works on his behalf and in whom 'God's saving promises are made visible and accessible' (ibid.). Richard Bauckham would agree with the revelatory and representative function of Jesus, but he also understands them to indicate Jesus' 'inclusion in the unique identity of God' – Bauckham, *Jesus and the God of Israel*, 40. Williams' own exegesis would seem to better support Bauckham's conclusions.

[13] Brown, *John*, 373.

[14] This is how Ball views the phrase in John 9:9 in his monograph on the 'I am' sayings – Ball, *'I Am'*, 172, 184, 281.

[15] Lincoln, *John*, 282. [16] E.g., Lk 24:39. [17] As Jn 9:9 is often translated.

[18] The 'I am' statement in 8:18 (ἐγώ εἰμι ὁ μαρτυρῶν περὶ ἐμαυτοῦ) may seem to have very limited divine associations, if any at all, but Williams notes that 8:18 is likely an echo of God speaking in LXX Isa 52:6 (Williams, *I Am He*, 272, n. 59).

[19] After making these observations on the use of εἰμι in John, I discovered Mikeal Parsons' essay where he presents similar findings: Mikeal C. Parsons, 'A Neglected ΕΓΩ EIMI Saying in the Fourth Gospel? Another Look at John 9:9', in *Perspectives on John: Method and Interpretation in the Fourth Gospel*, ed. Robert B. Sloan and Mikeal C. Parsons, NABPR Special Studies Series 11 (Lampeter: Edwin Mellen Press, 1993), 145–80, here at 175–79.

[20] 'I am not a Jew, am I?'

theology.[21] The only time the exact phrase is voiced in the Fourth Gospel by a character other than Jesus is in John 9:9. Can this singular instance be dismissed as thematically disjointed from the tactful way the evangelist has crafted his ἐγώ εἰμι trope?

The readers and auditors of John would have been conditioned by the foregoing narratival use of ἐγώ εἰμι to expect Jesus to be the phrase's unique vocal source. His use of the formula has appeared eleven times prior to John 9, with five of those occurrences found in the discourse immediately preceding the introduction of the man born blind. Over the course of these uses of ἐγώ εἰμι, the phrase has become increasingly associated with Jesus' divine status. The most theologically explicit use of the phrase up to this point in the Gospel has just been voiced in 8:58, πρὶν Ἀβραὰμ γενέσθαι ἐγώ εἰμι ('before Abraham was, I am'), in response to which Jesus is almost stoned (presumably for blasphemy). It could be argued that if the evangelist wanted to make clear the connection between the 'I am' statements of Jesus and that of the blind man in 9:9, the ἐγώ would not be absent from Jesus' εἰμι statement in 9:5. This conclusion, however, is unnecessary: Jesus' words – φῶς εἰμι τοῦ κόσμου ('I am the light of the world'), an echo of the most recent predicated ἐγώ εἰμι expression in 8:12 – still serves to interlink the ἐγώ εἰμι in 8:58 and 9:9, reminding the audience of the phrase's christological and theological import.

In spite of his assessment that the ἐγώ εἰμι saying in John 9 is non-theological,[22] Raymond Brown commented that 'the internal construction of the story [of the blind man] shows consummate artistry; no other story in the Gospel is so closely knit. We have here Johannine dramatic skill at its best.'[23] Given the evangelist's 'consummate artistry' and 'dramatic skill' in John 9, along with the intentionality behind the use of εἰμι in this Gospel and the narrative proximity of 9:9 to other 'I am' statements made by Jesus, some account must be given for why the healed blind man suddenly takes up a phrase that has been heretofore associated with the divine identity with an increasing degree of intensity.[24]

---

[21] Parsons conducted a thorough study of ἐγώ εἰμι in ancient Greek writings and discovered that the absolute, unpredicated use of the phrase only appears in Jewish literature, never in Hellenistic literature (Parsons, 'ΕΓΩ ΕΙΜΙ', 151–52).

[22] Brown, *John*, 373.

[23] Ibid., 376. Parsons also cites this quotation (Parsons, 'ΕΓΩ ΕΙΜΙ', 146).

[24] Scholars who acknowledge an intentional coordination of the 'I am' statements of the blind man and Jesus include Smith, *John*, 193 (Smith does not elaborate beyond observing an 'obvious connection'); and Frederick Dale Bruner, *The Gospel of John: A Commentary* (Grand Rapids, MI: Eerdmans, 2012), 577–78.

One such account is offered by Jo-Ann Brant. She regards John 9 as a 'miniature version' of the Gospel's large-scale story.[25] According to Brant, the account of the man born blind encapsulates key structural and thematic elements of the evangelist's wider story of Jesus. It is not merely incidental that such literary space is devoted to the man born blind while Jesus is absent from the narrative: 'the only other Gospel narratives of comparable length in which Jesus is not present appear in the infancy accounts of Matthew and Luke prior to Jesus's birth'.[26] Brant argues that the reason this anonymous character receives so much attention and space is because the story of the man born blind is a (partial) re-presentation of the Fourth Gospel's story of Jesus. Here is a duplication of her 'Table 4', a list of 'Parallels Between Jesus and the Blind Man':[27]

Jesus	Blind Man
Crowd repeatedly deliberates about his identity (e.g., 7:12, 25–27, 40–42)	Crowd deliberates about his identity (9: 8–9)
Series of scenes marked by exits and entrances in the trial before Pilate (18:28–19:16)	Series of scenes marked by exits and entrances in the interrogation by the Pharisees (9:13–34)
'I am', *egō eimi*, assertions (e.g., 9:5)	'I am', *egō eimi*, assertion (9:9)
Speaks frankly (e.g., 10:25–30)	Speaks frankly (9:25, 27, 30–33)
Argues with logic (e.g., 8:39–40)	Argues with logic (9:31–34)
Expresses sarcastic astonishment that Nicodemus, a Pharisee, does not understand (3:10)	Expresses sarcastic astonishment that the Pharisees do not understand (9:30)
Accused of being an invalid witness (8:13)	Treated as an invalid witness (9:18)
Accused of being a sinner (e.g., 9:24)	Accused of being a sinner (9:34)
Authority of his teaching questioned (e.g., 7:15)	Accused of trying to teach without authority (9:34)
Jesus throws out (*ekballō*) traders from the temple (2:15) and the 'ruler of this world' (12:31) but not his own (6:37). The good shepherd leads out (*ekbalē*) his own (10:4).	Pharisees throw him out (*exebalon*) of the assembly (9:34).

---

[25] Brant uses the phrase *mise en abyme* deriving from a practice in heraldry in which a smaller shield enriches the meaning of the larger shield in which it is set. See Jo-Ann A. Brant, *John*, Paideia Commentaries on the New Testament (Grand Rapids, MI: Baker Academic, 2011), 151–52.

[26] Ibid., 154.   [27] Ibid., 155.

To Brant's list of parallels could be added others,[28] including this riposte of the blind man to the Pharisees in 9:27 that anticipates a similar remark of Jesus to the Jews in 10:25:

> ἀπεκρίθη αὐτοῖς [the blind man]· εἶπον ὑμῖν ἤδη καὶ οὐκ ἠκούσατε[29]
> ἀπεκρίθη αὐτοῖς ὁ Ἰησοῦς·   εἶπον ὑμῖν   καὶ οὐ πιστεύετε[30]

Brant's interpretation of the numerous parallels between the blind man and Jesus means that the evangelist is 'showing his audience that imitation of Jesus is honorable'.[31]

This interpretation should be pressed further. Again, imitation is certainly a motif in John 9, but it remains an inadequate category for explaining the blind man's singular use of a recognized christological expression linked to the divine identity. I discussed in Chapter 5 the account of the blind man as a case study for the Gospel's 'ecclesial narrative script'. As an iteration of that script in the Gospel narrative, this scene, with its references to parentage and birth (9:1–2, 18–23, 34) and with the fate of synagogue expulsion, is designed to capture the challenging (and yet inspiring) realities of a christologically provoked communal exit and entry. The healed protagonist of John 9 undergoes a membership transfer from one social group into another that corresponds with a physical and perhaps even an ontological change.[32] Just as Jesus will wash the disciples in John 13, an act that allows them to participate in or share with Jesus (ἔχεις μέρος μετ' ἐμοῦ/'have a share with me' – v. 8), the blind man washes in the pool called Siloam. He 'comes seeing' (ἦλθεν βλέπων), an echo of 'come and see' from 1:39, 46, and 4:29. His new quality of sight reflects a physical transformation and

---

[28] See Parsons, 'ΕΓΩ ΕΙΜΙ', 170–73 for more detailed discussions on some of these parallels, plus a few others.

[29] '[The blind man] answered them, "I told you already and you did not listen."'

[30] 'Jesus answered them, "I told you and you do not believe."'   [31] Brant, *John*, 154.

[32] The 'sign' performed on the blind man results in a transformation that would fit Tyson Lee Putthoff's definition of a mystical and ontological encounter with the divine in early Judaism: 'A mystical change occurs when a human, upon encountering the divine in the present life, undergoes transformation such that the ontological state of either part or all of his or her being becomes altered in a positive, supernatural way … It must entail an alteration in the human body, mind or general state of existence.' See Tyson Lee Putthoff, 'Human Mutability and Mystical Change: Explorations in Ancient Jewish OntoAnthropology' (E-Thesis, Durham University, 2013), 10, http://etheses.dur.ac.uk/9395/ (last accessed 5 December 2016).

also implies a developing *internal* transformation as he enters the sphere of sight having been 'metaphorically a citizen of the dark'[33] – the figurative nature of the faculty of seeing in this Gospel is significantly accented here, especially in 9:35–41, which functions as a summative assessment of the preceding account. In John 8, Jesus has just reaffirmed that his faithful reception corresponds to transformation: the Jews are not able to hear Jesus because they have yet to undergo 'birth' from above, remaining 'from below' and having the devil as their generative source (8:23, 43–44; 3:3; see also 1 John 3:8). For the blind man, the imitation of Jesus assumes a gradual participation within a new social sphere that is divine and articulated with irony by the religious leaders: σὺ μαθητὴς εἶ ἐκείνου ('you are a disciple of that one'). As I stated in Chapter 5, this man who was born blind and accused of also being born in sin experiences a new 'birth' that is instantiated symbolically by explusion through a synagogue door. He is being inducted into the sphere of a divine community, a participation that entails filiation and deification in the Fourth Gospel and signalled as operative by his utterance of the bipartite formula ἐγώ εἰμι in John 9:9. The evangelist is intentionally implicating the transformed blind man within the divinity of Jesus.

But even though the 'I am' expression is indicative (or at the very least suggestive) of some participation in divine reality, the statement in 9:9 does not 'deify' the man born blind in such a way that his character is classifiable with the language of dyadic theology (i.e., 'the Word was with God and the Word was God'). If the Gospel's audience has indeed noted the theological overtones of ἐγώ εἰμι in John 4–8, then the appearance of the phrase in 9:9 would surely be received as striking, and perhaps confusing – does the blind man belong in the same divine category as Jesus? The divine–human boundaries discussed in the previous chapter are observable here in that *the only human character aside from Jesus to say 'I am', is also the only character in this Gospel to worship Jesus*: καὶ προσεκύνησεν αὐτῷ ('and he worshipped him' – 9:38). The inclusive parallel in John 9:9 associates the blind man with the divinity of Jesus, but, as seen in the Prologue (where believers are 'children' and only Jesus is the μονογενής), Jesus' unique divine status within the divine identity is still preserved.[34]

---

[33] Countryman, *The Mystical Way*, 70.

[34] Parsons describes the depiction of the blind man vis-à-vis Jesus as a theme of 'solidarity and subordination' that models the Gospel's theme of reciprocity: 'Jesus and the Father are One, yet the Son is clearly subordinate to the Father. Likewise, the Son and the disciple are one, but the disciple is clearly subordinate to the Son' (Parsons, 'ΕΓΩ ΕΙΜΙ', 174).

For Catrin Williams, the phrase in John 9:9 is a simple expression of self-identification: 'I am he'. She denies any theological connotations in the blind man's use of ἐγώ εἰμι and raises two important objections. First, she asks, 'why do his neighbours respond as though he had simply identified himself as the blind man who had been healed (v.10)?'[35] Added to this could be a related question: since Jesus' use of ἐγώ εἰμι often results in attempted persecution, why do no similar repercussions immediately occur after the blind man's use of the phrase in John 9:9? Second she asks, 'why should [the blind man], but not other followers of Jesus, pronounce ἐγώ εἰμι?'[36] In response to her first question, it should simply be observed that it is entirely fitting in this Gospel for a character's speech to be misundertood by the dialogue partners in the narrative while the audience immediately recognizes the deeper meaning.[37] Clearly, the passersby and acquaintances of the once blind man do not detect a claim to divinization. The issue at stake is whether the Gospel audience would detect a *Doppelbedeutung*, a common literary feature in John that Williams regularly discusses.[38] The answer is certainly in the affirmative.

My response to Williams' second question about why the blind man alone among the Gospel's human characters enunciates the 'I am' formula provides a transition into the next set of characters to be discussed. The point to make is that multiple figures in the Fourth Gospel are assigned attributes recognized as divine through inclusive parallelism, but these parallels are diverse and varied, perhaps expressive of the plurality constitutive of divine unity. A related occurence is found in John 12:21 where Philip is addressed by the Greeks as κύριος. This term is only used for Jesus except in this one isolated instance. Yet just as the blind man who voices the bipartite 'I am' formula worships Jesus, divine–human distinctions are also maintained in Philip's characterization: though he is the only character addressed as 'lord/sir' besides Jesus, he calls Jesus κύριος in John 14:8. Simply put, inclusive parallelism appears in varied forms. Just as Jesus says ἐγώ εἰμι, so also the blind man says ἐγώ εἰμι; just as the μονογενής is found in the bosom of the father, so the Beloved Disciple is found in the bosom of Jesus; just as Jesus dies as a shepherd of the sheep, so Peter will

---

[35] Williams, *I Am He*, 255, n. 2.   [36] Ibid.

[37] As Schafer points out *pace* Williams – Grant R. Shafer, 'The Divinization of the Blind Man: Egō Eimi in John 9:9', *Proceedings (Grand Rapids, MI)* 25 (2005): 157–67, here at 158.

[38] Williams acknowledges Parsons' study on John 9:9, but she seems too dismissive of his arguments for a 'reader-elevating' strategy by which the Gospel's audience would recognize theological connotations in the 'I am' saying that the blind man himself misses in the narrative (Parsons, 'ΕΓΩ ΕΙΜΙ', 167–68.).

die as a shepherd of the sheep. The blind man's 'I am' statement may be singular and unrepeated by any other human character in the Gospel, but it stands within the narrative among a handful of inclusive parallels by which believing disciples are called to 'come and see' and thereby participate in various forms of divine speech and action.

Peter and the Beloved Disciple: Ecclesial Conflict or Ecclesial Vision?

Attention now turns to the inclusive parallels found in Peter and the Beloved Disciple just referenced. The general interpretation of their narrative coordination is one of the former's subordination to the latter.[39] For many scholars, this subordination is so acute that it amounts to an outright programme of 'Petrine denigration'.[40] In the narrative juxtaposition of Peter's appearances alongside the 'disciple whom Jesus loved', the two could be labelled as rivals.[41] When these characters are understood within the Fourth Gospel's ecclesial vision of theosis, however, a new interpretation emerges.

The interpretative paradigm that is almost axiomatic in current Johannine scholarship is marked by conflict theories and matching historical reconstructions that attempt to explain why the Fourth Gospel would present Peter in an inferior position to the disciple whose testimony is foundational for the Johannine tradition. Rudolf Bultmann was among the first of major commentators to understand these two figures as representative of a clash taking place historically behind the curtain of the Gospel text.[42] He maintained that Peter represents Jewish Christianity and his counterpart Gentile Christianity, a Christianity

---

[39] See e.g., Snyder, 'John 13:16', 5–15; Cullmann, *The Johannine Circle*, 63–85; Colleen M. Conway, *Men and Women in the Fourth Gospel: Gender and Johannine Characterization*, SBLDS 167 (Atlanta, GA: Society of Biblical Literature, 1999), 163–99; Pheme Perkins, *Peter: Apostle for the Whole Church*, Studies on Personalities of the New Testament (Minneapolis, MN: Fortress, 2000); William W. Watty, 'The Significance of Anonymity in the Fourth Gospel', *ExpTim* 90, no. 7 (1979): 209–12. For a survey of the literature, see Bradford B. Blaine, Jr., *Peter in the Gospel of John: The Making of an Authentic Disciple*, SBLABib 27 (Atlanta, GA: Society of Biblical Literature, 2007), 8–18.

[40] Blaine, *Peter*, 1.

[41] This interdisciple rivalry contributes to the widespread suspicion, voiced strongly by Käsemann and widely held today, that the Johannine community was a wayward, sectarian offshoot of early Christ-devotion that found itself at odds with the mainstream Petrine Christianity of its day. See Käsemann, *Testament*, 28–29, 38–39, 40, 73, 75.

[42] Blaine, *Peter*, 8.

'emancipated from the ties of Judaism'.[43] For Raymond Brown, the historical conflict manifested in the narrative coordination of these disciples is that of Petrine or Apostolic Christianity versus Johannine Christianity.[44] For James Charlesworth, the Peter–Beloved Disciple tension is a 'global' issue in early Christianity. He argues that the anonymous disciple whom Jesus loved is none other than Thomas, and his superiority over Peter bespeaks 'a global rivalry for supremacy: Peter in the West and Thomas in the East'.[45]

Jewish Christianity versus Gentile, Apostolic Christianity versus Johannine, Western Church versus Eastern Church – these conflict theories by leading scholars in both Christian origins and Johannine literature are all largely premised on the Fourth Gospel's characterization of Peter and the Beloved Disciple. From Kevin Quast:

> The majority of scholars interpret the Gospel of John as reflect-ing a rivalry between the Beloved Disciple and Peter. *Operating from this perspective, they have gone on to reconstruct the community history and the origins of the Christian Church.* In addition, their understanding of the relationship between the Beloved Disciple and Peter has, of course, influenced their understanding of Johannine theology, particularly in the areas of ecclesiology and revelation.[46]

The predominance of this interpretative paradigm is evident in the following summary found in a popular New Testament introductory textbook:

---

[43] The mother of Jesus at the cross also represents Jewish Christianity for Bultmann (*John*, 484). Commenting on the race to the tomb: 'If Peter and the beloved disciple are representatives of Jewish and Gentile Christianity, the meaning manifestly then is this: the first community of believers arises out of Jewish Christianity, and the Gentile Christians attain to faith only after them. But that does not signify any precedence of the former over the latter; in fact, both stand equally near the Risen Jesus, and indeed readiness for faith is even greater with the Gentiles than it is with the Jews: the beloved disciple ran faster than Peter to the grave!' (ibid., 685).

[44] Brown writes, 'In counterposing their hero over the most famous member of the Twelve, the Johannine community is symbolically counterposing itself over against the kinds of churches that venerate Peter and the Twelve – the Apostolic Churches, whom other scholars call the "Great Church".' From Brown, *Community*, 83. Brown does not believe Johannine Christianity is 'anti-Petrine', but he does make clear his view that Peter 'did not understand Jesus as profoundly as did the Beloved Disciple' (ibid., 162.).

[45] Charlesworth, *Beloved Disciple*, 392.

[46] Kevin Quast, *Peter and the Beloved Disciple: Figures for a Community in Crisis*, JSNTSup 32 (Sheffield: Sheffield Academic, 1989), 12. (Emphases mine).

Designed to represent the Johannine community's special knowledge of Christ, the Beloved Disciple is invariably presented in competition with Peter, who may represent the larger apostolic church from which the disciple's exclusive group is somewhat distanced ... The disciple's 'brotherhood' would produce a Gospel promoting Jesus' theological meaning in ways that paralleled the Petrine churches' teachings but revealing, they believed, Jesus' 'glory' (1:14) more fully than other Gospel accounts.[47]

As to the historical evidence that these conflict theories are correct, however, Markus Bockmuehl asserts rather bluntly that there is none.[48] In a recent study on Simon Peter, Bockmuehl observes that 'F. C. Baur's critical legacy continues to loom large in many key debating points regarding the nature of early Christianity', one aspect of this legacy being the emphasis placed on 'conflict versus consensus'.[49] The impulse to detect interchurch antagonism informs the understanding of the interrelation of Peter and the Beloved Disciple in John. As stated in the Introduction, I am not opposed to hypothesizing about the historical realities that lie at the origin of Gospel texts. What I find problematic in this case is the concretizing in the interpretative process of an array of conflict theories that excludes or overlooks (albeit unintentionally) narrative or literary programmes *that are readily available within the text.*[50]

A number of scholars have begun to challenge paradigms in which the Peter–Beloved Disciple juxtaposition is antagonistic rather than 'complementary'.[51] Though Richard Bauckham grants Peter's

[47] Stephen L. Harris, *The New Testament: A Student's Introduction*, 5th edn. (New York: McGraw-Hill, 2006), 223–224.

[48] Bockmuehl, *Simon Peter*, 27. It should be noted that Bockmuehl does believe that Peter is subordinated to the Beloved Disciple in John's Gospel.

[49] Ibid., xv.

[50] In my view, the conflict theories and the alleged anti-Petrinism of the Johannine portrayals of Peter and the Beloved Disciple tend to mutually reinforce each other in a *historicizing hermeneutical circle.* Keen to unlock the historical facts veiled in mystery by the Gospel text, scholars have understood the Peter–Beloved Disciple contrast as symbolic and offered conflict theories as a way of historicizing a text that seems to play loose with history. Frustrated by the Beloved Disciple's tantalizing anonymity, this historicizing approach has filled in the textual gaps of his characterization, supplied interchurch conflicts for which there is no independent historical evidence, and in turn reread John's Gospel within this hermeneutical paradigm.

[51] See e.g., Bockmuehl, *Simon Peter*, 57–67; Nicolas Farelly, *The Disciples in the Fourth Gospel: A Narrative Analysis of Their Faith and Understanding*, WUNT 290 (Tübingen: Mohr Siebeck, 2010); Cornelis Bennema, *Encountering Jesus: Character*

subordination to the Beloved Disciple in John 1–20, he suggests that the contrast is markedly softened when it is noted that each disciple is intended to 'represent two different kinds of discipleship: active service [Peter] and perceptive witness [the Beloved Disciple]'.[52] His proposal can be expanded and enriched by identifying the comprehensive narrative programme of theosis in which they serve in these complementary roles. My argument in this section is that *their joint portrayal is primarily designed not to reflect an ecclesial conflict behind the text, but to depict an ecclesial vision within the text* – the same vision of participation in divine reality illustrated by the blind man's inclusive parallels in John 9. At the narrative level, the dual characterizations of Peter and the Beloved Disciple make sense within the evangelist's programmatic scheme of deification and participatory ecclesiology set forth in the Prologue. The Beloved Disciple is introduced with an inclusive parallel, and the Gospel closes with Peter in an inclusive parallel.[53] *These two figures therefore serve as complementary instantiations of diverse means by which believers participate in the activities of Jesus and in his intimate relation to the Father.* Before commenting on their respective inclusive parallels, I will offer a brief overview of Peter's characterization, then show how he and the Beloved Disciple are set in 'juxtaposing (but not opposing)'[54] relation to one another, together functioning not so much 'as competitors but as colleagues'.[55]

Peter and the Beloved Disciple in Negative Contrast: Assessing the Scholarly Consensus

Colleen Conway has labelled Peter's initial appearance in the Fourth Gospel as 'unremarkable'.[56] Similarly, Pheme Perkins draws attention to

---

Studies in the Gospel of John (Milton Keynes: Paternoster, 2009), 53–63; Quast, *Peter and the Beloved Disciple*. See the literature survey in Blaine, *Peter*, 18–22.

[52] Richard Bauckham, *Jesus and the Eyewitnesses: The Gospels as Eyewitness Testimony* (Grand Rapids, MI: Eerdmans, 2006), 395; and Richard Bauckham, 'The Beloved Disciple as Ideal Author', in Bauckham, *The Testimony of the Beloved Disciple: Narrative, History, and Theology in the Gospel of John* (Grand Rapids, MI: Baker Academic, 2007), 84.

[53] In his aforementioned study, Skinner uses Peter as a test case to show how the Prologue's theme of misunderstanding informs Peter's negative characterization in the Gospel. I certainly admit that Peter is shown as a figure lacking understanding in John. My own approach is to show how the deification themes in the Prologue contribute to the *positive* elements of his characterization. See Skinner, 'Johannine Characterization', 118–26.

[54] Bockmuehl, *Simon Peter*, 66.   [55] Blaine, *Peter*, 3.

[56] Conway, *Men and Women*, 164.

the order of the Johannine call narrative to point out that 'Peter is not the first disciple', a conscious decision on the part of the evangelist emblematic of his programme of Petrine denigration.[57] Though the other disciples in chapter 1's 'call narrative' address Jesus with some honorary title ('Rabbi', 'Messiah', 'the Son of God', 'the King of Israel'), Peter says nothing. Conway understands Peter as a passive character in John 1, brought to Jesus by his brother Andrew with his voice empty of christological titles and thus shown to be less christologically perceptive than the other disciples.[58] Against these negative readings, even though Peter offers no christological title in the call narrative of John 1, it is surely an act of honorific significance that the Christ gives Peter a title and a new name (1:42).[59]

Some interpreters have even viewed Peter's christological confession later in the Gospel, 'You are the Holy One of God', as inadequate (and perhaps even consciously associated with the demonic[60] – Mk 1:24; Lk 4:34[61]). But there is no critique of this title in the text and, unlike Matthew (16:23) and Mark (8:33), the Johannine Jesus does not rebuke Peter in this scene as 'Satan'.[62] Moreover, the closest this Gospel comes to the Synoptic Peter's rejection of Christ's violent fate is when Peter refuses to have his feet washed in 13:8; yet John has Peter dutifully relinquishing his resistance once Jesus explains the necessity of being washed. Also unlike the Synoptics, the Fourth Gospel does not have Peter reacting poorly to a Transfiguration scene or falling asleep in Gethsemane. His use of the sword in the garden is by no means a flattering portrayal, but we do find in Peter an allegiance that involves

---

[57] Perkins, *Peter*, 97.   [58] Conway, *Men and Women*, 164–66.

[59] Conway would explain, however, that Peter's naming has no import in John 1 on his role as founder of the church as in Matthew. It is true that Matthew's account of Peter's naming is directly given ecclesial significance, but I have already pointed out in Chapter 5 that this act of renaming resocializes Peter, implying a disassociation from his human parentage (ὁ υἱὸς Ἰωάννου) and entrance into a new filial domain (σὺ κληθήσῃ Κηφᾶς, ὃ ἑρμηνεύεται Πέτρος). Bockmuehl attributes the lack of details given to explain the name/ title of 'rock' to the Johannine audience's familiarity with Peter – Bockmuehl, *Simon Peter*, 58. Skinner's assessment is entirely contrary to Conway's, referring to Peter's introduction as 'positive' and 'favourable' (Skinner, 'Johannine Characterization', 119.).

[60] Snyder views the demonic associations with the christological title and the reference to a devil in 6:70 as a 'sly attack on the validity of Peter's confession' – 'John 13:16', 11.

[61] The Capernaum synagogue in John 6 where Peter makes his confession may be the exact site where demons use the same christological title in Mark and Luke – Michaels, *John*, 415.

[62] Peter here stands as a representative of the Twelve who have nobly refused to forsake Jesus after 'many of his disciples' withdrew (6:66). Skinner, again, views Peter's portrayal in this scene positively (Skinner, 'Johannine Characterization', 119–20.).

defending his leader against an entire Roman cohort. The Johannine Peter never denies Jesus by saying, as in the Synoptics, 'I do not know him.' His denials in John 18 are negative responses to the questions: 'are you not also one of his disciples?' and 'did I not see you in the garden?' He denies not Jesus directly, but only his association among his disciples. Though still grievous, it is nonetheless a curious difference from Mark, Matthew, and even Luke (whose portrayal of the disciples is normally more positive).[63] And only John gives such careful narrative space to Peter's restoration to Jesus and to his subsequent calling to pastoral leadership. Even if chapter 21 was added later to encourage Petrine loyalty among Johannine Christians after a possible falling out with mainstream Christianity (as is often suggested),[64] it is surely of some merit that the Fourth Gospel offers such a scene, which the Synoptics do not include in spite of their own (often negative) portrayals of Peter.[65] Indeed, Peter fares better in the Fourth Gospel than he does in the Synoptics *even without chapter 21.*[66]

When the Beloved Disciple makes his first explicit appearance in John's Gospel,[67] his position next to Jesus at table and his role as a mediator between Peter and Jesus is taken almost axiomatically as

[63] 'Peter comes off best in John' – Schnackenburg, *John*, 3:236. See also Blaine, *Peter*, 95–97; and Bockmuehl, *Simon Peter*, 63.

[64] Along with offering pastoral comfort to a community that seems to have lost its leader (21:20–23), it is also regularly understood that chapter 21 was added as an epilogue to rehabilitate Peter's negative presentation in John 1–20. See the discussion (and a list of sources) in Blaine, *Peter*, 127.

[65] Though it is widely understood that chapter 21 is a later addition to the Gospel (20: 30–31 seems like a fitting ending and the final depictions of Peter and the Beloved Disciple can be read as representative of a later church conflict), there are no extant MSS that end without this chapter. For a recent defence that chapter 21 is original to the Gospel text, see Stanley E. Porter, 'The Ending of John's Gospel', in *From Biblical Criticism to Biblical Faith: Essays in Honor of Lee Martin McDonald*, ed. William H. Brackney and Craig A. Evans (Macon, GA: Mercer University Press, 2007), 55–73.

[66] 'Peter is portrayed very positively in the Gospel, appearing as an exemplary disciple and hero of the Johannine community. His positive traits, which include courage, zeal, loyalty, love, resourcefulness, and determination, are meant to be emulated. His few lapses in faith – though considerable in scope – owe less to inadequate christology than to misdirected zeal. On the two occasions that Jesus rebukes him (13:8; 18:11), his purpose is to counsel him toward moderation rather than repentance. Peter does not represent Apostolic Christianity or any other rival or competing Christian faction, as most commentaries and monographs suggest, but is presented as an inspirational founding member of the Johannine church, equal in importance to [the Beloved Disciple].' From Blaine, *Peter*, 2.

[67] Some scholars believe that the unnamed disciple of John the Baptist in 1:35–40 is the Beloved Disciple. See, e.g., Brown, *Community*, 32; Cullmann, *The Johannine Circle*, 72; and Bauckham, 'Beloved Disciple', 83–84.

evidence of 'primacy' over his counterpart.[68] But this so-called 'mediation' could simply be understood as a mutual cooperation with Peter.[69] The Beloved Disciple takes his cue in asking Jesus about the traitor from Peter's initiative (13:24); and as for the former's superior perceptivity, the evangelist (somewhat confusingly) reports that *no one* at the table understood why Jesus sent Judas Iscariot out of the room, in spite of the fact that the Beloved Disciple seems to be privy to his identity (13:28).[70] It has been suggested that the unnamed ἄλλος μαθητής/'other disciple'[71] in 18:15–16 is a veiled reference to the Beloved Disciple whose mediation enables Peter's access to the high priest's courtyard.[72] If this is indeed the case, then a comparative contrast in which Peter's stature is being diminished may certainly be heightened. Ismo Dunderberg points out, however, that 'the potential of this contrast is not fully exploited in John since the admission of the Beloved Disciple to the courtyard is not explained in terms of his courage (as contrasted to Peter's denial), but "simply" as a consequence of his acquaintance with the high priest'[73] (and an association with the high priest should not necessarily be viewed as positive). The presence of the Beloved Disciple at the foot of the cross (19:26–27) ennobles his characterization remarkably, but the emphasis in John 19 is not on the absence of Peter but on the former's legitimacy as an eyewitness (19:35–37). In the so-called 'race' to the empty tomb (20:1–10), though the Beloved Disciple reaches the tomb first, Peter enters first. The Beloved Disciple is said to have believed on seeing the folded facecloth (20:8), yet both disciples are said to not yet understand the

[68] Raymond E. Brown, Karl P. Donfried, and John Reumann, eds., *Peter in the New Testament: A Collaborative Assessment by Protestant and Roman Catholic Scholars* (London: Geoffrey Chapman, 1973), 135.

[69] See David J. Hawkin, 'The Function of the Beloved Disciple Motif in the Johannine Redaction', *LTP* 33, 2 (1977): 135–50, here at 143. See also Quast, *Peter and the Beloved Disciple*, 59.

[70] From Ismo Dunderberg: 'John 13:21–30 should be read as a typical Johannine story of the disciples' misunderstanding. In John, their misunderstandings are usually related to the issues pertaining to Jesus' death and glorification, and this seems to be the case here too.' See Ismo Dunderberg, *The Beloved Disciple in Conflict? Revisiting the Gospels of John and Thomas* (Oxford: Oxford University Press, 2006), 145.

[71] In the MSS tradition the article ὁ sometimes appears in front of ἄλλος as if to clarify that this other disciple is the disciple whom Jesus loves (^{2}א, C, L, Θ, $f^{1.13}$, 33, M). The article is absent, however, in P^{66}, א*, A, B, D^s, W, Ψ, pc, sy$^{s.p}$, sa^{mss}, pbo, bo.

[72] E.g., Cullmann, *The Johannine Circle*, 72. For a close treatment of the arguments, see Frans Neirynck, 'The 'Other Disciple' in Jn 18:15–16', *ETL* 51, 1 (1975): 113–41.

[73] Dunderberg, *Beloved Disciple*, 134.

Scriptures (20:9). And it is difficult to fault the fourth evangelist (or his later redactor) with anti-Petrinism when we find Peter sharing with Jesus the role of a shepherd who lays down his life for the sheep – only in John does Jesus allow Peter's rash profession to lay down his life for his Lord to become a truthful prediction.

Inclusive Parallelism in the Characterizations
of the Beloved Disciple and Peter

Having offered grounds for mitigating the degree of antagonism interpreters regularly find in the Johannine interplay between Peter and the Beloved Disciple, I now turn to the respective parallels that associate their characterizations with Jesus and signify their shared literary role in the Gospel's vision of participatory ecclesiology. The Beloved Disciple's position in the κόλπος ('bosom') of Jesus (13:23), just as Jesus was depicted in the κόλπος of God (1:18), should be understood in terms of the blind man's proclamation of ἐγώ εἰμι. Both parallels include these characters in speech or activities formerly attributed to Jesus in the Gospel.[74] The role of the Beloved Disciple as a witness is undeniable in the Fourth Gospel, but his station in the bosom of Jesus need not symbolize his superiority over all the other disciples. Though his physical location at table is described in singular terms particular to the scene of the Farewell Discourse, his intimate relation to Jesus *is not altogether unique*. Others are associated with Jesus through specific instances of parallel language: the blind man (ἐγώ εἰμι), Philip (ἔρχου καὶ ἴδε/'come and see'; κύριος/'Lord'), the Samaritan woman (δεῦτε ἴδετε/'come see'), and of course Peter (see below). Though I view the Beloved Disciple as a unique character within the narrative,[75] the status of 'beloved' is not isolated solely to him: 'Although the Beloved Disciple is singled out as the "one Jesus loves," John does not consign him to a class by himself.'[76] The Gospel's audience has just previously learned of Jesus' love for Martha, Mary, and Lazarus in 11:5; and

---

[74] Just as there are many parallels between Jesus and the blind man (as pointed out above by Jo-Ann Brant), there are multiple parallels between Jesus and the Beloved Disciple besides 1:18 // 13:23. See Dunderberg's comments (ibid., 141–42).

[75] A standard interpretation of the Beloved Disciple is that he serves as an ideal character (who may or may not be an actual historical personage) who embodies ideal discipleship for the Gospel's readers. Again, see the discussion in Dunderberg (ibid., 128–32).

[76] Susan E. Hylen, *Imperfect Believers: Ambiguous Characters in the Gospel of John* (Louisville, KY: Westminster John Knox, 2009), 95. Keener makes similar observations in Keener, *John*, 918.

immediately before the Beloved Disciple's introduction in chapter 13, we are told that Jesus collectively 'loved his own' and 'loved them to the end' (13:1). In the Johannine Epistles, the addressees are referred to as 'beloved' (ἀγαπητός/ἀγαπητοί) on 10 occasions.[77] When viewed in relation to other parallels, the Beloved Disciple's 'privileged relationship'[78] with Jesus is actually more paradigmatic than exclusive. Since the ecclesial and soteriological vision of this Gospel is to include believers within the filial interrelation of Father and Son,[79] the Beloved Disciple's testimony actually makes his own relational access to Jesus available to all those who would believe (20:30–31).

Less noted, but no less noteworthy, is Peter's inclusive parallel with Jesus. Twice in the Gospel, Jesus' death was foreshadowed using the Greek phrase σημαίνων ποίῳ θανάτῳ ('signifying by what kind of death' – 12:33; 18:32). The exact phrase is used to describe Peter's forthcoming martyrdom in 21:19. Just as Jesus died as a Shepherd of the sheep, Peter will take up the pastoral task of feeding and tending the ecclesial entity of the flock and likewise die on their behalf. Given the magnitude of sacrifice required of Peter and the lofty significance placed in the Fourth Gospel on Jesus' own death as the Good Shepherd, this parallel must not be overlooked or in any way regarded as inferior to the parallel in John 1:18 and 13:23. Richard Hays points out that 'the "good shepherd" is not simply a consoler who promises to care for the souls of those who believe – as in later sentimental Chrtistian piety'.[80] The pastoral image is royal and messianic, drawing from Ezekiel 34 and 37. That Ezekiel's imagery is in view in John 21 is clear from the threefold command to 'feed my lambs', 'tend my sheep', 'feed my sheep' (vv. 15–17), language that suffuses Ezekiel 34. Jesus' appointment of Peter to a shepherding role should squash attempts to cast the latter within a programme of Johannine anti-Petrinism.

Christopher Skinner reads the Beloved Disciple's parallel with Jesus as the source of an antagonistic contrast with Peter.[81] Since he excludes John 21 from his treatment of Peter's characterization, Skinner misses the inclusive parallel in which Peter participates in the suffering of the Good Shepherd.[82] Peter's anticipated martyrdom in service of Jesus is more grim than the Beloved Disciple's intimate position next to

---

[77] 1 Jn 2:7; 3:2, 21; 4:1, 7, 11; 3 Jn 1, 2, 5, 11.

[78] R. Alan Culpepper, *John, the Son of Zebedee: The Life of a Legend*, Studies on Personalities of the New Testament (Minneapolis, MN: Fortress, 2000), 60.

[79] Van der Watt, 'Salvation in the Gospel', 122–28.

[80] Hays, *Echoes of Scripture*, 319.   [81] 'Johannine Characterization', 121–22.

[82] Ibid., 118, n. 32.

Jesus, but no less significant. Even if Peter's inclusive parallel was added later to the Gospel to rehabilitate his reputation and thus reconcile Johannine Christianity with Apostolic or Petrine Christianity, the redactor has nonetheless intentionally placed Peter within the programme of reciprocity and inclusive parallelism in the only extant version of this Gospel. The modifications John 21 may bring to the foregoing Gospel material exemplify the tension within the hermeneutical circle oscillating between the Gospel text and reconstructions of the history behind it. Though this circle is potentially helpful, emphasis has been placed more on the conflict theories than on the positive message about Peter this epilogue intends to convey. Though the *possible* addition of John 21 may *possibly* indicate some sort of inter-disciple tension, due emphasis should be placed on Peter's impressive portrayal that concludes the Gospel text.

Along with the Beloved Disciple's parallel with Jesus, Peter's sacrificial service to Jesus in John 21 is exemplary for others. His role as shepherd certainly implies a special vocation, but Bockmuehl denies that this role should be regarded as 'the Sole Vicar of Christ on earth to the exclusion of all other disciples'. He continues:

> In the Jewish and OT texts, the theme of God as shepherd delegating authority to human religious or political 'shepherds' is a commonplace (see, e.g., Jer. 23:1–5; Ezek. 34: 2–24; Zech 11:3–17), and within this received imagery, any singling out of just one divinely approved shepherd of Israel usually concerns specifically the Davidic messiah rather than one of his servants (2 Sam. 5:2; 7:7; 1 Chron. 11:2). The NT likewise affirms this derivative role for Christian leaders as shepherds more generally, including 1 Peter. In this respect, there is no implication here that Peter is the only proper shepherd; nor is there any hint of a succession of Petrine ministry so defined.[83]

Jesus is unquestionably the Ἀρχιποίμην, the 'chief Shepherd' (1 Pet 5:4). But Peter and other Christian leaders (surely the Beloved Disciple included) are undershepherds called to endure sufferings in the mission of loving one another, sacrificial hardships that in some cases can even result in death (15:3, 18–20; 16:2–3).

---

[83] *Simon Peter*, 65. See also Hylen, *Imperfect Believers*, 106; and R. Alan Culpepper, 'Peter as Exemplary Disciple in John 21:15–19', *PRSt* 37 (2010): 165–78.

Inclusive Parallels: A Summary

The narrative parallels between Jesus and multiple other characters (Philip, the Samaritan woman, the man born blind, the Beloved Disciple, and Peter) are all components of John's programme of 'narrative theosis' and demonstrate that participation in the divine interrelation of the Father and Son will be expressed in diverse ways for those who believe and are born from above into this family. Denying a participatory element to the blind man's proclamation in John 9:9 rejects the theological and christological connotations woven so carefully by the evangelist into the meaning of ἐγώ εἰμι. Likewise, placing Peter and the Beloved Disciple in opposition obscures their joint characterizations premised in the Prologue's template for participation in divine reality. The thematic programme in which these inclusive parallels collectively make sense is the Fourth Gospel's narrative ecclesiology of deification and participation. Such a narrative ecclesiology, however, is merely suggested or emblematized in the characters discussed above. The full enactment of Johannine theosis for the wider ecclesial community lies primarily beyond the Gospel narrative. This is because believers cannot be divinized apart from the Spirit-Paraclete whose role in Johannine theosis primarily lies beyond the glorification of Jesus.

11

NARRATIVE PNEUMATOLOGY AND TRIADIC THEOLOGY: THE SPIRIT-PARACLETE AS THE CHARACTER WHO DIVINIZES BEYOND THE NARRATIVE

As seen in the previous chapter, the thematic programme of participation is expressed through reciprocity and inclusive parallels *within* and *throughout* the Fourth Gospel. But 'narrative ecclesiology' is the presentation of a vision for communal life that a Gospel story limns, implies, or at times explicitly details; so the communal vision of what I am calling Johannine theosis is not to be fully realized for a corporate entity until Jesus begins his journey back to the Father. This envisaged concept of a Christian social identity that participates in the divine life is thus situated primarily within the *extra-narrative* setting of the evangelist's own ecclesial context. Though the characterizations discussed in Chapter 10 suggestive of divinization contribute to the rhetorical function of illustrating John's narrative ecclesiology, a tension persists between the narrative time within which those characterizations occur and the full enactment of the narrated vision, which, of course, is external to the Gospel's story frame.[1]

It is with respect to this tension that the ecclesial role of the Spirit-Paraclete in John must be understood. The man born blind, Peter, and the Beloved Disciple function within the evangelist's narrative ecclesiology by modelling Johannine theosis within the Gospel; but what they exemplify as individual characters is for a wider group and must be effected pneumatologically. Deification cannot be fully realized among the believing audience(s) of the Gospel until Jesus has died, surfaced from his tomb, and ascended to the Father (16:7).[2] The evangelist is clear: the promise that rivers of living water will flow from Jesus into believers' lives cannot be fully implemented in the

---

[1] The Prologue (1:12–13), however, does not entirely eliminate the possibility that a Spirit-generated re-origination can occur within the narrative (note that Jesus speaks in the first person plural to Nicodemus in 3:11, which seems to be the collective voice of the community beyond the narrative yet fused into the horizon of the text).

[2] These three elements are all central to the Johannine idea of Christ's glorification.

narrative,[3] 'for the Spirit was not yet [οὔπω γὰρ ἦν πνεῦμα], because Jesus was not yet glorified' (7:39).[4] So although the reciprocity statements and inclusive parallels occurring in narrative time are not directly attributed to the Spirit-Paraclete, this divine figure will actualize what they model for believers beyond the Gospel account. As will be shown, the Spirit is presented as the primary *source* and *agent* of Johannine theosis for post-resurrection believers. The decision to delay my treatment of the Spirit-Paraclete's role in Johannine theosis until now honours the extra-narrative dynamic of his activity, allows me to treat him as an identifiable literary character following on from Chapter 10, and (fittingly I think) permits me to conclude the formal body of this book on a (proto-)Trinitarian note.[5]

Integral to what follows is the recognition that the Spirit-Paraclete is both an onstage and offstage character in regard to the Gospel story. In the evangelist's sequential presentation of this figure (referred to below as 'narrative pneumatology'), links are made with both God and Jesus in such a way that the Prologue's dyadic theology enlarges and evolves to portray a *triadic* divine identity. It is precisely as a participant

---

[3] There is debate over the source of the living waters, whether Jesus or believers. Craig Keener, who views Jesus as the source, provides an overview of the discussion in Keener, *John*, 728–30. For a detailed treatment of John 7:37–39 that also identifies Jesus as the source for living water, see Maarten J. J. Menken, '"Rivers of Living Water Shall Flow From His Inside (John 7:38)"', in Menken, *Old Testament Quotations in the Fourth Gospel: Studies in Textual Form*, CBET 15 (Kampen: Kok Pharos, 1996), 187–203.

[4] Note the remark by Jesus to the disciples in 14:17 that the Paraclete 'is remaining with you and will be in you'. It is difficult to determine if μένω here is to be understood as a present (μένει) or a future (μενεῖ), but the future orientation of the Paraclete dwelling ἐν ὑμῖν accords well with John 7:39. See Brown, *John*, 639–40.

[5] The Spirit-Paraclete is regularly understood as central to Johannine ecclesiology. A sampling of works specifically relevant to my particular concerns of the Fourth Gospel's pneumatology are cited throughout this chapter. It is worth noting here, though, that John's portrayal of the Spirit has become a central feature of the historical reconstructions that, as argued in my Introduction, tend to displace ecclesiology (a theological vision for community) with aetiology (a historical investigation of a community's origins). These two enterprises should certainly be understood as interrelated, but the interesting observation to make is that the extra-narrative role of the Paraclete is sometimes attributed to the schisms scholars assume rocked and divided the Johannine community. The most influential exploration of this claim is probably Raymond Brown's *The Community of the Beloved Disciple*, esp. 138–44. For a recent development of Brown's ideas working from the Johannine Epistles, see Gary M. Burge, 'Spirit-Inspired Theology and Ecclesial Correction: Charting One Shift in the Development of Johannine Ecclesiology and Pneumatology', in *Communities in Dispute: Current Scholarship on the Johannine Epistles*, ed. R. Alan Culpepper and Paul N. Anderson, Early Christianity and its Literature 13 (Atlanta, GA: Society of Biblical Literature Press, 2014), 179–85.

of the Father–Son interrelation that the Spirit-Paraclete divinizes the 'church' by enabling believers to become joint participants. This chapter, and thus the formal body of the entire book, will therefore conclude suggesting a nascent Trinitarian understanding of ecclesial theosis.

Narrative Pneumatology: The Spirit-Paraclete as a Johannine Character

Having just devoted space to human characters divinized *within* the narrative, the Spirit-Paraclete can be understood as a divine character who divinizes human beings *beyond* the narrative. The use of the literary term 'character' is important – the Spirit is eventually depicted by the evangelist in personal terms and deserves treatment as a Johannine character in his own right. Even so, the Spirit receives little attention in recent narrative-critical studies on the Fourth Gospel's use of characterization.[6] The omissions in these recent studies may be due to the christocentric logic that governs the enterprise of finding and crafting suitable methods for understanding the Gospel's literary figures. At the cutting edge of this ongoing venture is Cornelis Bennema who affirms Stephen Moore's view that 'Johannine characterization ... is entirely christocentric'.[7] If we are to use Bennema's own methodology, among the more sophisticated means currently available for assessing characterization in John, the fundamental starting place is to 'evaluate the Johannine characters in terms of their response to Jesus'.[8] As Raymond Collins and R. Alan Culpepper noted several years ago in their pioneer studies on characterization in the Fourth Gospel, the evangelist

---

[6] The Spirit does not even feature amidst the more than 700 pages of the recently published volume edited by Steven A. Hunt, D. Francois Tolmie, and Ruben Zimmerman, *Character Studies in the Fourth Gospel: Narrative Approaches to Seventy Figures in John.*, WUNT I/314 (Tübingen: Mohr Siebeck, 2013). To be fair, it is important to note here that this impressive volume also does not provide literary sketches for the characters of God and Jesus, indicating that the emphasis is on the human characters of the Gospel. A brief treatment of the Paraclete's characterization in the Farewell Discourse in D. Francois Tolmie, *Jesus' Farewell to the Disciples: John 13:1–17:26 in Narratological Perspective*, Biblical Interpretation Series 12 (Leiden: Brill, 1995), 133–5.

[7] Stephen D. Moore, *Literary Criticism and the Gospels: The Theoretical Challenge* (New Haven, CT: Yale University Press, 1989), 49; cited in Cornelis Bennema, 'A Comprehensive Approach to Understanding Character in the Gospel of John', in *Characters and Characterization in the Gospel of John*, LNTS 461 (London: Bloomsbury, 2013), 53.

[8] Bennema, 'A Comprehensive Approach', 53; see further Cornelis Bennema, 'A Theory of Character in the Fourth Gospel with Reference to Ancient and Modern Literature', *BibInt* 17, 4 (2009): 375–421; and Bennema, *Encountering Jesus*.

establishes an unmistakable dualism that compels responses to Jesus ranging from acceptance or rejection.[9] Though Bennema's model (along with others[10]) advances this observation, accounting for nuances and complexities with his multiple continua for mapping 'the degree of characterization' applied to each Gospel figure, the christocentric orientation promoted by Culpepper and Collins remains in full force. This orientation is apt, *except when the focus on christocentricity proves a hermeneutical hindrance by eclipsing other thematic emphases* (a trend briefly analysed in this book's Introduction).[11] With accepting/ rejecting Jesus establishing the foundational rubric for assessing John's characters, the divine figure of the Spirit-Paraclete seems to lie, to some degree, outside the current frames of scholarly reference about Johannine characterization.

Further complicating the characterization of the Spirit-Paraclete is the phenomenon already noted above, that so much of his prominence lies offstage and outside the sphere of narrative time. Indeed, the extra-narrative nature of the Paraclete's prominence and work has at times been regarded as so manifestly disconnected from the intra-narrative presentation of the Spirit that the five sayings about the Paraclete in the Farewell Discourse are assumed to be later interpolations. One notable result of this reading is the tendency to regard the Spirit and Paraclete as distinct and separate (an unnecessary severance my frequent use of the hyphenated 'Spirit-Paraclete' is intended to work against).[12]

[9] Collins, 'Representative Figures'; Culpepper, *Anatomy of the Fourth Gospel*, 99–148. Culpepper revisits his earlier contributions in R. Alan Culpepper, 'The Weave of the Tapestry: Character and Theme in John', in *Characters and Characterization in the Gospel of John*, ed. Christopher W. Skinner, LNTS 461 (London: Bloomsbury, 2013), 18–35.

[10] See, for instance, the other essays alongside Bennema's in 'Part One: Methods and Models for Reading Johannine Characters' in Skinner, ed., *Characters and Characterization in the Gospel of John*, 36–58.

[11] See the discussion on pp. 12–14 inspired by Marianne Meye Thompson's critique of christocentricity in Thompson, *God*, 13–14.

[12] On this phenomenon in Johannine scholarship, see the discussion in Craig R. Koester, *The Word of Life: A Theology of John's Gospel* (Grand Rapids, MI: Eerdmans, 2008), 134 and in Gary M. Burge, *The Anointed Community: The Holy Spirit in the Johannine Tradition* (Grand Rapids, MI: Eerdmans, 1987), 3–45; Thompson, *God*, 146–49. Also contributing to the trend of severing the Paraclete from the Spirit is probably the tendency to regard the Farewell Discourse, which contains all references to the Paraclete, as a distinct literary unity. For a detailed argument against this reading, see Tolmie, *Jesus' Farewell*. Though Rudolf Schnackenburg views the Paraclete sayings as later additions, he recognizes the importance of reading them within their embedded literary position within the

I propose that the most fruitful means of assessing the characterization of this figure is found in attending to the evangelist's 'narrative pneumatology', that is, the unfolding continuum of the Gospel's story arc along which the presentation of the Spirit-Paraclete develops. Such an approach honours the energetic warning of Marianne Meye Thompson, worth citing here in full:

> On the whole, the various passages on the Spirit have not been treated within the flow of the narrative but have rather been extracted from the narrative to see if a synthetic 'theology' of the Spirit could be fashioned from them. This enterprise ... should not without further ado be eschewed. It ought to follow, rather than precede or substitute for, a close reading of the narrative itself, *for it is the logic of the Gospel narrative, as well as the theological reflection that shaped that narrative, that in the final analysis provides the framework that accounts for the Gospel's distinctive representation of the Spirit.* Explanations for the different functions predicated of the Spirit, and even for the different conceptions of the Spirit operative at various junctures in John, *must also be sought within the narrative progression of the Gospel* and in light of the functions of the Spirit that arise from each passage. That is to say, the Gospel ought not to be constructed as a sort of hodge-podge of mismatched statements about the Spirit-Paraclete that John never quite finished sorting through. There are genuine differences between statements about the 'spirit' in the narrative portions of the Gospel (chs. 1–12, 20) and statements about the 'Paraclete' found in the Farewell Discourses. *These can, and indeed must, be accounted for by the narrative movement of the Gospel itself,* as well as by John's theological reflection upon the identity of the Spirit.[13]

Though a detailed tracing of the evangelist's narrative pneumatology is beyond the scope of this chapter, what I presently offer are brief accounts of 1) the Spirit-Paraclete's onstage characterization as a divine figure gradually interrelated with the Father and Son and 2) the developing portrait of the Spirit-Paraclete's offstage role in effecting and sustaining Johannine theosis.

Gospel. See his 'Excursus 16: The Paraclete and the Sayings about the Paraclete', in Schnackenburg, *John*, 3:138–54.

[13] Thompson, *God*, 155 (emphases added).

The Spirit-Paraclete and the Triadic Divine Identity

It was shown in shown in Chapters 2 and 3 that the vague categorizations designating the divine figures in the Prologue – 'God' and 'Logos' – disambiguate in a process of filiation and enhanced personification. By John 1:18, God and the Logos are understood as distinct persons jointly sharing the divine identity and characterized by a familial interrelation. In the evangelist's narrative pneumatology, *a process of disambiguation is also underway for the* Spirit-Paraclete, the Gospel's other divine figure, but the unfolding process of development is stretched out over the course of the entire Gospel. The ambiguous and fluid terms θεός/God, λόγος/Word, and πνεῦμα/Spirit sequentially accrue personal specificity in the redesignations of πάτηρ/Father, μονογενής/the only Son, and παράκλητος/Paraclete (comforter), respectively. Though no familial terms are used for him, filiation is implied through the theme of mutual indwelling – the Spirit shares the same divine household as the Father, Son, and (eventually) the children of God.[14] The degree of personification in the evangelist's ongoing programme of characterizing the Spirit-Paraclete is critical enough that he seems willing to bend grammatical rules, possibly using masculine pronouns to modify the neuter πνεῦμα in the final references to this figure in the Farewell Discourse.[15]

Though emphasis has been placed on the dyadic nature of Johannine theology thus far in this study, it has been repeatedly observed that both the divine identity and the divine interrelation of the Father and Son who share that identity are marked by a social openness. Over the course of the narrative, the Spirit-Paraclete is so closely linked to the other two divine figures in the Gospel that Johannine theology must be recognized as *triadic*. These links are most succinctly expressed in the phrases πνεῦμα ὁ θεός ('God is Spirit') in 4:24 (pneumatology–theology) and ἄλλον παράκλητον in 14:16 (pneumatology–christology).

---

[14] The Spirit is introduced in the narrative by John the Baptist's testimony that it descended on Jesus and remained (ἔμεινεν) on him. The verb μένω becomes central to the household theme Mary Coloe has shown to be a central motif for Johannine ecclesiology. Again, see Coloe, *Household of God*.

[15] In 16:13, Jesus tells his disciples that whenever ἔλθῃ ἐκεῖνος [masculine], τὸ πνεῦμα [neuter] τῆς ἀληθείας, he will guide them in(to) truth. The masculine ἐκεῖνος, as opposed to the neuter ἐκεῖνο, reappears in 16:14. These masculine pronouns are probably intended to modify the previous reference to παράκλητος in 16:7, but the proximity of the ἐκεῖνος to the more immediate neuter πνεῦμα is striking.

First, I will take up the correlation of pneumatology and theology. Obviously, God and Spirit are closely interrelated in the Jewish scriptures so formative for the Gospel's audience.[16] The Prologue's re-narration of Genesis 1 may have been striking to early Jewish readers not only because of its reference to the Logos, but because of its omission of a reference to the Spirit (though an echo of Genesis 1:2 seems implied in John 1:32[17]). The Greek construction in 4:24, πνεῦμα ὁ θεός/'God is Spirit', resembles the construction θεὸς ἦν ὁ λόγος in John 1:1 – 'the Word was God'; and since the previous uses of πνεῦμα before John 4 have been in reference to *the* Spirit (1:32; 3:5, 8, 34), the phrase in 4:24 should be read as 'God is Spirit' (with the capital 's'), indicating the creative divine force active in Israel's scriptures that will later in the Gospel be personified through the use of the title 'Paraclete'.[18] The life-giving power of the Spirit, repeatedly referenced in John (3:3–8; 6:63; 7:37–39; 20:22) and bearing overtones from Ezekiel 36–37 in the background, locates Johannine pneumatology within the frame of Jewish theology. As the semantic range of the articular and anarthrous instances of πνεῦμα expands to accommodate the narrative pneumatology of personification, it becomes clear that, for the fourth evangelist, this life-giving force is ultimately a divine person coordinated with the divine person of God who is both 'Father' and 'Spirit'.

The evangelist's literary activity of correlating the Spirit-Paraclete with God coincides with the parallel programme of correlating him with Jesus. The post-Easter sending of the Spirit to the disciples is an event initialized by both the Father (14:16, 26) and the Son (15:26; 16:7). The Paraclete's associations with truth (15:26, 16:13) echo those made about Jesus (1:14, 17; 14:6; see also 1 John 5:7).[19] The reference to ἄλλον παράκλητον (*'another* Paraclete', emphases added) in 14:16

---

[16] The exact phrase πνεῦμα ὁ θεός, however, is not found in the LXX – Michaels, *John*, 251. For the wider background of the association between God and Spirit, see Barrett, *John*, 238–9.

[17] Brown, *John*, 57.

[18] Lincoln, *John*, 177; Raymond E. Brown, 'The Paraclete in the Fourth Gospel', *NTS* 13, 2 (1967): 113–32; Smalley, *John*, 228–33. George Johnston, however, opposes the idea of regarding the Paraclete as a 'person' – George Johnston, *The Spirit-Paraclete in the Gospel of John* (Cambridge: Cambridge University Press, 1970), see esp. 81. Johnston argues against the alternation between the personal and impersonal nature of the Spirit-Paraclete as understood by Otto Betz, *Der Paraklet: Fürsprecher im häretischen Spätjudentum, im Johannes-Evangelium und in neu gefundenen gnostischen Schriften* (Leiden: Brill, 1963), 159–64.

[19] Macaskill, *Union*, 255.

certainly means 'another' besides Jesus, who is explicitly identified as a παράκλητος in 1 John 2:1.[20] Brown has put it succinctly: 'Whatever is said about the Paraclete is said elsewhere in the Gospel about Jesus'.[21] Yet as indicated by the key phrase of pneumatology–christology, ἄλλον παράκλητον, Jesus cannot be simply *equated with* the Paraclete.[22] Like God and the Logos, the Spirit-Paraclete is an entity in his own right. As a divine figure directly linked to the Father and the Son (yet identifiable among them) whose presence continues the presence of Jesus among the disciples, it is not an exegetical stretch to claim that, in Johannine perspective, *the Spirit is somehow included within the divine identity.*

The dynamics of this inclusion receive no elaborate explanation by the evangelist – the outworking of the conundrums produced by this triadic theology are left for more formal treatments in the later centuries of the church. I acknowledge that modern-day scholars are hermeneutically apprehensive in discussing the Spirit as a 'person' and thereby risking a retrospective reading that imports later church doctrine into New Testament texts.[23] James Dunn has urged interpreters to 'let John be John' and resist reading the Gospel through third- or fourth-century lenses.[24] I am sympathetic to such resistance, but contemporary aversions to retrospective Trinitarian readings should not obscure the conspicuous exegetical fact that there are three divine beings in John's Gospel who are related, and yet distinct, personal entities.

---

[20] C. H. Dodd, *The Interpretation of the Fourth Gospel* (Campridge: Cambridge University Press, 1970), 414.

[21] Brown, 'Paraclete', 126.

[22] 'Calling the Spirit "another Advocate" does not mean he is "another Jesus"' – Koester, *Word of Life*, 148. The distinctiveness between the Spirit and Jesus is also emphasized by the descent of the former onto the latter in 1:32–33.

[23] This tendency is described in Watson, 'Trinity and Community', 168–70.

[24] Dunn, 'Let John Be John'. See also Johnston, *Spirit-Paraclete*. Affirming Dunn's comments on letting 'John be John', David Crump attacks the view promoted in social trinitarianism that the Fourth Gospel warrants the language of a perichoretic union between the Father, Son, and Spirit. Though for the most part I agree with Crump's arguments that the language of mutual indwelling is reserved for the triad of Father–Son–Disciples more so than for the triad of Father–Son–Spirit, he seems unable to acknowledge even the existence of the latter in the Gospel text. Crump actually may be operating within the anachronistic paradigm of later trinitarianism he is attempting to critique – since the language of interpenetration is not used in John, for Crump this amounts to a dismissal of any under-lying Trinitarian logic found within the text. See Crump, 'Re-examining the Johannine Trinity: Perichoresis or Deification?', *SJT* 59, no. 4 (2006): 395–412.

Narrative Pneumatology and Johannine Ecclesiology: The Spirit-Paraclete as Source and Agent of Corporate Deification

As the fourth evangelist's narrative pneumatology follows an identifiable literary and theological trajectory throughout the Gospel, it informs the narrative ecclesiology of participation and deification traced throughout this monograph. The agency of the Spirit-Paraclete in Johannine theosis can be summarily stated thus: 1) as a life force or creative divine power, the *Spirit* serves as the divine source and means of the re-origination of believers (an event I have identified as central to the participation motif); and 2) as the personified character of the *Paraclete*, he sustains the believers' post-Resurrection participation in divine reality through his abiding presence.[25] It should be clear from the logic argued above that re-origination by the Spirit and the Paraclete's preservation through indwelling are not two distinct activities governed by two different entities. They both comprehend within the cumulative portraiture of the one Spirit-Paraclete whose sending or giving from God is to be understood within the scope of Jewish eschatological expectations – though (unsurprisingly) these expectations are uniquely appropriated by the evangelist: 'since the Word has become flesh the new age of the Spirit has been inaugurated'.[26]

As repeatedly observed, the heart of Johannine soteriology and ecclesiology is an ontological transformation that amounts to re-creation. A new 'becoming' (1:12–13) takes place in which believers become divine beings sourced not in reproductive genetics or in ethnic heritage but in a supernatural creative act – ἐκ θεοῦ ἐγεννήθησαν ('out of God they were born'). This language is soon repeated and phrased within the language of pneumatology as Jesus explains to Nicodemus that to be

---

[25] Though David Crump adamantly argues against exegetically anachronistic Trinitarian readings of Johannine pneumatology in the article cited immediately above, he is surprisingly and ironically unapologetic about embracing 'the Eastern Orthodox doctrine of deification (divinization, or theosis)' (409) in his conclusions. His understanding of theosis differs from my own (curiously, he does not believe that Johannine divinization results in disciples being 'transformed into divinity' – 411), but he does claim that 'the Spirit/Paraclete is the agent of this soteriological deification' (409). See also Lawrence J. Lutkemeyer, 'The Role of the Paraclete (Jn. 16:7–15)', *CBQ* 8, 2 (1946): 220–29, here at 227.

[26] Smalley, *John*, 227; Stephen S. Smalley, '"The Paraclete": Pneumatology in the Johannine Gospel and Apocalypse', in *Exploring the Gospel of John: In Honor of D. Moody Smith*, ed. R. Alan Culpepper and C. Clifton Black (Louisville, KY: Westminster John Knox Press, 1996), 289–300.

born 'from above' (ἄνωθεν) means to be born ἐξ ὕδατος καὶ πνεύματος ('out of water and spirit' – 3:5), with ἐκ τοῦ πνεύματος ('out of the Spirit') occurring twice more thereafter (vv. 6, 8). In other words, deified believers derive their new ontology from the Spirit.

Along with being a divine source, the Spirit is also a divine agent. His role in the activities of re-creation/re-origination is made explicit in John 6:63 when Jesus claims 'the Spirit is the one who makes alive' (τὸ πνεῦμά ἐστιν τὸ ζῳοποιοῦν). The assertions that the Spirit gives life in both John 3 and 6 include contrasts with the flesh (σάρξ) that is 'useless' (6:63, NRSV) and capable only of futile self-replication (3:6). In drawing attention to these contrasts between flesh and Spirit as sources and agents the evangelist draws directly on the foundational statements in 1:12–13 in which believers become divine participants within the Father–Son interrelation. Furthermore, Jesus' death and resurrection are shown as integral events tied to the enactment of Johannine pneumatology from which believers derive some implied transformational benefit – from the cross he 'handed over the Spirit [παρέδωκεν τὸ πνεῦμα]'; 'water' soon flowed with blood from his side (19:34; cf. 7:38–39); and on the first Easter he breathed into his disciples as the risen Christ (20:22). These events enable the re-origination of believers and also offer the pneumatological means by which their abiding participation in divine reality is sustained.

As 'another Paraclete', the Spirit is shown to be not only a divine source for the believers' ontological transformation, but also a *person* who contributes to the ecclesial community's ongoing experience of deification through at least three ways. Since Johannine theosis is intensely relational (as a participation within the divine society of Father and Son), the Paraclete first will provide the gift of divine presence in light of Jesus' corporeal absence (14:16), which ensures the mutual co-dwelling of the Father, Son, and disciples.[27] Second, the Spirit-Paraclete will guide the ecclesial community into the truth Jesus embodies – central to the maintenance of Johannine participation is the discipline of abiding in Jesus' words (see e.g., 6:63–64; 8:31, 37, 43, 51–52), revelatory speech which the Paraclete will disclose (14:26; 16:13). Third, the Paraclete will allow believers to participate in the divine activities with which they are charged. In another inclusive parallel, the Spirit remains on the disciples (14:17) just as he was portrayed as remaining on Jesus (1:32). He will also enable them to bear testimony to Jesus (15:26–27) and to offer release from sins (20:23). The Spirit-Paraclete therefore

---

[27] Koester, *Word of Life*, 151.

divinizes believers external to the narrative that they may follow the paradigmatic roles of those characters suggestively divinized within the narrative.

Chapter Summary

With the characterization of the Spirit the fourth evangelist shows that the readers and auditors of his Gospel can participate in the narrative ecclesiology of theosis that extends beyond the narrative frame. 'Other sheep' and 'those who are believing' or 'will believe' through the disciples' testimony are invited to embrace the claim 'that Jesus is the Christ, the Son of God' and thus enter the eternal life of filiation and deification. What I have sought to provide throughout this chapter and, indeed, throughout this entire study on Johannine ecclesiology, is a robust interface with later theological interpretations that is nonetheless exegetically grounded within the Gospel text. The deification discourses and Trinitarian formulae of later patristic theologians certainly addressed specific controversies contemporary with their time of writing; but those writings also evidence the hermeneutical enterprise of trying to discern the theological logic at work in biblical texts. My own purpose here in this chapter has not been to offer a Trinitarian reading of the Spirit per se, but to provide a brief account of the Spirit-Paraclete's role in Johannine theosis by following the evangelist's incremental process of character-ization. And in that process the term πνεῦμα gradually disambiguates and acquires new layers of signification throughout the narrative resulting in a personification that cannot be jettisoned in the climactic scene of re-creation when Jesus blows on the disciples, re-enacting Genesis 2:7 (20:22) – the Spirit-Paraclete is a participant of the divine identity who divinizes believers, inducting and sustaining them in the divine community.

Conclusion

12

JOHN'S NARRATIVE ECCLESIOLOGY
OF DEIFICATION: A SYNTHESIS

The Fourth Gospel does not end conclusively. In what appears to be two attempts at narrative closure, the evangelist (or a later redactor) indicates in 20:30 as well as in 21:5 that the available material he could have potentially included exceeded the remit of his task. Jesus did more than space permits for description. Neither ending succeeds at providing a demarcated sense of closure because further reflection is invited either on what could still be written, as in 21:5, or on what has just been written, as in 20:20–31 where the readers and auditors are invited to consider the personal (yet collective) import of the foregoing account. The evangelist also indicates in that direct address to the audience that the material he *has* offered was done so on the basis of a clear agenda. An editorial programme was in force that determined the inclusion of some items and the exclusion of others.

In the spirit of the Gospel's (intentionally unsuccessful) attempts at narrative closure, I will identify here in my final chapter the key arguments central to my own editorial agenda that leaves the discussion open for ongoing debate and reflection. Listed below in the first section are a number of summary statements roughly correspondent with the sequence of the book that together serve as the foundation for these two overarching claims: 1) the Fourth Gospel's ecclesiology envisions the formation and ongoing life of a human community participating in the divine interrelation of the Father and Son; and 2) this relational participation is regularly depicted as filiation and requires a profound ontological transformation largely consonant with what later theologians would call theosis. The diverse evidence of these two claims is so embedded within the Gospel story and wields such force in the shaping of its plotline that John can be regarded as a 'deification narrative'. Cognizant – perhaps like the evangelist or redactor – that my study in no way offers definitive closure on the issues raised, I will bring the discussions to an inconclusive end by suggesting further lines of inquiry and noting potential areas requiring further clarification.

Eleven Summary Statements on Johannine Ecclesiology

My argument has for the most part followed this order of claims:

1. *Ecclesiology is a theme of paramount importance in the Fourth Gospel.* Though at times obscured in Johannine scholarship by questions of aetiology or eclipsed by an all-encompassing 'christocentricity', a robust ecclesial vision begins to emerge almost immediately in John – the Prologue is as much an introduction to the evangelist's ecclesiology as it is to his christology. The formation of a renewed people of God stands at the centre of the Gospel's unfolding developments alongside the portrait being offered of Jesus. Christology generates ecclesiology as the reconceptualization of God prompts a reconceptualization of the constituency of God's people.

2. *The Fourth Gospel's ecclesiology is a* narrative *ecclesiology.* Assumptions are regularly made about the historical issues concerning ecclesiology underlying the Gospels. Because Matthew provides a mechanism for managing sin within a communal context (18:15–17), it is understood that a recognizable church order was in force for Matthean Christians. John's reticence on such matters and a supposed sacramental ambivalence have been used to justify claims that ecclesiology is thematically marginal at best. Such an approach to early Christian ecclesiology demands too much of the genre of narrative. John provides (along with the Synoptics, I believe) a comprehensive vision for the ecclesial community as a social entity; but *narrative* ecclesiology is the presentation of such a vision through the cumulative, sequential development of a Gospel as 'story'.

3. *The plurality characterizing divinity according to the fourth evangelist generates a participatory ecclesiology.* The dynamic of participation is fundamental for Johannine ecclesiology because divinity is a category that is *social* and, with certain qualifications, *open.* The phrase 'dyadic theology' refers to the dialectic by which the Logos is identified *as* God while remaining identifiable *from* God. The divine identity comprises a community; and the interrelation of Father and Son is inclusive of humans who believe in Jesus and consequently undergo an ontological reconfiguration. Contrary to scholarly assertions that the Fourth Gospel promotes (a Western-style) individualism, the evangelist immediately establishes collectivity as a major dimension of his idea of 'church'.

4. *Participation is effected by the divine–human exchange of the Incarnation and expressed as filiation.* As derivative anthropology gives way to participatory ecclesiology throughout the Prologue's sequence, an

ontological reconfiguration of believers occurs that is directly linked to the Word becoming flesh. The divine re-origination of the children of God is made possible by the Logos' (literal) embodiment. These two 'becomings' are described in filial terms – what the Prologue depicts in 1: 12–14 is the formation of a divine family. 'Participation' can be an opaque theological term; but for the Fourth Gospel, participatory ecclesiology is given expression through the dynamics of family membership. Filiation is so important in the Prologue that it establishes the major classifications used in an unfolding process of disambiguation by which the abstract categorizations of θεός (God), λόγος (Word), and ἄνθρωποι (human beings) are eventually denoted as 'Father', the μονογενής, and the 'children of God'.

5. *The* Prologue *sets into motion an 'ecclesial narrative script' of resocialization that governs the plotline of the entire Gospel.* John's narrative is launched into an ecclesial trajectory by its opening lines, and the plot is resolved with the formation of a new community of people into which the evangelist's readers and auditors are invited as participants (20:30–31). The Prologue's account of the reception of Jesus resulting in the formation of a filial community (1:12–14), plus its converse of rejection and social division (1:10–11), form a template enacted repeatedly throughout the narrative proper. The words and actions of Jesus destabilize the social constructs within the text, though the invitation remains open for others to resocialize into the group centred around him. While some characters or character groups follow this positive dimension of the template (e.g., Peter), others continually waver between the two social domains (e.g., Nicodemus) or instantiate the negative option of social re-entrenchment (e.g., 'the Jews'). Ecclesiology is manifestly one of John's primary story arcs.

6. *The Johannine oneness motif is grounded in the Scriptures of Israel.* Within this script of resocialization the evangelist employs the term 'one' as a multivalent abbreviation expressing the identity of Jesus (christology), the resulting reconceptualization of God (theology), and the new community brought into being (ecclesiology) by these christological and theological revelations. Though various models of Johannine ecclesiology have understood the oneness motif as deriving from (proto-)Gnostic mysticism or as arising from a distressing historical situation of intra-church schism, the evangelist is relying on the sacred texts of his Jewish religious traditions. Jesus' claim 'I and the Father are one' is emphatically Jewish and draws from the monotheistic formula of the Shema in Deuteronomy 6:4 (and already referred to in John 8:41). The christological and ecclesial uses

of 'one' draw respectively on the messianic and nationalistic formulae found in Ezekiel 34 and 37. The evangelist alternates between the diverse meanings of oneness and their intertextual links in a complex narrative development. Over the course of John 8–11, the theological, christological, and ecclesiological resonances mutually reinforce one another and accrue multilayered meanings that eventually interfuse in John 17.

7. *The prayer 'that they may be one, as we are one' expresses an ecclesiology of divine association as the Johannine believers, at odds with their religious heritage, are coordinated with the 'one' God of Israel.* The prayer for ecclesial oneness in John 17 is not simply a call to doctrinal unanimity or internal social harmony; Jesus' request is an articulation of Jewish-Christian group identity. In spite of the ostracism faced by believers within the Gospel text (and likely also by the Johannine Christians behind the text), allegiance to Jesus does not amount to a desertion of the deity professed in the Shema: 'YHWH is one.' Jesus is the one messianic Shepherd of the one true God and the collective social entity of the disciples constitutes their one people. In John 17 Jesus prays a very Jewish prayer that associates the church with the divine identity.

8. *The prayer 'that they may be one, as we are one' also envisions an ecclesiology of divine* participation *as believers enter the Father–Son interrelation as family members newly generated and in the process of divinization.* In addition to associating believers with the God of Israel, the language of ecclesial oneness also suggests their deification. To be 'one' with this one God means more than correspondence, analogy, or association. The citation of Psalm 82 in John 10:34 indicates that the boundaries between humanity and divinity are porous – those to whom the Word of God comes are elevated to some form of 'god'-status. Jesus is that Word, the ultimate revelation of the one God, and those for whom he prays in chapter 17 share in his own consecration and participate in the divine glory. Oneness is deification as well as divine association. So when Jesus prays that his disciples may be 'one', he is essentially claiming for the church the assertion of Psalm 82:6 – 'you are gods'.

9. *Johannine theosis is Jewish, narrative, and communal.* Rather than imposing a set of terms and ideas alien to this Gospel, my application of later patristic theological concepts to John is in the service of articulating an ecclesial vision already present within the text. Theosis that is specifically Johannine is grounded within a Jewish religious framework, though this framework was admittedly

open to the influence of other religious ideas current at the time. The evangelist's rendition of deification is also grounded within a storied format, as opposed to the genres of treatise, homily, or pseudo-dialogue in which patristic theosis discourse often appears. Finally, Johannine theosis is communal in that it envisions divinization not as a personal experience of individualistic soteriology but as a corporate expression of ecclesial identity.

10. *Johannine theosis is illustrated in the narrative through the characterization of specific figures and groups.* If the Prologue frames the Gospel narrative with the expectation of human beings becoming divine through filiation and re-origination, then it should be expected that qualities or activities recognized as divine will be displayed or enacted by certain Johannine characters. Reciprocity statements and 'inclusive parallels' are employed precisely to that effect. Ecclesial reciprocity is roughly voiced through the formula *just as Jesus, so also the believers.* Inclusive parallelism occurs when certain figures or groups speak words or perform actions attributed to Jesus earlier in the narrative. Specific examples include the 'I am' saying on the lips of the man born blind, the positioning of the Beloved Disciple within the κόλπος (bosom) of Jesus (mirroring Jesus' earlier depiction in the κόλπος of the Father), and the means by which Peter's sacrificial death is signified echoing prior anticipations of the death of the Good Shepherd. When the characterizations of Peter and the mysterious 'disciple whom Jesus loved' are understood within the ecclesial vision of Johannine theosis, the need for conflict theories as a hermeneutical key for understanding their portrayals fades away.

11. *Johannine theosis is actualized beyond the narrative through the work of the Spirit-Paraclete whose characterization within the Gospel renders triadic the Prologue's dyadic theology.* A corrective to claims that John distinguishes between the Spirit and the Paraclete is offered by a recognition of the fourth evangelist's 'narrative pneumatology'. The process of disambiguation and enhanced personalization of God and the Logos in the Prologue is paralleled in the wider account as the spirit/Spirit gains increased personal qualities as the Paraclete, whose activity ensures the filial cohabitation of the Father, Son, and the children of God. The dynamics of Johannine theosis modelled by divinized characters within the Gospel narrative is made possible by the work of the Spirit-Paraclete beyond the narrative.

Questions for Further Reflection (and Implications for Biblical Studies, Theology, and Ecumenism)

Again, the Gospel of John ends noting its limited scope. The range of additional concerns and unaddressed material is stated at the narrative ending as inexhaustible (a fact well attested by the burgeoning array of secondary literature in Johannine studies!). I will bring my own work to a close by providing a list of questions raised by the foregoing chapters that require further or more adequate exploration. I envision fruitful discussions on Johannine theosis potentially emerging in interdisciplinary areas of academic research and also among local churches and their wider denominational traditions.

In the area of biblical studies, it should be asked how those ecclesial images in John that received only marginal attention in this study (such as the vine and the household or temple of God) might inform the vision of Johannine theosis. Also, my treatment of participatory ecclesiology in John's Gospel should be interfaced with a more focused study on filiation and deification in the Johannine Epistles. Though I have offered measured critiques on the scholarly impulse to reconstruct historical scenarios behind the text, the ecclesiology detailed in this study may provide new clues for sharpening (and perhaps modifying or even disqualifying) elements of those theories. My assertion that the Shema presents an ecclesial model for early Jewish Christianity bears import on the current dialogue concerning John's Gospel and anti-Semitism, since the Johannine self-identification of oneness is an explicitly Jewish move. Moving into wider areas of New Testament studies beyond John, it should be asked how comparative readings between the Johannine, Pauline, and Petrine literature might shed light on early Christian ideas of divinization. I suggest that another promising avenue of research is the application of narrative ecclesiology to canonical and extra-canonical Gospels. How might attentiveness to a storied ecclesial vision, however implicit or explicit, bring clarity to the self-understanding of early Christian groups?

I made the point in Part III that biblical scholarship's recent interest in deification has to some degree neglected the fourth evangelist as a resource alongside Paul and Peter. How might the construct of Johannine theosis inform the academic field of historical theology in the reading of patristic texts? I trust that I have provided sufficient warrant for a closer consideration of the exegesis of John in the ongoing work of discerning the New Testament's ideas about deification and divine union. My language of 'dyadic/triadic theology' and 'inclusive divine community' surely has implications in systematic theology, parti-cularly in current discussions on Trinitarianism. Pastoral theologians may wish to wrestle with the practical implications of Johannine theosis in local congregations. Given the popularity of the Fourth Gospel in contemporary ecclesial contexts, how might a vision of collective deifi-cation resound in homiletics and play out in the sacraments and in the exercise of spiritual disciplines?

I would certainly also hope that my study on Johannine theosis will inform discussions in the contemporary academic field of ecclesiology. Can we embrace theosis not only as a model of *soteriology* largely associated with Eastern Orthodox traditions but also as a more uni-versal model of *ecclesiology*? Furthermore, my argument that Jesus' prayer for oneness in John 17 refers to something more fundamental than social harmony or universal agreement on issues of doctrine raises a number of questions affecting ecumenicity. I would suggest that my understanding of *oneness as deification* in no way undermines the noble objective of ecclesial union; but I have largely left unexamined the question of how an interpretation of 'one' informed more by the Shema than by Greco-Roman ideals of social concord might supply the church with an understanding of corporate identity stronger than a joint cooperation in missional ventures or elusive quests for the lowest common denominator in doctrine. John certainly encourages christo-logical precision in the church's understanding of Jesus; but the fore-going study affirms that participation in the divine life should be regarded along with doctrinal discourse and shared mission projects as integral to the ecumenical promotion of unity. If Johannine theosis were promoted as a premise of ecclesial oneness and a goal of ecumen-ism, we would confidently rejoice in a plurality intrinsic to the divine community entailing such diverse members as a beggar born blind claiming 'I am' and comprising such theologically divisive characters as Peter and the Beloved Disciple. As the uncountable number of potential βιβλία ('books') envisioned at the close of John 21 continue to emerge on the shelves, I will be particularly grateful to those authors willing to take a closer and perhaps more learned look at Johannine theosis as a model for the contemporary church.

BIBLIOGRAPHY

Ackerman, James S. 'The Rabbinic Interpretation of Psalm 82 and the Gospel of John'. *Harvard Theological Review* 59: 2 (1966): 186–91.

Aland, Kurt. 'Eine Untersuchung zu Joh 1:3–4: Über die Bedeutung eines Punktes'. *Zeitschrift für die neutestamentliche Wissenschaft und die Kunde der älteren Kirche* 59 (1968): 174–209.

Anderson, Gary A. 'To See Where God Dwells: The Tabernacle, the Temple, and the Origins of the Christian Mystical Tradition'. *Letter & Spirit* 4 (2008): 13–45.

Appold, Mark L. *The Oneness Motif in the Fourth Gospel: Motif Analysis and Exegetical Probe into the Theology of John.* 2nd edn. Wissenschaftliche Untersuchungen zum Neuen Testament 2:1. Eugene, OR: Wipf and Stock, 1976.

Aquinas, Thomas. *Catena Aurea: Commentary on the Four Gospels Collected out of the Works of the Fathers by S. Thomas Aquinas.* New Edition. Oxford: James Parker, 1870.

Commentary on the Gospel of John: Chapters 1–5. Translated by Fabian Larcher and James A. Weisheipl. Washington, D.C.; London: The Catholic University of America Press, 2010.

Ashton, John. 'The Transformation of Wisdom: A Study of the Prologue of John's Gospel'. *New Testament Studies* 32 (1986): 161–86.

'Second Thoughts on the Fourth Gospel'. In *What We Have Heard From the Beginning: The Past, Present, and Future of Johannine Studies.* Edited by Tom Thatcher. Waco, TX: Baylor University Press, 2007: 1–18.

Athanasius. *On the Incarnation.* Translated by John Behr. Popular Patristic Series 44. Yonkers, NY: St Vladimir's Press, 2011.

Attridge, Harold W. 'Johannine Christianity'. In Harold W. Attridge, *Essays on John and Hebrews.* Grand Rapids, MI: Baker Academic, 2010: 3–19.

Augenstein, Jörg. *Das Liebesgebot im Johannesevangelium und in den Johannesbriefen.* Beiträge zur Wissenschaft vom Alt und Neuen Testament 134. Stuttgart: Kohlhammer, 1994.

Augustine, St. *Tractates on the Gospel of John 1–10.* Translated by John W. Rettig. Fathers of the Church. Washington, D.C.: The Catholic University of America Press, 1988.

Baldensperger, Wilhelm. *Der Prolog des vierten Evangeliums: Sein polemischer-apologetischer Zweck.* Tübingen: Mohr Siebeck, 1898.

Baker, Coleman A. 'A Narrative–Identity Model for Biblical Interpretation: The Role of Memory and Narrative in Social Identity Formation'. In *T & T Clark Handbook to Social Identity in the New Testament*. Edited by J. Brian Tucker and Coleman A. Baker. London: Bloomsbury T & T Clark, 2014: 105–18.

Ball, David Mark. *'I Am' in John's Gospel: Literary Function, Background and Theological Implications*. Journal for the Study of the New Testament Supplement Series 124. Sheffield: Sheffield Academic, 1996.

Baron, Lori. 2008. 'Reinterpreting the Shema: The Battle over the Unity of God in the Fourth Gospel', Paper at the Annual Meeting of the Society of Biblical Literature. Boston, Massachusetts, 2008.

Barrett, C. K. 'The Old Testament in the Fourth Gospel'. *Journal of Theological Studies*, 48 (1947): 155–69.

The Prologue of St John's Gospel. London: The Athlone Press, 1971.

The Gospel According to John: An Introduction with Commentary and Notes on the Greek Text. Second Edition. London: SPCK, 1978.

Barton, Stephen C. 'Christian Community in the Gospel of John'. In *Christology, Controversy and Community: New Testament Essays in Honour of David R. Catchpole*. Edited by David G. Horrell and Christopher M. Tuckett. Supplements to Novum Testamentum 99. Leiden: Brill, 2000: 279–301.

'The Unity of Humankind as a Theme in Biblical Theology'. In *Out of Egypt: Biblical Theology and Biblical Interpretation*. Edited by Craig Bartholomew, Mary Healy, Karl Möller, and Robin Parry. Scripture and Hermeneutics Series 5. Grand Rapids, MI: Zondervan, 2004: 233–58.

Bauckham, Richard. *Jesus and the Eyewitnesses: The Gospels as Eyewitness Testimony*. Grand Rapids, MI: Eerdmans, 2006.

'Monotheism and Christology in the Gospel of John'. In Richard Bauckham. *The Testimony of the Beloved Disciple: Narrative, History, and Theology in the Gospel of John*. Grand Rapids, MI: Baker, 2007: 239–52.

'The Beloved Disciple as Ideal Author'. In Bauckham, *The Testimony of the Beloved Disciple*: 73–91.

'Biblical Theology and the Problems of Monotheism'. In Bauckham, *Jesus and the God of Israel*: 60–106.

'God Crucified'. In Bauckham, *Jesus and the God of Israel*: 1–59.

Jesus and the God of Israel: God Crucified and Other Studies on the New Testament's Christology of Divine Identity. Grand Rapids, MI; Cambridge: William B. Eerdmans Pub. Co, 2008.

Gospel of Glory: Major Themes in Johannine Theology. Grand Rapids, MI: Baker Academic, 2015.

Bellinzoni, A J. *The Sayings of Jesus in the Writings of Justin Martyr*. Leiden: E. J. Brill, 1967.

Bennema, Cornelis. *Encountering Jesus: Character Studies in the Gospel of John*. Milton Keynes: Paternoster, 2009.

'A Theory of Character in the Fourth Gospel with Reference to Ancient and Modern Literature'. *Biblic. Interpret.* 17: 4 (2009): 375–421.

'A Comprehensive Approach to Understanding Character in the Gospel of John'. In Skinner, ed., *Characters and Characterization in the Gospel of John*: 36–58.

'Part One: Methods and Models for Reading Johannine Characters'. In Skinner, ed., *Characters and Characterization in the Gospel of John*: 1–127.

Betz, Otto. *Der Paraklet: Fürsprecher im häretischen Spätjudentum, im Johannes-Evangelium und in neu gefundenen gnostischen Schriften* (Leiden: Brill, 1963.

Beutler, Johannes, SJ. 'Das Hauptgebot im Johannesevangelium'. In *Das Gesetz im Neuen Testament*. Edited by Karl Kertelge. Quaestiones Disputatae 108. Freiburg: Herder, 1986: 222–36.

'The Use of "Scripture" in the Gospel of John'. In *Exploring the Gospel of John: In Honor of D. Moody Smith*. Edited by R. Alan Culpepper and C. Clifton Black. Louisville, KY: Westminster John Knox, 1996: 147–62.

Bieringer, Reimund and Didier Pollefeyt. 'Open to Both Ways ... ? Johannine Perspectives on Judaism in the Light of Jewish–Christian Dialogue'. In *Israel und seine Heilstraditionen im Johannesevangelium: Festgabe für Johannes Beutler SJ zum 70. Geburtstag*. Edited by Michael Labahn, Klaus Scholtissek, and Angelika Strotmann. Paderborn: Ferdinand Schöningh, 2004: 11–32.

Bieringer, Reimund, Didier Pollefeyt, and Frederique Vandecasteele-Vanneuville, eds. *Anti-Judaism and the Fourth Gospel: Papers of the Leuven Colloquium, 2000*. Jewish and Christian Heritage 1. Assen: Van Gorcum, 2001.

Blackwell, Benjamin C. 'Immortal Glory and the Problem of Death in Romans 3.23'. *Journal for the Study of the New Testament* 32: 3 (2010): 285–308.

Christosis: Pauline Soteriology in Light of Deification in Irenaeus and Cyril of Alexandria. Wissenschaftliche Untersuchungen zum Neuen Testament 2:314. Tübingen: Mohr Siebeck, 2011.

Blank, Josef. *Das Evangelium nach Johannes*. Geistliche Schriftlesung 1b. Düsseldorf: Patmos, 1981.

Bockmuehl, Markus. *Seeing the Word: Refocusing New Testament Study*. Studies in Theological Interpretation. Grand Rapids, MI: Baker, 2006.

Simon Peter in Scripture and Memory: The New Testament Apostle in the Early Church. Grand Rapids, MI: Baker Academic, 2012.

Boersma, Hans. *Heavenly Participation: The Weaving of a Sacramental Tapestry*. Grand Rapids, MI: Eerdmans, 2011.

Boismard, M.-E. *St John's Prologue*. Translated by Carisbrooke Dominicans. London: Blackfriars Publications, 1957.

Borgen, Peder. 'Logos Was the True Light'. In *Logos Was the True Light and Other Essays on the Gospel of John*. Edited by Peder Borgen. Trondheim: Tapir Publishers, 1983: 95–110.

'The Old Testament in the Formation of New Testament Theology'. In *Logos Was the True Light and Other Essays on the Gospel of John*. Edited by Peder Borgen. Trondheim: Tapir Publishers, 1983: 111–120.

Bornkamm, Günther. 'Die eucharistische Rede im Johannes-Evangelium'. *Zeitschrift für die neutestamentliche Wissenschaft und die Kunde der älteren Kirche* 47 (1956): 161–69.

'Towards the Interpretation of John's Gospel: A Discussion of *The Testament of Jesus* by Ernst Käsemann'. In *The Interpretation of John*. Edited and translated by John Ashton. Issues in Religion and Theology 9. London: SPCK, 1986: 79–98.

Boyarin, Daniel. 'The Gospel of the Memra: Jewish Binitarianism and the Prologue to John'. *Harvard Theological Review* 94: 3 (2001): 243–84.

Braaten, Carl E., and Robert W. Jenson, eds. *Union with Christ: The New Finnish Interpretation of Luther*. Grand Rapids, MI: Eerdmans, 1998.

Bradford B. Blaine, Jr. *Peter in the Gospel of John: The Making of an Authentic Disciple*. Society of Biblical Literature Academia Biblica 27. Atlanta, GA: Society of Biblical Literature, 2007.

Brant, Jo-Ann A. *John*. Paideia Commentaries on the New Testament. Grand Rapids, MI: Baker Academic, 2011.

Braude, W. G., and I. J. Kapstein (translators). *Tanna Debe Eliyyahu*. Philadelphia, PA: Jewish Publication Society of America, 1981.

Brown, Raymond E. 'Three Quotations from John the Baptist in the Gospel Tradition'. *Catholic Biblical Quarterly* 22: 3 (1960): 292–98.

'Unity and Diversity in New Testament Ecclesiology'. *Novum Testamentum* 6: 4 (1963): 298–308.

The Gospel According to John: Introduction, Translation, and Notes. 2 vols. The Anchor Bible 29, 29A. Garden City, NY: Doubleday, 1966.

'The Paraclete in the Fourth Gospel'. *New Testament Studies* 13: 2 (1967): 113–32.

'Johannine Ecclesiology: The Community's Origins'. *Interpretation* 31: 4 (1977): 379–93.

The Community of the Beloved Disciple: The Life, Loves, and Hates of an Individual Church in New Testament Times. New York: Paulist Press, 1979.

The Churches the Apostles Left Behind. New York: Paulist Press, 1984.

'The Heritage of the Beloved Disciple and the Epistles: Individuals Guided by the Spirit-Paraclete'. In Brown, *The Churches the Apostles Left Behind*: 102–23.

'The Heritage of the Beloved Disciple in the Fourth Gospel: People Personally Attached to Jesus'. In Brown, *The Churches the Apostles Left Behind*: 84–101.

Brown, Raymond E., Karl P. Donfried, and John Reumann, eds. *Peter in the New Testament: A Collaborative Assessment by Protestant and Roman Catholic Scholars*. London: Geoffrey Chapman, 1973.

Brown, Sherri. *Gift upon Gift: Covenant Through Word in the Gospel of John*. Princeton Theological Monograph Series 144. Eugene, OR: Pickwick, 2010.

Bruner, Frederick Dale. *The Gospel of John: A Commentary*. Grand Rapids, MI: Eerdmans, 2012.

Bruno, Christopher R. *'God Is One': The Function of Eis Ho Theos as a Ground for Gentile Inclusion in Paul's Letters*. Library of New Testament Studies 497. London: Bloomsbury, 2013.

Büchsel, Friedrich. *Das Evangelium nach Johannes*. Das Neue Testament Deutsch 4. Göttingen: Vandenhoeck & Ruprecht, 1937.

Bultmann, Rudolf. *The Gospel of John: A Commentary*. Translated by George R. Beasley-Murray, R. W. N. Hoare, and J. K. Riches. Philadelphia, PA: Westminster John Knox, 1971.

'The History of Religions Background of the Prologue to the Gospel of John'. In *The Interpretation of John*. Edited by John Ashton. Issues in Religion and Theology 9. London: SPCK, 1986: 18–35.

Theology of the New Testament. Translated by Kendrick Grobel. 2 vols. Waco, TX: Baylor University Press, 2007.

Burge, Gary M. *The Anointed Community: The Holy Spirit in the Johannine Tradition*. Grand Rapids, MI: Eerdmans, 1987.

'Spirit-Inspired Theology and Ecclesial Correction: Charting One Shift in the Development of Johannine Ecclesiology and Pneumatology'. In *Communities in Dispute: Current Scholarship on the Johannine Epistles*. Edited by R. Alan Culpepper and Paul N. Anderson. Early Christianity and its Literature 13. Atlanta, GA: Society of Biblical Literature Press, 2014: 179–85.

Burridge, Richard A. *What Are the Gospels? A Comparison with Greco-Roman Biography*. Grand Rapids, MI: Eerdmans, 2004.

Busse, Ulrich. 'Open Questions on John 10'. In *The Shepherd Discourse of John 10 and Its Context: Studies by Members of the Johannine Writings Seminar*. Edited by Robert T. Fortna and Johannes Beutler. Society for New Testament Studies Monograph Series 67. Cambridge: Cambridge University Press, 1991: 6–17.

Byers, Andrew. 'The One Body of the Shema in 1 Corinthians: An Ecclesiology of Christological Monotheism'. *New Testament Studies* 62: 4 (2016): 517–32.

Calvin, John. *Commentary on the Gospel According to John*, vol. 1. (Edinburgh: Calvin Translation Society, 1847)

Carson, D. A. *The Gospel According to John*. The Pillar New Testament Commentary. Grand Rapids, MI: Eerdmans, 1991.

Carter, Warren. 'The Prologue and John's Gospel: Function, Symbol and the Definitive Word'. *Journal for the Study of the New Testament* 39 (1990): 35–58.

Chapman, Seymour. *Story and Discourse: Narrative Structure in Fiction and Film*. Ithaca, NY: Cornell University Press, 1978.

Charlesworth, James H., ed. *The Old Testament Pseudepigrapha: Expansions of the 'Old Testament' and Legends, Wisdom and Philosophical Literature, Prayers, Psalms and Odes, Fragments of Lost Judeo-Hellenistic Works*, 2 vols. New York: Doubleday, 1983, 1985.

The Beloved Disciple: Whose Witness Validates the Gospel of John? Valley Forge, PA: Trinity Press International, 1995.

Chennattu, Rekha M. *Johannine Discipleship as a Covenant Relationship*. Peabody, MA: Hendrickson, 2006.

Chia, Roland. 'Salvation as Justification and Deification'. *Scottish Journal of Theology* 64: 2 (2011): 125–39.

Christensen, Michael J, and Jeffery A Wittung, eds. *Partakers of the Divine Nature: The History and Development of Deification in the Christian Traditions*. Grand Rapids, MI: Baker Academic, 2008.

Cohee, Peter. 'John 1.3–4'. *New Testament Studies* 41: 3 (1995): 470–77.

Cohen, Naomi G. *Philo Judaeus: His Universe of Discourse*. Frankfurt am Main: Peter Lang, 1995.

Collins, Paul M. *Partaking in Divine Nature: Deification and Communion.* London: T & T Clark, 2010.
Collins, Raymond F. 'Representative Figures of the Fourth Gospel'. In *These Things Have Been Written: Studies on the Fourth Gospel.* Edited by Raymond F. Collins, Vol. 2. Louvain Theological and Pastoral Monographs. Louvain: Peeters, 1990: 1–45.
Coloe, Mary L. *God Dwells with Us: Temple Symbolism in the Fourth Gospel.* Collegeville, MN: Liturgical Press, 2001.
 Dwelling in the Household of God: Johannine Ecclesiology and Spirituality. Collegeville, MN: Liturgical Press, 2007.
Conway, Colleen M. *Men and Women in the Fourth Gospel: Gender and Johannine Characterization.* Society of Biblical Literature Dissertation Series 167. Atlanta, GA: Society of Biblical Literature, 1999.
 'Speaking through Ambiguity: Minor Characters in the Fourth Gospel'. *Biblical Interpretation* 10: 3 (2002): 324–41.
Coogan, Michael D., ed. 'Ecclesiasticus, or The Wisdom of Jesus, Son of Sirach'. In *The New Oxford Annotated Apocrypha*, Translated by Daniel J. Harrington. Revised 4th edn. Oxford: Oxford University Press, 2010: 99–169.
Corell, Alf. *Consummatum Est: Eschatology and Church in the Gospel of St. John.* London: SPCK, 1958.
Countryman, L. William. *The Mystical Way in the Fourth Gospel: Crossing Over into God.* Revised edition. Valley Forge, PA: Trinity Press International, 1994.
Crump, David. 'Re-examining the Johannine Trinity: Perichoresis or Deification?' *Scottish Journal of Theology* 59: 4 (2006): 395–412.
Cullmann, Oscar. *The Johannine Circle: Its Place in Judaism, Among the Disciples of Jesus and in Early Christianity.* Translated by John Bowden. New Testament Library. London: SCM Press, 1976.
Culpepper, R. Alan. *The Johannine School: An Evaluation of the Johannine-School Hypothesis Based on an Investigation of the Nature of Ancient Schools.* Society of Biblical Literature Dissertation Series 26. Missoula, MT: Society of Biblical Literature, 1975.
 'The Pivot of John's Prologue'. *New Testament Studies* 27 (1980): 1–31.
 Anatomy of the Fourth Gospel: A Study in Literary Design. Philadelphia, PA: Fortress, 1983.
 John, the Son of Zebedee: The Life of a Legend. Studies on Personalities of the New Testament. Minneapolis, MN: Fortress, 2000.
 'Designs for the Church in the Gospel Accounts of Jesus' Death'. *New Testament Studies* 51: 3 (2005): 376–92.
 'The Quest for the Church in the Gospel of John'. *Interpretation* 63: 4 (2009): 341–54.
 'Peter as Exemplary Disciple in John 21:15–19'. *Perspectives in Religious Studies*, 37 (2010): 165–78.
 'The Weave of the Tapestry: Character and Theme in John'. In Skinner, ed., *Characters and Characterization in the Gospel of John*: 18–35.
Cyril of Alexandria. *Commentary on John.* Edited by Joel C. Elowsky. Translated by David R. Maxwell. Vol. 1. Ancient Christian Texts. Downers Grove, IL: InterVarsity Press, 2013.

Dahl, Nils A. 'The Johannine Church and History'. In Nils A. Dahl, *Jesus in the Memory of the Early Church: Essays by Nils Alstrup Dahl*. Minneapolis, MN: Augsburg Publishing House, 1976: 99–119.

'The Neglected Factor in New Testament Theology'. In *Jesus the Christ: The Historical Origins of Christological Doctrine*. Edited by Donald H. Juel. Minneapolis, MN: Fortress, 1991: 153–63.

Daley, Brian E. 'Christ and Christologies'. In *The Oxford Handbook of Early Christian Studies*. Edited by David G. Hunter and Susan Ashbrook Harvey. Oxford: Oxford University Press, 2008: 886–905.

Danby, Herbert. *The Mishnah: Translated from the Hebrew with Introduction and Brief Explanatory Notes*. Oxford: Oxford University Press, 1933.

Davies, Margaret. *Rhetoric and Reference in the Fourth Gospel*. Journal for the Study of the New Testament Supplement Series 69. Sheffield: Sheffield Academic Press, 1992.

Davila, James R. 'Of Methodology, Monotheism and Metatron: Introductory Reflections on Divine Mediators and the Origins of the Worship of Jesus'. In *The Jewish Roots of Christological Monotheism: Papers from the St. Andrews Conference on the Historical Origins of the Worship of Jesus*. Edited by Carey C. Newman, James R. Davila, and Gladys S. Lewis. Supplements to the Journal for the Study of Judaism 63. Leiden: Brill, 1999: 3–18.

De Boer, Martinus C. *Johannine Perspectives on the Death of Jesus. Contributions to Biblical Exegesis and Theology* 17. Kampen: Kok-Pharos, 1996.

Deeley, Mary K. 'Ezekiel's Shepherd and John's Jesus: A Case Study in the Appropriation of Biblical Texts'. In *Early Christian Interpretation of the Scriptures of Israel: Investigations and Proposals*. Edited by J. A. Sanders and Craig. A. Evans. Journal for the Study of the New Testament: Supplement Series 148. Sheffield: Sheffield Academic Press, 1997: 252–65.

Delling, Gerhard. 'ΜΟΝΟΣ ΘΕΟΣ'. In *Studien zum Neuen Testament und zum hellenistischen Judentum: Gesammelte Aufsätze*. Edited by Ferdinand Hahn, Traugott Holtz, and Nikolaus Walter. Göttingen: Vandenhoeck Ruprecht, 1970: 391–400.

Didymus the Blind. *Commentary on Zechariah*. Translated by Robert C. Hill. The Fathers of the Church. Washington, D.C.: Catholic University of America Press, 2006.

Dodd, C. H. *Historical Tradition in the Fourth Gospel*. Cambridge: Cambridge University Press, 1963.

The Interpretation of the Fourth Gospel (Cambridge: Cambridge University Press, 1970).

Du Rand, Jan A. 'A Syntactical and Narratological Reading of John 10 in Coherence with Chapter 9'. In *The Shepherd Discourse of John 10 and Its Context: Studies by Members of the Johannine Writings Seminar*. Edited by Robert T. Fortna and Johannes Beutler. Society for New Testament Studies Monograph Series 67. Cambridge: Cambridge University Press, 1991: 94–115.

'The Creation Motif in the Fourth Gospel: Perspectives on Its Narratological Function within a Judaistic Background', in *Theology and Christology in the Fourth Gospel: Essays by Members of the SNTS Johannine Writings Seminar*. Edited by P. Maritz, G. van Belle, and J. G. van der Watt.

Bibliotheca Ephemeridum Theologicarum Lovaniensium 184. Leuven: Leuven University Press, 2005): 21–46.

Dunderberg, Ismo. *The Beloved Disciple in Conflict? Revisiting the Gospels of John and Thomas.* Oxford: Oxford University Press, 2006.

Dunn, James D. G. 'Let John Be John: A Gospel for Its Time'. In *The Gospel and the Gospels.* Edited by Peter Stuhlmacher. Grand Rapids, MI: Eerdmans, 1991: 293–322.

'Was Jesus a Monotheist? A Contribution to the Discussion of Christian Monotheism'. In Stuckenbruck and North (eds), *Early Jewish and Christian Monotheism*: 104–19.

Elliott, John H. 'Phases in the Social Formation of Early Christianity: From Faction to Sect – A Social Scientific Perspective'. In *Recruitment, Conquest, and Conflict: Strategies in Judaism, Early Christianity, and the Greco-Roman World.* Edited by Peder Borgen, Vernon K. Robbins, and David B. Gowler. Emory Studies in Early Christianity. Atlanta, GA: Scholars Press, 1998: 273–313.

Emerton, J. A. 'Some New Testament Notes'. *The Journal of Theological Studies* 11: 2 (1960): 329–36.

'Melchizedek and the Gods: Fresh Evidence for the Jewish Background of John X.34–36'. *The Journal of Theological Studies* 17: 2 (1966): 399–401.

Esler, Philip F. 'Introverted Sectarianism at Qumran and in the Johannine Community'. In Philip F. Esler, *The First Christians in Their Social Worlds: Social-Scientific Approaches to New Testament Interpretation.* London: Routledge, 1994: 70–91.

Evans, Craig A. *Word and Glory: On the Exegetical Background of John's Prologue.* Journal for the Study of the New Testament Supplement Series 89. Sheffield: Sheffield Academic Press, 1993.

Falk, Daniel K. 'Jewish Prayer Literature and the Jerusalem Church in Acts'. In *The Book of Acts in Its Palestinian Setting*, vol. 4. Edited by Richard Bauckham. Carlisle: Paternoster, 1995: 267–301.

Farelly, Nicolas. *The Disciples in the Fourth Gospel: A Narrative Analysis of Their Faith and Understanding.* Wissenschaftliche Untersuchungen zum Neuen Testament 290. Tübingen: Mohr Siebeck, 2010.

Ferreira, Johan. *Johannine Ecclesiology.* Journal for the Study of the New Testament Supplement Series 160. Sheffield: Sheffield Academic Press, 1998.

Finlan, Stephen. 'Can We Speak of Theosis in Paul?' In Christensen and Wittung, eds., *Partakers of the Divine Nature*: 68–80.

'Deification in Jesus' Teaching'. In *Theosis: Deification in Christian Theology.* Edited by Vladimir Kharlamov, vol. 2. Cambridge: James Clarke & Co., 2012: 21–41.

Fletcher-Louis, Crispin. *Luke-Acts: Angels, Christology and Soteriology.* Wissenschaftliche Untersuchungen zum Neuen Testament 94. Tübingen: Mohr Siebeck, 1997.

All the Glory of Adam: Liturgical Anthropology in the Dead Sea Scrolls. Studies on the Texts of the Desert of Judah 42. Leiden: Brill, 2002.

Foster, Paul. 'Why Did Matthew Get the Shema Wrong? A Study of Matthew 22:37'. *Journal of Biblical Literature* 122: 2 (2003): 309–33.

Freedman, H., Maurice Simon, S. M. Lehrman, et al. *Midrash Rabbah* 2nd edn. London and Bournemouth: Soncino Press, 1951.

Frei, Hans W. *The Identity of Jesus Christ: The Hermeneutical Bases of Dogmatic Theology*. Eugene, OR: Cascade Books, 2013.

Gadamer, Hans-Georg. *Truth and Method*. 2nd edn. London: Sheed & Ward, 1989.

Gamble, Harry Y. *Books and Readers in the Early Church: A History of Early Christian Texts*. New Haven, CT: Yale University Press, 1995.

García Martínez, Florentino, and Wilfred G. E. Watson. *The Dead Sea Scrolls Translated: The Qumran Texts in English*. Leiden: E. J. Brill, 1994.

Genette, Gérard. *Narrative Discourse*. Translated by Jane E. Lewin. Ithaca, NY: Cornell University Press, 1980.

Gerhardsson, Birger. *The Shema in the New Testament: Deut 6: 4–5 in Significant Passages*. Lund: Novapress, 1996.

Glasson, T. F. *Moses in the Fourth Gospel*. Studies in Biblical Theology 40. London: SCM Press, 1963.

Gorman, Michael J. *Inhabiting the Cruciform God: Kenosis, Justification, and Theosis in Paul's Narrative Soteriology*. Grand Rapids, MI: Eerdmans, 2009.

'Romans: The First Christian Treatise on Theosis'. *Journal of Theological Interpretation* 5: 1 (2011): 13–34.

Gross, Jules. *The Divinization of the Christian According to the Greek Fathers*. Translated by Paul A. Onica. Anaheim, CA: A&C Press, 2002.

Gurtner, Daniel M. *Second Baruch: A Critical Edition of the Syriac Text, with Greek and Latin Fragments, English Translation, Introduction, and Concordances*, vol. 5. T & T Clark Jewish and Christian Texts Series. London: T & T Clark, 2009.

Haenchen, Ernst. *A Commentary on the Gospel of John*. Translated by Robert W. Funk. Hermeneia. Philadelphia, PA: Fortress, 1984.

Hakola, Raimo. *Identity Matters: John, the Jews and Jewishness*. Supplements to Novum Testamentum 118. Leiden: Brill, 2005.

Reconsidering Johannine Christianity: A Social Identity Approach. Bible World. London: Routledge, 2015.

Hallonsten, Gösta. '*Theosis* in Recent Research: A Renewal of Interest and a Need for Clarity'. In Christensen and Wittung, eds., *Partakers of the Divine Nature*: 281–93.

Hanson, A. T. 'John's Citation of Psalm 82'. *New Testament Studies* 11: 2 (1965): 158–62.

'John's Citation of Psalm 82 Reconsidered'. *New Testament Studies* 13: 4 (1967): 363–67.

'John's Use of Scripture'. In *The Gospels and the Scriptures of Israel*. Edited by Craig A. Evans and W. Richard Stegner. Journal for the Study of the New Testament Supplement Series 104. Sheffield: Sheffield Academic Press, 1994: 358–79.

Hanson, Stig. *The Unity of the Church in the New Testament: Colossians and Ephesians*. Acta Seminarii Neotestamentici Upsaliensis. Copenhagen: Einar Munskgaard, 1946.

Harnack, Adolf. *History of Dogma*. Theological Translation Library. London: Williams & Norgate, 1894.

What Is Christianity? Translated by Thomas Bailey Saunders. 3rd edn. London: Williams & Norgate, 1912.

'Über das Verhältnis des Prologs des vierten Evangeliums zum ganzen Werk'. *Zeitschrift für Theologie und Kirche* 2 (1892): 189–231.

Harris, Elizabeth. *Prologue and Gospel: The Theology of the Fourth Evangelist.* Journal for the Study of the New Testament Supplemental Series 107. Sheffield: Sheffield University Press, 1994.

Harris, Stephen L. *The New Testament: A Student's Introduction.* 5th edn. New York: McGraw-Hill, 2006.

Hauerwas, Stanley. *A Community of Character: Toward a Constructive Christian Social Ethic.* Notre Dame, IN: University of Notre Dame Press, 1981.

Hawkin, David J. 'The Function of the Beloved Disciple Motif in the Johannine Redaction'. *Laval théologique et philosophique* 33: 2 (1977): 135–50.

Hays, Richard B. *The Faith of Jesus Christ: The Narrative Substructure of Galatians 3: 1–4:11.* 2nd edn. The Biblical Resource Series. Grand Rapids, MI: Eerdmans, 2002.

'Reading Scripture in Light of the Resurrection'. In *The Art of Reading Scripture.* Edited by Ellen F. Davis and Richard B. Hays. Grand Rapids, MI: Eerdmans, 2003: 216–38.

The Conversion of the Imagination: Paul as Interpreter of Israel's Scripture. Grand Rapids, MI: Eerdmans, 2005.

Reading Backwards: Figural Christology and the Fourfold Gospel Witness. London: SPCK, 2015.

Echoes of Scripture in the Gospels. Waco, TX: Baylor University Press, 2016.

Hayward, C. T. R. '"The LORD Is One": Reflections on the Theme of Unity in John's Gospel from a Jewish Perspective'. In Stuckenbruck and North (eds), *Early Jewish and Christian Monotheism*: 138–54.

Hearon, Holly E., and Philip Ruge-Jones, eds. *The Bible in Ancient and Modern Media: Story and Performance*, vol. 1. *Biblical Performance Criticism.* Eugene, OR: Cascade Books, 2009.

Heath, Jane. 'Some Were Saying, "He Is Good" (John 7:12b): "Good" Christology in John's Gospel?' *New Testament Studies* 56: 4 (2010): 513–35.

Heckel, Ulrich. 'Die Einheit der Kirche im Johannesevangelium und im der Epheserbrief: Ein Vergleich der ekklesiologischen Strukturen'. In *Kontexte des Johannesevangelium: Das vierte Evangelium in religions- und traditionsgeschichtlicher Perspektive.* Edited by Jörg Frey and Udo Schnelle. Wissenschaftliche Untersuchungen zum Neuen Testament 175. Tübingen: Mohr Siebeck, 2004: 613–40.

Hengel, Martin. *The Johannine Question.* Translated by John Bowdon. London: SCM Press, 1989.

'The Old Testament in the Fourth Gospel'. In *The Gospels and the Scriptures of Israel.* Edited by W. Richard Stegner and Craig A. Evans. Journal for the Study of the New Testament Supplement Series 104. Sheffield: Sheffield Academic Press, 1994: 380–95.

'The Prologue of the Gospel of John as the Gateway to Christological Truth'. In *The Gospel of John and Christian Theology.* Edited by Richard Bauckham and Carl Mosser. Grand Rapids, MI: Eerdmans, 2008: 265–94.

Hill, Charles E. *The Johannine Corpus in the Early Church.* Oxford: Oxford University Press, 2004.

'Was John's Gospel Among Justin's "Apostolic Memoirs"?' In *Justin Martyr and His Worlds*, Edited by Sara Parvis and Paul Foster. Minneapolis, MN: Fortress, 2007: 88–94.

Hooker, Morna D. 'John the Baptist and the Johannine Prologue'. *New Testament Studies* 16: 4 (1970): 354–58.

'Beginnings and Endings'. In *The Written Gospel (FS, Graham Stanton)*. Edited by Markus Bockmuehl and D. A. Hagner. Cambridge: Cambridge University Press, 2005: 184–202.

Horsley, Richard, and Tom Thatcher. *John, Jesus and the Renewal of Israel*. Grand Rapids, MI: Eerdmans, 2013.

Hoskyns, Edwyn. *The Fourth Gospel*. Edited by Francis Noel Davey. 2nd edn. London: Faber and Faber Limited, 1947.

Hunt, Steven A., D. Francois Tolmie, and Ruben Zimmerman, eds. *Character Studies in the Fourth Gospel: Narrative Approaches to Seventy Figures in John*. Wissenschaftliche Untersuchungen zum Neuen Testament 1: 314. Tübingen: Mohr Siebeck, 2013.

Hurtado, Larry W. 'First-century Jewish Monotheism'. *Journal for the Study of the New Testament*, 71 (1998): 3–26.

One God, One Lord: Early Christian Devotion and Ancient Jewish Monotheism. 2nd edn. London: T & T Clark, 1998.

Lord Jesus Christ: Devotion to Jesus in Earliest Christianity. Grand Rapids, MI: Eerdmans, 2003.

'Monotheism'. In *The Eerdmans Dictionary of Early Judaism*. Edited by John J. Collins and Daniel C. Harlow. Grand Rapids, MI: Eerdmans, 2010 : 961–64.

Hylen, Susan E. *Imperfect Believers: Ambiguous Characters in the Gospel of John*. Louisville, KY: Westminster John Knox, 2009.

Instone-Brewer, David. *Prayer and Agriculture: Traditions of the Rabbis from the Era of the New Testament*, vol. 1. Grand Rapids, MI: Eerdmans, 2004.

Irenaeus of Lyons. *Against the Heresies*. Translated by Robert M. Grant. London: Routledge, 1997.

Against the Heresies. Translated by Dominic J. Unger. Ancient Christian Writers 64. New York: The Newman Press, 2012.

Iser, Wolfgang. *The Implied Reader: Patterns of Communication in Prose Fiction from Bunyan to Beckett*. London: The Johns Hopkins University Press, 1974.

The Act of Reading: A Theory of Aesthetic Response. London: Routledge & Kegan Paul, 1978.

Janzen, J. Gerald. 'An Echo of the Shema in Isaiah 51.13'. *Journal for the Study of the Old Testament* 43 (1989): 69–82.

Jeremias, Joachim. *The Prayers of Jesus*. Studies in Biblical Theology 6. London: SCM Press, n.d.

John Chrysostom. *John 1–10*. Edited by Joel C. Elowsky. Ancient Christian Commentary on Scripture, IVa. Downers Grove, IL: InterVarsity Press, 2006.

Johnson, Elizabeth A. 'Jesus, the Wisdom of God: A Biblical Basis for a Non-Androcentric Christianity'. *Ephemerides theologicae lovanienses* 61 (1985): 284–89.

Johnston, George. *The Spirit-Paraclete in the Gospel of John.* Society for New Testament Monograph Series 12. Cambridge: Cambridge University Press, 1970.

Jones, F. Stanley. *An Ancient Jewish-Christian Source on the History of Christianity: Pseudo-Clementine Recognitions 1.27–71.* Society of Biblical Literature Texts and Translation 37. Atlanta, GA: Scholars Press, 1995.

Jonge, Marinus de. 'Christology, Controversy and Community in the Gospel of John'. In *Christology, Controversy and Community: New Testament Essays in Honour of David R. Catchpole.* Edited by Christopher M. Tuckett and David G. Horrell, 209–29. Supplements to Novum Testamentum 99. Leiden: Brill, 2000.

Josephus, Flavius. *The Life. Against Apion.* Translated by H. St. J. Thackery. Loeb Classical Library. William Heineman, 1926.

Jewish Antiquities. Translated by H. St. J. Thackery. 2 vols. Loeb Classical Library. London: William Heinemann, 1934.

Justin. (Martyr). *Dialogue with Trypho*, vol. 3. Edited by Michael Slusser. Translated by Thomas B. Falls. Selections from the Fathers of the Church. Washington, D.C.: The Catholic University of America Press, 2003.

Kaminsky, Joel S. 'Paradise Regained: Rabbinic Reflections on Israel at Sinai'. In *Jews, Christians, and the Theology of the Hebrew Scriptures.* Edited by Alice Ogden Bellis and Joel S. Kaminsky. Society of Biblical Literature Symposium Series 8. Atlanta, GA: Society of Biblical Literature, 2000: 15–43.

Kärkkäinen, Veli-Matti. *One with God: Salvation as Deification and Justification.* Collegeville, MN: Liturgical Press, 2004.

Käsemann, Ernst. *The Testament of Jesus: A Study of the Gospel of John in the Light of Chapter 17.* Translated by Gerhard Krodel. Philadelphia, PA: Fortress, 1968.

'The Structure and Purpose of the Prologue to John's Gospel'. In *New Testament Questions for Today.* New Testament Library. London: SCM Press, 1969: 138–67.

Keating, Daniel A. 'Divinization in Cyril: The Appropriation of Divine Life'. In *The Theology of St Cyril of Alexandria: A Critical Appreciation.* Edited by Thomas G. Weinandy and Daniel A. Keating. London: T & T Clark, 2003: 149–85.

The Appropriation of Divine Life in Cyril of Alexandria. Oxford Theological Monographs. Oxford: Oxford University Press, 2005.

Keck, Leander E., ed. 'Derivation as Destiny: "Of-Ness" in Johannine Christology, Anthropology, and Soteriology'. In *Exploring the Gospel of John: In Honor of D. Moody Smith.* Edited by R. Alan Culpepper and C. Clifton Black. Louisville, KY: Westminster John Knox, 1996: 274–88.

Keener, Craig S. *The Gospel of John: A Commentary.* 2 vols. Peabody, MA: Hendrickson, 2003.

Kelber, Werner H. 'The Birth of a Beginning: John 1:1–18'. *Semeia* 52 (1990): 122–44.

Kerr, Alan R. *The Temple of Jesus' Body: The Temple Theme in the Gospel of John.* Journal for the Study of the New Testament Supplement Series 220. Sheffield: Sheffield Academic Press, 2002.

Klauck, Hans-Josef. 'Gemeinde ohne Amt: Erfahrungen mit der Kirche in den johanneischen Schriften'. *Biblische Zeitschrift* 29: 2 (1985): 193–220.

Klink, Edward W., III. *The Sheep of the Fold: The Audience and Origin of the Gospel of John.* Society for New Testament Studies Monograph Series 141. Cambridge: Cambridge University Press, 2007.

Koester, Craig R. *The Dwelling of God: The Tabernacle in the Old Testament, Intertestamental Jewish Literature, and the New Testament.* Catholic Biblical Quarterly Monograph Series 22. Washington, D.C.: Catholic Biblical Association, 1989.

'Messianic Exegesis and the Call of Nathanael (John 1.45–51)'. *Journal for the Study of the New Testament* 39 (1990): 23–34.

The Word of Life: A Theology of John's Gospel. Grand Rapids, MI: Eerdmans, 2008.

Koester, Helmut. *Ancient Christian Gospels: Their History and Development.* Philadelphia, PA: TPI, 1990.

Köstenberger, Andreas J. *John.* Baker Exegetical Commentary on the New Testament. Grand Rapids, MI: Baker Academic, 2004.

Köstenberger, Andreas J., and Scott R. Swain. *Father, Son and Spirit: The Trinity and John's Gospel.* New Studies in Biblical Theology 24. Downers Grove, IL: InterVarsity Press, 2008.

Kysar, Robert. *John, The Maverick Gospel.* 3rd edition. Louisville, KY: Westminster John Knox, 2007.

Labahn, Michael. 'Deuteronomy in John's Gospel'. In *Deuteronomy in the New Testament.* Edited by Maarten J. J. Menken and Steve Moyise. Library of New Testament Studies 358. London: T & T Clark, 2007: 82–98.

Labahn, Michael, Klaus Scholtissek and Angelika Strotmann, eds. *Israel und seine Heilstraditionen im Johannessevangelium: Festgabe für Johannes Beutler SJ, zum 70. Geburtstag.* Paderborn: Schöningh, 2004.

Lamb, David A. *Text, Context and the Johannine Community: A Sociolinguistic Analysis of the Johannine Writings.* Library of New Testament Studies 477. London: Bloomsbury, T & T Clark, 2014.

Le Donne, Anthony, and Tom Thatcher, eds. *The Fourth Gospel in First-Century Media Culture.* Library of New Testament Studies 426. London: T & T Clark, 2011.

Lemcio, Eugene E. *The Past of Jesus in the Gospels.* Society for New Testament Studies Monograph Series 68. Cambridge: Cambridge University Press, 1991.

Leonhardt-Balzer, Jutta. *Jewish Worship in Philo of Alexandria.* Tübingen: Mohr Siebeck, 2001.

Lieu, Judith M. *I, II, & III John: A Commentary.* New Testament Library. Louisville, KY: Westminster John Knox, 2008.

Lightfoot, R. H. *St. John's Gospel: A Commentary.* 2nd edn. Oxford: Oxford University Press, 1956.

Lincoln, Andrew T. *The Gospel According to Saint John.* Black's New Testament Commentary 4. New York: Hendrikson, 2005.

Lindars, Barnabus. *Behind the Fourth Gospel: Studies in Creative Criticism.* London: SPCK, 1971.

The Gospel of John. New Century Bible. London: Oliphants, 1972.

Litwa, M. David. '2 Corinthians 3:18 and its Implications for Theosis'. *Journal of Theological Interpretation* 2: 1 (2008): 117–33.

'Behold Adam: A Reading of John 19:5', *Horizons in Biblical Theology* 32 (2010): 129–43.

We Are Being Transformed: Deification in Paul's Soteriology. Beihefte zur Zeitschrift für die neutestamentliche Wissenschaft 187. Berlin: De Gruyter, 2012.

Louth, Andrew. *The Origins of the Christian Mystical Tradition: From Plato to Denys*. Oxford: Oxford University Press, 1981.

Lutkemeyer, Lawrence J. 'The Role of the Paraclete (Jn. 16:7–15)'. *Catholic Biblical Quarterly* 8: 2 (1946): 220–29.

Macaskill, Grant. *Union with Christ in the New Testament*. Oxford: Oxford University Press, 2013.

Malbon, Elizabeth Struthers. *Mark's Jesus: Characterization as Narrative Christology*. Waco, TX: Baylor University Press, 2009.

Malina, Bruce J., and Richard L. Rohrbaugh. *Social-Science Commentary on the Gospel of John*. Minneapolis, MN: Fortress, 1998.

Manning, Gary T. *Echoes of a Prophet: The Use of Ezekiel in the Gospel of John and in Literature of the Second Temple Period*. Journal for the Study of New Testament Supplement Series 270. London: T & T Clark, 2004.

Marcus, Joel. 'Authority to Forgive Sins upon the Earth: The Shema in the Gospel of Mark'. In *The Gospels and the Scriptures of Israel*. Edited by W. Richard Stegner and Craig A. Evans. Journal for the Study of the New Testament Supplement Series 104. Sheffield: Sheffield Academic Press, 1994: 196–211.

Martyn, J. Louis. 'A Gentile Mission That Replaced an Earlier Jewish Mission?' In *Exploring the Gospel of John: In Honor of D. Moody Smith*. Edited by R. Alan Culpepper and C. Clifton Black. Louisville, KY: Westminster John Knox, 1996: 124–44.

History and Theology in the Fourth Gospel. 3rd edn. The New Testament Library. Louisville, KY: Westminster John Knox, 2003.

Mealand, David L. 'The Language of Mystical Union in the Johannine Writings'. *Downside Review* 95 (1977): 19–34.

Meeks, Wayne A. 'The Man from Heaven in Johannine Sectarianism'. *Journal of Biblical Literature* 91: 1 (1972): 44–72.

The First Urban Christians: The Social World of the Apostle Paul. 2nd edn. New Haven: Yale University Press, 2003.

Meier, John P. 'The Absence and Presence of the Church in John's Gospel'. *Mid-Stream* 41: 4 (2002): 27–34.

Menken, Martinus J. J. '"Rivers of Living Water Shall Flow From His Inside (John 7:38)"'. In Martinus J. J. Menken, *Old Testament Quotations in the Fourth Gospel: Studies in Textual Form*. Contributions to Biblical Exegesis and Theology 15. Kampen: Kok Pharos, 1996: 187–203.

'The Use of the Septuagint in Three Quotations in John: Jn 10,34; 12,38; 19,24'. In *The Scriptures in the Gospels*. Edited by Christopher M. Tuckett. Leuven: Leuven University Press, 1997: 367–93.

Metzger, Bruce M. *A Textual Commentary on the Greek New Testament*. London: United Bible Societies, 1971.

Meyer, Paul W. '"The Father": The Presentation of God in the Fourth Gospel'. In *Exploring the Gospel of John: In Honor of D. Moody Smith*. Edited by

R. Alan Culpepper and C. Clifton Black. Louisville, KY: Westminster John Knox, 1996: 255–73.

Michaels, J. Ramsey. *The Gospel of John*. New International Commentary on the New Testament. Grand Rapids, MI: Eerdmans, 2010.

Miller, Edward L. *Salvation-History in the Prologue of John: The Significance of John 1:3/4*. Supplements to Novum Testamentum 60. Leiden: Brill, 1989.

Minear, Paul S. 'Evangelism, Ecumenism, and John Seventeen'. *Theology Today* 35: 1 (1978): 5–13.

'Logos Ecclesiology in John's Gospel'. In *Christological Perspectives: Essays in Honor of Harvey K. McArthur*. Edited by Sarah A. Edwards and Robert F. Berkey. New York: The Pilgrim Press, 1982: 95–111.

Moberly, R. W. L. 'Toward an Interpretation of the Shema'. In *Theological Exegesis: Essays in Honor of Brevard S. Childs*. Edited by Christopher Seitz and Kathryn Greene-McCreight. Grand Rapids, MI: Eerdmans, 1999: 124–44.

'"YHWH Is One": The Translation of the Shema'. In *Studies in the Pentateuch*. Edited by J. A. Emerton. Leiden: Brill, 1990: 209–15.

'How Appropriate Is "Monotheism" as a Category for Biblical Interpretation'. In *Early Jewish and Christian Monotheism*. Early Christianity in Context 263. London: T & T Clark, 2004: 216–34.

Old Testament Theology: Reading the Hebrew Bible as Christian Scripture. Grand Rapids, MI: Baker Academic, 2013.

Moloney, Francis J. 'John 18: 15–27: A Johannine View of the Church'. *Downside Review* 389 (1994): 231–48.

The Gospel of John, vol. 4. Sacra Pagina. Collegeville, ME: The Liturgical Press, 1998.

Moltmann, Jürgen. 'God in the World – the World in God: Perichoresis in Trinity and Eschatology'. In *The Gospel of John and Christian Theology*. Edited by Richard Bauckham and Carl Mosser. Grand Rapids, MI: Eerdmans, 2008: 369–81.

Moore, Stephen D. *Literary Criticism and the Gospels: The Theoretical Challenge*. New Haven, CT: Yale University Press, 1989.

Mosser, Carl. 'The Earliest Patristic Interpretations of Psalm 82, Jewish Antecedents, and the Origin of Christian Deification'. *Journal of Theological Studies* 56: 1 (2005): 30–74.

Motyer, Stephen. *Your Father the Devil? A New Approach to John and 'the Jews'*. Paternoster Biblical and Theological Monographs. Carlisle: Paternoster Press, 1997.

'The Fourth Gospel and the Salvation of the New Israel: An Appeal for a New Start'. In *Anti-Judaism and the Fourth Gospel: Papers of the Leuven Colloquium, 2000*. Edited by Didier Pollefeyt, Reimund Bieringer, and Frederique Vandecasteele-Vanneuville. Jewish and Christian Heritage. Assen: Van Gorcum, 2001: 92–110.

Moule, C. F. D. 'Individualism of the Fourth Gospel'. *Novum Testamentum* 5: 2–3 (1962): 171–90.

Mutschler, Bernhard. *Das Corpus Johanneum bei Irenäus von Lyon: Studien und Kommentar zum Dritten Buch von Adversus Haereses*. Wissenschaftliche Untersuchungen zum Neuen Testament 189. Tübingen: Mohr Siebeck, 2006.

Myers, Alicia D. *Characterizing Jesus: A Rhetorical Analysis on the Fourth Gospel's Use of Scripture in Its Presentation of Jesus.* Library of New Testament Studies 458. London: T & T Clark, 2012.

Neirynck, Frans. 'The "Other Disciple" in Jn 18: 15–16'. *Ephemerides theologicae lovanienses* 51: 1 (1975): 113–41.

Neyrey, Jerome H. '"I Said, You Are Gods": Psalm 82:6 and John 10'. *Journal of Biblical Literature* 108: 4 (1989): 647–63.

North, Wendy E. S. 'Monotheism and the Gospel of John: Jesus, Moses, and the Law'. In Stuckenbruck and North (eds.), *Early Jewish and Christian Monotheism*: 155–66.

O'Day, Gail R. 'Johannine Theologians as Sectarians'. In *'What Is John?' Volume I: Readers and Readings of the Fourth Gospel.* Edited by Fernando F. Segovia. Society of Biblical Literature Symposium Series 3. Atlanta, GA: Society of Biblical Literature, 1996: 199–203.

O'Grady, John F. 'Individualism and Johannine Ecclesiology'. *Biblical Theology Bulletin* 5: 3 (1975): 227–61.

'The Prologue and Chapter 17 of the Gospel of John'. In *What We Have Heard From the Beginning: The Past, Present, and Future of Johannine Studies.* Edited by Tom Thatcher. Waco, TX: Baylor University Press, 2007: 215–28.

O'Rourke, John J. 'Possible Uses of the Old Testament in the Gospels: An Overview'. In *The Gospels and the Scriptures of Israel.* Edited by Craig A. Evans and W. Richard Stegner. Journal for the Study of New Testament Supplement Series 104. Sheffield: Sheffield Academic Press, 1994: 15–25.

Origen. *Commentary on the Gospel According to John Books 1–10: A New Translation.* Translated by Ronald E. Heine. Fathers of the Church 80. Washington, D.C.: The Catholic University of America Press, 1989.

Otto, Randall E. 'The Use and Abuse of Perichoresis in Recent Theology'. *Scottish Journal of Theology* 54: 3 (2001): 366–84.

Painter, John. 'The Church and Israel in the Gospel of John'. *New Testament Studies* 25: 1 (1978): 103–12.

'Earth Made Whole: John's Rereading of Genesis'. In *Word, Theology, and Community in John.* Edited by R. Alan Culpepper, Fernando F. Segovia, and John Painter. St. Louis, MO: Chalice Press, 2002: 65–84.

Pancaro, Severino. '"People of God" in St John's Gospel'. *New Testament Studies* 16: 2 (1970): 114–29.

'The Relationship of the Church to Israel in the Gospel of St John'. *New Testament Studies* 21: 3 (1975): 396–405.

Parsons, Mikeal C. 'A Neglected ΕΓΩ ΕΙΜΙ Saying in the Fourth Gospel? Another Look at John 9:9'. In *Perspectives on John: Method and Interpretation in the Fourth Gospel.* Edited by Robert B. Sloan and Mikeal C. Parsons. NABPR Special Studies Series 11. Lampeter: Edwin Mellen Press, 1993: 145–80.

Perkins, Pheme. *Peter: Apostle for the Whole Church.* Studies on Personalities of the New Testament. Minneapolis, MN: Fortress, 2000.

Perry, Menakhem. 'Literary Dynamics: How the Order of a Text Creates Its Meanings'. *Poetics Today* 1: 1/2 (1979): 35–64 and 311–361.

Pester, John. 'The Gospel of the Promised Seed: Deification According to the Organic Pattern in Romans 8 and Philippians 2'. *Affirmation & Critique* 7: 2 (2002): 55–69.

Phillips, Peter M. *The Prologue of the Fourth Gospel: A Sequential Reading.* Library of New Testament Studies 294. London: T & T Clark, 2006.

Philo of Alexandria. *Works.* Edited by T. E. Page et. al. Translated by F. H. Colson. Loeb Classical Library, 10 vols. Harvard University Press, 1939.

Pollard, T. E. 'The Exegesis of John X. 30 in the Early Trinitarian Controversies'. *New Testament Studies* 3: 4 (1957): 334–49.

Porter, Stanley E. 'The Ending of John's Gospel'. In *From Biblical Criticism to Biblical Faith: Essays in Honor of Lee Martin McDonald.* Edited by William H. Brackney and Craig A. Evans. Macon, GA: Mercer University Press, 2007: 55–73.

Pryor, John W. 'Of the Virgin Birth or the Birth of Christians? The Text of John 1:13 Once More'. *Novum Testamentum* 27: 4 (1985): 296–318.

'Jesus and Israel in the Fourth Gospel – John 1:11'. *Novum Testamentum* 32: 3 (1990): 201–18.

John: Evangelist of the Covenant People: The Narrative and Themes of the Fourth Gospel. Downers Grove, IL: InterVarsity Press, 1992.

Putthoff, Tyson Lee. 'Human Mutability and Mystical Change: Explorations in Ancient Jewish OntoAnthropology'. E-Thesis, Durham University, 2013. http://etheses.dur.ac.uk/9395/.

Quast, Kevin. *Peter and the Beloved Disciple: Figures for a Community in Crisis.* Journal for the Study of the New Testament Supplement Series 32. Sheffield: Sheffield Academic, 1989.

Rainbow, Paul A. *Johannine Theology: The Gospel, the Epistles and the Apocalypse.* Downers Grove, IL: InterVarsity Press, 2014.

Rand, Jan A. du. 'The Creation Motif in the Fourth Gospel: Perspectives on Its Narratological Function within a Judaistic Background'. In *Theology and Christology in the Fourth Gospel: Essays by Members of the SNTS Johannine Writings Seminar.* Edited by J. G. van der Watt, P. Maritz, and G. van Belle. Bibliotheca Ephemeridum Theologicarum Lovanniensium 184. Leuven: Leuven University Press, 2005: 21–46.

Rasimus, Tuomas. 'Introduction'. In *The Legacy of John: Second-Century Reception of the Fourth Gospel.* Edited by Tuomas Rasimus. Supplements to Novum Testamentum 132. Leiden: Brill, 2010: 1–16.

Reeves, John C. 'Gnosticism'. In *The Eerdmans Dictionary of Early Judaism.* Edited by John J. Collins and Daniel C. Harlow. Grand Rapids, MI: Eerdmans, 2010: 678–81.

Reif, Stefan C. *Judaism and Hebrew Prayer: New Perspectives on Jewish Liturgical History.* Cambridge: Cambridge University Press, 1993.

Reinhartz, Adele. *The Word in the World: The Cosmological Tale in the Fourth Gospel.* Society of Biblical Literature Monograph Series 45. Atlanta, GA: Scholars Press, 1992.

'The Johannine Community and Its Jewish Neighbors: A Reappraisal'. In *'What Is John?' Volume II: Literary and Social Readings of the Fourth Gospel.* Edited by Fernando F. Segovia. Society of Biblical Literature Symposium Series 7. Atlanta, GA: Society of Biblical Literature, 1998: 111–38.

'Building Skyscrapers on Toothpicks: The Literary-Critical Challenge to Historical Criticism'. In *Anatomies of Narrative Criticism: The Past, Present, and Futures of the Fourth Gospel as Literature*. Edited by Tom Thatcher and Stephen D. Moore. Society of Biblical Literature Resources for Biblical Study 55. Atlanta, GA: Society of Biblical Literature, 2008: 55–76.

Rensberger, David. *Overcoming the World: Politics and Community in the Gospel of John*. London: SPCK, 1989.

Johannine Faith and Liberating Community. Philadelphia, PA: The Westminster Press, 1998.

'Sectarianism and Theological Interpretation in John'. In *'What Is John?' Volume II: Literary and Social Readings of the Fourth Gospel*. Edited by Fernando F. Segovia. Society of Biblical Literature Symposium Series 7. Atlanta, GA: Society of Biblical Literature, 1998: 139–56.

Resseguie, James L. *Narrative Criticism of the New Testament: An Introduction*. Grand Rapids, MI: Baker Academic, 2005.

'A Narrative-Critical Approach to the Fourth Gospel'. In Skinner, ed., *Characters and Characterization in the Gospel of John*: 3–17.

Ricoeur, Paul. *Time and Narrative*, vol. 3. Translated by Kathleen Blamey and David Pellauer. Chicago, IL: University of Chicago Press, 1985.

Ridderbos, Herman. *The Gospel of John: A Theological Commentary*. Translated by John Vriend. Grand Rapids, MI: Eerdmans, 1997.

Ringe, Sharon H. *Wisdom's Friends: Community and Christology in the Fourth Gospel*. Louisville, KY: Westminster John Knox, 1999.

Rowe, C. Kavin. *Early Narrative Christology: The Lord in the Gospel of Luke*. Grand Rapids, MI: Baker Academic, 2006.

Russell, Norman. *The Doctrine of Deification in the Greek Patristic Tradition*. Oxford: Oxford University Press, 2004.

Sanders, E. P. *Judaism: Practice and Belief, 63 BCE – 66 CE*. London: SCM Press, 1992.

Sanford, John A. *Mystical Christianity: A Psychological Commentary on the Gospel of John*. New York: Crossroad, 1993.

Schmithals, Walter. 'Introduction'. In Bultmann, *The Gospel of John*: 1–12.

Schnackenburg, Rudolf. *The Gospel According to St. John*. Translated by Kevin Smyth. 3 vols. Herder's Theological Commentary on the New Testament. London: Burns & Oates, 1968.

The Church in the New Testament. Translated by W. J. O'Hara. London: Burns & Oates, 1974.

Schneiders, Sandra M. 'The Raising of the New Temple: John 20.19–23 and Johannine Ecclesiology'. *New Testament Studies* 52: 3 (2006): 337–55.

Schnelle, Udo. 'Johanneische Ekklesiologie'. *New Testament Studies* 37 (1991): 37–50.

Scholtissek, Klaus. 'The Johannine Gospel in Recent Research'. In *The Face of New Testament Studies: A Survey of Recent Research*. Edited by Grant R. Osborne and Scot McKnight. Grand Rapids, MI: Baker Academic, 2004: 444–72.

'"Ich und der Vater, wir sind Eins" (Joh 10,30): Zum theologischen Potential und zur hermeneutischen Kompetenz der johanneischen Christologie'. In *Theology and Christology in the Fourth Gospel: Essays by the Members of the SNTS Johannine Writings Seminar*. Edited by Gilbert van Belle, Jan G. van der Watt, and Petrus Maritz. *Bibliotheca Ephemeridum*

Theologicarum Lovaniensium 184. Leuven: Leuven University Press, 2005: 315–45.

Schweizer, Eduard. 'The Concept of the Church in the Gospel and Epistles of St John'. In *New Testament Essays: Studies in Memory of Thomas Walter Manson, 1893–1958*. Edited by A. J. B. Higgins. Manchester: Manchester University Press, 1959: 230–45.

Segal, Alan F. 'Mysticism'. In *The Eerdmans Dictionary of Early Judaism*. Edited by John J. Collins and Daniel C. Harlow. Grand Rapids, MI: Eerdmans, 2010: 982–86.

Segovia, Fernando F. 'The Love and Hatred of Jesus and Johannine Sectarianism'. *Catholic Biblical Quarterly* 43: 2 (1981): 258–72.

'John 1: 1–18 as Entrée into Johannine Reality'. In *Word, Theology, and Community in John*. Edited by R. Alan Culpepper, Fernando F. Segovia, and John Painter. St. Louis, MO: Chalice Press, 2002: 33–64.

Shafer, Grant R. 'The Divinization of the Blind Man: Egō Eimi in John 9:9'. *Proceedings (Grand Rapids, MI)* 25 (2005): 157–67.

Skinner, Christopher W. *Characters and Characterization in the Gospel of John* (ed.). Library of New Testament Studies 461. London: T & T Clark, 2013

'Misunderstanding, Christology, and Johannine Characterization: Reading John's Characters through the Lens of the Prologue'. In Skinner, ed., *Characters and Characterization in the Gospel of John*: 111–27.

Smalley, Stephen S. *John: Evangelist and Interpreter*. Exeter: Paternoster Press, 1978.

'"The Paraclete": Pneumatology in the Johannine Gospel and Apocalypse'. In *Exploring the Gospel of John: In Honor of D. Moody Smith*. Edited by R. Alan Culpepper and C. Clifton Black. Louisville, KY: Westminster John Knox Press, 1996: 289–300.

'The Johannine Community and the Letters of John'. In *A Vision for the Church: Studies in Early Christian Ecclesiology*. Edited by Markus Bockmuehl and Michael B. Thompson. Edinburgh: T & T Clark, 1997: 95–104.

Smith, D. Moody. *Johannine Christianity: Essays on Its Setting, Sources, and Theology*. Columbia, SC: University of South Carolina Press, 1984.

'Salvation-History in the Prologue of John: The Significance of John 1:3/4'. *Journal of Biblical Literature* 111: 3 (1992): 542–44.

The Theology of the Gospel of John. New Testament Theology. Cambridge: Cambridge University Press, 1995.

John. Abingdon New Testament Commentaries. Nashville, TN: Abingdon Press, 1999.

'The Contribution of J. Louis Martyn to the Understanding of the Gospel of John', in Martyn, *History and Theology in the Fourth Gospel*: 1–23.

Smith, Morton. 'Ascent to the Heavens and Deification in 4QMa'. In *Archaeology and History in the Dead Sea Scrolls*. Edited by Lawrence H. Schiffman. Journal for the Study of the Pseudepigrapha Supplement Series 8. Sheffield: Sheffield Academic, 1990: 181–88.

Snyder, Graydon F. 'John 13:16 and the Anti-Petrinism of the Johannine Tradition'. *Biblical Research* 16 (1971): 5–15.

Söding, Thomas. '"Ich und der Vater sind Eins" (Joh 10,30): Die johanneische Christologie vor dem Anspruch des Hauptgebotes (Dtn 6,4f)'. *Zeitschrift für die neutestamentliche Wissenschaft und die Kunde der älteren Kirche* 93: 3– 4 (2002): 177–99.

Staley, Jeffrey Lloyd. *The Print's First Kiss: A Rhetorical Investigation of the Implied Reader in the Fourth Gospel.* Society of Biblical Literature Dissertation Series 82. Atlanta, GA: Scholars Press, 1988.

Stanton, Graham N. 'Jesus Traditions and Gospels in Justin Martyr and Irenaeus'. In *The Biblical Canons.* Edited by J.-M. Auwers and H. J. de Jonge. Bibliotheca Ephemeridum Theologicarum Lovaniensium 163. Leuven: Leuven University Press, 2003: 353–70.

Stendahl, Krister. *Paul Among Jews and Gentiles, and Other Essays.* London: SCM Press, 1977.

Sternberg, Meir. *The Poetics of Biblical Narrative: Ideological Literature and the Drama of Reading.* Bloomington, IN: Indiana University Press, 1985.

Stibbe, Mark W. G. *John as Storyteller: Narrative Criticism and the Fourth Gospel.* Society for New Testament Studies Monograph Series 73. Cambridge: Cambridge University Press, 1992.

Strack, Hermann L., and Paul Billerbeck. *Kommentar zum Neuen Testament aus Talmud und Midrash.* Munich: C. H. Beck'sche Verlagsbuchhandlung, 1965.

Stuckenbruck, Loren T. '"Angels" and "God": Exploring the Limits of Early Jewish Monotheism'. In Stuckenbruck and North (eds.), *Early Jewish and Christian Monotheism*: 45–70.

Stuckenbruck, Loren T., and Wendy E. S. North, eds. *Early Jewish and Christian Monotheism.* Early Christianity in Context. London: T & T Clark, 2004.

Tan, Kim Huat. 'The Shema and Early Christianity'. *Tyndale Bulletin* 59: 2 (2008): 181–206.

'Jesus and the Shema'. In *Handbook for the Study of the Historical Jesus.* Edited by Tom Holmén and Stanley E. Porter. Leiden: Brill, 2011, 3: 2677–707.

Tertullian. *The Five Books of Quintus Sept. Flor. Tertullianus Against Marcion.* Translated by Peter Holmes. Ante-Nicene Christian Library 7. Edinburgh: T & T Clark, 1868.

Thatcher, Tom. 'The Riddle of the Baptist and the Genesis of the Prologue: John 1: 1–18 in Oral/Aural Media Culture'. In *The Fourth Gospel in First-Century Media Culture.* Edited by Anthony le Donne and Tom Thatcher. Library of New Testament Studies 426. London: T & T Clark, 2011: 29–48.

Thatcher, Tom, and Catrin H. Williams, eds. *Engaging with C. H. Dodd on the Gospel of John: Sixty Years of Tradition and Interpretation.* Cambridge, 2013.

Theodore of Mopsuestia. *Commentary on the Gospel of John.* Edited by Joel C. Elowsky. Translated by Marco Conti. Ancient Christian Texts. Downers Grove, IL: InterVarsity, 2010.

Thompson, Marianne Meye. *The God of the Gospel of John.* Grand Rapids, MI: Eerdmans, 2001.

'The Breath of Life: John 20: 22–23 Once More'. In *The Holy Spirit and Christian Origins: Essays in Honor of James D. G. Dunn.* Edited by Bruce W. Longenecker, Graham N. Stanton, and Stephen C. Barton. Grand Rapids, MI: Eerdmans, 2004: 69–78.

Tobin, T. H. 'The Prologue of John and Hellenistic Jewish Speculation'. *Catholic Biblical Quarterly* 52 (1990): 252–69.

Tolmie, D. Francois. *Jesus' Farewell to the Disciples: John 13:1–17:26 in Narratological Perspective*. Biblical Interpretation Series 12. Leiden: Brill, 1995.

Troeltsch, Ernst. *The Social Teaching of the Christian Churches*. Translated by Olive Wyon. Reprint. 2 vols. Louisville, KY: Westminster John Knox Press, 1992.

Trumbower, Jeffery A. *Born From Above: The Anthropology of the Gospel of John*. Hermeneutische Untersuchungen zur Theologie. Tübingen: Mohr-Siebeck, 1992.

Van der Watt, Jan G. *Family of the King: Dynamics of Metaphor in the Gospel According to John*. Biblical Interpretation Series 47. Leiden: Brill, 2000.

'Salvation in the Gospel According to John'. In Jan G. van der Watt, *Salvation in the New Testament: Perspectives on Soteriology*. Supplements to Novum Testamentum 121. Leiden: Brill, 2005: 101–31.

Vanhoozer, Kevin J. *Biblical Narrative in the Philosophy of Paul Ricoeur: A Study in Hermeneutics and Theology*. Cambridge: Cambridge University Press, 1990.

Vellanickal, Matthew. *The Divine Sonship of Christians in the Johannine Writings*. Analecta Biblica: Investigationes Scientificae in Res Biblicas 72: Biblical Institute Press, 1977.

Vermes, Geza. *The Complete Dead Sea Scrolls in English*. Rev. edn. Harmondsworth: Penguin, 2011.

Verseput, Donald J. 'James 1:17 and the Jewish Morning Prayers'. *Novum Testamentum* 39: 2 (1997): 177–91.

Von Wahlde, Urban C. *The Gospels and Letters of John*. 3 vols. Eerdmans Critical Commentary. Grand Rapids, MI: Eerdmans, 2010.

Waaler, Erik. *The Shema and the First Commandment in First Corinthians: An Intertextual Approach to Paul's Re-reading of Deuteronomy*. Wissenschaftliche Untersuchungen zum Neuen Testament 253. Tübingen: Mohr Siebeck, 2008.

Warren, Meredith J. C. *My Flesh is Meat Indeed: A Nonsacramental Reading of John 6: 51–58*. Minneapolis, MN: Fortress, 2015.

Watson, Francis. *Text and Truth: Redefining Biblical Theology*. Grand Rapids, MI: Eerdmans, 1997.

'Toward a Literal Reading of the Gospels'. In *The Gospels for All Christians: Rethinking the Gospel Audiences*. Edited by Richard Bauckham. Grand Rapids, MI: Eerdmans, 1998: 195–217.

'Trinity and Community: A Reading of John 17'. *International Journal of Systematic Theology* 1: 2 (1999): 168–84.

Gospel Writing: A Canonical Perspective. Grand Rapids, MI: Eerdmans, 2013.

Watty, William W. 'The Significance of Anonymity in the Fourth Gospel'. *Expository Times* 90: 7 (1979): 209–12.

Webb, Robert L. *John the Baptizer and Prophet: A Socio-Historical Study*. Journal for the Study of the New Testament Supplement Series 62. Sheffield: Sheffield Academic Press, 1991.

Westcott, B. F. *The Gospel According to St. John*. London: John Murray, 1908.

Williams, Catrin H. *I Am He: The Interpretation of 'Anî Hû' in Jewish and Early Christian Literature*. Wissenschaftliche Untersuchungen zum Neuen Testament 113. Tübingen: Mohr Siebeck, 2000.

'John (the Baptist): The Witness on the Threshold'. In *Character Studies in the Fourth Gospel: Narrative Approaches to Seventy Figures in John*. Edited by Steven A. Hunt, D. Francois Tolmie, and Ruben Zimmerman. Wissenschaftliche Untersuchungen zum Neuen Testament 1. Tübingen: Mohr-Siebeck, 2013: 46–60.

Williams, Peter J. 'Not the Prologue of John'. *Journal for the Study of the New Testament* 33: 4 (2011): 375–86.

Wilson, Bryan R. *Magic and the Millennium*. St Albans: Paladin, 1975.

Wink, Walter. *John the Baptist in the Gospel Tradition*. Society for New Testament Studies Monograph Series 7. Cambridge: Cambridge University Press, 1968.

Wright, N. T. 'Monotheism, Christology and Ethics: 1 Corinthians 8'. In N. T. Wright, *The Climax of the Covenant: Christ and the Law in Pauline Theology*. Minneapolis, MN: Fortress, 1991: 120–36.

Wright, William M., IV. *Rhetoric and Theology: Figural Reading of John 9*. Beihefte zur Zeitschrift für die neutestamentliche Wissenschaft 165. Berlin: Walter de Gruyter, 2009.

Yoder, Perry B., ed. *Take This Word to Heart: The Shema in Torah and Gospel*. Scottdale, PA: Herald, 2005.

INDEX OF SUBJECTS

INDEX OF MODERN AUTHORS

INDEX OF ANCIENT TEXTS

4.200–201, 125
4.202, 125
4.212–13, 113, 114
5.111–12, 125
C. Ap.
2.193, 125

Philo
Praem.
163–72, 142
Spec.
I.67, 125

IV.137–39, 115
IV.159, 126, 151

Rabbinical Writings
Berakoth
1–3, 112
Exod. Rab.
32:1, 189
Lev. Rab.
11:1, 3, 190
Tamid
7.4, 191